The Aquarian Guide to African Mythology

Jan Knappert

Illustrations by Elizabeth Knappert

THE AQUARIAN PRESS

This edition published 1990

British Library Cataloguing in Publication Data

Knappert, Jan
The Aquarian guide to African mythology.
1. African myths
I. Title
299.62

ISBN 0-85030-885-2

The Aquarian Press is part of the Thorsons Publishing Group, Wellingborough, Northamptonshire, NN8 2RQ, England

Printed in Great Britain by Mackays of Chatham, Kent
Typesetting by MJL Limited, Hitchin, Hertfordshire.

1 3 5 7 9 10 8 6 4 2

Contents

Preface

This modest guide to African mythology does not pretend to give more than an anthology of myths and mythological figures. There are many myths, legends and fables in the more than one thousand languages of Africa. A severe selection has been necessary, and often it has been necessary to summarize a wealth of mythological material under general headings like 'Gods', 'Goddesses', 'Sorcery' and so on. In some entries a myth or fable is told as an illustration of the mysterious character of some animals, e.g. the frog.

The reading list at the end of this book is likewise only a selection. This writer had to study hundreds of articles and books before he could put pen to paper — not to mention the happy years in Africa, of working with my many friends/informants.

The illustrations too, have been inspired by numerous sources. They represent works of traditional African art, some of them very old, so that in many cases not only the artist and his family, but his entire ethnic group have long since died. These art works are now safely stored in the museums of Europe and elsewhere. Miss Elizabeth Knappert has drawn these vignettes especially for this book, after making sketches of the ancient African effigies. It has not always been possible to select illustrations that refer to one of the entries under the letter which accompanies them. So, Jinn is for J and Owl is for

O, but the L is not represented by a picture of a lion or leopard, because we found no suitable examples. African gods are mostly represented as masks in an abstract manner, highly stylized, unlike the humanized gods of Antiquity. It is hoped that the reader will become as absorbed in African mythology and its mysteries as is the author.

Jan Knappert

Introduction

It is with fear and trepidation that I begin this guide, not so much because I am frightened of the many spirits, as rather because it is a bold enterprise in a much debated field. Many experts will say it is much too early to compile a general survey of a subject that is still full of lacunae and unknown territory. That is true, but it will be many years before those lacunae have been filled and it is not fair to let the students of this important subject wait so long. Precisely because there are still so many blank pages in our catalogue of African religions, an attempt at a guidebook may show up the limits of our knowledge and understanding of Africa.

Africa is still not adequately appreciated in the Western world, not even in scholarly circles. Learned works on the 'World Religions' will discuss African religions in a few paragraphs in the chapter on the 'primal' religions. This new word means that African religions, like north Asian and Amerindian religions, are comparable to primeval, prehistoric spheres of beliefs and ritual practices, without the sophistication and systemization of the real world religions of our times.

The present writer has found, on the contrary, that African religions (the term 'religion' will be discussed in the chapter on terms) are intricately complex systems of thinking, in which the beliefs, myths and cosmology of an ethnic group are interwoven with their moral code and rules of behaviour, into one infinitely variable organism of living religious ideas and actions.

In a volume like this no complete system of myths can be described in any detail. Only a few glimpses of insight can be shown to give the reader an idea of the inexhaustible wealth of African myths and legends, cosmology and narrative imagination.

Mythology is the study of myths. The word myth can be defined in more than one way. Here it will only be used in the meaning of a description of the deities and other spiritual beings which, in Africa, populate the 'other' world, the world of invisible creatures and forces, where only prophets and shamans are at home, and only under special precautions. These spiritual beings may be found in dangerous places, such as whirlpools, or in trees and even in the houses. Numerous myths are told about them. Many people I consulted refused to discuss them, but some African scholars have no objection to mentioning the spirits' names.

Those years in Africa were the best years of my life, during which I learned to think in an entirely different manner. In Africa, many people never read or write, but they have keen and clear brains, uncluttered by all the useless data with which we fill our storage cells. I have found my African preceptors exceptionally sagacious, their remarks to the point, their human knowledge full of wisdom and understanding of the world around them. Some African peoples have not yet broken all connections with nature, as we have. They approach their environment with awe and respect, not as destructive exploiters. They revere the elephant and the lion as kings of the forest and the savannah, by no means inferior to man. People are only one of the numerous species of Creation permitted to walk on the face of the earth, not as divine regents, but as fellow eaters of the earth-food. Life in the wilderness is a struggle between equals who have equal rights to live and eat, and equal chances to die and be eaten. Life is hard in Africa, so it can only be lived by those who are endowed with a grim determination to survive and a boundless energy to enjoy every day. This makes African people more cheerful than the gloomy northerners, more inclined to dance, feast and make merry. Here we can learn a little wisdom-of-life.

It may be that some of that energy is gained by staying close to nature, or by listening to the counsels of the spirits who know more than we, and are tremendously strong and powerful. More research is needed here into the psychological reality of this nature mysticism. Much more research is also needed into the dark aspects of spiritual life: witchcraft, black magic, and sorcery. We also need teams of researchers to study the trees, herbs and other vegetation from which African doctors make the medicines which they use for curing the many diseases of Africa.

In this work, these doctors are assisted (so we have been told) by the spirits which help them find the right medicinal herbs. We are a long way from understanding these spiritual methods of healing, which can only be approached when we know the cosmology in which they function. A people's cosmology describes their world-view, their belief in gods and spirits, their convictions regarding dream and reality, their relations toward the world of nature surrounding them, and their own place and function in that world. A cosmology is a description of the world we live in, not from a physico-scientific point of view, but as a spiritual world.

It is from this cosmology, which makes the physical environment into a meaningful spiritual world, that a person derives his purpose in life. This purpose may be to venerate the ancestors, to live in harmony with nature, to marry and raise a family so that one's children may venerate the ancestors including their parents in order to continue the chain of living generations in the world of the living. A purpose in life is dependent on a cosmology, such as, in this case, the belief in a spiritual life after this life. On this purpose in turn is based the morality which guides a man and a woman through their lives and makes these lives meaningful. Without such a cosmology embedded in religion, there would be no morality, since there would be no purpose in life, no faith in anything.

These simple facts explain much of the turbulence in modern Africa. The impact of the colonial period has been to destroy the fine fabric of beliefs and morality in the traditional societies. Africans were told by Europeans that they were simple idolaters and that ancestor worship is foolish, primitive nonsense. But what have they been given in return for the devaluation of their religions? Every human being needs something of value in his or her life, something to live for, a rule for life, a purpose, a meaning. When that is destroyed, life itself becomes valueless, and there is nothing left to control the forces of destruction, no fear of punishment by the gods.

We cannot create a new philosophy of life for Africans. What we can do is to reassemble the known fragments of the old religions. Much of the good faith has been overgrown by sorcery and witchcraft in the last hundred years, precisely because the old true religions crumbled. Good gave way to evil. Fortunately, there are numerous sources for the study of the religions of Africa. In spite of the attrition by modern 'civilization', many religions are still alive or, at least, are still remembered by the elders of the clan. Scholars have, during the last hundred years, left us good descriptions of the rites and ceremonies they witnessed, and others have given summaries of what the elders told them about their gods, their history and their relations with the gods. Other scholars have written down religious songs, hymns and prayers to the gods in the original languages and added translations and explanations.

Narrative myths, fables and fairy-tales have also been taken down and published, though much work remains to be done in this field. This author has spent the past 35 years editing the oral religious traditions of Africa, after carefully collecting them. Obviously no author can study all the cultures of the entire African continent, not even superficially visit them. More than a thousand completely different languages are spoken in Africa, where almost every nation is composed of numerous ethnic groups with distinct cultures and religions, speaking mutually unintelligible languages. In Somalia only three languages are spoken, in Zimbabwe only nine, but in Kenya 39, in Uganda and Ghana 22 each, in Tanzania 46, in Ethiopia and Eritrea together 76 and in Zaïre 326. All these are distinct languages; dialects are not counted in this survey. Nigeria, Cameroun and the Sudan speak some two hundred languages each. Unknown languages are still being described by diligent linguists, while missionaries are busy translating the Bible into all the languages of Africa. Some languages are spoken by millions of speakers, like Yoruba, Hausa and Igbo (Ibo) in Nigeria, others by only a few dozen speakers, like !Kung (the ! is a click) a language spoken by some Bushmen in Namibia. The languages of the pygmies in the dense forests of Zaïre and Gabon are also spoken by very small groups of people. However, as soon as a scholar arrives to stay with these peoples, learn their language and record their oral traditions, suddenly an unknown world is opened, populated by gods and spirits, fairies and witches and all the imaginable creatures of human literary creativity. Wherever scholars have worked among the speakers of a language, they discovered so many folk-tales, songs of every type, proverbs and riddles, that they could fill tomes with their recorded material, translations and explanatory notes, dictionaries and grammars. Epic poetry, recited during long nights of festive celebrations, has filled volumes of scholarly works. Far from being primitive, as some people think, African languages are extremely complex and difficult to learn, full of idiom and complicated structures, while African conversation is interspersed with proverbs referring to every aspect of their culture, religion, behaviour and history.

The complete collection of all the myths of the African peoples would fill hundreds of thousands of pages, even with our incomplete knowledge. This writer has had to choose and select until only the most important aspects of some of the African religions remained, including all the common aspects which distinguish African religions from European, Asian and American religions. Mythology, the backbone of religion, will constitute the major part of the contents. Other aspects of religion, such as ceremonies, hymns and prayers, shrines or spirit-houses, sacred places and objects, will be mentioned only when indispensable for the understanding of the myths. Since every myth belongs to a particular people, or group of peoples, the name of the people will be mentioned in every entry. The major ethnic groups of Africa all have an entry giving their habitat, numbers, language and a few more details.

The word tribe is no longer used except in a special well-defined meaning: an endogamous group of intermarrying clans which share a language and a religion. The only practical criterion by which an ethnic group can be defined is its common language, so 'the Hausa' will mean 'the speakers of Hausa'. Note the prefix *Ba-* for 'people', e.g. *Bakongo*, *Baganda*, *Baluba*, meaning 'the Kongo people', 'the Ganda people', 'the Luba people'.

Several useful anthropological terms can no longer be used, but they have not been replaced by a word of equal clarity. For instance, the word Bantu for a large group of peoples speaking a well-defined family of languages and so belonging to clearly related cultures, is now 'out' among some people. The word Hottentot, which honestly means nothing else except a person belonging to a certain type of people, has also been discouraged. But the word that is being promoted to replace it, Khoi, does not mean the same. The Khoi form only a section of the large family of Hottentot speakers. The term San for the Bushmen is even worse. 'San' is a small group of people in West Namibia who speak a Khoi language, not a Bushman tongue which is quite different. The term 'ethnic group' for tribe is worse, not better. It has no precise meaning, nor is it less denigratory. 'Ancestor worship' is another term that is being discouraged by some as if it was something to be ashamed of. Professor Noel King of UCLA has suggested we should refer to it as 'communicating with one's forebears'; it can be that, for instance, when a *nganga* or shaman listens to the voices of his father and grandfather when they give him advice. However, when people go to the graves of the ancestors, pray to them at their shrine, bring food, beer and other offerings, this must be referred to as worship.

There is another problem in the use of English words for forms of magic practices, which are totally different. The word 'witch' is the most hotly debated term in anthropology. The English word 'witch', like the German *Hexe*, is inescapably associated with the Christian Middle Ages. Witches keep cats, tell fortunes, put spells on people and fly on their broomsticks to the annual gathering under the leadership of Satan himself, the Prince of Evil. There is nothing comparable to this anywhere in Africa, least of all the idea of a central organization of Evil opposing the Good Christian hierarchy of the Church.

In Africa, a witch has been defined as 'a person whose body contains . . . witchcraft substance and who is supposed to practise witchcraft' (Evans-Pritchard, *Witchcraft*, 1937, p. 9). Witchcraft is: 'a supposed psychic emanation from witchcraft-substance (see *Mangu*) which is supposed to cause injury to health and property' (ibid.). It is obvious that this definition is totally inapplicable to any witch-beliefs in a European context. I have tried to overcome this problem by introducing a Bantu word like *Baloi* (q.v.) but to discuss all the words in African languages for magic practices and those who use them would be impractical. By reiterating the word 'supposed', Evans-

Pritchard demonstrates that he does not believe in witchcraft; nor can anyone who was not born into such a culture. When, many years ago, as a green researcher, I ventured that I had never seen a ghost, I was told curtly: 'You have not been here very long yet.' However, it is the duty of the anthropologist to try and understand the people he lives amongst in so far as his limited time permits. Every culture is a different world, so there are at least as many different worlds as there are religions. Every religion has its own cosmology, its own cosmos, i.e. its own universe of reality, the familiar world of the believers.

African peoples are more religious than Europeans, readier to dedicate time and energy to worship. This is good news for Christianity and Islam, religions to which now more than half the African population belongs. The study of Islam lies entirely outside the scope of this book. (See for this Knappert, *Islamic Legends*, Leiden, Holland, E. J. Brill, 1985.) Christianity prospers in most countries south of the Sahara, the Roman Catholic Church especially in 'French-speaking' African countries such as Zaïre. The Protestant churches are also richly represented in Africa. None of these come within the purview of this work, except in one respect: many African communities have split off from one Christian church or other and have set up churches of their own. In other cases African religious leaders have founded communities which they call churches, in many cases after seeing Jesus or an angel who spoke to them. Many African usages and beliefs are incorporated in the communal services of these churches or sects. In this field we are evidently on the borderline between African and Christian religions. Though many African religious leaders claim that their churches are Christian, many Christian theologians maintain that there is too much non-Christian belief and practice in these so-called free churches to call them Christian. This author is no partisan to this dispute. Some of the names of these leaders and their movements will be included in this dictionary because of their huge influence on their fellow Africans.

The purpose of this work is firstly to be a guide in the maze of African myths and beliefs, secondly to give students of Africa an introduction to the numerous very beautiful religious and literary motifs in African myths. Thirdly I sincerely hope that Africans as well as others will realize how rich the African heritage is, and that African religions deserve to be studied in their own right, side by side with other religions, in Europe and Asia.

Scope and Arrangement

Frequent references to the Bible, and to Greek mythology will demonstrate the obvious and numerous parallels between many African religions and those of the ancient peoples of the Mediterranean Basin. The Romans and Phoenicians built cities in North Africa where they worshipped their gods. Many Africans no doubt followed their example. The single most brilliant culture and religion in Africa before Christianity is that of ancient Egypt, where the gods are often depicted with the heads of African animals: crocodile, hippopotamus, ibis, lion and jackal. It is true that the Greek gods, too, have an animal aspect, but they are not shown in Greek art with their animal features, whereas the Egyptian gods, like those of many African nations, have prominent animal appearances.

There can be no doubt that this highly complex and sophisticated religion has profoundly influenced the religions and mythologies of the African peoples. On the other hand, the origin of the Egyptian religion itself may have to be found in Africa, where traces of related deities abound.

The lexicographer of African mythology is faced with the problem of the choice of entries. No African gods and heroes are known to the public like Jupiter and Hercules or Isis and Osiris. How many readers will look for Lianja or Liongo, two great heroes of African mythology? How many have heard of the great Yoruba gods with their formidable names like Olodumare and Obatala? It has seemed better, in writing for an English-reading public, to arrange the subjects under English headings, and under the names of peoples and provinces, though I have assumed that the reader knows a little about the geography of Africa, so that he can find, for example, Buganda or Kasai.

Even professional Africanists are often confused by the many names by which each people is known to its neighbours. Their gods and heroes, too, are referred to by a variety of names, many of which are praise names, such as Mukulu Ijulu 'the Great One Above', the Old Swahili name for God, quoted by the Arab traveller Al-Mas'udi in the tenth century.

Using what may seem to be English equivalents leads to other problems. For instance, the English witch is associated in popular consciousness with cat and broomstick, toad and lizard, but an African witch is no joke. She or he (in Africa, witches can be men) can terrify people without even knowing it.

Some articles in this guide will therefore begin by giving the reader a definition of the English word, in so far as a neat definition is possible in myth and folklore; after that the 'equivalent' of the same idea in Africa is described, subject to the restrictions mentioned above. 'Ghosts' do not differ much in Africa and Europe, except perhaps that in Africa they are more malicious, in Europe pitiful. This is a Greek idea: that the poor dead no longer participate in the enjoyments of life and company on this sunny surface.

Some head-words are illustrated by means of the beliefs of a particular people somewhere in Africa. In other entries examples have been adduced from a number of regions in different parts of Africa. It is hoped that this varied treatment will give an idea of the incredible diversity and richness of African mythology. Yet, there seems to be a mysterious unity hidden in these numerous views of the divine: the proliferating tales of magic beings and wild animals all focus on the problem of Man's place on this earth where he seems hardly welcome, and his relations with his fellow beings, which are not always happy. For instance, the terror and anxiety about witchcraft reflects the sadness over the loss and suffering of loved ones, and anger which is really disguised fear.

At the other end of the scale there is the joy of life, expressed in dancing and singing, and in sacrifices out of unspoken gratitude to the deities of earth and high heaven. The same truth can be expressed in many ways, in art or myth. This is the basic truth of human existence in love and fear.

A Note on Sources

This work represents in the first place the results of fieldwork in Africa during 11 journeys undertaken between 1957 and 1988, some lasting only a few weeks, some more than a year, taking me to all the corners of Africa, from Casablanca to Cape Town to Cairo. Since it is impossible even to visit all the peoples of Africa in a lifetime, numerous written, published and unpublished, sources have been consulted as well as various experts in the field of mythology and African religion. A selected bibliography is included, but this does not reflect the enormous amount of available material. The potential for confusion created by the fact that there are so many different peoples in Africa, each with their languages and their dialects, is aggravated by the fact that the majority of these are known by more than one name, depending on who is speaking. The problem is not helped by the fact that some African states have been renamed, sometimes with names which already had another meaning, and that some writers refer to the same peoples with different hames. For example, Dahomey was renamed Benin, which is the name of a city in Nigeria. The Gold Coast was named Ghana, which was the name of a long-lost city in Mali. The Swahili people used to be called Coastal Arabs or Afro-Arabs, or Coast-Muslims. Nowadays, they are sometimes included in the Miji Kenda, which is in fact a comprehensive name for nine tribes speaking different languages, all in eastern Kenya.

Apart from their multiplicity, African names present problems of pronunciation. The Bantu languages are the easiest to pronounce, since they are comparable to Italian or Hawaiian. Their words are composed of open syllables, as in Japanese, so the name of King Solomon becomes Sulemani, with the stress on *ma*, almost always on the penultimate syllable of the word.

The letter *y* is always a consonant, as in yes. *Ny* is thus pronounced as *gn* in French and Italian, e.g. *Nyang*, the word for crocodile in the Nilotic languages, which have a totally different structure. Most of the languages of South Africa have clicks which are written in a variety of ways; so, in Zulu (Natal) and Xhosa (Kossa) in Transkei, the letters *c*, *q*, and *x* are in use to represent different types of clicks.

The Bushman languages (including San) and the Hottentot languages (including Khoi) use other characters to indicate the clicks. Thus the name !Kung for one of the peoples of Namibia is pronounced beginning with clicking the tip of the tongue, but in pronouncing Xhosa one clicks with the right side of the tongue, followed by the *h* which is pronounced.

In West African languages the big problem is the implosive consanants *gb, kp, ngb, ngmb* and others, which defeat the learner of African languages who does not persevere.

The biggest problem in African languages is their melody. Almost all the languages of Africa are tone languages, which means that every syllable has its own tone, as if they are sung. The tone depends on the meaning of the word and its grammatical structure, e.g. the past tense of a verb may be pronounced on a higher or lower tone than the present tense.

The reader of this book should not be discouraged by these linguistic details, but just pronounce the names as he sees fit. Remember that every letter has to be pronounced; it is there for a purpose.

A

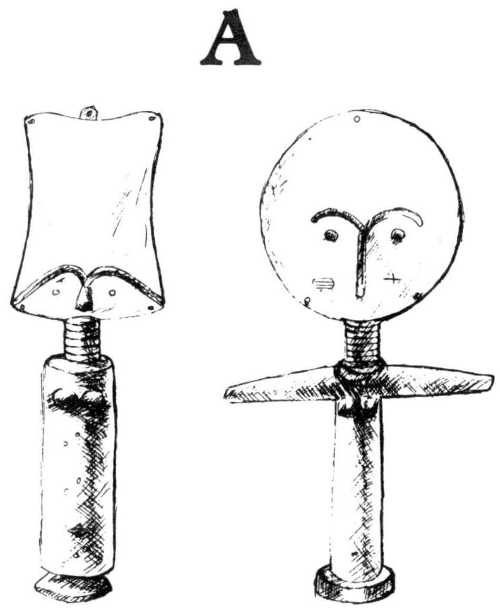

Ashanti fertility figures from Ghana

Aardvark In African folklore the aardvark, or ant-bear, has a good name not only because it is unafraid of armies of soldier ants but also because it digs diligently searching for food all night, an example and model for lazy cultivators.

The Hausa magicians can make a charm which is very much sought after by thieves and lovers. With the root of a certain tree, they pound up the heart, a piece of skin from the forehead and the nails of a *dabgi* (Hausa for ant-eater or ant-bear), which, wrapped up in a piece of skin, is worn on the chest. The owner can now lean against a wall in the middle of the night, and the wall will give, allowing him to enter the courtyard of the house he wants to burgle. If he sits down on the roof, he will go through it and so visit his paramour without her father's consent.

Acholi (Religion, Uganda). The Acholi are a Nilotic people speaking a language that is closely related to Alur, Lango, Luo and Shilluk. They call themselves Lwoo, 'Noblemen'. During the migration southward of these proud cattle-owners, they remained on the eastern (right) bank of the Nile, whereas the Alur (q.v.) crossed over westward.

The Acholi have a famous term, *jok* (q.v.), which is seldom used in the plural but which can be compared to the Latin word *Di* for the gods as a collectivity, although it is often translated as 'God'. *Jok* live or lives in a cave between the hills Alela and Baka, where offerings of food and beer are brought. Every clan has its own *jok* which for this reason has been referred to as 'totem-god' (see *Totemism*). Every clan has its own *abela* or lineage shrine, a small hut for the local *jok*. Each *jok* had its animal name, and if a child was descended from a *jok* called *kwach* 'leopard', he could change himself into a leopard and even go into the bush and play with the leopards. Only his mother would know and she would not tell anybody. Some members of the clan called Ngech related that their ancestor was one of twins. The other twin ran away into the bush where he turned into a monitor lizard (*ngech*), hence the name of that clan. Not all spirits are animals, though. Some are associated with mountains, wells, woods or rivers. Certain elders are charged with the care for the deities, the *latedo* 'priest'. There is also a *latedo-tiim* 'bush-priest' who performs the necessary rites for good hunting, and the *latedo koot* 'rain-priest', who prays for rain. The *won-ngom* 'Earth-father', is a descendant of the aboriginal people who 'came out of the earth'; he is especially in charge of the deities of the earth and the water. He is jointly responsible with the *latedo-koot* for rain-making (q.v.).

Afterlife All traditional African peoples agree that the soul of an individual lives on after death. Some people distinguish more than one spiritual essence living within one person, the life-soul or bio-spirit which disappears at the moment of definitive death, and the thought-soul which keeps his individual identity even after it is separated from the body. The life-soul can, according to some peoples in Africa and Asia, be separated during a person's life, in times of danger, and be kept hidden in a safe place, so that its owner can be harmed, mortally wounded even, but not killed, as long as his life-soul is safe. When the danger is past, the life-soul can be restored to the body and the person is hale and hearty again. The thought-soul lives on after death, but not for ever, it may gradually die and be forgotten. Souls of little children who died young, those of weak minds and insignificant persons will fade away after some years lingering.

If, however, an individual had a strong personality, a rich and famous man, a mother of many children, a chief, someone who was loved or admired, that soul will live on for many generations. Evil souls, too, may have a long afterlife: witches (q.v.), sorcerers (q.v.), the souls with a grudge, who have a score to settle, will wait for their revenge and haunt the living for years.

The oldest concept of the place where the dead continue their existence is the forest (q.v.). The impenetrable depth of the great forests of Africa is the heartland of the spirits and of all magical beings.

Where there are steep rocks, the dead reside in deep, dark caves, where their souls flutter about disguised as bats (q.v.). Below the surface of rivers and lakes is the habitat of many souls. Many others linger on near the graveyards where they were buried. The good souls of the loved ones who have died, the wise parents' souls still accompany their living children and grandchildren. (See also *Ancestors; Burial; Death; Rebirth; Reincarnation*.)

Afterlife (Yoruba, Nigeria). The Yoruba believe that each person has at least three spiritual beings. Firstly there is the spirit, *emi*, literally 'breath', which resides in the lungs and heart and is fed by the wind through the nostrils, just as the fire is fed through the twin openings in the blacksmith's bellows. This *emi* is the vital force which makes a man live, that is, breathe, rise up, walk, be aware, be active, work, speak, see, hear and make love. There is also the shadow or shade, *ojiji*, which follows its owner like a dog. When he dies, it awaits his return in heaven. The third is the *eleda* 'spirit' or *ori* 'head', also translated as 'guardian soul'; from time to time it has to be 'fed' by sacrifices. At death these spiritual aspects of a person leave the body and wait for him or her in heaven. An individual is expected to return to his clan as a newborn baby. Babatunde, 'Father returns' is a name which is given to a child when it resembles his father's father; Yetunde 'Mother returns' for a girl. Physical resemblances determine the identity of the baby.

Before death, the *emi*-spirit may visit relatives, clan-members who will thus learn in a dream that their kinsman or -woman is going to die soon. Even in daytime, the cold presence of a dying relative may be felt from far away, as if he were close by.

The ghosts of those who died in mid-life may go and live in distant towns and assume a quasi-physical existence there. A man who died early in life might even marry, his wife would not even know that her husband was dead already, a mere ghost. When the final hour arrives, the man dies a second time.

After death the guardian soul arrives in heaven and confesses to the Supreme God Olorun (q.v.) what it has done on earth. The good souls will then be sent to the Good Heaven, Orun Rere. The souls of the wicked, those who are guilty of theft, murder or cruelty, poisoning, witchcraft or slander, will be sent to Orun Buburu, the Bad Heaven, as punishment.

Akan (Ghana). Akan is the name of a beautiful language which includes a number of dialects or rather, varieties, such as Twi and Fante. It is spoken all over the ancient kingdom of Ashanti (q.v.). All these peoples have comparable religious beliefs.

Onyame or Nyame is their Supreme God (see for a related name for God: *Nzambi*); originally the word may have just meant 'the sky', hence the proverb: 'No one shows a child the sky (or God).' Onyame helps all those who cannot help themselves, and His wisdom overcomes all human problems. Onyame is Borebore 'the Maker' and Totrobonsu 'the Giver of Rain', Onyankopon 'the Great and Shining One', Odomankoma 'the Giver of Boundless Abundance'. People say: 'No one will see the end except Onyame,' and: 'Fear no one except Onyame.' Onyame was worshipped in the shape of a tree trunk, like Diana-Artemis in Greek antiquity. Food offerings were brought to him.

Asase Yaa was the Earth Goddess (see under *Earth*). A cock was sacrificed to her by the farmers every year, to ensure good crops.

In the south, the Ocean God Opo, son of Onyame, is venerated by the coastal people. Opo has special priests and mediums. The great bodies of water in Akan country, the Lake Bosomtwe and the River Tano, are both sacred, and revered by the people.

The Asamanfo (plural of Osaman) are the spirits of the dead, most of whom live in Asamang, the World of the Dead, which is thought to be far away in the mountains, where they live much the same lives as they did on earth: kings are kings and the poor will be poor. The spirits of the ancestors are invoked by their descendants, to grant prosperity, by libations and food.

It is said that everyone receives his *mogya* 'blood', i.e. his physical body, from his mother's *abusua* or maternal ancestors, but his *sunsum* or personality comes from his paternal ancestors whose clan, *ntoro*, descended from a divinity.

Albinos see under *Children*.

Alexander the Great (Sikandari, Iskender). In the Islamic legendary tradition numerous sagas circulate describing the peregrinations and exploits of Alexander – in Arabic Al-Iskandar, Sikandari in Swahili, to which are added his praise names Dhuli Karineni, the Horned One; this phrase is much corrupted in the oral traditions. It refers to Koran 18, 83-98, which alludes to his conquests. God had given to Alexander the empire of the whole earth, so the young ruler set out to assume command in all the countries, and also in Africa. Numerous tales are told by the Islamic story-tellers about Alexander's adventures in Africa. After his romantic meeting with the Queen of Andalucia, Alexander crossed over to Africa, where on the extreme western cape of the known world there is a huge building full of machinery, where a dozen angels pump the seawater into the ground from where, through a network of tunnels, it finds its way to the source of the three great rivers then known: Nile, Niger and Zambezi which, it was believed, shared a common source, in the Mountains of the Moon, where water from heaven is added to make the rivers 'sweet'. No doubt this Arabian tale was inspired by an Aristotelian or Archimedean theory of the circulation of the earth's water supply. From there, Alexander and his army marched south-east through the Sahara for 40 days. In the centre, they came upon a vast lake, probably Lake Chad, which saved them from certain death of thirst.

After that they arrived in the country of the black people, Ethiopia or Abessynia, Habashia in Arabic. Its king, Azimu by name, followed the religion of Abraham; his rival worshipped speaking idols. Alexander marched on to the Jabali Lamma, the Gleaming Mountain, which is the source of five rivers (perhaps Ruwenzori?). Further south he met the king of the Zuru (Zulu or Zezuru?) who were a strong, able-bodied nation, and the Wakongela, who were converted to Alexander's religion: they may be the modern Walemba. On the west coast, Alexander slew the terrible sea-serpent Tinnin.

Algeria see *ghoula*.

Alur (Religion, Uganda-Zaïre). The Alur number over 200,000 persons living astride the Uganda-Zaïre border to the west of Lake Albert and the Nile. They speak a Nilotic language closely related to Acholi. The Alur believe in Rubanga the Creator, whose name is of Bantu origin, and who is associated with the ibis, the bird that was once sacred to the ancient Egyptian god Thoth-Hermes. *Jok* (q.v.) is the Alur word for the spirits collectively, especially the spirits of nature, tree-spirits, but also wicked spirits. In pre-colonial times the Alur nation, then undivided by frontiers, had a sacred kingship system. The king was chosen from a particular clan, and his first act would be to pray to his ancestors' shrines in his father's graveyard. Then he would be carried on the chiefs' shoulders and the women would ululate. He would then be secluded for some days, sitting in the laps of two of his father's widows who would feed him milk, like a newborn baby. He must not eat meat of the *ruda*, the bushbuck sacred to the Alur, nor any foreign food such as sugar.

In order to wield power, the king has to be in full possession of four objects representing the four elements: the *kidikoth*, the rainstones hidden in a bag made of a frogskin; the *tong*, the royal spear which shines like fire on the battlefield; the *vul*, the royal drum, the king's voice carrying his command; and the *kom*, the royal stool symbolizing possession of the land, *ngom*.

In those days the king was the chief rain-maker and only the sacred rainstones ensured him the veneration a king needs in order to reign. Without them there would be no rain. The spear was the legalization of the king's authority over the nation's warriors. Without the drum the king's orders would not be listened to. Finally, the *komdongo* 'the chair of food', the royal throne, was the most essential of the *jamker*, 'the instruments of royal dignity', without which the king could not 'grow', i.e. prosper, and the nation could not eat, nor give birth. (See also *Cattle; Months; Rain-making*.)

Amazonas (Amazons, West Africa). The Greek word *amazona* seems to mean 'woman without breast' (*mazos*). The myth of the Amazon women warriors is very old; it was said they used to cut off the right breast so that they could draw their bowstrings more effectively. The

Arab authors, however, maintain that they were born with one male and one female breast. Others again wrote that their breast was more like a cow's udder, in the middle of the body. 'But only God knows.' It was believed that they lived in the western desert along one bank of a river (the Senegal?), while the men lived on the other bank. Only once a year, during the dry season, could the men wade through to visit their women and make them pregnant. Others again have quoted yet greater and older authorities who have said that the climate out there was so harsh that only daughters survived; the women became pregnant by simply bathing in a certain pool. (This is a well-known mythical motif: in the pool there lives a male being, usually a jinn, who mates with the women.) According to this account, the Amazon women were devoid of physical desire; they never permitted men to have carnal relations with them. They were, according to Islamic writers, faithful Muslim women, who lived strictly according to God's law. The Koran states that God can make a woman pregnant without a man if He so wishes (3: 47). Nor did these women have a desire for ornaments, gold or jewels of any kind; they lived frugally from the labour in the fields and shared the fruits of their hard work. Thus they never sinned for it is only desire for wealth and the flesh that makes us sinful. No author states whether these women were Berbers or negroes, nor have they been found by any traveller since Alexander (q.v.).

Amma (Dogon, Mali). Amma is the Creator in the mythology of the Dogon of Mali. He first created the sun as a pot from clay which he fired until it was white hot. He surrounded this gigantic pot with a spiral of red copper which he wound around it eight times. Then he created the moon in the same fashion but smaller and wound a spiral of brass ('white copper') around it. Later, Amma created the shining black people out of sunlight, and the white people out of moonlight. Then Amma took more clay and created the earth in the shape of a female body lying with its head towards the north and its legs towards the south. Its *mons veneris* is an anthill, its clitoris is a termite hill, which Amma circumcized. Now, Amma, the god of heaven, could have sexual intercourse with the earth. She gave birth to the first animal, the Golden Jackal (*Thos aureus*), which is reminiscent of the Egyptian Anubis.

The Creator fertilized the earth a second time by means of rain. As a result she gave birth to twins, half human but with tails like green snakes and with forked tongues. Their name was Nummo 'Water'. They together became the grass, the plants and the trees. They joined their father in the sky and, looking down, saw their mother naked, so they began to clothe her with reeds and shrubs. As the first wind, which the twins' movements caused, stirred in the leaves and branches, language began to be heard on earth. Amma created the stars by scattering pieces of sun across the sky. Then

Amma modelled the first man and woman out of clay and gave them life. He circumcized each of them. The man's prepuce became a black and white lizard. Afterwards the woman's clitoris became a scorpion. The first couple mated and the woman gave birth to four sets of twins in succession, four boys first, then four girls. From these eight children descended all the people of Dogon.

Amulets Amulets are used almost universally in Africa, by Muslim as well as non-Muslim peoples and by many Christians as well. The original meaning of the word amulet was 'a piece of food', from the Greek *amylon* 'food'. This food was placed at the place where a certain spirit was thought to pass, so that it might be fed and become friendly or at least not be harmful. The Latin word *amuletum* was associated with the verb *amolire* 'to ward off, avoid, protect', and this has always been the true purpose of an amulet: to protect its owner against specific dangers. In modern times there are amulets against failing exams and against losing a football match. Numerous amulets will protect the wearer against the evil eye, the evil tongue (i.e. someone mumbling curses against the wearer will see them come back upon his own head), and the evil hand.

The great majority of amulets are intended to protect their owners against witchcraft and sorcery and any other forms of black magic, which are all thought to cause illness in people or their animals, including infertility. Every amulet thus has a certain inherent power, like magnetic energy, that can arrest and reverse the evil forces attacking its owner. Thus Hausa magicians can make an amulet from the skin of an electric eel, *munjiriyya*, which lives in the Niger. Its owner cannot be caught by robbers nor arrested by the police, but will slip out of their hands, and their weapons will be ineffective against him. Many of their amulets are written antidotes (*makarii*) against poison (*sammo*). Children especially have to wear rows of amulets against ailments of every limb or organ.

Anansi the Spider (Ghana). One unlucky day fire raged in the savannah. All the animals were running around frantically; some were already surrounded by fire and doomed to perish. An antelope was looking for an escape route, when she heard a tiny voice: 'Please let me sit in your ear so we can escape together from here!' It was Anansi the Spider, who, without waiting for an invitation, jumped down from a branch and settled in the antelope's ear. The antelope had no clue where to go but the spider knew the way out. There seemed to be fire everywhere, but the spider directed the antelope confidently: 'Now to the left, now straight on. . .' until the antelope's swift legs had carried them both to safety, across streams and brooks and swamps. When the fire was far behind them, the spider ran down to the ground along the antelope's leg, saying: 'Thank you very much for your kindness. We shall meet again some time.'

Not long afterwards the antelope gave birth to a little baby antelope, which spent most of its first weeks hiding in the shrubs while its mother was grazing; later, it could be seen grazing beside its mother. One unlucky day two hunters arrived and spotted the mother antelope. While the little one crouched down under the shrubs, the mother leaped up to catch the hunters' attention, limping away but staying just out of range of the hunters' arrows. After an hour the hunters gave up the pursuit and went back to the young antelope, but they searched in vain and left the forest empty-handed. A long time later the mother came back but she could not find her young either. After a long search she heard a familiar voice calling her. It was the spider Anansi who led her to a thicket surrounded by a dense network of spider's threads. Inside, there lay, quite invisible and quite safe, the little antelope. Anansi had been very busy weaving webs all round the bush where it hid, so that the hunters passed it over.

Ancestors In many regions of Africa the ancestors are remembered and even worshipped. The spirits of parents and grandparents live on after death – that is not in doubt. They remain near their graves, emanating an invisible but always active power for the benefit of their descendants, provided they are not forgotten. At regular intervals, usually annually, an animal has to be ritually slaughtered and offered to the ancestors, or to a particular father or grandfather, in a family ceremony during which the spirit or spirits are invoked to remove disease and bless their children with children, with good health, with good crops, with increasing flocks or herds. In many households the husband and wife have their own ancestor shrines, where they perform their own rituals, just as Jacob and Rachel had their own god each. African religions are far more tolerant than Islam and even Christianity. It has even been said that ancestor worship is not really worship, since it is 'only' a trade-off between the living and the spirits, the latter being persuaded with sacrifices to remove the illnesses they have caused. It should be remembered that we meet a similar situation in ancient Rome, where the relations between people and their gods was almost commercial. The idea of worshipping a god in the sense of loving him or her is a very late development. Even in Islam the love of God is only mentioned by the mystics. Among the Zulu the spirit (*idlozi*) of a beloved father may be persuaded to come back after a year in the grave, and to take up permanent residence in the kraal of his children who can now come to him in times of need and worry. For chiefs, and especially for kings, the ceremonies instituted to appease their spirits were celebrated more frequently and more elaborately, with lavish meals for the worshippers.

The Kipsigis believe that every human spirit has existed for several generations. After death, the spirit of an ancestor will reincarnate in the body of a newly born descendant, so that the spirits will continue to live as long as the family survives. (See also *Afterlife; Burial; Death; Rebirth; Reincarnation*.)

Angels In Islamic Africa, angels are created by God from pure light in order to help people remain virtuous. In other parts of Africa, angels are good spirits or kind genii, sympathetic beings who may appear in any shape or form to help mortals in distress and despair. Very often a good genius appears to be the spirit of a compassionate relative who has died but still wants to help.

There was a girl in Zaïre whose mother had died. Her stepmother did not want to give her stepdaughter any food, so the poor girl often sat crying on her mother's grave. One morning a tree had grown up from the grave, bearing delicious sweet fruits in abundance, which kept the girl alive and healthy until the wicked stepmother persuaded her husband to have the tree cut down. The starving girl cried on the grave again, until she saw a pumpkin growing from the earth which was sweet and refreshing. A new one grew every morning, until the stepmother dug it out. Then a stream appeared, the water of which was fresh and nutritious, until the stepmother had it filled in with earth. The girl went back to her usual place to weep, until a hunter appeared who saw the dead tree lying on the grave and asked if he could make arrows from the wood. The girl said yes and the hunter fell in love with her because the mother's good spirit was putting him under her spell. The arrows killed a herd of buffaloes which was enough for a bride-price, so the girl married the hunter.

Angola see *Donna Beatrice; Fetish; Kalunga; Kianda; Kindoki; Kishi; Moonking; Ndoki; Nzambi; Ovambo; Ovimbundu; Spirits; Tebo.*

Ani see *Earth*.

Animals Animals play a vital role in African tales, religion and mythology. From an early age, African children hear the fables (i.e. stories with a lesson) in which the chief characters are the Hare (Bre'r Rabbit), the Tortoise, the Squirrel, the Jackal (q.v.), the Hyena (q.v.), the Lion (q.v.), the Leopard (q.v.), the Elephant (q.v.), the Crocodile (q.v.), the Spider (see *Anansi the Spider*), the Hedgehog and many others.

The student of African tales has to be a zoologist, so many animals, birds, reptiles and insects populate the African myths. African storytellers know a great deal about animals and much of what they weave into their tales is based on correct observation. On the other hand, there are many tales of animals who behave like human beings because they have human spirits. Many animals marry human beings in myths and have often children with them who have characteristics of both human and animal creatures, so they will catch prey or gnaw juicy bones. Animals speak many languages, which only King Solomon and very few others could understand.

Animism Animism is the belief that there is a soul (*anima*) or spirit (*animus* in the natural world or even in every separate natural phenomenon. No African informant could answer specific questions on such problems as: 'If that stone has life, does it breathe?' 'Is there a spirit in every single tree or is the whole forest together one spirit?' 'Can trees think?' Yet the man who stumbles over a tree root may think that the tree stuck it out on purpose, to trip him. Only living things have their own spirits, whereas stones and rocks may be *inhabited* by spirits. Since a spirit is invisible, the animal or the tree may be seen as only the habitat of the spirit, so that there is no definable difference between the phrases 'the tree *has* a spirit' or 'the tree *is* a spirit'. Sometimes a whole family of spirits is believed to live in a tree, e.g. the baobab in Kenya, the tree that never dies (q.v.). Animism is one of those terms that have been so over-used that they become difficult to define for the professional. Animism, as a blanket term for all religions that are not Islam or Christianity in Africa, is certainly misleading. Not all African religions are animistic.

Antara (North Africa). Antara (also Antar, Antari) is an Arab hero whose exploits in North Africa are still sung in Egypt and as far west as Morocco. Antara's father is Shaddad or Shadadi, an Arab who, during his conquest of the Sudan, 'liberates' a young woman called Zabiba ('Raisin'), who later turns out to be the King's daughter. She bears him Antara, a boy who at 2 is already strong enough to pull down a tent; at 4 he slays a large dog, at 9 a wolf and at 15 a lion, with his hands. Antara is the typical model of the poet-hero, like Liongo (q.v.). Some 27 poems and fragments are extant, in several of which there occurs the name of Abla, his cousin whom he loves ardently. However, he has to fulfil many arduous tasks before he is deemed worthy of marrying her. These tasks, and the accompanying exploits he performs, are described in ten volumes, which were composed probably during the thirteenth century. Antara conquers Morocco and Algeria, then turns on the Negus (Najusi), King of Habashia (Abessynia or Ethiopia), who appears to be his grandfather, his mother's father. When he wants to penetrate deeper into Africa he has to go through a huge tree, a baobab (q.v.), which is believed to be the abode of spirits. He finds himself in a palace in the sky surrounded by pomegranate trees in blossom. Deeper in Africa he comes upon a king called Humâm. This may be the word *umwami* 'king' in Rwanda and Burundi. Professor Norris, however, identifies this Bantu kingdom with Zimbabwe (q.v.) since the description fits in many details. In his numerous adventures, Antara discovers a witches' kitchen, the country of the Amazons, the warrior women in the far west of Africa (see *Amazonas*), whom Alexander the Great (q.v.) also met on his conquests. The historical Antara lived in the sixth century, before Islam. He may even have been a Christian and, according to the saga, he married a Christian princess and had a son called Jufran (Geoffrey).

Ants see under *Solomon, King*.

Ashanti (Religion, Ghana). Ashanti is the name of a people, their language and their kingdom, whose centre, the capital city Kumasi, was founded in 1665; the nation itself was considerably older and forms part of the Akan-Ashanti-Twi group of nations in South Ghana.

For the Ashanti people the ancestors, *nsamanfo* are ever-present, so that the world of the spirits is very close to the world of the ordinary people. At the other end of the scale of spiritual beings is Onyame or Nyame, the Supreme God, who is praised in Ashanti with many names: Onyankopon, the Great One, Otumfoo, the Powerful One, Odomankoma the Eternal One, the Wise One, the First and Oldest One, and many other descriptive names.

Every Obosom, god, has his or her priest, but Onyame has no priest; however, every worshipper has direct access to him, because he is not far but lives immediately above this world. Before Christianity there was a shrine dedicated to Onyame in every village where the people would bring offerings or wine.

The children of Onyame are, of course, also gods; they are in the first place the great rivers of Ashantiland, the Tano and the Bea, further the Lake Bosomtwe and the Ocean in the South. Onyame sent his children, the river-gods, to earth so that the waters might benefit all living beings and give them life, and so that people might honour the gods and show their gratitude.

Apart from a geographical area such as a river or lake, every god has a temple or shrine, and often a statue, where devotees congregate to worship. Every priest has been chosen by the god whom he serves. A famous case was that of Di Amono, a man who saw a stone in the forest. The stone was burning with high flames which clearly revealed the presence of a divinity. These visions still occur in Ashanti where the people are deeply religious. The god or goddess will from time to time take possession of a man or woman and use that person for the promulgation of the divine will. Such a person will be found in the forest, having spent several days in solitude there, alone with the deity, receiving the words of divine revelation. Such a chosen person will then come back to the world of people and be initiated into the priesthood by the senior priests of the same or other gods. Then he will be established as the new priest of the god who has revealed himself, and receive worshippers. The people will come with requests for good health or children and the priest will receive offerings and interpret the will of the god either on the basis of direct revelations, or of divination by means of cowrie shells, carved sticks and so on.

Spirits also live in the *asuman* (singular *suman*), a type of talisman in the form of beads, medicine balls or horns.

A very special deity is the Earth Goddess Asase Yaa (for whom see under *Earth Goddess*). Music and hymns are performed for her, since people know that we all depend on the earth.

There were believed to be ghosts and other terrifying spiritual beings living in the forests, called the *mmoatia*. These spirits possessed medicine and other magical powers. In the forest also there lived the Sasabonsam, a hairy and monstrous giant with large blood-red eyes, long legs and prehensile feet which would hook up any unwary traveller who took those dangling legs for lianas and aerial roots.

The hunter has to be on good terms with all these horrifying monsters. If he is, they may teach him magic and medicine, so he can manufacture and sell talismans and become a famous man. The need for such charms will remain as long as there is belief in the spirits, who can do harm as well as good, as they wish. (See also *Golden Stool*.)

Astrology Astrology as it is known in Europe, is a Greek invention. The Arab scholars of the Middle Ages eagerly translated the Greek books into Arabic. Extracts of those early works still circulate in North and West Africa. The Swahili and Malagasy peoples have developed an astrology of their own on the classical basis. Here are the names of the signs of the zodiac as they are known and used in East Africa, Zaïre, Nigeria, Mozambique and Madagascar.

Latin	*Swahili*	*Hausa*	*Malagasy*	*Meaning*
Aries	Hamali	Dan Tinkiya	Alahamady	Ram
Taurus	Thauri	Sa	Adaoro	Bull
Gemini	Jauza	Dami	Adizaoza	Twins
Cancer	Saratani	Kaguwa	Asorotany	Lobster, Crab
Leo	Asadi	Zaki	Alahasaty	Lion
Virgo	Sumbula	Zangariya	Asombola	Ear of Corn
Libra	Mizani	Ma'auni	Adimizana	Pair of Scales
Scorpio	Akarabu	Kunama	Alakarabo	Scorpion
Sagittarius	Kausi	Baka	Alakaosy	Bow
Capricornus	Jadi	Dan Akuya	Adi jady	Buck
Aquarius	Dalu	Guga	Adalo	Pail
Pisces	Hutu	Kifi	Alohotsy	Fish

According to the astrology of Madagascar, Aries, the Ram, is the most auspicious of all the signs; it is while the Sun is in Aries that the feast of the annual lustration is celebrated. Taurus is a little less auspicious; persons born under this sign are believed to be proud and unsympathetic.

Gemini is a good sign under which to undertake a journey or a voyage, to start a business or build a residence. Those born under it will live to a ripe old age, they say. Cancer is auspicious for the performance of religious rituals, whereas Leo is favourable for taking important decisions in life. Virgo is the best of all the signs: those born under it will be rich, having large and healthy families and enjoy good health themselves. Libra is the time for meditation and circumspection. Scorpio is the season of abundance assuring 'a fortune', good crops and for women pregnancy. Sagittarius, on the contrary, is a time of adversity, very inauspicious, indeed dangerous, for children born under this sign will cause disaster to the elders as well as to themselves. Elaborate expiation ceremonies will be necessary to remove the threat of bad luck hanging over such a child. In the old days children born under Sagittarius used to be executed in a custom which used to be called ritual infanticide. Later this was replaced by the removal of one digit of the right ring finger. Persons born under Capricorn are supposed to be cautious, proud and satisfied with themselves; they may expect to attain high functions in society. Aquarius predestines people for tears and sorrow, though it is not quite as bad as Sagittarius. Finally, Pisces is very favourable and beneficent. It is a time for important ceremonies, such as the first cutting of a baby's hair and the circumcision of boys. The days of the week also have a predestinatory charge: Monday is red, violent; Tuesday is favourable, light; Wednesday is inauspicious; Thursday is favourable; Friday is black, Saturday regretful; Sunday is good.

Atlantis There are tales told in Africa of the Queen of the Mountains, whose beauty is such that men will risk their lives and riches to find her in her palace in the wilderness. The French call her *l'Atlantide*, the Arabs *Hiya*. She will destroy the men who come to love her.

Azande see *Zande*.

B

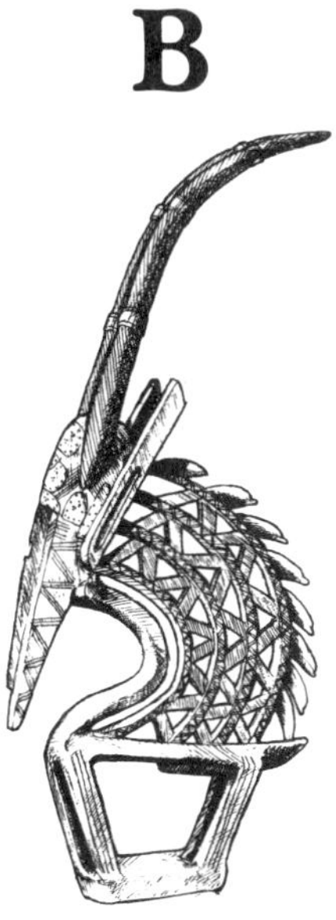

Bambara antelope head-dress from Mali

Bakongo (Creation myth, Zaïre). The Bakongo tell the following myth of the creation of people: Nzambi (q.v.) created the first man, who was called Ndosimau, and the first woman, who was called the Breaker of Prohibition. Nzambi told the couple what to do and set them free in the world. They built a hut and in due course of time they had a baby. Nzambi came to see them and said: 'If the baby dies, do not bury it, but cover the body under layers of firewood. After three days he will revive.' The baby died the next day, so the parents buried it under the firewood, but after a time it began to smell, so they buried it in the earth. Nzambi came back and said: 'You will have other children but they will all die and none will revive after that. Look at the moon! I restore it every month to its former splendour.'

Another myth relates that Nzambi first created Mahungu 'Breath', a human being who was both male and female, and so: *Muntu Walunga* 'The Complete Person'. It had the shape of a palm-tree with two heads. Wooden statuettes show the tree with breasts on one side, with a woman's head, and on the other side a bearded head, the two coming out of a spathe, like a spadix emerging from a sheath of palm-leaf. This double person lived a happy life since it knew no jealousy or hatred, no desire or want. One day Mahungu saw the tree called Muti Mpungu, the tree of the Supreme Being. Mahungu went up to the tree trying to embrace it, but the tree split Mahungu into two equal personalities, who were henceforth called Lumbu (Man) and Muzita (Woman). After this event they always wanted to be together and to embrace one another. Man was brave but violent, a good hunter; Muzita was fearful, gentle and hard-working, a good cultivator. (See *Donna Beatrice; Kimpasi; Kindoki; Ndoki; Nkisi; Tebo; Warlocks*.)

Baloi see *Mulo(y)i; Night Witches; Warlocks*.

Bambara (Creation myth, Mali). The Bambara people form a branch of the great ethnic tree of the Mande-speaking peoples of Mali, around Bamako. They grow maize, millet and rice; they breed cattle, goats and fowl.

The Bambara myth of creation is almost pure philosophy. In the beginning there was the great Empty, *fu*. At some time there started *glan* 'movement', 'awakening'. All movement has to go in two directions, going and coming back, so the first movement can be *zo nyami*, breath. That makes the next stage possible in the chain of creation, namely *yo*, the voice, the Word in the biblical sense, i.e. the Word which creates all. This word is the action which is the effect of thinking, *tasi*. It creates *yereyereli* 'vibration', which is the essence of a voice. But *yo*, like the classical concept of *verbum, logos*, is not just the word as part of a language. It is the spirit itself which is free to create whichever it wishes and when. There is also *nugu* 'entrails, contents, substance', which in its turn contains the elements: *yalan* 'air', *fayan* 'wind', *sani* 'water', *yeren* 'fire', *yelengu* 'earth'. The elements have an effect on each other ('work upon one another') because of *mana* 'attraction, magnetism, power', in a concentric spiral.

At one time there was generated Pemba or Fem-ba 'Great Thing', the principal of creation, the spirit of the whirlwind-spiral. Pemba descended on earth as a seed of the acacia tree. It grew into a tree, *balanza, Acacia albida*, then dried up and withered. Pemba created *ni*, the human souls, from softened wood, then a female being with a tail, a snout and long ears, but still a little human. Pemba mated with his creation, after which she gave birth to all the animals, birds and insects so that the earth teemed with them. They all worshipped Pemba, calling him Ngala, God.

Faro was the god of the waters without which no being can live. Faro came to earth after a long period of drought in which most of the trees and people had died. His voice was like the first fresh wind at the end of the hot season. Faro spoke to the assembled people: 'I will give rain to feed the rivers, wells, lakes and streams and, most of all, the great River Niger. Remember that water is sacred and must be revered. I cannot save you from death but I can help you.' He taught them speech and language. Faro fertilized the women so they gave birth to twins. But Faro had not yet won the struggle for life on earth.

There was Teliko, the arid spirit of the hot desert wind, who suffocated people so they had to worship him. Faro waited patiently until his moment came: Teliko in his pride forgot that he must never cross a river. When he did, Faro, who lives in the water, seized him and smashed him against a mountain.

Faro, now master of the world, proceeded to create order in it. He fixed the cardinal points of the compass, the seasons and the regular succession of days and nights, the opposition of left and right. Then he placed himself in the centre and created the seven heavens; the first, *Kaba noro*, 'soft sky', is formed by the rain clouds where Faro resides as god of the waters. The second heaven, *Kaba dye*, 'white sky', is fresh and clear. Here live the souls (*ni*) of people and animals, and the Kwore or genii. The third heaven, *Kaba fii*, 'black sky', is the spirit abode, and in the fourth Faro keeps his accounts of the world. In the fifth, the Red Heaven, Faro gives judgement against those who have broken the taboos. Here he keeps Fire, Blood and Smoke. In the sixth, the Sleep-heaven, Faro keeps the world's secrets. Here, the spirits of people and genii sleep until he wakes them. In the seventh heaven Faro resides and stores the rain. Here he holds the cord by which he pulls the sun up every morning. (See *Muso Koroni*.)

Bangala (Religion, Zaïre). The Bangala lived along the right bank of the Congo (Zaïre) River, from its confluence with the Ubangi (Oubangui) to Liboko in the East. Their main occupation was fishing and trade on the rivers. There are traces of a belief that the chimpanzee was the ancestor of the Bangala; once he came to a village, spear in hand, to claim homage.

The sun and the moon are lovers. Once a month they come together, when the moon hides herself for a few nights to be together with the sun.

The two principle Bangala gods are Libanza and his sister Nsongo, who is probably also his wife. Libanza is known as the Rich One; he lives in a misty region below the waters of the river and possesses everything one may wish for. He travels constantly along the river and controls its level so that he can punish people with floods when he likes. The deceased hope to join him, and to this end they want to be buried together with their wealth and their slaves, weapons and a boat so that they may make the long journey to Libanza's abode of opulence. A man's wives, too, were killed in order to accompany him in the other life. The name Libanza, or Ibanza (see *Lianja* under *Mongo*) seems to mean 'The Creator'. He is the good god who gives people what they need.

Jakomba or Nzakomba is the name of a god who rules people's

thoughts. He is the god of moral decisions, and is called the God of Hearts.

Likundu or Ikundu is the god of evil; his other names are Ndoki, Ekundu, the red sorcerer, or Nzambi (q.v.). He inspires witchcraft and murder. Nzambi or Njambe is perhaps a separate deity, whose work is destruction.

Many people possess fetishes (q.v.), small images or other 'Containers of Spirits'. They are used to cure sickness, remove spells and discover thieves. Big chiefs possess powerful fetishes for the purpose of warfare. Inducing the spirits to act is the work of the *féticheurs*, some of whom work full-time as witch-doctors. Their ceremonies are accompanied by constant drumming, loud singing and shouting, and tireless dancing.

The preparation for war is the greatest of all these ceremonies; the dancing fetishist is believed to be capable of discovering the plans of the enemies, and of 'cooking' their weapons, as a result of which they will become useless. The fetishist received several slaves as payment. One of the principal tasks of the fetishist, even after the advent of the Europeans, was to expel Likundu, the Devil, who made people ill or insane. After complex ceremonies, the fetishist removed Likundu from the sick body in the form of a knife or arrowhead, with great skill.

Bantu philosophy This is the philosophy of life as it has been brilliantly formulated by Fr. Placied Tempels in his book of the same title (published by de Sikkel, Antwerp 1946). Fr. Tempels had lived with the Baluba in Kasai for many years. What he writes is considered by many scholars to be applicable to all of black Africa. Others have denied its validity. Tempels states that the essence of every living being is its strength, its ability to survive, grow and multiply. A man's strength is in his limbs, his brain and his quick eye when it sees the game and aims the arrow at it. The crocodile's strength is in his eye peering keenly above the water's surface; the lion's strength is in his enormous teeth which can crack his victim's bones. Thus survival is the ability to find food every day. The elephant is admired for his enormous size, the swallow for his swift flight. Not only what a creature *is*, but also what it *has*, makes it strong, in the first place many children and other relatives. A lonely person is pitied for his weakness: who will help him? A strong woman will have many children so that she will not be hungry when she is old, for they will help her then. A rich man has more strength (we would probably say power) than a poor man: he owns animals, land and crops, all of which will keep him alive. His wealth maintains his wives, who will give him children who add to his life-power, simply by being there.

'Magic' in this philosophy is nothing else but all that which adds to a man's strength, e.g. hunting magic which helps him to kill more game, or medicine which restores his strength if he is ill, or black magic, which will diminish the strength of his enemies. For the living beings can influence each other either purposefully as does the doctor or sorcerer, or unwillingly as does a 'witch' or other being with infectious bad luck.

Banu Hilal The Banu Hilal or Hilali were the sons of Hilal, Arab warriors who invaded Africa in the eleventh century, riding west (*taghriba*) until they arrived in the West, i.e. the Maghrib or Morocco. Their history was turbulent enough, but the North African storytellers have added numerous details and uncounted miraculous events making the sagas of the Banu Hilal (*Sirat Bani Hilali*) into vast romances comparable to the Arabian Nights Entertainments, printed in Cairo in nine volumes. There is no complete translation. Parts of this romance go back to the thirteenth century and are still narrated in the vernacular in Tunisia, Egypt, Morocco and Algeria, interspersed with romantic songs and many praise poems. It all begins with Hilal's son Al-Mundzir who has two wives who give birth in the same night (a clear sign of their husband's virility) to two sons, Jabir and Jubayr. Jabir's son (or grandson) Rizk 'Sustenance' marries Al-Khadra 'Green' who bears him a son Barakat 'Blessings', who becomes famous as Abu Zayd, the great leader who rides west to Tunisia because there is a famine in Arabia. Abu Zayd, who is black though his parents were pure Arabs (or so the saga says) routs the Zanati king of Tunis (Ifrikiya), then conquers the seven thrones and fourteen castles of the West, belonging to the tribe of the Zinatiya; the original object of the expedition is *riyada*, the search for green pastures, typical for the harsh life of the Bedouin warriors. The noble ethics of the Bedouin sheikhs permeate the entire saga. Barakat can only be wounded from behind, but since he, of course, never flees from battle, and his equally noble enemies never attack him from behind, he survives until a traitor hits him in the back, like Siegfried. The romance of the Banu Hilal is thus full of chivalresque adventures, when noble knights fight villains, often *ifrits*.

Baobab The baobab tree, *Adansonia digitata* of the Bombacaceae family, grows in the African savannah. Its fruit is the calabash, Swahili *buyu*, which is widely used as a receptacle for all liquids: water, milk and blood; the contents are edible. Some people carve eyes and a mouth in the hollow fruit and put a candle in it so it looks like a living skull in the night. In some countries the baobab tree is thought to be inhabited by spirits. In Kenya the baobab may not be cut down before the spirits have been given proper notice in writing 14 days in advance so they can migrate to another tree. Monkeys also live in the baobab, hence its name 'monkey-bread tree'. The baobab is known for its endurance. It lives on even when felled by a storm, as long as a few roots still unbroken, lead from the ground to the tree. In periods of prolonged drought the baobab sheds its leaves and just waits. Its bark is thick and shiny so it reflects the sunlight while not permitting any evaporation of the tons of water it has stored in its porous flesh. As soon as rain falls, the baobab sprouts leaves.

The Fulani of Mali narrate that a mother when she felt she was dying, went up to a baobab tree and begged it to help her lonely daughter. The tree could speak and answered: 'By the grace of God! I will help your child.' The mother died and her daughter came to the tree every night. It dropped a fruit which the girl ate so that she could live, for her stepmother gave her nothing. The stepmother even persuaded her husband to have the tree cut down. That night, the girl cried on the heap of firewood the cutters had left behind. When she picked up a piece it became cheese which she ate, so she lived on. The stepmother had the wood burnt, but when the girl wept in the ashes, she noticed the ashes had become sugar, so she could live by eating ashes. She found one undamaged fruit and decided to go and live somewhere else. She took the fruit and planted it far away on a riverbank. Soon, a new baobab tree grew up and fed the girl with its fruits until one day, a prince watered his horse there and fell in love with her.

Baptism Among the Zionists, baptism has a central place; preferably it is baptism in the Indian Ocean because the Ocean has the mightiest spirit (or is the greatest god?) of all the South African bodies of water — the Atlantic being too far away from the religious centres in Natal and the Rand. From all parts of Transvaal and Natal the faithful arrive in buses on Sunday mornings at sunrise. First, they form a circle to sing with candles in their hands, and to dance while praising God. Next, they undress and are invited by the preacher, one after the other, to be baptized by immersion in the sea, so that the sea-god may remove their sins and the evil spirits which may possess them. The preacher will beat the candidates while they are submerged, hoping to beat the evil spirits out of their bodies. All the time he goes on preaching eloquently. In the end even the preacher himself may go down into the surf to be purified of all evil. He is still preaching, but by now he seems to be in trance, as if the deity is speaking through his mouth. It should be noted that here baptism has acquired a new significance. It is not a once-only death-and-rebirth into the new community of Christ. In South Africa baptism has become a regularly needed purification ceremony to deliver the faithful from sin and from devils.

Basuto Sotho-speaking people in Lesotho.

Bats The Swahili people say that after death the spirit, *roho*, of the dead man hovers around the house where he died like a bat, *popo*. It stays near the body until Doomsday. In Uganda the bats live in certain trees, and in Zimbabwe in deep caves. Some people say that when the bats leave their hiding at nightfall, they are the spirits of the dead who are on their way to haunt the houses of the sleeping living.

In Ghana, there is a giant bat, Sasabonsam, called in English a flying fox (sub-order *Megachiroptera*). It is a fruit-eating bat, harmless except for doing some damage to crops. The people say that it is evil, lurking in the branches of the forest from where it will suddenly attack unwary travellers. It has long hindlegs which it can unroll to make them even longer. With its claws it is believed to seize people under their armpits and take them away to wherever evil spirits take their victims. Its feet point backwards like the devil's. It is believed to have come from far away because it has a beard and red hair, and its wings have hooks on them. It is said to be in league with the Mmoatia, the dwarf sorcerers of the forest, and with the *abayifo*, the witchcraft experts.

In Egypt, the gipsy women used to go round to perform certain operations on girls, such as tattooing. They used the blood of bats to apply on the skin around the private parts of a newborn girl; it was believed that no hair would ever grow there, so she would be more attractive to her husband. Such a girl was called *muwatwata* 'visited by a bat'.

In South Africa bats seem to frequent graveyards. Some people used to tell stories about bats who were little people with almost human faces. Some were evil spirits bringing disease, others would help brave young men to find a hidden treasure, but only after they had given them some blood to drink.

Benin, Province of Nigeria see *Edo; Ehi; Oba; Olokun; Vodu*.

Benin, Republic of see *Dahomey; Vodu*.

Biloko see *Eloko*.

Birds In Ancient Egypt it was believed that the soul after death could fly around in the shape of a songbird. This belief is still widespread in Africa. There are many tales about the good young wife who was killed or bewitched by a rival or enemy, but comes back to her husband in the shape of a songbird, singing her sad tale to him, until his sister or mother interprets it for him. While he is out, the little loving bird will fly into his house like a swallow, take her feathers off, become a woman again, sweep the floor, grind the corn, cook her husband's meal for him, then again put her bird-clothes on and fly away. The reason for her falling into the power of a witch is her husband's neglect. He has to 'recapture' her now, by luring her back with love.

Sometimes the wife is a bird in daytime, but a wife at night, who sleeps with her husband (or is it a dream) but flies away just before dawn. Her son will come out of an egg.

The Basotho relate how a pigeon gave a woman two seeds which she had to plant in a calabash: out sprang handsome twins.

The Berbers of the High Atlas Mountains relate that there is a bird called *sheerree* (*Strix nocturna*) which screeches *sheerree*! in the night and comes to suckle young babies, because it has breasts: one breast will make the child healthy, but the other will cause its death. Another bird, the wryneck, *Ixeutica*, is believed to lie down near ants' nests, pretend to be dead, and let the ants creep into its mouth by attracting them with magic. It puts a *jynx* on them, from the Greek word for this bird. A big bird, called *amdda* in Berber, probably an eagle, mates with the female wolf or a vixen in the mountains. The fruit of this copulation is a griffin or gryphon, a beast with the head of an eagle but the body of a wolf or fox, which will split its mother open when it is born. Others say it is the male fox mating with the female eagle.

Birth In Africa so many children die in the first few weeks of life that little attention is paid to them until they pass this initial stage. Their mothers are often confined to the home until the child makes its first appearance in the big world. There are numerous taboos and restrictions on pregnant women lest their babies be affected by some unfavourable influence.

In many African religions there is a belief that a child is an ancestor reborn in a new body, a dead grandfather or a revered aunt whose spirit is still strongly alive. Certain features of the child's body may be signs of his reborn, new identity. Later, he or she will also acquire the wisdom of the old person. Now the child will receive his or her name.

Otherwise the child's name may be taken from some event that took place during or just before his or her birth, which is believed to be an omen. I knew a man in Tanzania whose first name was Mvua 'rain', because just when he was born, the rains had started which was, of course, a very auspicious omen. Mchwa ('Termite') was born when the termites started swarming — also a good omen, for termites are collected and eaten.

The Ewe people in Togo relate that before it is born, a child has to visit Ngolimeno, 'the Mother of the Spirit People', who rules the invisible world where unborn souls live until their time arrives. If they obey her and worship her, she will grant them happy lives on earth, if not they will be unlucky for ever. (See also *Destiny; Predestination; Pre-existence; Rebirth; Reincarnation*.)

Bisimbi see *Nymphs*.

Blood It is thought that the spirit of the wounded man flows away with his blood; it does not die, it stays in the earth and calls for revenge. Blood-brotherhood is the mixing of blood so that the two souls merge and neither can harm the other, nor their descendants.

Even touching blood may be dangerous as it might make us ill, not by contagion, but magically, since blood has soul-power. The spirits are hungry and thirsty; their food is flesh, and their thirst can only be slaked by blood, to stay alive. In the Christian ritual, wine replaces blood for the communion. The spirits which possess persons also have to drink blood; that is why spirit possession rituals in Bantu Africa occasionally include drinking blood from a freshly killed animal. To that end the possessed must kill the animal, often with axes or, in the case of a hen, by biting its head off. Each spirit requires its own special animal blood. In the old days it was human blood, as in the case of the Singilla queen Nzinga in Angola (c. 1680). The possessed persons drink the blood at the height of their ecstasis; without it the spirit will not speak through the medium's mouth. A coven of spirit-carriers will drink blood ceremonially so as to swear each other to secrecy about crimes committed when possessed. Blood makes accomplices. Blood is also drunk by the victors, together with the livers of the vanquished enemies, latterly in Zaïre in 1964-5. Blood of enemies was also drunk once by young men during the war-dance ritual before going to war, to make the warriors literally blood-drunk. The Maasai in East Africa give blood to drink to the young warriors, mixed with milk, an excellent source of protein.

Boats Boats have names and the Swahili boat-painters, who are great artists, paint eyes on all their boats. Are boats living beings? We shall see that they are. Fishing by boat is well developed on the Atlantic Coast of Ghana, Benin, Sierra Leone, Senegal, Gambia and elsewhere. The Swahili sailors voyaged as far as Egypt, India and Madagascar, Iraq and Iran. River transport was conducted by means of special boats on the Niger and Congo-Zaïre rivers and their tributaries. The Nilotic peoples (Luo, Padhola, Acholi, Alur, Nuer, Dinka and Shilluk) have fished on the Nile and its lakes since time immemorial. Each people has its own tradition of boat-building. In Zaïre, the boat-builder has to observe certain taboos before he can enter the forest to select a tree that is suitable to be made into a boat. He will pray to the spirit who lives in the tree (or who *is* the tree) for permission to cut the tree down, and when he has done that, he will beg the spirit to remain in the wood, so as to keep it alive and energetic. He will then start hollowing out the tree with fire and axe, until it is ready to be launched. The wood-spirit is asked to protect the owner and the rowers against crocodiles and cataracts, against drowning and attacks by hippopotamuses.

Thus the boat *is* a living being, which , if well cared for, will protect its inmates. The Ntomba hero Mokele (q.v.) went to fetch the sun in his boat after the falcon had caught it. It is astonishing how close we are to the ancient Egyptian tradition of the sun-god Horus travelling in a boat from the night-world to the people-world. Horus was himself the falcon (q.v.). Osiris and Ammon-Ra also travelled by boat out of the world of the dead to new life. Thus the boat itself became a deity to whom the people prayed. The boat saves its inmates, just as the Ark saved Noah and his sons, i.e. all humanity, from death.

Bones see *Diagnosis; Diviners; Oracle.*

Bori (Hausa, West Africa). Bori has been described as a secret society or a coven of witches, or even a community of spirits spreading evil. The Bori are spirits of a type that possess persons who want to be possessed or who are prone to spontaneous trances. It is believed that most illness and most ill luck is caused by specific spirits, *al jannu*, and that these spirits can be exorcized — that is, controlled and placated — by regular dances, to be performed by persons who are ritually and frequently possessed by one of the spirits. The dances are accompanied, and the possession induced, by drumming and playing stringed instruments; each spirit has its own rhythm so that the 'regulars' know which spirit is being danced. The choreography of every spirit is also peculiar to its character and to the disease or discomfort it causes. The trance or cataleptic fit causes the medium to speak with the voice of the spirit and in its language.

A person who displays the spirit-caused disorders is placed under the observation of a cult member who can identify the spirit and placate it, hoping that the visitations will be limited henceforth to the time and place of the big dance. In this way the patient is protected against harm from the spirit but he will never get rid of it and so he has to join the Bori cult. Many others will try to join it voluntarily, wanting to be possessed during the dance. There are a number of officiating spirit experts who, for a fee, organize the dance, pay the musicians and perform the sacrifices. The performances can be held in the town square or in a private house. Some participants show signs of ecstasies when they feel touched by this unknown world of spiritualism. Tremearne lists 178 names of spirits, each with its own habits, most of them nefarious, who 'ride' their 'mounts' during the dance often until the latter collapse, exhausted. (See also *Hausa*.)

Botswana (Origin of People). In the beginning of time there was a cave in the centre of Botswana called Lowe. In it lived the first man, whose name was Tauetona. The gods had created him first, then his brothers, then the animals, for which they told Tauetona to invent names. They named their country Taya-Banna 'the Beginning of People'. The men lived in peace with the animals but they had no wives since the gods had created the women in another valley called Motlaba Basetsana 'the Plain of Women'. One day, the gods sent a messenger to the people to tell them: 'You will all have to die like the animals but you may come back later if you wish.' The messenger was slow: it was the chameleon Tread-Carefully. The gods changed their minds and sent another messenger, the lizard Run-in-the-Sun to tell the people: 'Your spirits will not die but your bodies will die forever.' People had to accept this last message as the definitive one, because it came first. The gods promised, however, that the men would be able to have children. But how? One day Tauetona was out hunting and discovered the footprints of an unknown animal, smaller than his own, but very similar. He asked the wolf: 'Have you ever seen this biped?' But the wolf, seeing that the biped must be too big to eat, went away. Then the man asked the giraffe who can see wide and far from his height. The giraffe said: 'Yes, in yonder valley there are a dozen of them. I can go and tell them you want to meet them!' So, the wise giraffe went to the women and told them: 'Go to yonder cave where some nice men are eagerly waiting for you.' The women followed the giraffe. On the way they sang a song: 'We are the mothers-to-be, men rejoice.' In Heaven meanwhile the old Mother of the Gods took the seeds of the mimosa tree, pounded them and made an ointment which she placed on the men's tongues, one drop each. This gave the men the gift of language so that they could propose to the women and marry them. (See *Heise; Modimo; Night Witches*.)

Buffalo Since the white hunters brought their guns the buffaloes have been decimated, but before those days African hunters did not find it easy to down a buffalo, and those large mammals were regarded with great respect because of their size and strength. In African idioms till the present day 'buffalo' (*mbogo* or *nyati* in the Bantu languages) refers to a man of muscular force, bravery and endurance. The following myth illustrates the close relation of man and buffalo.

A hunter was stalking game along the River Sara near its mouth in Lake Chad (Tsade). Suddenly he saw a group of buxom women bathing in the river. As he was slowly coming closer he came across a row of buffalo hides neatly laid out on the bank. He chose the finest and softest and took it away, wanting to keep it for his bedcloth. Great was his surprise when the nude women emerged from the river and started walking in his direction. As an experienced hunter he managed to remain invisible behind the bushes, while the women approached. They picked up the buffalo hides and proceeded to put them on, whereupon they became buffalo cows. Except one, a lovely big girl who searched frantically for her skin, but in vain. The buffaloes finally walked away and the hunter came out of his hiding place. When the girl saw him she wanted to run away but he quickly caught up with her, talking soothingly to her. He persuaded her to marry him and took her home. They had a son, but when they went to visit his grandparents in the buffalo-bush, the hunter asked his parents-in-law to change him into a buffalo too, for he no longer wanted to live in the wicked world of people.

Buganda (Gods, Uganda). In the days before the advent of Islam and Christianity, that is until the end of the nineteenth century, the Baganda of Buganda worshipped their own gods; each god had his own temple(s), rituals, priests and mediums.

Mukasa was the name of the supreme god of the Baganda. He was a benign god, which means he did not demand any human sacrifices; on the contrary, he gave people food, cattle and children. His chief temple was on the island of Bubembe in Lake Victoria; many other temples had been built for him throughout Buganda. Anyone could go and consult the oracle in those temples but only the king could consult the oracle at Bubembe. In that temple there was a stone which had fallen from heaven. It pointed east or west, according to the phase of the moon at that moment. The god's emblem was a long oar or paddle; there was one placed in each of his temples. Mukasa was the son of Manema Mairwa; his mother was Nambubi, who descended from the Lungfish in the Lake. Mukasa ate only the hearts and livers of the sacrificial animals and drank their blood. Mukasa was born on the island Bukasa (hence his name), but soon moved to Bubembe, where he was found by a man called Semagumba, who became his first priest, when the people discovered that he was a god. Soon people came from all over Buganda to consult the god concerning their troubles, worries, the future and difficult decisions. Both the king and the local chief would send nine oxen for the annual inaugural celebration. The blood was drunk by the god; the meat was eaten by his children, the people; the hides were cut into strips for tying the posts of the people's huts. The king would be conducted into the god's presence by his Gabunga, or 'Chief of the Canoes'. A channel was dug along which the blood of the sacrificial animals was led into the lake. As soon as the bloodstream reached the lake, the priests who were posted there would call out: 'He has drunk it!' The god himself had already disappeared from the island, but left a medium, Mandwa.

Kibuka the War-god was a brother of the Supreme God Mukasa, son of Manema. He lived on the island Sese. Centuries ago there was a terrible war between the Baganda and the Banyoro of Bunyoro (q.v.) during the reign of Kabaka Nakibinge. The Baganda were hard-pressed so the King sent messengers to the oracle of Mukasa. The god answered that the King should pray to his brother Kibuka Kyobe. He did and Kibuka was sent by his brother Mukasa to help the Baganda in battle. Kibuka assumed the appearance of a cloud hovering above the Banyoro, raining down arrows and spears. The enemy fled. In another battle, Kibuka fought on the ground. Suddenly he disappeared, leaving his shield behind. The enemies who tried to lift up the beautiful shield found it too heavy and died. It was later discovered by the priests and carried to the new temple of Kibuka, where it was placed as his emblem or symbol, just as the shield of the Roman war-god Mars was kept in his temple.

When King Nakibinge died in battle, his son Mulondo built a huge temple for Kibuka in which he appointed his own brother as supreme priest. There were 40 mediums in this temple; some of them accompanied the army to the battlefield. Many slaves and cows had to be offered to the god by the kings of Buganda in war. Whenever a new temple was built for Kibuka, a priest would go to a nearby rock with a reed and beat fire out of the rock. This fire would be kept going in the temple until the king died, when it was extinguished. In the temple there was a statue of the god, which only the builders were allowed to see, once. The god stood on a dais covered with leopard skins; in front stood the spears which had been taken in battle by previous kings. There was also the god's fly-swish, his knife, his paddle, his shield, a copper axe, a harp named Tanala and an umbilical cord named Semutega. Thirty drums would be beaten in front of the temple when the god was being carried to a new residence.

Bunyoro (Gods, Uganda). Before the colonial period, Bunyoro was about twice the size of the present district of Bunyoro in Uganda as it included the district of Butoro and a segment of what is now Buganda. Bunyoro was ruled for centuries by a dynasty of kings which was related to the kings of the Alur (q.v.) across the lake, and of Acholi. The Banyoro have a myth, which is as follows. Their first king descended from heaven together with his cattle. He vanished one day, leaving only a daughter, who was one day visited by a handsome stranger, Simbu, who also vanished, leaving the princess pregnant. Nyina Mweru (that was her name) gave birth to a boy, Ndaula, who became a herdsman and later accidentally killed the king with a spear. He made it a law that as soon as the king felt too old to rule he would hand over power to his son and retire to the country. Later, the king had to take poison as soon as he was no longer fit, and the princes would fight for the throne until only one survived. The others would be killed or flee into exile for ever.

The Banyoro people are divided into 46 clans, each with its own totem-name which can be an animal, e.g. Kiroko, 'hippopotamus', or a plant, e.g. Bulo, 'millet', a utensil, e.g. Kaibo, 'basket', or a part of the body, e.g. Amara, 'stomach'. The clans were exogamous, i.e. no one was allowed to marry a member of his own clan, except the royal clan. Kings could only marry their own cousins, and it is known that several kings married their sisters, a custom that was already well known in ancient Egypt, and in Zaïre as well.

Absence of pregnancy in a young newly married wife might be attributed to the influence of a ghost who was owed a sacrifice. The diviners held great power since they not only diagnosed absence of pregnancy but also other illnesses which were usually attributed to a sorcerer having hidden a bone with a curse in the patient's yard.

The Banyoro used to have an elaborate pantheon of gods and goddesses, which is exceptional in East Africa (see also *Buganda*). Every god is served by specially trained professional priests who observe traditional rituals. They also hear the god's oracles and deliver the messages to the worshippers who come for enlightenment. Every god has a temple or temples at each of which a medium is available to 'receive' the god's possession and speak when he wishes.

Ruhanga was the Creator and Initiator of this world, and the supreme god, but he was seldom invoked or prayed to. Every clan in Bunyoro had its own protective deity. Mulindwa was the goddess who protected the royal clan. Muhingo was the god of war. Every field-marshal had to sacrifice to Muhingo before marching off to battle. If he returned victorious, sheep had to be sacrificed to Muhingo, just as the Roman emperors sacrificed sheep to Mars when triumphant. Ndaula was the god of epidemics, usually smallpox. His main temple was on the frontier so that offers could be brought to him when a disease raged over the border in the hope of keeping it outside the country. Mugizi was the god of the lake (Lake Albert). His medium wore garlands of shells. Anyone wanting to travel by boat had to bring offerings to Mugizi for a safe voyage. Kigare was the god of cattle, whose priest advised the king regarding negligent herdsmen whom he had to wake every morning. Kaikara was the goddess of the harvest; her medium was a woman. People would bring her offerings of millet before harvesting. Lubanga was the god of health; his temple had to be surrounded by rows of living trees. Prayers for health to the god had to be accompanied by offerings of beer for blessings. Munume was the god of the weather who was invoked in time of drought or conversely when there was too much rain. The king would send a sacrifice of an ox, while the people would send sheep and fowls which would be sacrificed and eaten as a sacred meal at the temple door for the priests and the people, after the priests had sprinkled the blood in the temple.

Wamala was the god of plenty who could help to increase the number of children, calves, crops and all other living beings. He had his temple near the royal palace where his medium (see *Mediumship*), who was dressed in a special costume, gave oracles (q.v.). The king and the noblemen of the realm would come with cows and bull calves as offerings when they wished to consult the oracle. The cows would be milked and the milk would be placed in the temple, after which the god would possess the medium, i.e. the latter would go into a trance and afterwards deliver the god's message, regarding the sickness of the cattle or the failure of the crops. The sacrificial meal would be eaten by the priests and the people, while the medium would receive special portions. After this the people would light fires and spend the night singing and dancing, until the medium, in a deep trance, would join in the dance bellowing like a cow and exclaiming: 'Peace, peace!' These were the same words the priest had used when addressing the god during the ceremony when meat was offered to the god.

As in ancient Greece, pythons were regarded as sacred in certain parts of Bunyoro and were referred to as 'calves'. The king had a special temple at Kisengwa where the pythons (q.v.) were fed daily on milk. These divine pythons would never kill human beings.

Earthquakes were caused by the spirits of old kings stirring in their graves, which were well kept for that reason.

Burial Bantu chiefs received special treatment but commoners were — in pre-colonial days — simply left in the bush. Children were told: 'Grannie has gone on a journey with Mr Hyena.' (Reported by Willoughby 1882, p. 27.) In some places, a man who had before dying expressed the intention of coming back as a ghost was buried in a very deep pit. This may be the origin of the custom of interment. If a man dies far from home, for instance on a hunting expedition, and the corpse is never found, his relatives will slaughter an ox and bury its bones wrapped in the skin together with his possessions, for there is fear that he might cause sickness in the village. In most parts of Africa there lingers a belief in the continued presence of the soul near the tomb. The graves are covered with flat stones on which sacrifices may be performed: these may be the oldest altars. According to A. Cardinall, when the tribe removes to another locality, they take some sand from the graves, presumably taking the souls of the dead with them in the sand. In North Africa, sand from the tombs of saints is worn as an amulet, sewn in a little bag, to protect its owner by means of the saint's spirit.

The custom of leaving an opening in the grave through which wine can be poured directly into the dead man's mouth is reported from among the Bateke in Zaïre as well as from the Mediterranean countries in antiquity. This proves that many primitive peoples already believed that the soul remained close to the body even in the grave and this is still believed by Muslims. In Nigeria it is believed that the skull remains the seat of the soul. In many parts of Africa the dead haunt the place where they died or lie buried until the moment when all the proper funerary ceremonies have been completed. In Zimbabwe and Lesotho when a man has died the completion of the funerary rites are at the same time a request to his soul to take its place among the spirits of the ancestors. Meat and beer are offered to the deceased, who is now a god. The Zulu used to institute a special ceremony called *ukubuyisa* 'to bring back', hoping to induce the spirit of a venerated chief or a helpful and dependable father to take up his residence in his own village again, about a year after his death. A goat is killed and its stomach is burned. A similar ceremony is reported from the Mashona, and the Vandau further east. Most peoples of equatorial and southern Africa believe that the soul lingers near its body's grave, and that souls of strong characters will continue to have influence on the lives of their descendants, for which reason good relations must be maintained. In Botswana, a dead man is given an ox's rope and milking utensils, a dead woman a pestle, a winnow, a spoon and a plate before burial. In north-west Zambia an eye-witness of a funeral was struck by the fact that all the relatives acted in such a way as to show they knew the deceased was alive and present. The Wachagga of north-east Tanganyika would wrap the body of a man in a freshly slaughtered bull's hide and bury him under the floor of his senior wife's cabin. In the banana orchard the following prayer would be recited to the clan's founder: 'Great grandfather, our father who guards this village, receive this bull, may you eat it with your fathers. Take this son of your son's son, open for him the door to the villages of the ancestors and protect him for ever after. He was taken from your hands.' This last sentence implies that the ancestors (q.v.) did not prevent the man's death, so now they are asked to protect him in the next life.

Burkina Faso (Upper Volta) see *Dausi; Gassire; Swords*.

Burundi (The Origin of the Kingdom of Burundi). The people of Burundi believe in God, Imana, who commands everything: even Death obeys Imana. One day Imana created the first man, called Kihanga, and sent him to Earth to live. Kihanga descended from heaven like a spider along its thread. Kihanga was both black and white, his skin was like a zebra's. Kihanga landed on earth with such force that he bounced up again and again, so that even today when there is an earthquake, people say: 'Kihanga is bouncing.' Kihanga is called 'the one who makes the families grow like the crops'. His children have the names of nations: Kanyarundi (for Burundi). Kinya-Rwanda, and Katwa, the ancestor of the pygmies of the forest. Kihanga's daughter Inaruchaba lost her way in the forest one day and lived on wild strawberries for many days until she discovered the cows of Kibira ('Forest') who were bathing in the cool swamps. Inaruchaba saw the milk of one cow which had just calved, flowing freely from the udder, and tasted it. It was so delicious that from that day on she wanted to drink nothing else. At last Kihanga found her there on the lake-shore with the cows in the meadows. Suddenly, they heard a deep voice speaking. It was Rutenderi, the bull of the herd, or, according to other narrators, it was the voice of Imana speaking through the bull: 'Take these animals and look after them. Your children's children will drink milk for ever after and become a great nation. I, your Father Imana, bless you all.'

Kanyarundi, son of Kihanga, was also called Chambara-Ntama, 'Dressed in Sheepskin'. His Grandfather Imana used to appear to the people frequently in the shape of a lamb or young ram. Kanyarundi had an uncle, Mashira the Diviner, a very learned man who introduced sorghum and its cultivation into Burundi. Mashira told Kanyarundi: 'Imana has revealed to me in a dream: ''Go to the weaponsmith, tell him to forge you a great sword, Inkoto. Take this sword to the mountains. There in a cave lives a serpent guarding the source of the River Ruvuvu. If you can kill that serpent you will become King of Burundi. You will recognize the place for there is a large boulder there.'' ' Kanyarundi did everything Mashira had told him to do. He found Ibuye the rock as tall as a man, near the summit of the mountain. Just below it was the cave where the serpent lived. Kanyarundi entered the cave, and, with his new sword, slew the serpent. Exploring the cave, he found it very large and deep, with many rooms containing all the treasures a man could dream of, so he decided to stay, and lived in the cave.

Once a year the people had to sacrifice a maiden to the serpent and that year the lot had indicated the daughter of a chief. She was brought to the entrance of the cave by her guides and left there to be devoured by the serpent. Great was her surprise when, instead of the ugly serpent, she found a handsome prince in the cave. Kanyarundi fell in love with her and together they travelled to her father the chief. The latter agreed to giving him his daughter since Kanyarundi could pay a large bride-wealth from the treasures in the cave. While he was there, his hair had grown long, so the people called him Intare Rushadzi 'Long Locks', and he is known to historians as Intare I, first king of Burundi. He at once sent word to his father Kihanga who sent him an important present: two royal drums — one male, Kagenda, and one female, Mukakagenda — carved from the same tree.

Burundi (King Intare II). Intare I and his queen Inaruchaba had a son Mwezi 'Moon', who had a son Mutaga I, the first king to play a musical instrument, like King David. He wanted his queen Inabizoza to dance to his strings but she refused, so he danced his own dance. They had a son, Mwambudza I, who in turn, had a son, Intare. Prince Intare stayed with their kinsman Ruhaga, King of Buhaa to the east of Burundi, who had two daughters but no son. One day Ruhaga had a dream in which he saw a big bull being defeated by a bull-calf. The next night he dreamed that he saw Intare sailing on the lake in two boats. The King called his court-diviner, Indwano, who interpreted both dreams as follows: 'Your Majesty will be succeeded by Prince Intare who will become king of two kingdoms.' Ruhaga was furious, so Intare had to flee back to Burundi, where his father Mwambudza had just died. In those days it was the custom for the kings of Burundi to celebrate their wedding and their enthronement on the same day. Intare asked for the hand of Ruhaga's elder daughter, Juru 'Sky', whom he had never seen, since in those days princesses were kept secluded. King Ruhaga, still fretting over his dream, sent the younger of his two daughters, Kikore 'Bean', who was born from a concubine. The wedding ceremonies were performed, but Intare heard the ambassador from Buhaa whisper: 'Beans are good enough for servants.' Intare said nothing, but that night he demanded to know from his bride who she was. Kikore confessed that she was not Juru but that she had been told to keep the fact a secret. Intare sent messengers to Ruhaga 'asking for the Sky', but the king was heard to murmur: 'We do not even know that he can fertilize a bean yet.' Upon hearing this terrible insult, Intare disguised himself as a herdsman and penetrated Ruhaga's court where he was at home. He bribed his way into Juru's quarters and persuaded her to elope with him, thus avenging the insult. (See also *Nile; Ryangombe*.)

Bushmen The Dutch settlers in South Africa called these small men *Bosjesmannen*, because they hid in the bushes, where they could not be found. The Bantu peoples attribute this to the magic arts which the Bushmen are said to possess. The word *Bosjesman* became Bushman in English. Some people thought this term denigrating, preferring the word San, properly Saan, plural of Saa, the name given to a people in Namibia who are not Bushmen at all. The Bushmen call themselves Ju, 'People', so we should follow their example.

The Ju are divided into a number of groups or clans, seldom more than a hundred per group, which nomadize in the Kalahari desert of Botswana and the adjacent areas of Namibia, South Africa and Angola. Each group has its own dialect, such as Kung and Auni, and some even have a separate language, such as the Cham. (Note that the spelling of all these names has been simplified, for they all begin with clicks which can be pronounced only by the native speakers or by phonetic experts.) The best-known art form of these people are the famous rock paintings which are found all over southern Africa, since in the Middle Ages the Ju expanded all the way from the Cape to Kenya. The Ju are physically and linguistically quite distinct from the Hottentots or Khoi (q.v.). They keep no domestic animals except hunting dogs. They are also experts in finding water-bearing roots buried in the desert.

The Ju have 'Words in their Bodies', which means they have premonitive dreams, so they are often consulted as diviners (q.v.). The Ju once worshipped the Moon Goddess, singing beautiful hymns to her. They have a myth showing that the animals descended from people who preferred to live wild in the bush than to be human.

The old Bushman, Mr Qabbo (Mr Dream) has told the following tale: 'We, the Ju, as we call ourselves, were the first people who ever lived on earth. Once all the people who lived were young, but there was only darkness. At one time they saw a red glow in the distance gleaming and disappearing again. They went out in search of this light (they had never seen light). They found an old man asleep who from time to time would stretch and as he raised his arms, from his armpits there would shine forth this red glow. The young people decided to throw him up in the sky so that everybody could benefit from this new light. They took him by the arms and hoisted him on their shoulders, then swung him round and launched him upwards. There he soared into the sky with his arms outstretched, his armpits shining bright white light. All the land was wonderfully visible so the hunters could hunt. After six hours the sun-man began to descend until he finally landed on earth in red flames. The next day he reappeared and by that time he was shining brightly all over his body, as the sun.

In the earliest times the Moon Goddess disappeared after 25 days, then reappeared three days later, born again. She decided that human beings too, should die and be born again. She asked the quickest animal, the hare, to go and tell the people, but the hare's mother had just died and Hare could not believe that she would ever live again. He said so to the Moon Goddess. That was foolish. She revoked her decision and declared that henceforth people would just die and would never live again.

C

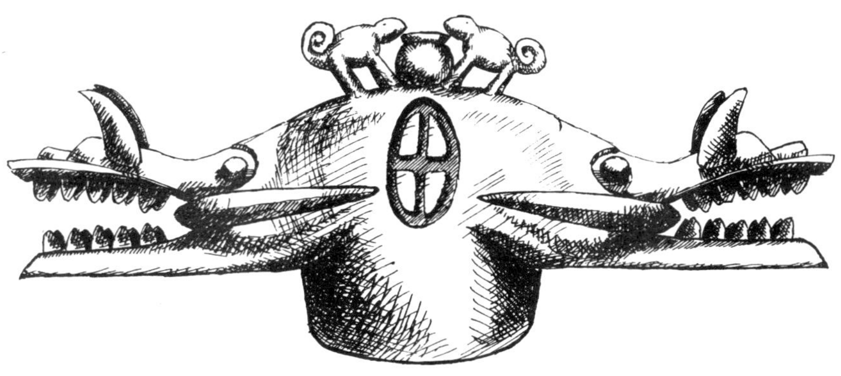

Crocodile dance head-dress from Burkina Faso

Cameroun see *Monkeys; Wute*.

Cannibals Cannibals in African tales look like ordinary people but they are not, although they sometimes have human daughters or even granddaughters. These cannibals can be of either sex. When uncertain one has to look sharply at the thumbnail of the left hand. Cannibals have this very well developed with a horny cutting edge suitable for carving meat, even for crushing human skulls.

In southern Africa some cannibals have a long tail with a mouth at the end of it; while the head is talking pleasantly to a fellow woman, or so it seems, the tail-mouth is quickly devouring the woman's baby. In reality (in so far as there is reality in myth) these tail-mouth monsters are monitor lizards, a species that loves carrion. They can disguise themselves as graceful girls, impersonating the bride at a wedding procession, in order to eat her.

All cannibals are expert talkers in human language, though they are not considered as really human. They sometimes marry human wives who will then discover that the meat the husband brings home for cooking is human. Escaping is impossible: cannibals are quick magicians who can turn themselves into swift vultures. In Nigeria the cannibals are handsome young men who tempt nice girls to follow them. Then on a lonely road they turn into skulls and devour the innocent maidens.

Castle of Light The Castle, or Palace of Light is familiar to students of European mythology (the Castle of the Grail) and of oriental mysticism (Persian Koh-i-Noor, the Mountain of Light, where the Divine Presence is revealed to the persevering pilgrims). In the Swahili tradition of Travellers' Tales, the Castle of Light, *Kusuri ya Nuru*, is in the east, it can be reached only by ship and only a devout and righteous captain will be able to sail the ship to its shore and land safely. There he will find fresh water, fresh fruit, shade to rest in, and all his wishes fulfilled by invisible hands. Other sailors, nearly drowning when their ship was wrecked, were suddenly picked up by white birds and carried to the Island with the Palace of Light which looks like the rising moon just after sunset when the sky has the colour of pomegranates.

In North Africa, a young prince, Habbat ar-Rumani, who has been made blind by order of his stepmother, meets a flock of seven doves, one of whom is also blind. The prince takes pity on the wounded dove and carries her along the seashore. The eldest dove brings a herb which restores eyesight and cures both the prince and the young dove in his hand. The white doves then bring him to the Castle of Light which he had not previously seen. It stands high on a rock overlooking the sea, all its arches and windows shining brightly. The prince lives in the Castle happily with his sisters the seven doves, with all his wants attended to — though there is one room forbidden to him, because from that room one can see the market-place, the world of people.

Cattle Cattle, cows, bulls and calves, have been sacred since well before the Children of Israel worshipped a calf in Sinai. For the Ancient Egyptians the night sky itself was a cow, the goddess Nut (pronounce: Noot) who was standing protectively over Egypt. Isis too, was a Cow-goddess, and the bull Apis was the emanation of her husband Osiris when he came back to earth, as food.

Many peoples of the Sahel and Savannah-Belts in Africa depend entirely upon cattle for their livelihood, so that their cultures are structured around their animals. A young man who has to bring his biggest bull or his finest cow to his father-in-law in order to marry his daughter, will sing to his precious animal a tender goodbye song in Nuer or Dinka. In Zaïre, the chief's daughter Tangalimlibo is held by the river-god who will only allow her to breast-feed her son once a night. She can only be saved by the cows that were given to her father in exchange for her. When her special cow is sacrificed, the river-god lets her go back to her husband. The Alur (q.v.) of Uganda also tell a tale about the girl whom the Nile-god had claimed. She is told by her mother to hold on to the tail of her father's leading cow, the one that was given in exchange for her. She can put one hand out of the water to hold the cow's tail. In this way, the cow that made her marriage legal pulls her out of the water with the strength of her special relationship with that cow, which has magic power stronger than the river-god.

The young prince of Lesotho who had the sun on his chest, showing that God had destined him to become king, was put on the dungheap by his jealous stepmother to die, but he was saved by his father's favourite cow, who fed him and carried him to safety. Bulls, too, have a special relationship with boys, like Matong, whose mother left him nothing but a bull. The bull carried Matong to safety and fought the lions in the bush for him.

Central African Republic see *Mangu; Ngband; Tule; Zande.*

Chad (Tchad) see *Buffalo; Elephant.*

Chameleon The chameleon occurs in almost all countries of Africa, and everywhere its curious ability to change colour has fascinated the story-tellers. In Zulu the chameleon is called *Unwabu* 'Mr Slow'. In Afrikaans they say *Trapsoetjies* 'Tread-Carefully', which is what the chameleon does: gripping the twigs with its fingers, it moves on very cautiously without speaking. This has given the chameleon a reputation for wisdom. It was no doubt for this reason that God when He had decided to create people, sent the chameleon down to earth with the important message: 'People will not die for ever but come back to life like the moon.' The chameleon memorized the message, took leave from God and set off on his long walk to earth.

After a long time, God decided that maybe he should send another messenger with the same vital message to make sure that people would get it. So God sent Hare with the same message. Hare hopped away before he had memorized the message and when he arrived in people's town, he garbled it, saying: 'God says you will all die for ever.' When finally the chameleon arrived and delivered the correct message, it was too late: God's word cannot be changed once it has been delivered, even incorrectly. The moral of this fable is that haste may lead to disaster; we should have patience. The slow chameleon was the good messenger. (For other versions of this story, see under *Botswana* and *Wute*.)

In the days before letters were written, the chiefs had to rely on trustworthy messengers, who therefore had a crucial job in the life of the tribe. Adaptation to changing times is also wisdom, as is well known in African proverbs like this one in Swahili: *Kigeugeu geuka, ulimwengu huzunguka* 'Change, chameleon, the world turns round.' Many people in Zaïre regard the chameleon as a god who can appear in different aspects demonstrating great power and knowledge. Some clans believe they descend from the wise chameleon.*

*The importance of the chameleon can be seen in the artefact on the cover of this book.

Charms Charms are magical objects with a power one degree stronger than the amulets (q.v.). Whereas amulets merely function as a shield against the evil influences assailing their wearer, a charm exercises (or so we are told) positive or negative influence upon the target person or animal. Even in regions where African religions have been entirely replaced by Christianity or Islam, charms are still in use. The Hausa word *laya* is probably from *al-aya* 'a miracle, a verse from the Koran', verses from the Koran being most frequently used to make charms, both in West and East Africa. In Swahili this is called *azima*; *hirizi* is the common word for protective amulet; *tego* is a special charm that prevents a man's wife from committing adultery with another man (see *Uchawi*). A thief in Tanzania once stole a man's watch. Unfortunately for him the man was a magician who could make a *kibabi*, a special charm which influences thieves. The effect (so I was told) was that the watch hurt the thief's wrist, so he brought it back, trembling with fear of reprisals. There is in Zaïre a special mirror which permits its owner to see the spirits (see *Tebo*). *Nkondi* is the Kikongo word for a charm which returns stolen property to its owner. *Kapiangu* is a special charm (see *Nkisi*) in western Zaïre, which will pursue thieves until they fall and die. This type of charm is already practically in the class of fetishes (q.v.). Love charms are numerous in Africa, both for men and for women. Some are aphrodisiacs, i.e. they have to be eaten or drunk, and are often made of the most extraordinary ingredients; some are written charms in Arabic script, to be hidden in a place where the loved one is likely to sit or sleep.

Chiefs In Africa, a chief of a traditional tribe or clan is much more than a political leader or an administrative mayor. Like the Old Saxon kings, African chiefs used to be war leaders as well as justices of the peace reconciling feuding parties. Political units in Africa before the colonial period were of very different sizes: the smallest was one village, totally sovereign in its isolation from other villages speaking quite distinct languages. The chief of such a village was responsible for its defence against raiders as well as neighbouring tribes. The many large political units in African history were real kingdoms, like Ashanti, Benin, Buganda, Burundi, Ife, Kwazulu, Kongo or Lesotho. Islamicized rulers styled themselves sultans, like the ones in Kilwa, Pate, Sokoto or Darfur.

The Safwa from the Lake Tanganyika area relate that in the past a terrible famine caused the people to dismiss their king. A prophet arose who led the people to a sacred pond, which became agitated and jetted water over the young man whom the water-god had chosen as the future king. The young man then found the royal stone in his hut.

The Alur kings had to be in possession of the royal stones for rain-making (see *Alur;* see also *Rain Making*). Many other chiefs were responsible for rain, which they made with magic tools (a buffalo tail for the Nyakyusa chief north of Lake Malawi), or by praying and sacrificing to the ancestors or the rain-god. For other purposes too, the chief had to perform the proper rituals for the propitiation of the ancestors, especially the clan-chief of a patrilinear clan. Fire, too, had to be ritually 'drilled' by the chief at specified moments in the life of the tribe. When the chief or king dies, his royal drum may no longer be played (see *Drums*). The new king has to be recognized not only by his people but also by the animals. The sacrificial cow knelt for the King of Ukuru in Uganda. Elephants, leopards and monkeys were seen mourning the death of the Nkundo king Itonde (q.v.).

Chikanga (Malawi). Chikanga 'Little Guineafowl', also called Kiganga 'Little Doctor', was a famous diviner who lived in Rumpi District in the village of Ihete in northern Malawi. He became so famous that people came to consult him from five countries: Tanzania, Malawi, Zambia, Zimbabwe and Zaïre.

He was originally called Chunda and belonged to the Henga tribe. In about 1956 he had a serious illness and went to see a medicine man called Muzegeva Simwaka who treated him with success. This was seen, as it often is, as a sign that Chunda himself should become a diviner and a healer specializing in the type of illness from which he had just recovered. He was reasonably well educated with seven years of primary school. He was a member of the Church of Central Africa Presbyterian, a church with a venerable history, having originally been founded by David Livingstone more than a century previously.

It was believed by some that he had gone to South Africa to work, that he had quarrelled with his brother, fallen ill and died. After he was buried he rose from the dead and took a new name, which, he said, means 'Courage': Chikanga. It was said that God had charged him with the task of eradicating all witchcraft and sorcery in Africa, and that if he succeeded there would be no more sickness there. There were so many people waiting in line to see Chikanga every day, till well after dark, that the surrounding farmers began to specialize in growing food for those patients, some of whom travelled 700 miles to see Chikanga for a cure.

Chikanga not only knew, according to his patients, what ailed them, but also which sorcerer had caused that ailment, and by his magic he could force that sorcerer to come and be *kumogwa* 'washed' by him. Those who refused suffered such pains that they soon came.

Children Children are by far the greatest wealth, the most treasured asset of life in Africa. Absence of children is compared in songs and proverbs to death and decay, to the silence of the grave, the relapse of the village to wilderness. Childless couples will spend fortunes to consult diviners (q.v.), to offer sacrifices to the gods, ancestors or other spirits, they will pray to Allah, his angels and his saints, and perform all the required rituals to have children. Absence of children is regarded as a punishment by the gods in many parts of Africa, and women who have a series of miscarriages or stillbirths, may be suspected of witchcraft and be tried.

Malformed children likewise are considered by some peoples to be a punishment by the gods for the parents' sins, in the case of the mother often supposed to be adultery. There is a fine sculpture from Cabinda showing a mother with a malformed child, which illustrates the proverb: 'Even a malformed child has someone to care for him.' This proverb admonishes the judge to exercise lenience, since criminality, like malformity, is caused by destiny. Yet, even the Christianized peoples still see it sometimes as a punishment for the parents.

Women who have many children are highly respected and are asked to assist in health ceremonies intended for the healing of other women who are barren or poorly (mostly undernourished). The Acholi (q.v.) of Uganda have a special dance for the 'Mothers of Many', in which the ladies stride solemnly along the square.

Squint-eyed children are often regarded as prone to witchcraft in Mpangu, Zaïre, because it is believed they have 'double sight', they can see the spirit-world as well as the people-world. Albinos were treated with deep respect, since they were believed to be spirits born as human beings. The belief that children are reborn ancestors is almost universal in Africa. (See also *Reincarnation; Itonde*.)

Chimpanzee (Makere, Zaïre). The word chimpanzee comes from Malawi. The Swahili equivalent would be *ki-mpanzi* 'little climber', from *panda* 'climb'. The peoples of the rain forests of Central Africa have many tales about the chimpanzees, whose habits they have watched with wonder. Some say that chimpanzees were more human in ancient times when people were more ape-like, but that the chimps preferred a life in the trees whereas man liked hunting in the open savannah. Other people say that the chimpanzees are gods who look after us. The Mambese are a sub-clan of the Makere in central Zaïre. They are hunter's but they will never harm a chimpanzee since the chimpanzee once protected their people. Their ancestor was a Babwa called Mbese, an elephant-hunter.

One night Mbese was tired and lost in the forest. It was getting dark so he tried to climb a tree with a sling, but lost his foothold and there he hung, clutching a branch with one hand. He shouted for help but no man heard him — only an ape. A huge chimpanzee climbed down, took the hunter's hand and put him gently down on safe ground. Mbese was exhausted and had to sit down and rest. The chimpanzee went away and came back with sweet berries which he gave the man. Mbese felt much better after eating the berries. Suddenly the chimpanzee picked him up and carried him to the nearest village, no more than a hamlet, of the Makere. The village headman's daughter saw what had happened and told her father.

He said: 'Look after that man, for you can see that the gods love him.' She cared for him until he had recovered, and they were married. Mbese went back to hunting so the village never lacked meat. They had many children, who learned to speak both the Makere and the Babwa language. (See also *Monkeys*.)

Congo see *Fetish; Ghosts; Kimpasi, Kindoki; Ndoki; Nkisi; Nymphs; Nzambi; Spirits*.

Copper City In northern and eastern Africa there are legends about the city of copper or brass, Baladu Nuhasi, which it was said King Solomon had built somewhere in Africa, perhaps in the Sahara not far from the Nile, or on the coast of the Red Sea, or even in Cyrenaica on the Mediterranean. It was built on top of a rock called Jabal Lamma, 'Gleaming Mountain', and this feature was explained by the numerous poisonous snakes that were found on this rock and whose coppery scales reflected the sunlight. There may here be a confusion of Arabic *nuhas* 'copper' with *nahas* 'snake'. When Alexander the Great arrived at the brass gate, an inscription stated that the Copper City was built by Solomon. There were 40 palaces with beautiful gardens. The inhabitants were the Dahari, children of the jinn Sakhar, 'rock', who built the city for Solomon. Another legend gives the name of the rock as Jabal Saa, stating that the city was built by Yafat (Japhet, son of Noah) entirely from copper plates. More probably it was Yafat's brother Ham (q.v.) who rebuilt the ancient cities. In the centre of the City of Copper there was a tall building, surmounted by an enormous copper dome, on which stood a brass horseman on a circular, movable platform. It was so constructed that whenever enemies were approaching, the horseman would turn in their direction and raise his gigantic spear which would jet forth fire at the invaders. This explains why ancient Egypt was never invaded from that side. Alexander (q.v.) entered the copper city, since he was King of the World by divine decree.

Creation Myths There are many myths of creation told among the more than a thousand African peoples. The Shilluk (q.v.) of the Sudan say that Juok, God, created people from earth. He took white loam for the white men, brownish earth for the Arabs, but for the black people he used the best earth: the fertile black clay of the Nile banks. God spoke: 'I will give people long legs so they can run in the shallows like the flamingoes while fishing; I will give them long arms to swing their hoes the way monkeys swing sticks to reach for fruits; I will give them mouths to eat millet and tongues to sing; I will give them eyes to see their food, and ears to hear the songs.' And thus it happened.

The Pangwe of Cameroun narrate that God first fashioned a lizard, then the body of a man, similar, but without a tail. He left it in the river to soak; after a week God called: 'Man, come out!' The body rose up and emerged from the water.

The Ewe (q.v.) in Togo maintain that God still creates good people out of good clay and bad people out of stinking mud. First, the gods made man, then they made a woman, and when those two saw each other, they both laughed, for nakedness is funny.

For the creation myth of the Dogon see under *Amma*, the Creator. The Efe of the great forest in Zaïre assert that God created the first man, Baatsi, out of loam which he kneaded into shape, then covered with a skin and finally infused with fresh blood. God told man: 'You may open your eyes now. You and your children may eat all the fruits of the earth, except the *tahu* fruit.' Then God created a woman and gave her to the man. She soon became pregnant and began to crave particular foods. She insisted that she must have a *tahu* fruit, or else the child would die, she said. Baatsi went and picked a *tahu* fruit for her. When God discovered that the *tahu* fruit was missing, He spoke to Baatsi: 'For your punishment you shall both die: I am taking immortality away from you.' The *tahu* or *sau* fruit belongs to the spirits of the dead.

Kono (East Guinea). In the beginning there were two creators, Alatangana, who lived above the earth, and Sa, who lived in the earth, together with his wife and only daughter. Sa lived in the muddy, murky waters of the primeval swamps, before there was light or sky, before there was earth or vegetation.

Alatangana began by creating solid land in the muddy sea. After that he decorated these lands with greenery and trees. Sa was grateful for the labours of Alatangana and offered him hospitality at his house while he was working on earth. Alatangana gratefully accepted and so he met Sa's lovely daughter with whom he soon fell in love. Her father, however, refused to give him his daughter in marriage, so she eloped with her lover to a remote corner of the earth where they lived happily and raised fourteen children, seven boys and seven girls, three of each black and four of each white.

As they grew up the children started speaking different languages so that their parents no longer understood them. Alatangana went to consult Sa, who told him that it was a punishment for 'stealing' his daughter. However, Sa agreed to give the children the tools they would need in order to survive and prosper. So he gave the three black boys a hoe, a matchet and an axe, and the white children received paper, pen and ink, to write down their thoughts. The white children travelled to Europe while the black children stayed at home and started cultivating. They all multiplied and spread out.

One dark day Alatangana felt he needed light. He sent the cock to Sa with the request to bring light into the world. Sa taught the cock to sing a certain song and sent it back, telling it to start singing at a specified time. When the cock sang its song for the first time, Alatangana saw dawn breaking and the sun rising over the earth.

Nandi (Kenya). In the beginning Asis, God, created Kiet, the World

Order, that is, the unison of each member with the whole. Then Asis divided this world into two, and the sky went upwards. The earth stayed; God took some of it and made a manchild. Then he took some more and made a girlchild. Then God went up to the sky to live. When he came back, the man and the girl had children. God said: 'Why have you borne children?' The man answered: 'I did not know you had forbidden us to have children.' God said: 'Go!' God created the sky and the earth first, then fire and water, and thunder with lightning. After these four elements, God created the first four living beings on earth: man, elephant, snake and cow. And God created trees on the hills and grass in the valley. Thunder was a gigantic bird flying through the sky with in his talons a spear with a long flashing blade, or a sharp matchet: lightning, which can kill people in a flash, so they fear the mighty black cloud that thunders, but it also brings rain-water. Asis, God, made the sun and the moon, and people with living souls. There are the *oiik*, the spirits of the ancestors, who live under the earth, in hills and waterfalls, who watch people's deeds.

Swahili (Kenya). In the beginning there was only God, the only being who was never created. When He had lived in the universe for many centuries, He decided to create light. When God saw His light he looked at it and He loved it so much that it blushed: the first colours of daybreak. God took the brightest part of His light in His hand, and created the souls out of it: the souls of the angels, and all the human souls. The angels are entirely created out of light, so that the eye can see right through them, they have nothing to hide, their nature is pure and simple. Their food is the worship of the Lord, their daily prayers. In some human beings, however, the divine light is hidden rather deeply behind their frowning foreheads, so that their aspect is frightening.

After the light, God created the Canopy, a vast indigo-coloured tent or pavilion which He spread out beneath the light. Some scholars have said that this is the night-sky and that the stars are in reality tiny apertures through which we can see glimpses of the divine light from which the dark tent-cloth protects us, for whose eyes can tolerate the brightness of God's light? So, they say, the sky is really a curtain.

Furthermore, God created a throne for Himself but no one knows what it looks like. All we know is that He will sit in judgement on it after Resurrection. Then God created the Lauh that is the Tablet made of Emerald, on which all the things that will happen, are written, and He created also the Kalamu or Pen, an obedient angel, who writes in white ink all the events that will ever take place, on the Lauh. This is the Mother of Books, in which all the wisdom of the world is written. Who would not want to know what is written in the Book about himself? Everything that will happen to you, all your good and bad deeds, are already in that Book, clearly readable for whoever can come near it. Many devils try to enter Heaven only in order to get a look into the Book of the future, so that God had to appoint special angels who will chase those devils away with special arrows called *shihabu*, that is, falling stars or shooting comets. Beneath His Throne, God created the Lotus Tree of the End, the leaves of which have all our names written on them. As soon as a leaf falls, the angel of Death will go and take the soul of that person whose name has fallen, so that he dies.

The roots of this huge tree are in Paradise, and from it spring the never-ending rains which feed the source of the Nile. God alone knows! No created being may pass above the Tree of the End, no matter how strong his desire is to see God. Other scholars say that from its roots spring the rivers Euphrates and Tigris, as well as the Jayhun or Oxus. This tree is so large that on every leaf an angel can kneel down to worship God, and its shadow falls across Paradise so that its people are protected from God's light. (See also *Bakongo*.)

Crocodile In Ancient Egypt, the crocodile was the animal which belonged to the god Set or Seth, in Arabic *Shayth*. In the oldest strata of Egyptian myth, Set *was* the crocodile: he lurked on the bank between the reeds until his brother Osiris came floating past in a state of suspended animation. Set seized his brother's body and tore it to pieces. The Egyptian myth seems to be a parallel to the biblical tale of Cain and Abel. In most African tales, crocodiles behave in this way. In several areas of tropical Africa, the crocodile is believed to be an evil spirit, not just voracious but treacherous.

The Bakongo tell the tale of an old lecher who used to watch the girls bathing in the river and became so desirous to have them that he went and bought a 'crocodile-fetish'. He ordered his wife to make porridge with which he re-created himself. The porridge man went to bed, while the real man changed into a crocodile to eat the girls. The village elders ordered a yet more powerful fetish from a *nganga*, who administered some powder which he scattered on the water so the crocodile had to come out of the river and resume his human form.

In Lesotho the story is told of the good girl Selekana who met the River King, a gigantic crocodile. Selekana had been thrown into the water by her envious peers, and on the bottom she saw the River Woman, who had only one hand and one leg, shaped like a fish-tail. The River Woman made Selekana work in the palace. When Selekana had cleaned the River King's palace, the old woman let her choose some jewellery. When Selekana came back to her village, the daughter of the chief was jealous of the jewels and plunged into the river to try to get similar jewels. The River Woman asked her to clean the palace but she would not do any work, so the woman went away and the chief's daughter was found by the River King, who devoured her. Here the myth describes the crocodile as the guardian of justice, and in the old Egyptian myth of Set there is also that element: Set is the god who punishes sinners.

D

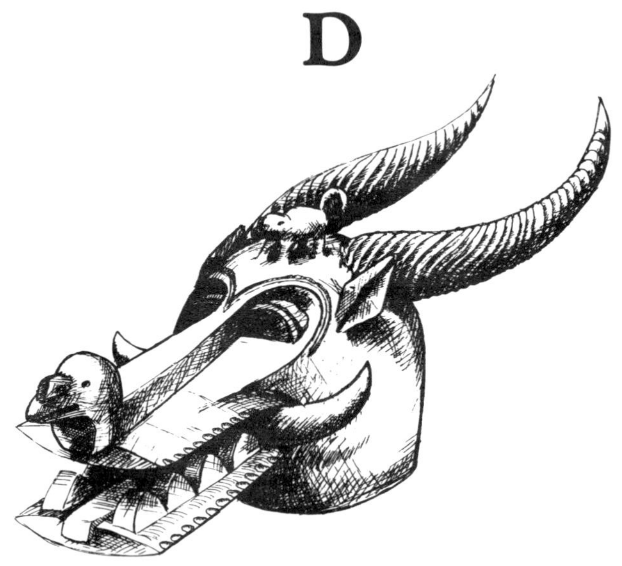

Demon Kponiugo as a Senufo mask

Dahomey (Religion, Benin). Dahomey, the country which is now called Benin, although its people are quite distinct from those of Benin in Nigeria, owes its name to that of the palace of King Bossa Ahadee, who reigned more than 200 years ago in Whydah (Ouidah), and had over a thousand wives. Human sacrifices were performed for the gods at the great annual festival in town. Their sun-god is called Lisa (or Whi in the Fon dialect). Lisa's messenger is Agamma the chameleon. Lisa has human wives, women who dance with corkscrew-shaped staves. Lisa is married to Gleti the moon-goddess and together they have a large number of children called *Gletivi*, 'Moon-children', who became the stars. Sometimes when Lisa approaches Gleti in the night, his black shadow can be seen to glide over her face.

Some Ewe people used to greet the appearance of the moon with salutations, cries of welcome, chants and cheerful processions.

Nesu was the god of the royal family and tutelary deity of the kingdom; his temple Nesu-we 'House of Nesu', stood near the royal palace. The god's 'wives' carry water for his worship.

Wu was the sea-god, also known as Hoo or Hwu. His chief priest, the Wu-no, went to the beach whenever the surf was so bad or the sea so stormy that the surfboats could not land. He prayed: 'Oh Wu

Wu the terrible! Oh Wu the immense! Be less angry! If you want cowries, if you want palm-oil, here they are!' With these words, the said offerings would be thrown in the sea. From time to time an 'ambassador' was sent by the king to the sea-god in full regalia, and thrown overboard in mid-ocean, as a sacrifice.

Avrikiti was the god of the fishermen who sacrificed to him for a good catch. His statue, in a sitting position, stood on the beach, where every year the notables honoured him with a meal on the beach, begging him to 'steal the keys of the fish store from Wu', so that they might have a good catch.

Dausi (Djerma, Niger, Burkina Faso). The Dausi is an epic song of at least seven cantos, first sung by Gassire, son of Nganamba, King of Jerra, of the dynasty of Fasa. It is said that an old sage told Gassire: 'Prince, you will never be king. Jerra your city will one day be a ruin. Go to the savannah and listen to the woodcock. He will sing the first lines of the Dausi for you.' Gassire went and studied the songbirds of the bush until he understood their language. Then the old diviner told him: 'Prince, now go and buy a lute.' Gassire went to the lute-maker and ordered a lute. When it was ready he struck the strings but no sound came. 'It does not sing!' cried Gassire. 'No, Sire,' answered the lute-maker, trembling for Gassire's wrath. 'I can make the wooden lute, I cannot make its spirit. You must give it spirit, like the wind makes the woods rustle. It has no heart. You must give it to drink from your own blood. Only living beings have voices, beings that can breathe and bleed. Take this lute into battle, hang it over your shoulder. There it will learn to sing.' The next day Gassire rode into battle. Before nightfall, his eldest son had been speared. Gassire carried him home over his shoulder so that his blood flowed into the lute. Five more sons died in battle and were carried home in this way. Their blood flowed over the lute and made it one of the family. Not long afterwards Gassire was exiled so instead of being a king he became a herdsman, watching over his beasts in the starry night. There, where silence reigned over the distant hills, Gassire heard a voice singing. Was it in his heart? Gassire trembled: it was his lute singing. The lute had a voice and it sang the epic of Dausi, in a language lovelier than any ever heard before. The Dausi was born from sorrow, like all true beauty, like all real poetry. (See also *Dragons*.)

Death Three major questions are recurrent in all African cultures: How did Death come into the world? Why does a person die? And, most important: What happens after death?

There seems to be a consensus among the peoples of Sub-Saharan Africa about the answers to these agonizing questions. Firstly, death was not part of the original creation, but arrived later, when people were already living in the world, usually as a result of a mistake, a garbled message, a slow delivery, an accident, an irreparable, disastrous blunder. Secondly, most people accept dying of old age as the normal, unavoidable conclusion of a busy, long life. A man or woman who leaves grandchildren behind in this world is usually resigned to dying when the vexations of old age begin to make life less pleasant or no longer worthwhile. As for infant mortality, which still takes a heavy toll in most parts of Africa, all people know that there is a price to pay for life: one must die so that his brothers may live. If, however, there is a series of deaths among the children of one family, then it is time to consult a trusted diviner. When people die in middle age, or worse, in the flower of youth, that is reason for serious concern that something is wrong in the relations between this world and the other one. Like people all over the world, Africans are constantly worried about health, either their own, or that of their children. The belief that ill health and mortality are caused not by natural factors but by spiritual powers is universal in Africa. Early death is caused by spirits or by God. Thirdly, there is a universal belief in Africa that death is not the end of existence, but a transition to spiritual life. See also *Ancestors; Rebirth; Reincarnation*.)

The origin of death: Long ago, people did not die, or at least, not all people died. The Baluba have a tale in which an old woman says to her granddaughter: 'Do not disturb me today for I have to slough my skin.' The little girl either did not understand what her granny said, or she had forgotten it as the day wore on. In any case, when she wanted to ask something, she just opened the door of the old woman's room, to find her stripping off her skin, a secret activity which should not be disturbed. This tale is also found among the Chaga and other peoples. The commonest myth in southern Africa dealing with the problem of death is associated with the immortality of the moon, which comes back after having 'died' slowly during the preceding two weeks. The Moon Goddess, who may have been the principal deity of some of the oldest peoples in southern Africa, was the divinity who decided between life and death for human beings. She promised them that they would all be revived after death and rise from their graves. The message is sent to earth; usually the tales name the chameleon (q.v.) as the one who was charged with it, though in the version told by the Dama of Namibia it is the praying mantis. So, the chameleon (or mantis) took an inordinately long time to arrive. Meanwhile the rapid hare had been sent with the same message. The hare overtook the slower messenger but garbled the message. Gods can never correct or revoke a message once it has been delivered. The spoken word stays. People have to die because the Moon's message was distorted. More than a solemn myth, this tale is a fable teaching young Africans the practical lessons of management: if you have an important communication, make sure that it arrives in good time and correctly, in other words, choose your personnel for speed and intelligence. African story-tellers are teachers rather than myth-makers.

The Kono of Guinea relate that death came into the world as a punishment for Alatangana, who had eloped with the daughter of Sa, the Earth-god, without paying bride-price. Again, the intent of the tale is moral rather than cosmological.

The cause of death in daily life, of mortality in the family, is, on the other hand, a vitally important problem, around which every nation or tribe in Africa has constructed its own philosophy. Since mortality is still high in Africa, as a result of illness and also of physical afflictions, there is a daily fear of omens and symptoms that may point at health problems. (See *Amulets; Charms; Diagnosis; Ill luck and Illness*).

Almost everywhere in Africa untimely death is attributed to evil magic, either evil spirits or wicked people, or other agents of misfortune (see *Muloyi; Uchawi; Warlocks; Witches*). The Islamicized peoples of northern Africa accept that God gives and takes whatever and whenever He wishes. But in sub-equatorial Africa there is a more rebellious attitude — of 'Why me?' so that people attribute their illnesses, their failing crops, their dying flocks to the influence of witchcraft.

This is where the diviner (q.v.) has a job to do. Infant mortality is the biggest single cause of deaths in Africa. What people, especially women, want most in their lives, is children. It is therefore understandable that their children's health is foremost in people's minds and arouses more emotions than anything else. This all-pervading fear provides work for the *nganga* (q.v.), the shaman (q.v.), the makers of charms (q.v.), amulets (q.v.), and fetishes (q.v.), the witch-doctors (q.v.) and the men of medicine (q.v.).

What happens after death? The people of Africa all seem to agree that death is not the end of existence, not even of earthly existence. It is simply the moment at which the person can no longer dispose of his physical body, so that what is left of him becomes invisible, except as a ghost, in other people's dreams or in the body of another person, i.e. a medium (q.v.), or of an animal (see *Hyena; Lion; Snake*), or a tree, a plant, a river or a wind. A zombie (q.v.) is in a curious transitory state between life and death, a condition of having died to the world whilst remaining mobile, of having been buried, exhumed and put to work in the body.

Many African peoples have different traditional ways of treating the bodies of the dead, depending on who the deceased was, whether old or young, man or woman, infant, chief or witch. Most peoples believe that the spirits of the dead remain near the place where they were buried, or left behind, so that some spirits linger in the forest, some in the rivers, some in the bodies of the hyenas who have eaten the corpses. The spirits, which emit light, can be seen through the luminous eyes of the hyenas, so I was assured in East Africa by several persons. It should not surprise us that loved ones are often buried right under the floor of the house, so that the blessing from that love-rich soul may continue to emanate from his or her spiritual presence and benefit the living who are all descendants. In a corner of the house or the garden there is often a modest shrine where the descendants will place offerings of food and beverages for the deceased, and pray to keep the spirit happy. The ancestors (q.v.) will influence their descendants' lives for many generations, always for the best, unless their rites are neglected. See also *Burial.*

Mongo (Zaïre). In the elaborate mythology of the Mongo-Nkundo-speaking peoples of central Zaïre, Itonde (q.v.) is the God of Death, Darkness and the Poison Oracle. The rats which teem in the stagnant pools and swamps of the Middle Zaïre Basin, are his daily food. If a man walking in the forest meets a youth with fiery eyes blazing in the darkness, he will not escape Death that night. In the eternal semi-darkness of the Great Forest, Itonde is the hunters' god. He it is who kills the game so that sacrifices have to be made to him. Therefore he is also called Ilele-a-Ngonda, Ilele of the Lianas, for he taught the hunters to construct traps and snares from lianas in which the animals die. Itonde possesses an *elefo*, a magic bell with mysterious letters engraved on it, signifying probably the signs of the zodiac, so the bell signifies the universe. With it, Itonde can predict the future, so he knows who is going to die soon. Like the sorcerers, Itonde dances with his bell, whose sound can kill people.

Itonde is also the god of the coppersmiths who serve him. When he sings his song to the bats and other winged mammals who fly at night, the spirits of the ancestors, the copper will melt and become red-hot so it can be forged into ankle-rings.

Sunset is the foreboding of darkness and night; it has the colour of copper with which it is associated. One one of his hunting expeditions, Itonde saw a light in the forest, a sun burning between the trees. It was the Sunset Serpent, the Copper Dragon Indombe as long as many men and three feet across. Itonde knew he must catch the serpent before sunset, so he quickly made a giant bird-trap to catch the setting sun. Then he caught the serpent but it burnt him badly. Itonde rang his bell and felt better. Finally, he killed the monster and its spirit swam away in the river.

Meru (Kenya). After death, the body of the deceased person used to be carried out to the bush and left there. Only a man who had lived long enough to become a grandfather was buried properly. They believe that the spirits of strong characters live on after death and are called *nkoma* (Swahili *koma*). A death in the family infects the survivors with a sort of contamination called *rukuo*. The man who has carried the body away to the bush has to have ritual intercourse and a shave in order to remove the contamination. It is believed that in the afterlife the spirits eat and drink, own cattle and cultivate their fields. They are normally happy, but if dissatisfied, they will reveal themselves to the living who will offer them sacrifices.

Demoness see *Ghoula; Jinn; Karina*.

Demons Swahili: *jini* (q.v.), *nundu* (q.v.), *shaitani* (q.v.); Hausa: *bori* (q.v.); Arabic: *jinn* (q.v.), *shaytan* (q.v.); Kongo: *tebo* (q.v.), *nkisi* (q.v.); Kimbundu: *kishi* (q.v.); Mongo: *eloko* (q.v.); Nubian: *dogir* (q.v.); Zulu: *tikoloshe* (q.v.).

Demons are pagan spirits, whereas devils operate in a Christian context, to tempt people away from Christ's church. Demons are spirits with more status and power than most others. Originally, Greek *daimon* meant 'god' in the sense of he who divides, gives to each his lot, like Kikuyu *Ngai*, Swahili *Mgawanyi*. In Christian times, the Greek gods were condemned as evil demons, so that ever since, demons have been vicious but very powerful. Ever since, the word demon has remained associated with destiny. Every man has his own demon who is at the same time himself and his enemy, as the Swahili say: *Kila mtu na roho yake*: 'Every man has to come to terms with his own spirit', his desire, his envy, his grudge (Swahili: *Fundo la moyoni* 'A knot in one's heart').

The Ancient Egyptians already knew of numerous demons, both male and female, headless men, jealous ghosts, incubi, bad demons causing epilepsy and other diseases, and good demons to help us.

The Bammana of Mali relate how a hunter met a demon who befriended him and took him to his own city, which was surrounded by three walls with well-guarded gates, where demon-herdsmen herded antelopes, the demons' cattle. Demons, like people, live in hierarchical societies, ruled by kings. If a woman is childless, they say that she has 'known' a demon. The Ninimini (Malinke: *Ninginanga*; Khasonke: *Samano*) is a demon with horns and large fiery eyes who lives in the mountains. If the king of that country keeps on good terms with Ninimini, then Ninimini will vomit gold and silver for the king; if not, the demon will coil round the king and choke him. (See also: *Devils; Familiars; Ifrit; Incubus; Monsters; Spirits*.)

Destiny The Yoruba believe that the success or failure of a man in life depends on the choices he made in heaven before he was born. If a person suddenly becomes rich, they will say that he chose the right future for himself, therefore poor people must be patient because even if they have chosen the right life, it may not have arrived yet. We all need patience. The word *ayanmo* means 'choice', and *kadara* means 'divine share for a man'; *ipin* means 'predestined lot'.

The Yoruba believe that there is a god, Ori, who supervises people's choices in heaven. Literally, *ori* means 'head' or 'mind', because that is what one chooses before birth. If someone chooses a wise head, i.e. intelligence, wisdom, he will walk easily through life, but if someone chooses a fool's head, he will never succeed anywhere. Ori could be considered as a personal god, a sort of guardian angel who will accompany each of us for life, once chosen. Even the gods have their Ori which directs their personal lives. Both men and gods must consult their sacred divination palm-nuts daily in order to learn what their Ori wishes. In this way, Ori is both an individual and a collective concept, a personal spirit directing each individual's life, and also a god in heaven, who is feared even by Orunmila (q.v.).

In heaven, there is a curious character called Ajala, a very fallible man whose daily work is fashioning faces (*ori*) from clay. Sometimes he forgets to bake them properly, so they cannot withstand the long journey to earth prior to the beginning of life; especially in the rainy season the clay might be washed away and there would be a total loss of face!

Devils Devils are found in all African countries, we are told. For similar beings see *Demons; Ghosts; Jinns;* and *Shaitans*. The devils of the West African forest are perhaps comparable to the North African ghouls (q.v.) and ifrits (q.v.), though no story-teller is able to give precise detailed descriptions of the many strange creatures that populate his vivid imagination.

Many tales are told about the forest devils in Liberia, Sierra Leone and Ghana. Some say they have only one eye, one leg, one arm and one big ear, but they can run very fast. Others say the forest devils look more like chimpanzees (q.v.).

A man from the Gola people in Liberia once cut down a forbidden forest and planted rice; when it was ripe, he saw that someone had eaten from it, so he decided to stay the night in the field. Suddenly he saw a devil, then a second one with two heads, and a third one with three heads and so on: the tenth devil had ten heads. Each head carried a basket. They quickly picked all the rice and put it in their baskets. The man meanwhile had lit fires all around them, so they all perished in the flames. That is why people burn the forest.

There lived a lovely girl in Gola-land who turned down all her suitors. A forest devil disguised himself as a handsome young man and arrived in the girl's village. She liked him at once and told her mother: 'He will be my husband. I will go with him to his town.' In spite of her mother's warnings she went with her devil-husband, till they arrived in his town. There she saw that all the men had only one eye and one leg; even her husband had resumed his devil's shape. She burst into tears, but he growled: 'Stop crying or I will kill you!' Finally, the girl's brother arrived, fixed the devil's sole hand in a rock, by magic, and took his sister home.

Diagnosis When a calamity of any type occurs, the father of the household, or even the chief of the village, will call a diviner (q.v.). A diviner (Swahili *mwaguzi*) is a specialist in some areas, but in other, poorer regions he has to combine the function of diviner, i.e. diagnostician, with that of healer or herbalist. In South Africa this specialist is called, among other names, the *isanusi*, i.e. the professional who can smell witches, and it is the witches who make people ill, especially children and women.

Another South African expert of the unseen world is the thrower of bones, a specialism that is of Khoi (Hottentot) origin, we are told. The South African diviner will throw them on the floor in front of his client, then look at the way they have fallen, with the hollow side up, on their sides, etc. From this he can conclude the culprit, i.e. the witch or sorcerer, or the ancestral spirit, who caused the illness.

In Zimbabwe, the Shona *nganga* (diviner, herbalist, witch-doctor) throws 32 *hakata*, wooden staves with carved decorations on them, which look like meaningful characters. However, he does not look at the carving, except to identify the individual staves; the *nganga* again mainly watches the way they fall: face up, or hollow side up. From the 1,024 possible combinations – the *nganga* can conclude who was the perpetrator of the disease – man or ghost. In Zimbabwe, a *nganga* may also divine by means of possession. This means that this category of specialized *ngangas* have each a spirit whom they can call to possess them. The spirit will 'ride' or 'mount' its host and finally enter his head, where it informs the *nganga* about culprit and cure.

Diamonds Diamonds are found in many parts of Africa, as indeed the Ancient Greeks knew. The origin of our word diamond, as well as of the Swahili word *alamasi* 'diamond', is the Greek word *adamas* 'unconquerable', hence also the word adamant. It is related that in the Central Sahara there was a city called *Burju Alamasi* 'Tower of Diamonds', (the reading of the name is not certain in the Arabic manuscripts), which was built entirely of diamonds on top of a hill called the Gleaming Mountain. It was also called the City of Death, since any man trying to scale the walls would see a pool of clear water inside and plunge to his death because it was a polished floor of crystal. No one ever came out of the castle. It was one of God's ways to test a man's domination over his own greed. They believed that inside the castle there lived a queen of great beauty, but others said she had long since died and lay in a crystal coffin.

In the central Sahara there is also what is known as Bahr ar-Raml 'the Sea of Sand', but according to other writers those hills are composed of diamonds. Alexander's army had difficulty marching across it. The king spoke: 'If you take you will regret it, if you do not, you will also regret it.' Those who picked up some diamonds regretted not having taken more; those who took many regretted it too, because they could not move and perished of thirst; those who took none regretted not having taken at least a few. Later travellers, having heard the saga of Alexander's men and the diamonds, went in search of that immeasurable wealth, but all failed.

In south-western Namibia there is also a vast diamond field, near the coast. Sailors who were shipwrecked there were overjoyed to have found enough wealth for a lifetime, only to realize that a thousand diamonds did not buy them a pint of water: they died.

From South Africa comes the tale of that priceless diamond that was found in a farmer's field. The farmer sold it for a fraction of its value, but at least he lived to tell the tale. Each successive owner of that diamond was murdered for its possession, before it reached Cape Town.

Disease (Bangala, Zaïre). The Swahili identifications of disease and their treatment look very scientific when compared to those of the Bangala people in Boloki and Libinza in the equatorial province of Zaïre, as reported by John Weeks in about the same period (1912). Dr Weeks lists (pp. 345-6) 42 diseases for which there are names in the Boloki language; all of these are caused by spirits, according to the people (p. 269): 'Each sickness has its own spirit (*bwete*), hence the native names for debility, anaemia, rheumatism, sciatica, ague fevers and sleeping sickness are not only the names of diseases, but really denote the names of those spirits responsible for sending them. They cannot tell me from whence these spirits emanate, but the only means of luring them out of the body of the patient is to set up specially prepared posts for some of them, for others a saucepan of small sticks, and again for others a saucepan of medicine water. . . For the spirit of sleeping sickness they prepare a saucepan in which they put small sticks, and the whole is decorated with yellow, red and blue spots and stripes. These. . .often have little shelters built over them which are coloured with various paints, and every time the owner takes a meal he throws some of his food on the roof of his house for the spirits to eat. From time to time he pours sugar-cane wine over the posts, or into the saucepans. . . Not to make these offerings is to invite a return of the spirit or spirits to the body of the owner, i.e. to have a relapse.' (See also *Hausa; Illness*.)

Diviners Whereas the prophets (q.v.) serve the One God who speaks to them or sends His angel to them, the diviners hope to receive knowledge of the future from any spirit or deity. Furthermore, the prophet receives revelation, that is true, immediate knowledge which he can directly prophesy to his people, whereas the diviner receives only signs, so-called omens (q.v.) from the gods, which he still has to interpret correctly. The medium (q.v.) does not work consciously at all but repeats or writes down mechanically what the spirit inspires her to say or write. A priest or interpreter (called 'linguist' in Ghana) is needed to translate the medium's words into human language. All these seekers of hidden knowledge have one thing in common: they will be asked to reveal knowledge that is concealed ('occult') to ordinary people, knowledge of the future or of the hidden past, of events that are vital to human life. Equally important are the events that take place at a distance where dear ones may have gone whose whereabouts and well-being are unknown. Most important of all is the avoidance of disasters such as sickness, starvation, infant mortality, sterility and barrenness, floods or droughts, enemy invasions and raids, and, if these have occurred already, how to remove the evils.

Modern governments have ministries of health and defence, and meteorological services to advise and warn them of impending diseases and disasters. African kings used to have diviners to explain the causes of misfortune. Ordinary people will consult a diviner mainly for health problems, including barrenness in women and in the flocks or herds they own. Drought is important enough to be a matter for the local chief or clan head to call upon the rain-maker (q.v.) to do his job. Diviners also have to advise the chiefs regarding good times for hunting, sowing, harvesting, migrating, fishing or performing religious rituals such as slaughtering an animal. In the old days diviners had to fix an auspicious time when the king wanted to lead his warriors against neighbouring enemies. Many tales are told of rulers who ignored the dark predictions of the diviners, went to war, and fell in battle.

The methods of the African diviners differ from country to country; some African methods of divining are unknown in Europe. The Arabs have exercised a powerful influence on the divination of Africans, from dream-interpretation to the throwing of lots and divination by means of letters and numbers. There are more than sixty known methods of divining practised in African countries. Amongst the more common are: astromancy, by reading the stars for the right time to sow, etc; cleromancy, by throwing lots, usually made of short sticks; geomancy (q.v), by studying lines in the sand made by non-initiates; haematomancy, by observing the blood trickling from a victim; and ornithomancy, by observing the flying and perching of birds.

All forms of divining are based on spirit beliefs, because the assumption that there will be a sign showing truth or falsehood, guilt or innocence, implies the belief in a conscious, deliberate, honest, intelligent will-power that can and will change the objects or substances used so as to represent the truth or to express the will of the deity. The Swahili diviner (*mwaguzi*) has a divining board, *bao* or *loho* by means of which he divines with Arabic letters and numbers. He also possesses books on astrology, usually in Arabic, and books on the interpretation of dreams and other signs or portends. He will insist that all his divining is in accordance with the will of God but many Muslim scholars do not agree. They maintain that the will of God may not be known before God will let us know. Especially our death-hour (*saa*) remains His secret. In essence, therefore, all divining is really stealing divine secrets.

Djerma see *Dausi; Gassire*.

Dogir (Nubia, Sudan). The Nubians in the northern Sudan have numerous tales about the Dogir, a race of spirits who live in the River Nile, where they have their well-ordered society and even pay taxes to their king. From time to time a Dogir man may emerge from the waters and capture a human woman, take her into his element and marry her. So, women may wash on the riverside but they should not bathe in the water. Near the town of Umbarakab there lived in the late 1950s a woman who had a Dogir lover, who came to visit her at night in the shape of a little man. The woman's husband had to put up with this water-sprite, after whose visits his wife was so exhausted that she never had any children with her husband.

Some of the Dogirs were once people but they were changed into water-sprites by witchcraft. A midwife recounted that she was once called to help with a difficult birth. She was terrified when her guide led her into the river. However, everything went well, and when she had safely delivered the Dogir baby, she was guided back to land and paid a basketful of lupin seeds, a delicacy in the Sudan. A few of the seeds turned out to be grains of gold. Further south, we are told, the Dogirs are not so friendly but are habitual eaters of people and look like horrible monsters. Some Dogirs appear at night as hyenas or werewolves with luminescent eyes. In 1929 in the village of Dabod, the police searched for persons with a swelling in the lower back, which, it was believed, was a sign that such a one changed into a man-eating predator at night, the swelling being the stump of a carnivore's tail. Such persons changed themselves, by rolling in the ashes, into a *salue* or werewolf. Some Dogirs live in human villages as seemingly normal human beings, but at night they perpetrate their horrible deeds.

Dogon see *Amma*.

Dogs The dog is man's first domesticated animal and his companion while hunting. Dogs are kept as pets in African houses, but they do guard compounds and plantations. Even dead dogs are used as a protection against evil spirits by hanging the corpse at the gatepost.

In Liberia, a Kpelle medicine man once slaughtered a black dog on the grave of a child who had been killed by witchcraft. The evil spirit who had killed the child was chased away by the dead dog's spirit, so that the child revived.

Hunters' tales in Africa are full of magic since no game can be killed without magic; so, the hunter's hounds also possess magic. Some can make themselves as big as bulls. Others can run as fast as swallows can fly, others can swim like otters. Flying dogs are believed to be spirits of dead people; scientists call them bats (q.v.). Good dogs will hear their master even when he is calling them from hell.

A certain hunter's sister had been foolish enough to accept as a husband a man who turned out to be an ogre (q.v.), that is, a man-eating monster. The hunter owned three fine hounds called Finder, Tackler and Killer; with them he went to find the ogre's village. There he and the ogre greeted each other quasi-politely as brothers-in-law. When the hunter said he wanted to see his sister, the ogre insisted the dogs must be chained. The hunter proposed a compromise by suggesting that raffia chains would be as good as iron. The dogs were tied in a small hut, and the hunter went to see his sister who was sitting in another small hut, being fattened for the ogre's feast. The hunter was locked up there too, so he called his dogs. After three calls the dogs could free themselves. They tackled the ogre and tore him to pieces.

Donna Beatrice (Angola). Donna Beatrice was a prophetess of the Bakongo people whose Kikongo name was Kimpa Vita; Beatrice was her baptismal name. She was born in or near San Salvador, the capital of the kingdom of the Congo, i.e. of the Bakongo and the Mani-Kongo, their king, to whom she may have been related; she was of noble birth. At about 20, she had dreams and visions in which she died and was reborn as a different person, an experience that is well known among the Bakongo (see *Kimpasi*). She was reborn as St Anthony; i.e. this saint, who is much venerated at San Salvador, took possession of her body and spoke through her mouth. This experience is also common among African prophetesses. She now had a new life and devoted it to preaching, but not Christian doctrine — on the contrary. It is true she gave away her possessions and preached the coming Judgement of God. But she forbade her followers to fast during Lent and to pray Ave Maria. She ordered crosses and crucifixes to be destroyed, perhaps because the cross had become a new sort of fetish among African Christians (see *Nkisi*). She taught that Christ was born as an African in San Salvador and that his apostles were black. Her hope was the restoration of the ancient kingdom of the Congo which would help her people to regain paradise on earth. She tried to create her own church with its own priestly hierarchy. Her new African-Christian movement spread rapidly as a result of the people's despair at the decline of the kingdom of the Congo, and the weakness of the Church. It was especially her strong nationalism that led to conflict with the Church. Her movement, sometimes called Antonianism or the Antonian sect, spread to the far corners of the kingdom; from far afield people came to see and hear Beatrice and venerate her as a saint. Her close associates were called 'angels' or 'apostles', whom she sent to all districts to preach her message. She gave birth to a boy who, she claimed, was conceived of the Holy Ghost. Under pressure from the Capuchins, King Pedro IV had Beatrice arrested. The Capuchins had her sentenced and burnt at the stake together with her baby, in 1706.

Doomsday (Swahili). The Holy Prophet explained to his followers what would happen at the end of the times and how one was to foresee this. In those days, he said, people will no longer study the Holy Koran nor keep the law; everybody will be interested only in satisfying his own greed and lust. There will be an epidemic in Jedda and famine in Medina, the plague in Mecca. There will be earthquakes everywhere in North Africa, thunderstorms in Egypt and all over Europe so terrible that entire regions will be laid waste. Iran and Iraq will be destroyed by murderers and vandals in great numbers. Floods will cause the rivers to rise and sweep away thousands while disease will exterminate the Asians of the East. There will be no more morality or discipline. Then God will cause a monster to appear created from people's bestiality. It will be ugly and horrifying to see. Its name is Dajjal, whom the Europeans call the Anti-Christ. He will ride on a giant ass and subject all the peoples of the earth to his will, causing even more filthy behaviour than is already there. He will rule for only 40 days with terror and force. Then God will send Jesus, the Prophet Isa, down from heaven on a white horse with a lance in his hand. His throne too, will descend from above and he will seat himself on it, so that the faithful believers will rejoice. From them Isa will recruit an army and ride out against Dajjal who will be defeated but escape and run for his life. Then God will intervene and command the earth to hold the monster. Suddenly, Dajjal's feet will be glued to the ground so that Isa can approach and kill him with God's lance. The army of sinners and godless men will be annihilated by the followers of Jesus, who will become king at last and rule with justice for 40 years. Each year, however, will be as long as two years and two months are at the present time, so that there will be a long period of peace and righteousness, following the second coming of Jesus. At the end of his period of reigning for 84 years, Jesus will return to Jerusalem and pray to God in the Dome of the Rock to surrender his soul again to God, and die there. Seven days later Yajuj and Majuj, God and Magog (Revelations 20:8) will finally break through the brass wall that Alexander built to contain them (Koran 18:89). Waves upon waves of barbarians will come tumbling down from the mountains of the east where they breed in their millions and destroy civilization, especially all the waterworks, so that the people will perish of thirst. The earth will become dry and dusty except for the filth of the barbarians.

Doves The doves are widespread in Africa, divided into about half a dozen species, including the Mediterranean ringdove (*Streptopelia decaocto*) and the oriental domestic dove (*Str. risoria*) in northern Africa, the latter also in eastern Africa, especially in Kenya where it is a symbol of mutual love, as it was in ancient Greece. In Swahili love songs a pair of doves often appears, helping each other and sharing everything.

For the Yoruba people the dove is a very important bird which symbolizes honour and prosperity in the ritual offerings. Originally the dove was a forest bird, says the Yoruba myth, which could be heard lamenting that she had no children. So, Eji Ogbe, the king of the Odu divinities, arrived, took pity on the dove and promised her children if she followed his advice. The dove obeyed him and became a domestic bird, building her nest next to his house. Eji Ogbe decreed that she would always have two children at any time, so she became the Mother of Twins. Here is a passage from the Song of the Dove,

Eshe Eyele in Yoruba, a splendid hymn to Nature: 'When she was weeping in the bush, the Dove Eyele:/ Her nest was without baby doves, for she was childless./ She sacrificed two hens, two eggs and two bananas;/ when soon she had two baby birds, she thanked God who gave them.'

Dragon of the Lake (Fula, Mali). Many years ago there was a town near the lake which was so vast that one could not see the other shore. Nevertheless, the citizens of that town could draw water only once a year, during one day and then not again for a whole year. Every house had a large cistern in its cellar where the people stored their water for the year, so that they had only just enough to last the year. Every year a virgin had to be offered to the dragon who lived in the lake, for permission to draw water for one day.

The day came when there were no more virgins available except the king's only child, Fatouma, a girl so beautiful that even in neighbouring countries her name was known. There lived a prince, Hammadi, who, upon hearing her fame, decided he must go and marry her. When he arrived in the town on the lakeshore he found the whole town in mourning. He entered an old woman's house but she would not give him any water, saying: 'Here, prince, water is worth more than its weight in gold. Go to the lakeshore; there you will find our princess all tied up and waiting for the horrible dragon to devour her. We have no time for guests!'

So Hammadi went to the shore where he found the princess. All the other people had fled, but Hammadi was not afraid even of a dragon. He talked to the princess and untied her, saying: 'Only over my dead body will the dragon eat you.' She fell in love with him. In the middle of the night they suddenly heard peals of thunder, after which a drenching rain came pouring down. There came the monster out of the water, with fiery eyes and flames spraying sparks out of its maw. The prince attacked the monster fearlessly with his dagger, which he plunged in its side. The monster died by God's decree, and the princess was free. She took her saviour by the hand and brought him before the king her father saying: 'I will marry no other man. He is the bravest of all men and he really loves me.' The king agreed.

Dragons (West Africa) Dragons feature in the oral traditions of several West African peoples, in Chad, Burkina Faso, Niger and Mali. The most elaborate, and apparently the oldest, version is the narrative in the second canto of the great Epic of the Dausi (q.v.). When King Dinga was dying he sent for his eldest son, to tell him the secret of kingship, but the prince was too lazy, rude and proud to move, so the king sent for his next son, and the next one, but only the youngest one cared for his dying father and so he earned the kingdom, since he arrived before the king had died. His last words were: 'Find the nine jars of water which will make the one who washes in it, rich, obeyed, and king. Then go and find the royal drum Tabele and strike it, out in the northern desert. The young prince, Lagarre, went and found the vulture which could fly to heaven to unhook the royal drum Tabele. When Lagarre struck the drum in the desert, he suddenly saw a city rise out of the sand, with domes and date palms. But his way was barred by the dragon Bida, who encircled the city with his long body. Lagarre had to promise him one girl every year as a sacrifice for access to the city. He promised and rode into the ancient city of Wagadoo, which had been re-revealed by God to a just prince, as its king. Every year King Lagarre kept his promise and ordered lots to be drawn to see which family would have to deliver a girl up to the dragon Bida. In return, once a year the dragon flew over the city and spewed gold on it so that its streets were paved with pure gold. Three generations of kings reigned after Lagarre over Wagadoo in peace. One day, when it was time for the girl to be sacrificed to the dragon, she arrived all dressed up like a bride, to be devoured by Bida. The dragon appeared out of its lake near the Niger, when suddenly her lover, Mamadi Sefe Dekote, Mamadi of the Silent Sword, stepped forward and slashed his sword through the dragon's neck. Its head flew away to the Gold Coast where gold is now plentiful. (See also under *Ghana*.)

Dreams In Africa, dreams are of tremendous importance, even in Islamic Africa, where dreams are known to have changed history. Many peoples believe that during a dream the soul visits the spirit world, which may be under the earth, under water or in heaven. In dreams the spirits of the ancestors, the saints, and other persons may appear and give a message to the dreamer. If it is not for himself, he will have to deliver it to the person for whom it is intended. Nightmares may be caused by evil spirits (see *Eloko; Incubus; Tikoloshe*) or by foreboding of doom. In Burundi, in such cases, the dreamer may rinse his mouth with a concoction of the roots called *musendabazimu* 'spirit-chaser', and spit it out on the fire, saying: 'I extinguish my dreams.'

Some peoples have an elaborate system of dream interpretation; e.g. in Burundi dreaming that one is eating meat or marrow means that somebody in the family will soon die and be buried. Some Hausa people believe that when a person dreams, his soul is travelling outside his body, but as soon as someone touches that body, the soul, which has the same shape of the body but cannot be seen (*ukurua*), will hurry back to enter its body and so the dreamer wakes up. If he dreams that he is falling this means that a *maye* (sorcerer) has been trying to catch his soul, so it ran quickly back to its body and jumped in, head first. The Hausas say that if a man has a sexual dream this means that his female *bori* (familiar spirit) is having sex with him secretly. If one dreams of a man who is sitting alone while passers-by do not seem to notice him, that man is going to die soon.

The Hausas believe that all dreams will come true some time later. North Africans may go to sleep near the tomb of a saint, expecting the saint to appear in a dream and tell them what to do. Ancestors often appear in dreams to claim the sacrifices due to them which must be performed forthwith. Both Jesus and Muhammad have appeared in dreams, to convert the pagan dreamer to their faith.

Drums Drums are by far the commonest musical instrument in Africa. Even the smallest village has at least one drum, to accompany the frequent dances. In many Bantu languages the word for drum is *ngoma*, which also means 'dance'. Almost every clan has its own dance, its own song and, to accompany these, its own drum. A chief of substance has his own drum which only he or his appointed drummer may touch. Such drums are used for conveying messages and orders across the forest; most of them should really be called gongs. In Alurland (Uganda) and Burundi, the king's drum is called the king's voice. In the latter country, the king is not enthroned but placed with his feet on the royal drum. In Buganda and Burundi the king's drums could no longer be touched after the king had died. They were kept in a house of their own. Drums are, or have in them, spirits. A drum's name is in 'reality' the name of the spirit that lives in it. So, in Swahili *tari* is the name of a drum as well as the dance that is played on it and danced with it. Tari is also the name of the spirit who comes and possesses people there.

In Zaïre, the drum-maker has a very special profession. He has to go to the forest, select a tree and perform a ritual in order to beg forgiveness of the tree-spirit for cutting the tree down. Having done that, he has to beg the spirit to stay in the wood from which he is going to carve a drum. When the drum is ready and the great moment comes for it to be struck, *if* it gives a sound, *that* is the voice of the spirit. It is for this reason that so many taboos and cautions surround the drum: it is, or contains, a spirit, which can easily be displeased when 'touched' by the wrong person. When the drum is played for a feast and the dancers become absorbed in the dance, that is the moment when the spirit of the drum itself is dancing. Then the expression 'the spirit moves them' has to be taken literally.

Dwarfs Dwarfs are beings who look like humans but are half the size of fully grown persons. Note that dwarfs are not the same as pygmies. Pygmies (Swahili *watwa*) are small human beings, but dwarfs (Swahili *mbilikimo*) are not human at all, but either semi-simian, or spirits in ugly disguise. In central Zaïre the dwarfs of the forest are particularly vicious cannibals (see *Eloko*). In East Africa the dwarfs are expert magicians. If you are talking to one in the wilderness, he will go on talking while he is gradually disappearing, and suddenly you will find yourself talking to the bushes. In South Africa the dwarf called Ucakijana or Uhlakanyana is born with an adult intelligence and a ruthless character, from a human mother. He stands up as soon as he is born, cuts his own umbilical cord with his father's best knife, then walks away to his father's meatstore where he steals all the beef and mutton. He plays tricks on everybody and when he is almost caught he simply disappears. He strongly resembles the English changelings and the Irish leprechauns of yore, children looking like wizzened old men in midwives' tales. In Ancient Egypt the god Bes was an ugly dwarf whose protection was invoked by women in labour against the evil spirits.

The Bammana in Mali relate that there are spirits in the bush who look like dwarfs, only three feet high, whom they call Wokulo. They have big heads surrounded by abundant hair, but are mostly invisible – which helps them to steal food from people's kitchens. A Wokulo has sharp eyes which can see through walls and trees. They are very strong so they can easily throw any man; their feet point backward, so that most people never find them when they follow in their tracks. The Wokulos live very long, but not happily since they are the slaves of the devil Dume.

E

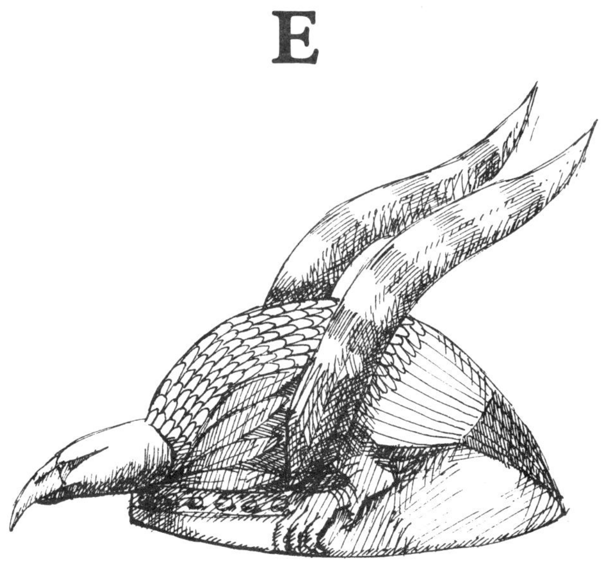

Eagle mask of the Mossi in Burkina Faso

Eagle see *Birds*.

Earth Many African peoples regard the earth as a female deity, a mother-goddess who rules all people and is the mother of all creatures. The earth lives and gives birth to ever new generations of beings. She will make the grass grow when heaven gives her rain and if there is no rain, she withdraws into her own depths, waiting for better times to come. Many regions of Africa have to endure a dry season when nothing grows and death reigns. As soon as the new rains begin, life begins miraculously. Grass sprouts, flowers open and the frogs croak, creeping out of the earth who hid them. Thus the earth conceals life, protects it against desiccation and revives it as soon as better times arrive. Without the gifts of the earth no one lives. Many African peoples believe that the ancestors live in the earth, in houses very similar to the ones they had here, on the surface of the earth. They also own cattle and goats there. Indeed there is a Zulu myth in which people go in search of the milk-lake under the earth, from where the milk is absorbed by the grassroots so that the cows and goats have milk from the earth. Where else could the milk come from? Our own flesh is earth; even the name Adam means 'earth'. All creatures are earth. Fire too, lives in the earth, which sometimes spits it out when in anger. Fire comes out of wood, so it, too, must come from the earth. Wind too, it is believed, comes out of caves in the earth. Thus all four elements come out of the earth. Yet, the earth is seldom worshipped; the libations which are poured down during numerous ceremonies are more addressed to the ancestors than to the earth as a whole. Nevertheless, the earth has a very powerful spirit which rules over our life and death. Sometimes, when she is perturbed, she moves, forests and mountains and all. Unlike man, the animals understand their mother and obey her, although sometimes she will have to punish a disobedient creature.

Akan (Ghana). The earth-goddess of the Akan is called Asase Yaa and in the Fante dialect Asase Efua. She is also generally known as Aberewa, 'Old Mother'; she ranks second only to God in the Ghanaian pantheon. On the special days that are dedicated to her, no land may be ploughed and libations are made to her. Yet there are no temples built for her, nor does she have priests serving her, nor does she give oracles. Fowls are sacrificed in her name and the blood is sprinkled on the earth, especially by the farmers when they need to beg her for permission to plough, to plant and to harvest the crops. Asase Yaa is also the goddess of truth. When a speaker is met with disbelief, he may pick up some earth and touch his lips with it, thus swearing that he is speaking the truth. Asase Yaa is also the goddess of peace: when there is murder or war or when in any other way human blood has been spilled, very substantial sacrifices are necessary to appease the Earth. The Earth is also the goddess of the dead. Whenever a grave has to be dug, the relatives of the deceased have to make an offering to the Earth with libations, to ask for permission. Asase Yaa literally means 'Earth Thursday', because Thursday is her sacred day, when work on the land is taboo. Before planting the farmers have to knock on the earth as if she were a door.

Igbo (Nigeria). For the Igbo, the Earth is a goddess called Ala, Ana, Ale or Ani. Shrines are dedicated to her in many places in Igboland. Offerings are brought to her frequently because the people know that without the Earth helping them to survive they would all perish. The Earth Goddess is the Queen of the Underworld, where she rules over numerous deities, as well as the ancestors buried in her womb, so that the cult of the dead is closely associated with her own. She is also a judge of human morality and truthfulness in disputes between people, and she punishes offenders. Homicide, poisoning, kidnapping, stealing and adultery are offences against Ani. Laws are made and oaths are sworn in her name. The priests of Ani are the guardians of public morality in their society, which is to some extent held together by her. She is the most loved deity and the one who is closest to the people. The most important festival in Igboland, the Harvest Festival or Yam Festival, is celebrated in her honour. During this ceremony, offerings of yams, eggs and other produce are given to her. At that time she also hears prayers for good crops and many children. There are also ceremonies at the time of the planting of the crops and the First Fruits Festival. Ani or Ala is especially venerated in her own temple, called Mbari, where there is a prominent statue in her image, showing her seated with a child in her arms and the crescent moon on her or near her and flanked by her twins; opposite her presides the god of storms.

Edo (Benin — Bendel, Nigeria). The Edo people of the former kingdom of Benin have many gods. Whereas Olokun (q.v.) and his father Osanobua are believed to be good gods, giving prosperity, health, happiness and long life, Ogiuwu is the bringer of death who is no longer worshipped but is still feared. Human sacrifices were once offered to him at his shrine in the centre of Benin City, for Ogiuwu is said to be the owner of the blood of all living beings, which he applies on the walls of his palace in the Other World. He never emerges from his palace, sending his servant Ofoe whenever he needs a human life. Ofoe is represented in the famous brass artwork of Benin as a grotesque head on two legs so that he can pursue the souls of those who are doomed to die, wherever they run, and two long arms so that he can grab them from afar. 'Ofoe has no mercy and yields to no sacrifices,' say the people.

Esu is another god of harsh character who confuses people with tricks. He stands outside the gate of the gods' abode with its keys in his hand. Osanobua does not allow him inside because he is an ambiguous, obscure character, feared by many.

Ogun (q.v.) is the patron of the farmers, craftsmen, hunters and warriors. He represents the strength and power inherent in all metals, a power with the potential to destroy but also to build. Thus Ogun is represented in the swords and metal staffs used for ritual purposes where his power manifests itself. Heaps of metal are found in Ogun's shrines near the gates of the temples for all other gods. Osanobua sent Ogun out very early in the history of human beings to open up the land with his cutlass, so that the people could start planting their crops. He is also sent out to war with his sword to slay the enemies of the people. Thus Ogun is depicted as a furious warrior with red eyes, in armour.

Osun (q.v.) is the god of the *ebo*, the herbalists, who go and collect leaves and roots in the forest from which they brew medicines, but which are also used for divining and even for bewitching others.

Egypt see *Karina; Lion; Nile; Pyramids; Vulture*.

Ehi (Benin — Bendel, Nigeria). The Edo (q.v.) believe in predestination (q.v.). Every living person has an *omwa* 'life, spirit', and an *Ehi*, or Spirit of Destiny. Before he goes down to earth to be born as a human being, every person, or, as we would say, his soul, is called before the god Osanobua, the Creator, who will ask him what sort of life he wants to lead. The soul has to make a statement there and then about life, about which he knows nothing as yet. If he is unable to say what he wants, he will have a life of poverty waiting for him. If he is eloquent and can persuade Osanobua to give him many acres of land and many head of cattle, or to give him many children, then that soul will become a rich and respected person on earth. This pre-life conversation with the Creator is called *hi*, to predestine oneself, to fix one's life. By so doing the soul creates for himself an Ehi. An Ehi is thus a type of spirit who stays with Osanobua, while the soul goes to earth to begin its terrestrial life. The Ehi will remind Osanobua from time to time of the life which that soul has been allotted. If on earth that person finds himself living in poverty and squalor, he will have to offer sacrifices to his Ehi, in order to improve his personal destiny.

Elephant Numerous myths are told in Africa about its biggest animal, the elephant, whose very size makes it unassailable in nature, except by man, who has weapons and magic to kill it. In the African fables the elephant is always the wise chief who impartially settles disputes among the forest creatures. A hunter in Chad found an elephant skin near Lake Chad and hid it. Soon he saw a lovely big girl crying, because she had lost her good 'clothes'. The hunter promised her new clothes and married her. They had many big children, for the son of an elephant cannot be a dwarf. One bad day when the grainstore was empty, his wife found the elephant skin at the bottom, where the hunter had hidden it. She put it on and went back to the bush to live as an elephant again. Her sons became the ancestors of the clan whose totem was the elephant. They do not have to fear elephants.

A myth of the Kamba in Kenya tells us how elephants originated. A very poor man heard of Ivonya-Ngia, 'He that feeds the Poor'. He decided to go and find Ivonya-Ngia but it was a long journey. When he finally arrived, he saw uncounted cattle and sheep, and there, amidst green pastures, was the mansion of Ivonya-Ngia, who received the poor man kindly, perceived his need and ordered his men to give him a hundred sheep and a hundred cows. 'No,' said the poor man, 'I want no charity, I want the secret of how to *become* rich.' Ivonya-Ngia reflected for a while, then took a flask of ointment and gave it to the poor man, saying: 'Rub this on your wife's pointed teeth in her upper jaw, wait until they have grown, then sell them.' The poor man carried out the strange instructions, promising his wife that they would become very rich. After some weeks, the canine teeth began to grow and when they had grown into tusks as long as his arm the man persuaded his wife to let him pull them out. He took them to the market and sold them for a flock of goats.

After a few weeks the wife's canine teeth had grown again, becoming even longer than the previous pair, but she would not let her husband touch them. Not only her teeth, but her whole body became bigger and heavier, her skin thick and grey. At last she burst out of the door and walked into the forest, where she lived from then on. She gave birth to her son there, who was also an elephant. From time to time her husband visited her in the forest, but she would not be persuaded to come back, although she did have more healthy children, all elephants. It was the origin of elephants and it explains why elephants are as intelligent as people.

In Southern Africa there is told the tale of the girl who grew up so tall and fat that no man wanted her as a wife because she was accused of witchcraft. She was exiled from her village and wandered into the wilderness on her own. There she met an elephant who began speaking to her politely in good Zulu. She agreed to stay with him and he helped her to find wild cucumbers and other fruits of the forest. She gave birth to four human sons, all very tall and strong, who became the ancestors of the Indhlovu clan of paramount chiefs.

In the African fables, the elephant is usually described as too kind and noble, so that he feels pity even for a wicked character and is badly deceived. The Wachaga in Tanzania relate that the elephant was once a human being but was cheated out of all his limbs except his right arm, which now serves as his trunk. He paid for nobility! The Ashanti of Ghana relate that an elephant is a human chief from the past. When they find a dead elephant in the forest, they give him a proper chief's burial.

Elixir see *Alexander; Khadir; Solomon, King; Water of Life; Well.*

Eloko (pl. Biloko; Mongo-Nkundo, Zaïre). The Biloko are dwarfs, which would seem to indicate that they are the spirits of the ancestors, or at least of the dead who still have a grudge to settle with the living. That explains why they are so vicious. They live in the densest and darkest part of the rain forest in central Zaïre. They guard their treasures, that is, the game and the rare fruits of the forest, jealously and ferociously. Only intrepid hunters can enter the deepest forest and survive, because in order to be successful, hunters have to possess strong magic, without which they would never see any game at all. There are many tales about wives who insist upon joining their husbands in the forest only to faint as soon as they see their first *eloko*. The Biloko live in hollow trees and are dressed only in leaves. They have no hair; only grass grows on their bodies; they have piercing eyes, snouts with mouths that can be opened wide enough to admit a human body, alive or dead, and long, sharp claws. They possess little bells which, in Central Africa, have the function of putting a spell on passers-by, except on those who possess very strong counter-magic in the form of an amulet (q.v.) or a fetish (q.v.).

One day a hunter took his wife, at her own insistence, into the forest, where he had a hut with a palisade around it. When he went out to inspect his traps, he told her: 'When you hear a bell, do not move. If you do, you will die!' Soon after he had left, she heard the charming sound of a little bell coming closer, for the Biloko have a good nose for feminine flesh. Finally, a gentle voice asked to be let in. It was like the voice of a child. The woman opened the door and there was an *eloko*, smelling like the forest, looking small and innocent. She offered him banana mash with fried fish but he refused: 'We eat only human meat. I have not eaten for a long time. Give me a piece of your arm.' At last the woman consented, totally under the spell of the *eloko*. That night, the husband found her bones.

Eshu (Yoruba, Nigeria). Eshu is one of the oldest deities of the Yoruba pantheon. He has been described as the Satan or Dark Demon of Yoruba religion, but that seems to be a Christian reinterpretation. Eshu is a servant of Olodumare the Supreme God (q.v.), who sends Eshu out to the world of people to test them, to see what their real character is. Eshu wanders round the habitations of people, 'inspecting' their lives all the time. It is said he can make kinsmen quarrel, or even set a wife against her husband, and so, punish those people for some previous sin. He can even force a debtor to pay his debt. He can even make arrogant people insult the gods so that they have to perform purificatory ceremonies and pay a sacrifice to the gods to atone for their offence. He also is invoked by barren women for whom he sometimes provides a baby. Whoever does good is richly rewarded by Eshu. Almost every traditional household has the symbol of Eshu, showing that he is worshipped there, because people are afraid that Eshu might spoil an undertaking if he is not propitiated. At the same time Eshu is expected to ward off evil from the home. Eshu's special devotees wear black or dark brown beads round their necks. Dogs are sacred to Eshu because they eat the food that is placed on dishes near Eshu's shrines. When the offerings are not satisfactory to the god, a brawl may break out, or a fire, or an epidemic. Therefore palm-oil is offered to Eshu regularly, otherwise the god would become 'dry' and certain disaster would follow. The concept of this deity expresses the wisdom of the Yoruba people who perceive that good and evil spring forth from the same spirit at different times and for different reasons, that there must be a balance in our views of people and in our beliefs in the gods.

Esu see *Edo*.

Ethiopia (The Queen of Ethiopia). In the days of King Solomon, three thousand years ago, there lived in Ethiopia a dynasty of queens, who reigned with great wisdom. One queen, the Malika Habashiya or Abyssinian Queen of old legends, had a dream in which she held a kid in her lap. On waking up she found herself pregnant and in due course she gave birth to a baby daughter. But alas! The child had one goat's foot. When the queen died, Princess Goat's Foot succeeded her, since she had no other children. One day she heard of King Solomon and his great wisdom, so she wrote him a letter announcing her arrival at his court. She was hoping that his great knowledge might enable him to cure her foot but she did not mention that. The King, however, always knew in advance what was going to happen, so, in front of his new palace he had a large pool dug, so that all his visitors had to rinse their feet before arriving. When the Queen of Abyssinia arrived, she had to raise her skirt before wading through the pond, so that the King could see her legs, one normal and one caprine. In the pond was a piece of ironwood which was placed there on the King's orders. When the Queen's cloven foot hit it, she was cured. When she stepped out of the water, she noticed that she had two human feet. She was now a very attractive woman and Solomon fell in love with her. She wanted to go home, having achieved her purpose, but Solomon persuaded her to stay. He proposed marriage, but she refused. However, Solomon knew the answer to that too. He gave some orders to his servants and an hour later the cook served a very spicy meal. That night the Queen felt very thirsty but there was no water in the palace. The pond had been drained and the servants told her that only the King had water, so she had to go and beg Solomon for water in his bedroom.

There is a version of the tale which says that she had agreed to marry King Solomon only if she took something vital from him. She therefore stole into his bedroom like a thief, hoping to find water without waking him. However, Solomon was wide awake like every man in love. As she was drinking from his water jar, she felt his hand holding hers in the dark, while the King's voice asked: 'Is water not vital, my dear Queen?' She had to agree to marry him there and then, but the next day she insisted on going home. Solomon gave her a ring, saying: 'When you have a son, send him to me when he is grown up, and I will give him half my kingdom.' The Queen of Ethiopia took the ring and travelled back by boat along the Red Sea.

In due course she gave birth to a son whom she called David, after his father's father. When he came of age, his mother sent him to King Solomon, with numerous presents. When David entered Solomon's court, he noticed an empty chair next to the King's and sat down on it. Solomon asked him: 'What have you come for, handsome young man?' He replied: 'I am David of Ethiopia, I have come to ask you for half of your kingdom, and here is the ring which you gave my mother.' Solomon embraced him when he recognized his ring, and spoke: 'So be it. I will give you Africa, which is half my kingdom.' According to the legend, the King was in his right to do so for God had given him the whole world as his realm. No one knew at that time how big Africa really was. Since that time, the kings of Ethiopia have styled themselves 'The Lion of Judah'.

Ethiopia see also *Janjero; Kafa; Oromo*.

Evil eye The belief in the evil eye seems to be universal in Africa.

The Egyptians take many precautions against the evil eye and anxiously endeavour to avoid its imagined consequences. When a person expresses what seems to be envious admiration for anything, its owner will reprove him by saying: 'Bless the Prophet!' The admirer must obey by saying: 'May God bless him!' That will remove the danger from the thing admired, which may be a child. If someone is seen staring at a child, its parents will cover it, hurry home with it and burn some alum, salt and coriander seed to ward off the evil consequences from their little treasure.

The Kikuyu of central Kenya call the evil eye *kita*, 'saliva', in Swahili *kijicho*, 'little eye'. A person is born with it and is unable to remove the harmful effect from his eyes, it is even believed to run in some families. If such a person has 'looked' at a fine cow, its owner will insist that he remove his evil influence, lest the cow fall ill and die. This is done as follows: the 'owner of the evil eye' rubs some of his saliva into the mouth of the cow with his finger; this will neutralize the evil. Only the owner of the evil eye can remove the spell; not even a medicine man has that power. If an evil eye falls on a pregnant woman she will abort, or her breasts will become inflamed so that the owner of the eye has to rub saliva on them. If his eye falls on a spear, it will break, if it falls on his neighbour's corn, the rats will eat it. If such a person enters a village he must spit into the mouths of all the children so as to remove his own influence.

Ewe (Religion, Togo). The Ewhe or Ewe (both *E* and *e* pronounced as in *pet*) are a people speaking closely related dialects (including Anglo), living east of the River Volta in southern Togo in a wide area around Lome, the capital. Most Ewe are now Christians but thanks to Dr Jakob Spieth we have a good knowledge of their original religion. The Ewe express their concept of religion by means of the phrase *wo mawu* 'To carry out God's commandments', for, they say, we have to serve God as his servants. In the old days, they revered more than one god. They used to distinguish between Sky and Earth gods. There are also lesser protective deities, who are collectively referred to as Ngunuwo 'the Fates'.

We can mention here only two of the sky gods. Sodza is the great god who lives in heaven and to whom the priests pray for rain. Yams are offered for him at least once a year. Prayer ceremonies are performed for Sodza every week. His priests wear white and sacrifice a white sheep annually. Sogblen is the messenger god who carries the prayers from the people to heaven and returns with the gods' promises of good crops and good health for the worshippers, as well as offspring, for which reason he is also known as the God of Growing. He, too, receives a white sheep every year.

The gods of the earth are associated with death, the other world and the trials of life such as disease, war and famine. They were worshipped collectively with the annual sacrifice of a goat, concluded by a communal meal for the entire tribe. Soului is the god of the crops, of wealth and of the magic sound of music, and of medicine, the noblest form of magical art.

Exorcism In Zimbabwe, if a person has been bewitched, the evil spirit has to be driven out by transferring it to an animal or fowl, just as Jesus did. Alternatively, the patient can be taken to a crossroads away from the village, where the exorcist will command the spirit to leave the body of the patient and to wait there at the crossroads until some unlucky traveller passes who will then in turn be possessed by the spirit. That is why strangers are often distrusted.

In southern Mozambique there is a very elaborate ceremony for the expulsion of a spirit. For a whole night, drummers and others make such a noise that even the evil spirits must be frightened. Towards dawn the chief exorcist will conjure the spirits to go away. A goat is slaughtered and the patient has to drink its blood, after which he is induced to vomit it up and, by so doing, remove the spirit from his stomach. After this the patient is thoroughly washed and is said to have 'risen from the sea', implying a new birth and a purification.

External souls In many countries there are stories circulating about mysterious persons who cannot be killed because their souls are not in their bodies, and to kill a person is to take his soul, in African philosophy. A sorcerer, i.e. a person who, by his evil magic practices, has made many enemies, may take his soul out of his body and put it in a safe place. 'Soul' or 'life' are regarded as concrete objects or substances, like the Water of Life in a small bottle, or the Bird of Life, a little songbird on the wing. This 'soul substance' will be hidden in a box, or in a 'Russian doll' i.e. a series of boxes inside each other, and this in turn may be hidden in a living being, like a bird or a tree, or in a faraway place, like a fish on the bottom of the ocean. Yet, since every man dies, there will always come the hero in the tale who will find the sorcerer's soul and crush it so that the wicked man dies, and his prisoner, the heroine, marries the hero. A king in southern Nigeria hid his soul in a little brown bird which lived in a tree near the palace. The secret was betrayed by the queen to her lover who shot the bird and so killed the king, married the queen and became king himself, for this had been the prediction.

The Baronga in southern Mozambique tell the story of Titichane's Cat. The cat was the family totem; i.e. if it were to die the whole family would die with it. Upon her marriage, Titichane persuaded her relatives to let her take the cat to her new home, since marriages are 'virilocal', i.e. the wife lives at her husband's home. She took the cat with her in a wicker cage wrapped in a cloth, and in her new home, hid it under her bed, without telling her husband. Of course he killed it as soon as it escaped to attack one of his chickens. At once his wife died and her entire family with her, the whole cat-clan.

Eye see *Evil Eye; Karina*.

F

Fetish of the Bakongop in Zaïre

Falcon For the ancient Egyptians, the falcon was the symbol of the young sun-god Horus, whom the Greeks identified with the young Apollo-Kouros, the god of the rising sun. Horus is born after his father Osiris has died. The Ntomba of Lake Tumba in Zaïre relate the myth of Mokele (q.v.) who was born from an egg and went out in a boat to catch the sun-falcon, so that the world could become light, just as Horus went out in a boat in search of his father. When the falcon was caught in the world of the death-god, and was released in the world of animals and human beings, it rose up in the sky, and with it rose the sun.

The sun-bird of the hero Lianja, whose myth is told by the Mongo and Nkundo peoples of central Zaïre, is called Nkombe, which is translated as 'sparrowhawk'. Lianja is told by the people that the earth is too dark for them to work. Lianja calls a meeting of all the creatures of the earth. The fishes say they are not interested. Nor are the animals of the dark forest. Nor are the bats and owls in their caves. Only the birds and insects love the light. Their leader is Nkombe, who comes forward and offers to go in search of *Jefa* the Sun. He flies away and finds Yemekonji (God) in heaven. Yemekonji offers him three parcels, two of them brightly painted. The fly who accompanies Nkombe says quickly: 'Take the plain grey parcel. I am Lontsingo the Fly who can hear what people deliberate in secret!' Nkombe picks up the grey parcel and flies away with it to the place where earth and sky meet. He unwraps the parcel and all the people cheer when they see the sun breaking through the clouds. The sun rises as Nkombe flies up into the sky, singing: 'I am Nkombe who has changed the lifeless villages!'

Fall of Man The story of the Fall of Man is well-known in many parts of Africa. The Baganda of Buganda relate that, after their creation, Kintu, the first man and Nambi, the first woman, travelled to earth from heaven; the Creator had told them that they must not try to come back, or else a great disaster would happen. When they were on the long journey down, the woman who was carrying her chicken, her vital asset for life on earth which was still fallow, suddenly remembered that she had forgotten the millet to feed her hen. So she went back, in spite of the repeated warnings of her husband. After waiting a long time he finally saw her reappear over the horizon, carrying a basket of millet on her head. They arrived on earth and Kintu started building a hut where they settled. The woman fed millet to her hen and planted some of the seeds from heaven. Alas, when she had reached the bottom of her basket, there she found a snake lurking. It was Death who had come with them from heaven in the basket. Since that time, people have died.

The Yoruba relate that in the beginning heaven was hanging just above our heads, so that people could touch it, but they had been told to touch the beautiful clear sky only with clean hands. One day, however, a woman touched the sky with mud on her hands, and the sky withdrew, with all the gods in it, to a place well out of reach of human beings, who, since that time, have had to die. (See also *Creation; Death*.)

Familiars A familiar is a serving spirit attached to a sorcerer. In Europe we can only think of the black cat sitting on the witch's shoulder. In Egypt too, the familiar spirit is usually a cat or dog. Edward Lane mentions Sheykh Khaleel El-Medabighee who lived in Cairo before 1860. The sheikh owned a black cat, which could open the front door and answer questions in fluent Arabic. Some people are said to keep snakes in their basements. In Zimbabwe the witches ride on hyenas and in Zaïre a very evil sorcerer employed a ferocious leopard to kill his enemies for him. Marain Jagu in Senegal owned a calabash in which he had conjured three hounds who, at his order, would leap out and kill his enemy. (For familiars in human shape see also under *Zombies*. For the woman who kept a snake see under *Mamlambo*.) Often familiars get out of hand, like the Tikoloshe (q.v.), who was too strong and too evil to be controlled without strong magic. Such spirits indulge in wanton killing and often dominate their former masters. Such tales repeat the lesson of the sorcerer's apprentice: do not conjure up a spirit that you cannot control. The Lunda and Luvale peoples of north-west Zambia tell us of the *baloi* (sorcerers, see *Muloyi*) who raise newly buried corpses at night and revive them with a *mwana-nkishi*, a fetish-spirit (see *Nkisi*) from a calabash. Such a walking corpse will then go and kill its master's enemies, and, when apprehended, will die, so that the police will be blamed for their prisoner's death in custody. *Tuyebela* are spirits in the shape of jackals, hyenas or little wooden men, who are so powerful that they demand human meat from their owner. If he refuses, they will go and kill one of his own relatives. A *linkalankala*, also in Zambia, is a tortoise whom its owner will send to kill his enemy; but it is not a real tortoise, only an empty shell with a knife sticking out where its head was.

Fetish (West- and West-Central Africa). A fetish is an object in which a spirit lives. The spirit may be an ancestor of the owner or the maker (who may not be the same person), or it may be an alien spirit 'caught' by the fetish-master in the forest, by means of magic, like birdlime, or the spirit may be that of a dead man or woman exhumed from a grave and revived to become the master's mute slave (see *Zombie*). The object which houses the spirit may be anything from an elaborately sculptured statue, a true idol, to a calabash, or a pouch, usually made of the skin of a magically powerful animal, a cat, a frog or a big lizard. It may also be a box made of wood or bamboo, or a skull. Most fetishes, like most gods and privately owned spirits, are kept for self-protection. They protect their owners against disease, theft, the evil eye (q.v.) and attack, by wild animals or by enemies, including adulterers and thugs. Fetishes owe their bad name to the evil character of some of their owners who started using their servant-spirits to harm their neighbours (see also *Tikoloshe*), by making them attack at night. A man in the possession of a fetish can enter a house without being seen, and lie with a woman who will think that it is her husband who is making love to her; or he can so frighten a pretty girl with his flying monster-image, that she will consent to anything and never dare to talk about it; or his fetish will kill the chief for him and frighten the elders into electing him chief. A fetish can do anything for its owner, but there is a price to pay for these services. In order to stay alive, alert and active, the spirit in its container has to be fed and it only drinks human blood, its food being human flesh. The more evil the owner wants his fetish to perpetrate, the more human bodies it will devour. So the owner has to work for his fetish, his idol, his devil. This is when the roles are gradually reversed and the owner becomes the slave. The more evil the fetish is allowed to do by its owner, the more he will be in its power so that in the end he will even have to give up his own relatives to be devoured by his fetish (not physically but through their becoming ill and dying). This development explains why the word fetish also means an idol, something one worships, something one is enthralled by. In the end the fetish will destroy its master.

A fetish is manufactured by a professional sorcerer or a medicine man (see *Nganga*), who will prepare the container, leaving a hole open for the spirit to enter when it is ready. The spirit is lured to approach with incantations and by pouring blood from a victim inside the container. The hole is quickly plugged to keep the spirit captured. Pins are stuck into the fetish to make the spirit angry because its job will be to kill its owner's enemies. A special incantation will instruct the spirit what it must do, and for whom: its owner will be introduced to it by name. (See also *Fingo; Kishi; Nkisi*.)

Fingo (East Africa). A *fingo* is the nearest thing to a fetish in East Africa. A *fingo* may be a pot or calabash, a horn or other container filled with pieces of vegetable and animal matter, all according to definite rules which are kept secret, which protects a building, a town, a farmer's field or a pregnant woman. Dr James Kirkman found one in the medieval city of Gedi, under the doorstep of a room in the palace, as he writes (*Man and Monument*, 1964, p. 107): '. . . a *fingo* or spell which consisted of a pot containing a piece of paper with words written on it which was buried in the floor with appropriate incantations and by which it was believed that a jinn had been induced to take up residence in the pot. If anybody came in with evil intentions he would be driven out of his mind. The pot was buried near the door, so that the miscreant would not have an opportunity to do very much before the jinn got him. Once a week incense was burned over the pot, just to remind the jinn that he was there for a purpose. Two other pots have been found in similar positions at Gedi, one in the north-east gate, presumably aimed against political undesirables.' (For the *tego*, 'trap', a charm to protect one's wife against a sorcerer intent on adultery, see under *Uchawi*. See also *Nkisi* and *Fetish*.)

Forest It seems that all the peoples of Africa regard the forest as the abode of spirits. These spirits are of very different types, but the majority are evil. The Mongo-Nkundo peoples of central Zaïre relate that the forest is inhabited by *biloko* (see *Eloko*), evil dwarfs who eat human flesh. There are also ogres (q.v.) in the forest, hideous giants who devour people after tearing their limbs off. The Yoruba tell tales about forest demons who appear to men in the shape of lovely girls, and to girls in the form of handsome men. These spirits marry human beings and have children with them who later become sorcerers and witches because they know their way in the forest and can find the magic substances they need for their nefarious practices. They also become hunters in the forest, whose phenomenal success in catching game results from their blood relations with the forest demons. They often have to pay for these services with the flesh of human beings, of which the demons are particularly fond. Some people with lugubrious inclinations make friends with the animals of the forest, such as the leopard, the gorilla or the monitor lizard, and become like them in appearance. Many people believe that the spirits of the dead live in the forest.

Fox see *Amma; Omen*.

Frog (Fable, Mozambique). The theme of resurrection, of rising from the dead, is very well known in Africa, and very old. In the oldest myths we find the frog revered as a god, and this fable which is no doubt the relic of a very old myth, tells us why. Frogs possess magic power!

One fine day at the beginning of the dry season, the gazelle Impala challenged the frog Chura to a running competition. Of course the frog lost — it was an unfair competition. The gazelle now claimed a pot of beer from the frog as a prize, but the frog said: 'Wait, give me a chance to win the next round! Can you rise from the dead? Burn my house over my head and see what happens!' Of course the gazelle could not believe that, so when the frog and his wife were in, the next day, the gazelle arrived and set fire to the frog-house. It burnt to ashes. Many animals in the village mourned the frogs, for they had been good neighbours. After six months the rains came and soon the place where the frogs' house had been was submerged. That night, when the gazelle came to drink, there he saw the frog in the water, with his wife, and surrounded by numerous young frogs, all croaking merrily. The gazelle, irritated by all that noise, asked: 'What are you doing?' 'We are singing, we and our children. We are happy that the rains have come, so we have come back to this earth.' 'Where have you been?' the gazelle wanted to know. 'In the country of the dead, of course, since you killed us in the fire.' 'What is it like down there?' 'Oh, very pleasant! Don't you see we are looking healthy? Look at our children, they were all born in the Land Under the Earth. The God of the Dead has blessed us!' The gazelle, who had no children, was jealous, went home to his wife, and lit the walls of his house. He burnt to ashes, for he did not know that frogs, in the dry season, dig themselves into the earth and sleep there until the rains come.

Fula (Fulani), also called Fulbe, plural of Peul or Pullo. West African people nomadizing between Senegal and Cameroun. See *Dragon of the Lake; Hydra*.

G

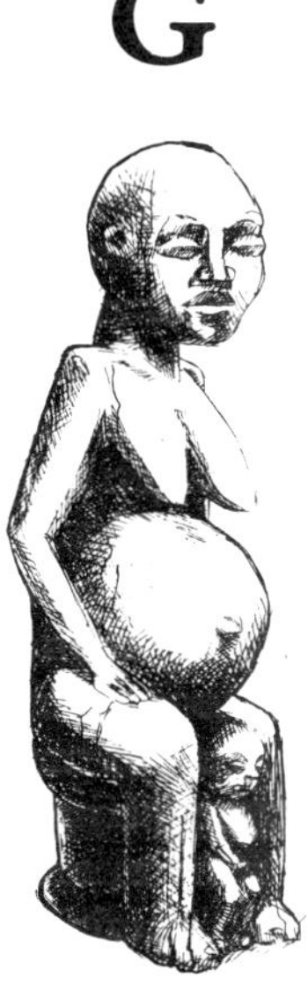

Goddess: mother statue from Cameroun

Ga or Gan (Religion, Accra, Ghana). The Gan people live in Accra and its surrounding districts; they may by now number half a million. They speak a separate language, also called Gan, related to Ashanti, but distinct. The Gan are a very religious people who worship a pantheon of gods. The Supreme Being is called Ataa Naa Nyongmo, an extremely difficult expression to interpret. It probably means: 'Father who looks after us'. The word Nyongmo means 'rain', which is not an unusual name for God in Africa. Perhaps it means 'sky'. The sky was there first, they say, and from there the earth was created, and from it the waters ran down as rivers and formed the ocean. Ataa Naa Nyongmo also rules the sun and the rain. In their prayers, the Gan appeal to Him through the mediation of the gods and the ancestral spirits, for food, for children, for abundant crops, for success in their work, and for peace. Ataa Naa Nyongmo may punish those who neglected to perform the necessary rites or to keep His commandments, by causing earthquakes, epidemics or other disasters. He is immortal, as are all the gods. They may manifest themselves by possessing female mediums or by revealing their will to the priests who are men.

Nai is the next-in-rank god at Accra; he is revered as the God of the Ocean (Bosobro). He is also addressed in the hymns sung by his worshippers as 'Owner of the Land (Shitse), King of Kings, the Ruler of the City, Father of many children and also the Father of the creatures in the Ocean, the Great Whale'. The goddess Ashiakle is Nai's eldest daughter, born in the ocean, from where she travelled to the coast in a canoe, in order to obtain a gong from the people. She is the goddess of wealth (*shika*, 'money'). Her colour is red or white like the seashells. Sakumo is the god of war and defender of the Gan people. Buadza or Olila is the god of the wind who covers the sky in storm-clouds.

Gabon see *Mvet*.

Gambia see *Sunjata*.

Gana see *Dausi; Ghana*.

Gandi see *Buganda*.

Gassire (Djerma, Niger, Burkina Faso). Gassire (also spelled Ghasiri, Rasser) was the son of King Nganamba of Jerra (or Jara or Gara, the name may be identical with Djerma) in the early Middle Ages. Gassire was one of the great heroes of West African epic songs: the first canto of the great epic of Dausi (q.v.) deals with Gassire's exploits. Nganamba was the last king of the Fasa dynasty which had come from the north (Morocco?) and had settled along the River Niger. There they had built Jerra, the first of the four cities of Wagadoo, with high walls to ward off its numerous enemies. The Burdama were a particularly hostile tribe of uncountable warriors who attacked every day. Every day Gassire killed hundreds of them with his good sword Dama Ngile, and the next morning fresh troops faced his army. One day a famous diviner told him: 'Prince, you will never be King, but you will be famous. Learn singing from the woodcock in the savannah. One day you will play the lute and sing the epic of Dausi. But the lute will not sing without sacrifices.' Indignant, Gassire went back to battle, until six of his seven sons had been killed in battle against the swarms of Burdama. The elders of the city said: 'Prince, we are tired of war. Go with your family and retainers, take your animals and migrate to another nation.' Indignant, Gassire left with his men and all the womenfolk, his horses, cattle and camels, to the desert. The old sage predicted: 'Men who are tired of war will soon lose their land and their towns. There is no secure life without the sword. Proud Jerra will be a ruin where the owls hoot at night.' He was right again. When the Burdama attacked again, they overran the city and plundered it so it became a city of death. Meanwhile, Gassire kept watch in his desert camp where his only surviving son and all the others slept. Gassire watched the starry sky. That is when the lute began to sing.

Genesis see *Creation*.

Geomancy Geomancy is divination (q.v.) by means of sand, hence its Swahili name *ramli*, 'dry sand'. Geomancy is widely practised in Africa and was introduced, we are told, by the Arabs in the seventh century. However, it is doubtless much older. In Egypt geomancy is practised by means of drawing secret signs on sand: these are based on the astrological symbols. In Kpelle (Liberia) this art is called *tel-kpe* 'beating the sand'; the Swahili expression *kupiga ramli* means the same. The Kpelle diviner or *telkpenu* (Loma *ngadobenu*) is always a Muslim; in Bamana he is called *kenyelala* 'sand operator'. These men are found all over Liberia, Guinea and Mali. As soon as a case or problem is brought before a diviner, he will withdraw into his hut and reflect on a solution. He will then draw lines in the sand which, in Arabic letters, spell out his thoughts on the solution to the problem laid before him. This work may take him 24 hours. He will advise regarding the most auspicious date for a public sacrifice; he will know whether a murder has been committed by a man-leopard or by a real (bush-) leopard; he knows why the hunter has had so little luck in the forest; he knows where thieves and robbers are hiding, and who is a sorcerer.

Sand-divining in Nupe-land in Nigeria is called *hati* (in Swahili *hati* means 'handwriting', from Arabic *khatt*). *Hati* is, however, not practised with lines but with dots in the sand. After a series of complex additions and deletions, the diviner may tell his client whether he will be rich, or will find a good wife or husband and have many children.

The Dogon of southern Mali divine by studying the footsteps of a jackal in the sand in a sacred place during the night, where previously the diviner has made certain marks in the sand.

Ghana (West Africa). The ancient city of Ghana lay well to the north of the present republic of Ghana. Ghana was the Arab spelling of the African name Gana, the meaning of which is unknown. In vain have archaeologists searched the vast spaces of West Africa for its site. Many stories are told of its wealth, of the power of its kings and the beauty of its buildings. Other tales are told about the cause of its fall. Here is one.

The city of New Wagadoo, now called Wa-Gana was the capital of 80 chiefdoms, but when the king died leaving only a daughter, the 80 chiefs made themselves independent. The princess, Annalia Tu-Bari, was a lady of unequalled beauty; she promised her hand in marriage to the man who would subdue the 80 rebellious chiefs. Many princes who had heard of her beauty came and tried, but none was successful. Finally, there arrived the King of Gana, by name Samba, 'Strong'. He vanquished the 80 rebellious barons one after another, and sent each one to Queen Annalia to submit as her vassal.

When the last chief had surrendered, Annalia agreed to marry Samba, who became King of Gana and Wa-Gana. A few years later there was a devastating drought in the land, threatening famine. The drought was caused by a dragon called Isa Bere, which lived in the mountains of Futa Jallon and drank all the Niger water. King Samba had to go and fight the dragon. He went with his famous bard Tarafe, who had been the first to sing Annalia's fame. For eight years King Samba fought the dragon, breaking 800 spears in its scaly skin. Finally he hit its heart with his long sword so that the monster died and the Niger flowed once more, the holy River Jollibe. Tarafe sang a praise song on the sword. King Samba loved the mountains, the wooded slopes and decided to stay there. Old Gana, in his absence, fell into neglect. (See also *Akan; Ashanti; Earth; Ga or Gan; Goddess Akonadi; Golden Stool; Gratitude; Hua*.

Ghosts A ghost or shadow may be the principle of life as in some African languages the word for shadow is used in both meanings (cf. 'shades'). When a person 'gives up the ghost', this ghost, escaping with his last breath, assumes a life of its own. It is usually believed to remain near the body in or above the earth. Wherever a person has died, there his ghost, we are told, is still to be found if one is unlucky. That is why ghosts are to be expected at graveyards. Whole processions of ghosts can be seen in Congo in the bush (see *Tebo*). Many ghosts are ancestral spirits who are so powerful that they still rule the clan generations after they have died. Shrines may be erected for them, either in the villages or in the forest, where food and other offerings may be placed for their enjoyment. Such shrines may be built in the form of small huts or cabins, called ghost-huts. This custom is widespread in Zaïre, Congo and Cameroun.

Ghosts are seldom seen in daytime, but at night their appearance is so common that many people in Africa lock their doors at night and never go out for fear they may meet one. A ghost has the shape of the person he once was, and is clearly recognizable, except that ghosts are white, like the bones of the dead. Ghosts are feared because they may cause madness. People who have foolishly gone out at night and met ghosts, go on talking to themselves for ever. They are, of course, talking to the invisible ghosts who go with them everywhere. 'He goes with ghosts' is the Swahili expression for 'he is mad'. Ghosts can speak and often warn people of impending dangers or deaths in the family. They may also want to take revenge for any wrong a still living person did to them. (See also *Mizimu; Spirits*.)

Congo. A hunter walked through the forest with his three dogs, whose names were Ntuntu, Mbwa and Kapakala. Well-trained dogs they were, loyal and faithful. They stayed an antelope so the hunter could shoot it with an arrow. They headed for home, but it was late and darkness was spreading rapidly. The hunter saw an old house and decided to spend the night there. The house belonged to a ghost, but the hunter did not know that. The ghost came home late that night and found the hunter asleep surrounded by his dogs, and a big dead antelope hanging from the ceiling. (These ghosts love antelope's meat, but they love man's meat even more. For the purpose of carving man-meat, ghosts have a huge thumbnail, looking like an axe such as butchers use to cut animal bones.) In order to prepare his thumbnail for rapidly cutting through human bones, the ghost held it in the fire until it was glowing red. The pungent odour woke the dogs, who growled so that the hunter woke up. Seeing his host with a large red-hot nail on his left thumb the hunter suspected witchcraft and asked: 'What do you want?' 'I only wanted to carve a piece of this delicious antelope,' answered the ghost, disappointed but looking innocent. The hunter pretended to go back to sleep, knowing that he would be carved up himself if he did fall asleep. Before dawn, the ghost wanted to disappear with the antelope, but the dogs would not let him. They tore him to pieces, discovering that a ghost is nothing but bones — which dogs love to gnaw. Thus they saved their master.

This delightful Congolese tale illustrates all the essential aspects of ghosts in Africa. Old abandoned houses and villages are usually haunted by ghosts, the spirits of the inhabitants of the past. Therefore, one should never go near such places, but hunters are fearless, strong and wise. A ghost can speak human language and present a human appearance at night. Ghosts have no smell, except their nails, a curious feature of ghosts in many African tales. All ghosts in Africa have an insatiable appetite for human flesh. They hope by eating it to regain their own lost flesh.

Ghoulas (Algeria). Although grammatically the word *ghoula* is the feminine of *ghoul* (q.v.), in the Algerian myth of Bousetta the ghoula is a very different being. Bousetta was a prince born on the same day his father's finest mare gave birth to a white filly. Both grew rapidly: at two years Bousetta had the stature of a man. His name means 'Owner of Six', because he had six fingers on each hand, which is usually interpreted as an ominous sign.

In the mountains there lived a ghoula in her castle, with her daughters. We do not learn what these ghoulas looked like but they could disguise themselves as ordinary women if they wished; their favourite food was human meat, especially princes' flesh, hence the French translation of ghoula: ogresse. Bousetta's brothers were jealous of him, so they led him one day, during a hunting expedition, deliberately in the direction of the ghoulas' castle. Before they could turn round quickly and desert him there as they had planned, the mother ghoula met them with her daughters, all disguised as beautiful women. They invited the princes with smiles and fair words so that the latter could not refuse but entered the castle, Bousetta unafraid, his brothers trembling, because they knew that they would be devoured. In the middle of the night, all the brothers except Bousetta were asleep together on the carpet. Bousetta had gone to tend his horse, who kept him awake by licking his forehead. His sleeping brothers were softly carried away one after the other, each by one of the ghoulas, who can fly and are immensely strong. For a long time, the princes travelled through the air until the ghoulas alighted on the terrace of an even bigger castle higher up in the mountains. They have not been seen since, though they are probably not dead but married to ghoulas. Bousetta was not caught because he stayed awake.

Ghouls Arabic *ghul* or *ghool*, Swahili *ghuli*, plural *maghuli*. The ghoul were a race of giants who took to robbing graves at night and eating the corpses. God condemned them for this sin and made them look as ugly and as black as the carrion they ate. In Kenya, I was assured that in the mountains there lived a race of creatures who were people (*watu*), but not children of Adam, i.e. not human beings. The Nilotes in northern Uganda call them *bima*. From this word *ghoul*, sometimes mispronounced as *ghrool* or *ghorool*, the word gorilla (q.v.) was derived. The *ghoul* are evil spirits in animal form, almost human and intelligent but desirous of human flesh at all times. They are dark and hairy with sharp tusks in their big mouths. They are said to have built the enormous prehistoric dolmens found in many parts of North Africa. When the Prophet Muhammad sent his first followers to Ethiopia, he sent Ali to accompany them, and there, in the mountains, Ali had to do battle against the ghouls who blocked their path, until Ali slew their king with his double-bladed sword and drove them away. They still live in the deepest forests, we are told. Their females sometimes fall in love with human hunters lost in the forest, and carry them away to their caves in the hills to make love to them. Male ghouls also pick up human girls when they risk themselves out on the verandah at night, and carry them off to their caves deep in the mountains, where they seduce them with gold and diamonds and other ornaments. The fruits of these unions are a new race of savages, fierce and fast in hunting and killing, and prone to raping human girls.

In the Sahara, the ghoul has one eye like a cyclops, and a long snout with sharp teeth, a long neck, a body like an ostrich, with ostrich legs and arms like wings with stumps for hands. He entices travellers calling to them from a distance, looking like a pretty girl, but hoping to eat human flesh.

Gishu (Bagesu) (Religion, Uganda). Weri (or Mweri) Kumbamba or Kibumba was the Creator to whom offerings were made before circumcision took place, and in order to pray for the recovery of a patient. He was associated with rocks but it is not clear whether he was the god of *all* the rocks. Gibini was the god of the plague. Trees were planted for him in front of the house and offerings of vegetables were placed beside them, when the first cases of plague were observed. Enundu was the god of smallpox to whom a goat was offered whenever the first cases of the disease appeared in the area.

For the rain-god, see below. The Bagesu had the custom of eating the flesh of a deceased person. The body would be carried to a secret place in the bush where at nightfall the men of the clan would make the noise of howling jackals by blowing horns. The women would come and carve the piece they wanted for cooking and eating. The bones would then be burned, except the skull which would be placed in a shrine (*mboge*) in the house, as residence for the ghost.

Rain-making. A rain-maker had a hazardous job for he might be punished if he failed to deliver rain. Two fowls had to be brought to him in time of drought, one of which he slit open to 'read' the entrails concerning the weather in the near future. The second fowl was used as a 'check' to confirm the 'reading' of the first. If in spite of his efforts, rain still did not fall, the rain-maker might decide to climb the mountain to visit the sanctuary of the rain-god near the summit. Accompanied by the elders leading a black bull and carrying big jars of their best beer, he would stop at the place of sacrifice where the bull would be slaughtered by the men and eaten, the blood being offered to the god. One bull's leg would be taken further up to a priest who used to live at a sacred pool in which the god resided in the shape of a large snake. Several streams ran from this pool down the mountain. The beer is here offered to the snake-god, a huge python. Water may not be taken from this pool without the god's consent, for it has magical qualities.

God The notion of the One God, first propagated in Africa by King Echnaton in Egypt in the fourteenth century BC, had no remaining influence outside Egypt. Christianity was the first major monotheistic religion in Africa, spreading all over North Africa, Nubia and, from the fourth century, Ethiopia, where it survived. Islam spread from the seventh century to West and East Africa. Those religions have influenced African mythology fundamentally. In Tanzania and Kenya the notion of God in Heaven is well established. The Janjero (q.v.) believed in a Supreme Being, Hao. The Swahili word for God, *Mungu* or *Mulungu* is widely used, whereas the Kikuyus and the Masai call Him *Ngai*, the Nuer in the Sudan pray to God as *Kwoth*, and the Nupe in Nigeria also say that God, *Soko*, is in the sky. *Tilo*, Sky, is also a vague notion for the Thonga in southern Mozambique, as a directing principle of their lives. The Ibo in Nigeria know *Chiuke* in the Sky as the Creator, as well as the Earth Goddess *Ale* (see *Earth*). For the Congolese notion of God see *Nzambi*. The peoples of Zambia often refer to God as *Lesa*, a word which originally may have meant 'rain', revealing what they needed most from heaven. Similarly in Angola. In eastern Africa the Kipsigis used to organize an elaborate annual ceremony called Kapkorosit for the worship of God, in which the worshippers face east while they pray, since the rain always comes from there.

Goddess Akonadi, The (Accra, Ghana). One day, three brothers, sons of one father, appeared before the shrine of the goddess Akonadi near Accra, and requested an oracle from the goddess. There had been several recent deaths in the family: an aunt, a wife, three children. Did the goddess know the answer? She did. The priestess interpreted: 'The goddess spoke: ''Go to the house of your grandmother (the goddess gave her name) and search it. I know you respect her deeply but she is in league with thieves and robbers, so I, goddess of justice, decided to punish her by causing five deaths in her family.'' This cryptic message hardly put the brothers' minds at ease, but they obeyed it and went to their revered grandmother's house. No one was home, so they searched the house wondering what they might find. Under the old woman's bed they found a metal box which they opened with a crowbar. In it they found incredible treasures: golden bangles and bracelets, necklaces and earrings full of jewels, and silver coins. They lifted the box and carried it together to the goddess' shrine in the full confidence that she knew who the rightful owners were. She did. She told the men through her priestess: 'I thank you for your honesty. This was stolen property. Now that it is no longer with you there will be no more deaths in your family. Leave it with me. The rightful owners will soon come here.' They did. Not long after that day, two gentlemen arrived and complained that a metal box containing a large number of golden women's ornaments, silver coins and precious stones had been stolen from their mother's estate. Did the goddess know who the thieves were and where the box was? She did. She gave the answer through her priestess: 'I know. The box is here. You may take it or you may leave it as charity for the poor women and children in this town.' The men decided it would be better not to touch those treasures which had caused so much suffering, so they left the box as payment for the oracle. Thus Akonadi functions as goddess of justice and protectress of women and children.

Goddess Dzivaguru, The (Korekore, Zimbabwe). According to one tradition in the country of the Korekore, a Shona-speaking people of northern Zimbabwe, Dzivaguru was once worshipped as the great Earth Goddess, the most ancient deity of the Korekore. She lived in a valley near the present Dande, where there was once a lake; at its shore stood her palace. There she owned many cattle and goats, pastures and forests. She was dressed in goatskins and had a commanding voice which all the people obeyed. She possessed a long horn filled with magical substances which gave her whatever she wished. One day Nosenga, the son of the sky-god Chikara, became jealous of Dzivaguru's wealth so he decided to drive her away. He descended into her valley but Dzivaguru had surrounded herself with fog, so all Nosenga could see was the lake and the mountains. Nosenga tied a magic red ribbon round his head so he could see Dzivaguru's palace. He entered it but Dzivaguru had already withdrawn to the hills, taking all the light of the earth with her. Nosenga, surrounded by darkness, cut fibres from a certain plant and constructed a bird snare which he set near the lake. Soon it snapped shut and the first Sunbird (q.v.) was caught. Nosenga set it again and soon it snapped again: the second Sunbird was caught too. The cocks crew, dawn came. As the sun rose Nosenga could see Dzivaguru standing on the hillcrest. She spoke: 'You have driven me away from my lake, Nosenga, so I will take it with me. You have brought the sun out which will soon become so hot that the forest will dry out. If any of your sons commit incest, I will withhold rain. If they want to pray to me they will have to slaughter a sheep first. You will be punished. For a time you will be worshipped but one day men whose knees are not visible will come and bring another god so you will be forgotten.' She vanished for ever.

Goddesses (Yoruba, Nigeria). 'The earth is venerated in Yorubaland because it is believed to be inhabited by a spirit,' writes Omosade Awolalu. Such a huge spirit, who gives us all the food we need, and grass for the animals as well, is surely to be regarded as a goddess, one of the most powerful divinities, one who rules life and death. Human beings were formed from earth by Obatala (q.v.) before Olodumare (see *Earth: Yoruba*) gave them breath; we eat food that comes out of the earth one way or another; finally we are buried in the earth for good. Since the earth is everywhere, if two persons conclude a treaty they will invoke the earth as a witness and believe she will punish the party that breaks the covenant. Ile, the goddess of the earth, receives special sacrifices at the time of planting and harvesting. Like the ancient Greeks, the Yorubas have the good custom of pouring a libation of wine or other beverage on the earth as an offering to the spirits of the dead below. The blood of all the sacrificed animals also flows into the earth.

Yemoja is the goddess of the water, she is the mother of all the rivers in Yorubaland, in particular the River Ogun, the country's chief river. She is worshipped especially in Abeokuta, where a jar of Ogun water is kept for barren women as a remedy. Female devotees bring her offerings of goats, yams, maize, hens, ducks and fish. Her symbols are the cowrie shells for wealth.

Oya, the first and favourite wife of Shango, is the goddess of the River Niger. She accompanies her husband on his travels with his thunderstorms, as the goddess of the winds and squalls, uprooting trees and blowing roofs off houses. Her symbol-animal is the bushcow or buffalo, whose horns she is depicted with. For these reasons we can compare her to Hera, Zeus' consort. In the Niger and its delta the people refer to her as Mammy of the Water, and believe that she has hoards of cowrie shells.

Gods The essential difference between gods and other spirits, even great and powerful ones, is that the gods are worshipped. Spirits are propitiated, appeased, even magically compelled to act on behalf of the magical expert, but not worshipped. It is true that many ancestral spirits are worshipped and so, they too, deserve to be called gods, as indeed in ancient Rome they were called *di* 'divinities'. Many African gods, on the other hand, are referred to as 'spirits', just as the Great Spirit whom the American Indians worshipped was not referred to as God. The reason is that the Christian missionaries, and in Africa also the Islamic scholars, refused to accept that the gods of the pagans were worthy of the epithet 'divine'.

The simple definition: 'Your god is what you worship,' though workable, does not solve all our problems. Many peoples in Africa know of the existence of the Creator, the High God of the Sky, but do not worship Him, because He is too far away; they approach Him only through intermediaries such as the spirits of the ancestors. Islamicized peoples similarly pray to the good spirits of saints and angels who, they believe, will intercede with God on their behalf. Yet there is no doubt in such religions that the High God is a god, not a mere spirit. Here another difference comes into focus: gods are far greater than spirits, higher and more powerful, more universal, multifunctional, multi-aspectual. Many of the names for God are known across tribal borders, such as Mungu (Mulungu), Nzambi (Nyambe), Ngai, Kalunga (Karunga) or Imana. (See also *God*.)

Gods and spirits (Igbo (Afikpo), Nigeria). There does not seem to be a belief in a supreme god in this society, and no hierarchy of deities, so they all work independently. There are two major types of spiritual forces: the ancestors or *Ndiche Nwe-Ale*, the 'Elders in the Ground' and the *Erosi* spirits. The ancestors are thought to be, or want to be, reincarnated in their descendants over whom they have great power so that these sons and daughters perform regular, prescribed ritual sacrifices. Neglect of these duties may be punished with sickness. When a descendant is in trouble, an ancestor may appear to him or her in a dream and suggest a solution for the problem. There are also evil ancestor spirits, called *Ndema*, who do not want to be reincarnated, but haunt their descendants and make them ill with magic. This behaviour may be very unlike that of the same spirit when it still resided in a living body. A good man may become a bad spirit; the latter may, after some time, give up its wicked ways and become good, whereupon it will reincarnate in a child. If a person is haunted by Ndema he must make a sacrifice in the Bad Bush, the part of the forest where the dead babies and those who died of horrible diseases have been left. Burning the bones of such a haunting ancestor will punish him and silence him.

The Erosi or impersonal spirits may dispense fertility, prosperity and health; they have shrines where sacrifices in the form of food in pots are placed for their enjoyment. People can own such a spirit, in which case they will appoint a priest to serve the spirit, act as an intermediary and perform the ceremonies.

Ibini Okrabi is the spirit of the Aro Chuku oracle which is very powerful, so that some people say it is Chineke, God in Heaven. Very powerful also is Ale, the Earth Deity, who watches carefully over people's behaviour and punishes the wrongdoers. For instance, sexual intercourse on the ground is not permitted. There are numerous taboos, transgression of which is castigated.

Golden Stool, The (Ashanti, Ghana). In Africa, some important develop a close relationship with their wooden stools, as if part of their personality is in them. A man may bring his own stool to a meeting, saving himself and his host the embarrassment of offering someone else's stool to an uninvited but prominent guest. No one may sit on a man's stool except his eldest son after his death. For a king his stool represents his authority over the Earth on which it stands. In English, too, one may refer to 'the Throne', meaning the Sovereign.

More than two hundred years ago Osai Tutu was made King of all the Ashanti peoples. This happened as follows. One day there appeared before Osai Tutu a famous medicine man called Anochi who spoke: 'Great Chief Osai, it has pleased Nyame (God) to give you the kingdom of Ashanti and all the Akan-speaking peoples. If you convene the Grand Council of all the clan-heads of the realm, I will perform the ceremony that will confirm you as the national sovereign. God wills it.'

As soon as the Grand Council was in session, Anochi prayed to God that He show a sign to express His pleasure with Osai Tutu as King. As all the eyes were raised upwards, there descended from the sky a stool made of pure gold, touched the ground and placed itself right in front of Osai Tutu. Anochi spoke: 'This stool contains by God's will the soul of the Ashanti nation. No one may ever sit on it, and no one may ever remove it from Ashanti or else great misfortune will happen to all people.' The kings of Ashanti defeated all their enemies from that day forth, until the British came a century ago and besieged Kumasi, their capital. After a fierce defence, the Ashanti king surrendered, lest the Golden Stool be damaged by gunfire, since the soul of the nation resided in it.

Gorilla Contrary to much popular belief, gorillas are very peaceful and rather shy vegetarians. They live in close-knit family groups and treat their young ones with apparent strong love and affection. Since much of their habitat, the dense rain forest in their native Uganda, Rwanda and Burundi, is now being destroyed, they have to come out in the open and are being hunted for trophies.

In Ethiopia there was a myth relating the existence of a race of men who were not sons of Adam, but lived in the darkest forest. The Arabs took up this myth and called the animal *ghoul* (q.v.), describing it, of course, as a *jinn* (q.v.). From *ghoul* we have the word 'gorilla'. In their myths the gorilla is represented as a very strong animal (true) with genitals bigger than a man's (not true), who will, if given a chance, pick up a human woman (not true), carry her into the forest and rape her. A more sophisticated form of this myth relates how the male gorilla approached a beautiful white woman, disguised as a gentleman, well-mannered and soft-spoken. The woman was charmed and consented to go with him, only to find that her new husband lived in a tree. The Arabs also tell lewd tales about neglected wives who have secret trysts with tender male gorillas. There are also tales about hunters who meet attractive females in the forest, only to discover they have married a gorilla. The offspring of such unions, we are told, is a race of sub-human rapists who raid human villages to round up buxom girls. Such tales are told by Muslim fathers who want to frighten their daughters so that they stay inside.

Graveyards In northern Africa, the Islamic belief that God will call the dead to rise one morning, makes it necessary for graveyards to remain undisturbed until that day. Graveyards in Islamic countries are, as a result, peaceful places where old cypress trees grow amidst the graves.

The Tsonga in southern Mozambique used to bury their dead deep in the heart of the forest in separate graveyards for each clan, *mitimu*, where on special days the guardian of the graves, *mutameli*, penetrates, walking carefully along the forest path, to perform a ritual, such as the slaughtering of a goat. This is necessary if, for instance, a man has lit a fire which swept over a grave. The sacrifice is performed to extinguish, not so much the fire as the wrath of the old king who lies there. No one may cut firewood in that sacred grove, only the priest may walk through it. No man (and certainly no woman) may look upon the graves, they have to avert their eyes, for the spirits are dangerous.

The Merina people of Madagascar buried their kings in a separate graveyard for each king: he reigned alone, so he was buried alone. On or near the grave they built a *trano masina*, a Holy House for the spirit to live in. Originally just a hut the Holy House grew into a sumptuous mausoleum for each of the nineteenth-century kings.

In Zimbabwe and Zambia, we are told that the graveyards are visited at night by sorcerers, sometimes in the shape of hyenas who dig up the corpses to dissect from them the parts which they need to bewitch their victims. Whether the sorcerers actually eat human flesh is still a disputed point.

The Zulu used to bury a loved father or grandfather in the floor of the hut, and perform a ceremony, *ukubuyisa* 'to bring back', hoping to persuade the spirit to stay close to his loved ones.

Guinea see *Creation Myths*.

H

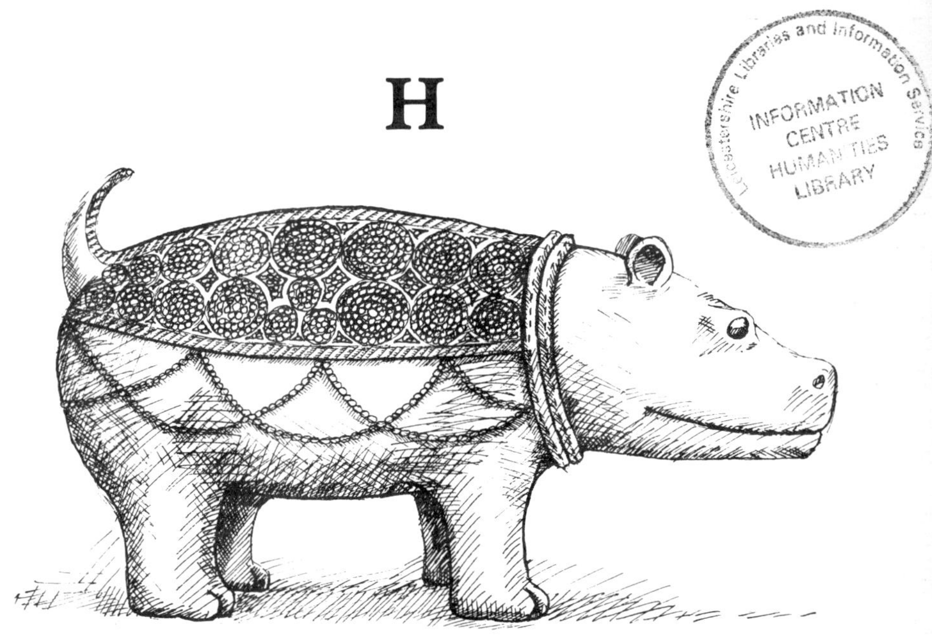

Hippopotamus made of bronze from south-east Nigeria

Hades Most African peoples agree with the ancient Greeks that the country of the dead is under the surface of the earth. It is easy to enter the land of the dead, but it is difficult to find one's way in it, let alone to find a loved person there. It is quite impossible to find one's way out again once one is under the earth, unless one possesses special magical powers. Only a very wise man who has taken specific precautions can return to the surface after a visit to death-land in the Underworld. The Swahili word for Hades is *Kuzimu* 'Cool Place' (see *Mizimu*). The souls or spirits (*mizimu*) of the dead are shivering in their dark misty habitat of dripping forest, fungus, big toadstools and bats.

The Alur of Uganda relate that their King Mola found his father in Hades, who asked him to bring fire from the upper world where it was warm. Mola did, so his father gave him many cows and showed him the way out. Mola found himself in a deep cave not far from his own village. The Ronga of Mozambique and the Xhosa of Transkei relate that the way to the other world is by diving in a river. The Yoruba say that there must be a deep pit in the forest which leads to Deadtown. The Kimbundu of Angola tell the tale of King Kitamba, who mourned his queen, Muhongo. He sent a *kimbanda*, a famous magician and herbalist to find her. The *kimbanda*, after collecting medicines in the forest, lay down in his fireplace, ordered his wife to water him every day, and told his men to shovel earth on top of his body. When he had completely disappeared, he found there, under the earth, a path that led to the hut of Queen Muhongo. She said: 'We dead people are the prisoners of Kalunga-Ngombe the King of the Dead. We can never come back to earth.' The wife, meanwhile, went on watering the earth-heap, until she recognized her husband's nose coming up like a courgette. He began to breathe so she harvested him, digging him out like a big sweet potato.

Hakata carved wooden plates used for divining in Zimbabwe. See *Diagnosis; Oracle*.

Ham (North Africa). Ham was the son of the Prophet Noah. In the later Jewish and Islamic traditions, Ham became the ancestor of all the peoples of Africa. During the voyage of the Ark, Noah commanded his sons to abstain from intercourse with their wives. Sem (Shem) and Japheth obeyed, but Ham was so full of ardent love for his wife that he embraced her in the middle of the darkest night during the rainstorm. For his disobedience, God made him black, and his sons as well. Thus say the Arabian scholars. When the Ark had safely landed, Noah sent Japheth to the north and Ham (in Swahili: *Hamu*, 'Worry') to the south, to become king of Egypt. Ham and his wife had nine sons, who became the ancestors of the 900 tribes of Africa.

Hatifu voice in the desert. See *Sahara*.

Hausa (Spirits causing illness, West Africa). The Hausa people suffer from many diseases and other problems that are not classified as medical in textbooks of medical science. For each of these problems the Hausa know the name of a particular evil spirit that is blamed for causing this harm. Each spirit may possess a dancer who specializes in dancing for that spirit so that people may know what caused the trouble and what will cure it.

Here follows a list of the most prominent evil spirits.

1. Dakaki or Mai-ja-Chikki, a serpent-spirit which causes the evil eye, which in turn may cause stomach ulcers.
2. Kuri, Yerro or Yandu, a black hyena spirit who causes paralysis.
3. Ba-Maguje is the spirit of drunkenness, a scourge for Muslims. He causes ever more thirst and renders his victims insensible.
4. Mai-Gangaddi or Sarikin Barchi, the spirit of sleeping sickness, danced by a woman who slumps on the floor like a real patient.
5. Bidda causes stiffness, probably the result of blood-poisoning.
6. Taiki causes swelling of the stomach, probably food-poisoning.
7. Rako is the spirit of old age: it causes weakness and doziness.
8. Kworrom lives under the tree-roots in the traveller's path, so that his foot is caught and he stumbles repeatedly.

9. Sarikin Bakka rules the animals of the bush and causes madness.
10. Jigo or Jihu causes fever, prickly heat and fits of shivering.
11. Mahalbiya is a female spirit who causes sores and tropical ulcers.
12. Jato or Nakada or Janziri is a dirty spirit who lives in the gutters and sewers. He causes venereal diseases and therefore insanity.
13. Ba-Toye is the spirit of fire, burning houses, fields and trees.
14. Makeri (blacksmith) and Masaki (weaver), who represent the professional illness of craftsmen who use their arms and backs till they hurt and become stiff.

Every spirit has its own animal that must be sacrificed to it, normally a fowl of a particular colour, breed and gender, by anyone who is afflicted by the spirit's illness.

Heise (Bushmen, Botswana). Heise is the great hero of the people who used to be called Bushmen, now often erroneously called San, but calling themselves Ju. Heise was half man, half god; he was a wanderer in the wilderness and so familiar with the animals that he knew them all by name. He had a wife who was a *gemsbok*, an elegant grey antelope with long curved horns, grazing peacefully in the *veld* with her two young ones who were half human, half antelope.

In those days there were no mountains yet, only plains. Heise was walking about when he came upon a pool shaded by a tree. He sat down and broke off a branch to make a fire, but the tree would not let him. A voice from inside complained: 'Please let me out! This strong tree will not release me! I am a prisoner. Help!' Heise simply commanded the tree to open itself. It had to obey him, for he was God. Inside there was a lovely girl who stepped out and agreed to become Heise's wife. They had a son, a handsome child but too delicate to live in the searing sunshine. So, Heise cut off some of his own hair and swung it round in all directions, speaking: 'There shall be trees everywhere, and hills and rocks for shelter!' At once the countryside all round was covered with thick forest, while big rocks became visible and distant hills rose out of the horizon. In the rocks there were caves with cool springs where they could live.

Hell (North Africa). The original African religions did not know of a place where the souls of the departed would be punished for their sins. The Islamicized peoples, however, have many tales about the horrors of hell — more than about the blessings of heaven.

In Swahili literature, hell is located beneath this earth and is constructed in the form of a building with seven floors, but much bigger. At the very bottom there are the worst sinners, those who during their lives have consistently denied the existence of God. They shiver eternally in the perennial ice which is crushing them for ever. On the first floor, that is, the upper floor of hell, there are the sinners of moderate wickedness, the drinkers of wine who were otherwise good Muslims. They will be forgiven after a spell in hell, and then go on to purgatory, Matahara or Jahannamu, where they only suffer thirst and drink discharge. Ladhaa, the second floor as one goes down, contains the misers who are dragged by their hair into a river of blood, the blood which they squeezed out of their victims, and which they must now drink or else drown in. Hutama, the third floor, is for the hypocrites and liars. Sairi, the fourth floor, is for embezzlers and deceivers. Sakari, the fifth floor, is full of fire and smoke, for the adulterous women who will have fire in their bellies for ever. Here also are the *sahiri*, the sorcerers who put spells on their victims, or those who dig up bodies and eat human flesh. Jahimu, the sixth floor down, is for the idolators who worship *sanamu*, false gods, in defiance of the One God. Hawiya, the seventh and bottom layer, is for the atheists, who live in a never-ending polar night.

Hereafter see *Ghosts; Hades; Hell; Judgement; Kuzimu*.

Hippopotamus In Ancient Egypt, the hippopotamus was worshipped as a goddess named Taweret, in Greek Thoueris, the special protectress of pregnant women and women in childbirth, very popular with all the women in Egypt, who used faience images of the goddess as amulets (q.v.) to protect them against demons.

In the River Ubangi there lives a large animal called Sangu in the Ngbandi language (see also *Ngbandi*). Sangu attacks the fishermen if they have not sacrificed to her before starting out in their boats in the morning. She protects pregnant women.

In southern Mozambique there are also traces of worship of the hippopotamus as a goddess. The Ronga tell a tale of a young woman whose rival wanted to kill her baby son. The baby was handed over to the Hippopotamus-goddess, who was already surrounded by a happy crowd of babies, her protégés. Every night the young mother would come to the riverbank and sing: 'Manana Mpfuvu! Mother Hippopotamus, strong and big!' Mother Hippopotamus would emerge from the water with the baby and give him to his mother to suckle. He grew rapidly. Under water, she rules a kingdom of lush, flowered meadows.

In Gavoland (capital Gao, now in Mali, but once a kingdom) there was once a huge hippopotamus, a monster which could change itself into any shape. It devoured all the rice in the fields so that the people were hungry and frightened as well. Fara Maka was a great hero, who decided to destroy Mali, the monster hippopotamus. He took his javelins and threw them at it, one after another, but the monster devoured all the blades, which melted as soon as they touched her hot body. Then came the hunter Karadigi with his 120 dogs, all black and as big as horses. They went for the monster howling, but the hippopotamus devoured them all. Fara Maka went home and slept with his wife Nana Miriam. She went the next morning and put a spell on the hippopotamus so that it was paralysed.

Hlakanyana (Zulu, Natal). The best-known character in Zulu mythology is Hlakanyana, or, with its grammatical prefix, Uhlakanyana, also known as Ucakijana or Icakijana, with a different prefix. He is well known among the Xhosa too, whereas the Tsonga of Transvaal call him Mpfundlwa, the Hare. The Zulu name seems to mean a weasel or a marten, a clever, quick predator, but more often he is described as a dwarf, an impish character who always outwits his enemies and gets free meals out of his friends. Dwarfs (q.v.) in the mythology of most nations are originally the spirits of the ancestors, which explains why they are so wise and why they live in the earth, like the Swiss gnomes who hid gold in the hills.

Like Lianja (q.v.) and Mokele (q.v.) in Zaïre, Hlakanyana spoke to his mother while he was still in her womb, telling her to give birth to him at once because he was ready for life. As soon as he fell on the floor, when she did give birth to him, he stood up, took his father's spear — which no one was allowed to touch — and cut off his own umbilical cord. Without asking the way he went to the cattle kraal for he could walk already; there, a beast had just been slaughtered for the elders, the wise men of the village. Hlakanyana took a piece of meat without asking, and devoured it at once. He then offered to deliver the meat portions at home for each of the men, but ate them all himself on the way, so that he had the whole cow as his first meal, deceiving the elders.

Next, Hlakanyana left the village in search of adventure. He fell in with a hare, offered him friendship, then proceeded to devour him. When he met a cannibal, he suggested they build a house together, whereupon he captured the cannibal by weaving his hair into the roof from the inside. The cannibal was hit by lightning and died, while Hlakanyana devoured his cattle.

Horses In Africa, the horse prospers only in North Africa, in South Africa and parts of West Africa, but not in the tropics. The horse was adopted by the Ancient Egyptians c. 1600 BC from Palestine. Its original homeland is the Asian steppes. From Egypt, the horse spread to north-west and west Africa as a domestic animal; it has not gone 'wild' as it did in North America. Famous horse-races are held by the More (Mossi) in Upper Volta (Burkina Faso) and in northern Nigeria. The great time of horse mythology began with the Islamic invasions of the seventh and following centuries. The great warrior-poet Antar had a miracle horse called Abjar, 'Having a big Navel'. The Egyptian story-tellers know of a fairy horse made of ivory that can fly; some say it was a jinn in the form of a horse, others that it was a flying machine moving its wings mechanically by magic power. When Alexander the Great had to travel underneath the Sahara in search of the Well of Life, his sages told him to ride a mare, for only mares can find their way to water in total darkness.

In the Indian Ocean there occurs a species of green horses, Farasi

Bahari in Swahili (from Arabic), quite unlike the tiny sea-horses of tropical waters. The green mares are highly prized for their beauty and endurance. There is an island off the East Coast of Africa, where the sea-stallions come to graze only in certain nights during the year. Horse-breeders take their mares in heat to this island in a boat, and leave them there for the night, hoping they will be covered by the sea-stallions, who will not emerge from the sea if they smell human beings. The young horses resulting from such unions are a rider's dream. They have the ability to run on and on without ever getting tired, because they have no lungs, so they are never out of breath. History does not relate how they acquire oxygen because that question was never posed to myth-makers. These horses were known to the Greeks as Hippocampus, in Egypt as Sabgarifiya.

Hottentots see *Khoi*.

Hua (Religion, south-east Ghana). The Hua distinguish between two types of gods, *dzi-mawu* or sky-gods, from *dzi* 'sky', and the earth gods. The lesser deities are called *ngunu-wo* 'fates'. The Hua express the concept of religion by means of the word *wo-mawu* 'to obey the gods', 'to worship'.

Sodza is the great god who lives in heaven and to whom the priests pray for rain. Yams are offered to him at least once a year. Prayer ceremonies are performed for Sodza every week; there is also a monthly ritual in his honour. The priests wear white robes and apply white clay on their faces before the annual sacrifice of a sheep.

Sogblen is the god who mediates between the high god Sodza and the priests. He carries the prayers of the worshippers to heaven and returns with promises of good crops, so he is regarded by some as the god of vegetation and fertility, living between heaven and earth.

The gods of the earth, *Anyi-mawu-wo*, from *anyi* 'earth' and *mawu* 'god', are associated with such trials as war, disease and famine. When disaster struck, the entire tribe came together for the sacrifice of a goat in the town which was under the earth-god's protection. The goat was duly dedicated and killed in a pit filled with water. The mud from the pit, mixed with the blood, was given to the worshippers, who applied it generously on their bodies, with the priests' blessings. A ceremonial meal concluded the proceedings. It was hoped that the sacrifice would induce the gods to remove the disaster.

Soului is the god of the crops on the fields, of wealth and of the magic sound of wind and music. He was also the god of medicine, which is the highest form of magic. If someone shakes beans in a pot, praying to Soului in the right manner, then, the next morning, Soului may have filled the pot with cowrie shells. But the lucky man may make no one partner to his fortune. If he tells even his best friend, Soului may take the shells back again. Secrecy is the key to success, the guardian of good luck. The god's favourite wears white clothes, daubs white clay on his face and scatters ashes on his shells.

Hunger (Kran, Liberia). On the day when God had created people, He also created food, in two forms: Rice and Cassava. Then He spoke to them: 'You must now go to the villages of the people and be their food, so that My people can live happily.' Rice agreed, but Cassava was just wondering: 'My brother Rice and I know that we are very important, being the Keepers of the people's lives. What do we do when we are not treated with proper respect?' God answered: 'Have no fear. I will give you my son Hunger to accompany you on all your journeys through people's lands. Whenever you approach a village he will precede you to announce your arrival.' Hunger arrived. His skin was as dry as a drumskin, and his bones could be seen sticking out through it. God spoke: 'You will travel ahead of these two foods and announce their arrival. If in any town they are not given respectful treatment you will teach the townspeople a lesson so that they will honour their food. If the people do not demonstrate their devotion to their foods by carefully and persistently cultivating Rice and Cassava, you will make them as thin as you are yourself. Remember, Cassava, that people have to eat you properly cooked, otherwise you will be poison for people. And you, Rice, must be boiled, or eaten in soup or gravy, but never raw.' So, the three of them set out on the road to people's land. Whenever they arrived near a village, Hunger would blow in its direction. A terrible dry wind would dry the leaves and stalks, and people would feel faint with hunger. Some would fall down and be unable to get up. As soon as they could see Rice and Cassava coming down the path, the people would rush towards them, fall at their feet, offer them all their possessions, begging them to come and stay in their houses, organizing ceremonies to thank God for keeping Hunger from their doors. Soon, they would be cultivating their fields again with great effort. Hunger is God's son who was created to teach us gratitude.

Hunting Hunting is by far the oldest occupation and the only one which all the peoples of Africa practise. Hunting provided the biggest source of food for mankind until well after the invention of agriculture. A successful hunter was highly honoured in his community, and even today hunters will be welcomed by the women of some villages, who will sleep with them if they bring game. Many hunters are believed to possess magic by which they can put a spell on the game; in any case hunters have a reputation for bravery because they risk the dangers of the forest, even sometimes at night. Rock paintings of prehistoric (Bushman, San) peoples show the use of magic to deceive the game. Before the hunt dances are performed named after the chosen animal, which, they hope, will fail to see the difference between its own species and the hunters, who will walk and behave exactly like the game. Numerous rites and taboos are observed to make the hunt successful, e.g. sexual abstention, bathing, hairdressing, rubbing of the body with magic oil, painting it, food taboos, etc. Neglect of these rules will make the game shy and invisible.

In the forests of northern Cameroun, the animals belong to the Bedimo, the Ancestral Spirits; the hunter must pray to his ancestors so that they may release the game from their 'stables'. Some hunters have to pray to the Game-Lord of a particular species to ask permission for hunting it; elsewhere they have to promise a piece of the game to the Lord of the Forest, the God of the Wilderness, who will otherwise hide all his animals. In central Zaïre, the hunter may have to face terrifying monsters who will claim half his catch, or else devour the hunter himself. If the Forest God is favourably inclined, he will 'send' the game into the hunter's nets, but only if the hunter obeys him.

The God of Hunting (*Gongola, northern Nigeria*). There was once a very skilled hunter whose name was Indaji. His arrows never missed, his spear always killed. Any animal he aimed at was doomed. When he whistled the animals would come to him, for he possessed magic power. One day he killed 10 animals, then 20 and finally he killed 100 animals every day. He was so rich and so famous that every chief in the district was in his debt. However, he became too greedy. He killed for pleasure. He already owned horses, fields, cattle and goats, as many as he could oversee and he had several wives and many children. What more did he want?

Finally the god of the forest became incensed about this hunter's pride. One day he appeared to Indaji in the forest and spoke to him: 'Indaji, you are a famous hunter. From now on you may hunt no more than one animal every day. That will be more than enough to feed your family. You already own more tame animals than any other man. If you go on killing animals like this, I shall soon have none left. You know the art of killing animals but not of keeping them alive. If you do not obey me you will not live long.' Not long after that day Indaji shot three antelopes who were grazing peacefully together in the forest. Suddenly he heard a voice: 'This sin will cost you your life.' At the same moment the three dead antelopes changed into three fierce lions who attacked Indaji. But Indaji, who possessed magic, changed himself into a songbird and flew away. But the lions changed into hawks and soared up after him. The bird changed into a tree. But the hawks changed into fire and burnt the tree to ashes. Fire is always too quick for the tree. We all must respect the forest.

Hydra (Fulani, Nigeria). A Hydra is a water-monster with seven heads. The Peul or Fulani of Mali call it the Waterlord and bring it small offerings, knowing that if it is displeased it will stop the river's flow of water so that people and animals will die.

One day a pregnant woman, whom her co-wife had teased by filling her water jar with mud, pleaded to the River Spirit in a song, to come and help her, pledging her child to him. The Waterlord rose out of the river and helped her, cleaning her jar and putting it on her head. That night at home she gave birth to a daughter, Jinde Sirinde 'the one whom the Water Spirit will claim'. When she was big enough to carry a full jar on her head, her mother sent her to the river to fetch water mornings and evenings. One day, as Jinde was standing in the water cleaning her jar, the Waterlord took her by her ankles and dragged her down in the deepest part of the river. There she had to live with him, as her mother had 'given her away'. As a special favour she asked her new husband to be allowed to pay a last visit to her mother and to see the sun for the last time. The Waterlord permitted her to go for one day, but, he said, 'If you do not come back, I will come and take you.' Jinde Sirinde quickly escaped and swam to the bank before the Waterlord changed his mind. She went to her mother but her mother did not open the door for her own daughter: a married woman belongs to her husband. Her father did not answer the door either: he was afraid of the monster.

Finally, she went to her lover. He was a true lover, for he came out with his father's old sword, ready to risk his life for his true love. In the distance the monster could already be heard rising up from the river like a storm roaring across the fields. He had a scaly skin and seven heads, but the lover slashed off all seven.

Hyena The word hyena is used for at least four quite distinct species of carnivore. Three of these are carrion eaters, but the fourth, the spotted hyena, is a hunter, for which its large and powerful physique makes it more than fitted. Hunting in packs, these hyenas are not afraid to attack lonely travellers at night.

In the Sudan, we are told, evil sorcerers may employ hyenas to hunt down their enemies for them, who, when they hear the blood-curdling howling in the dead of night, know that their doom is sealed. In East Africa it is believed that the glowing spirits of the dead can be seen inside the hyena who has eaten them, through its luminous eyes. Some peoples put their dead out in the bush where the hyenas will devour the bodies. Hence it is believed by some that the spirits of the ancestors can use a hyena to ride on at night, to visit their relatives as ghosts.

In Zimbabwe the witches travel at night riding hyenas. Witnesses have given sworn statements in court to testify they had seen so-and-so, accused of killing his or her enemies by witchcraft, riding on a hyena at night, which is considered proof positive of the accused's nefarious practices. In Zambia, the sorcerer (see *Sitondo*), may enter the body of a hyena, go and devour his victims, then resume his human form, looking quite innocent. (See also *Burial; Death; Taboo*.)

Hyena men (Mali). Hyena men are evil spirits which can assume form of a man or a hyena at will, depending on what they want to do at any given moment: to confuse people or to devour them or their animals. The purpose of a hyena man is to eat big meat.

Two young men went to see an old man who had once been a man-eater, or so people said. They told him: 'We never get enough meat to eat, can you help us?' He gave them a medicine which enabled them to become hyenas after dark. They went to live in the bush, sleeping in daytime. At night they would visit the graveyard outside the town and dig up the corpses but soon this high meat bored them. So, one night they fell upon a shepherd who was asleep outside the fold he was supposed to be guarding. They devoured the old man raw, then helped themselves to the fattest sheep, took that to the bush and roasted it over the fire, having resumed their human form just to enjoy the roast. They had a carving knife which they called *ala jugu*, 'God's enemy'. The next night they went back to the village in hyena form, taking each a child from a nursery. Having eaten that they were still hungry, so they jumped a fence, found a sheep and took it to their lair. They sang a song while eating it: 'There is no god today, we can do what we like.' The next night one man-hyena went to his own home and caught his mother; his friend jumped the enclosure of the chief's compound and grabbed the chief's wife and ate her, after raping her, while his friend devoured his own mother.

There are a few exceptions to the wickedness of hyena men. One very poor man with a numerous family lived in the village of Sofara. At night he changed himself into a hyena and went hunting to provide his children with meat. When he became too old for such an active night-life, he changed his eldest son into a hyena and told him to hunt. That same night he died, leaving his son without the necessary magic formula for regaining his human form. So, the young, innocent hyena man wandered around the village at night, howling sadly, until the villagers took pity on him and started feeding him daily.

Some girls from Macina wanted to go to the night fair at Bandiagara, but there was, they said, a huge hyena waiting for them in the bush. They went to a young man called Jolima 'Love-maker', who had a reputation for bravery. He agreed to accompany them that night, and as soon as they were near the hyena's den, Jolima walked in front with the girls at a respectful distance. Suddenly the big hyena appeared with eyes glowing red in the night. Jolima kept saying to himself: 'I am Jolima, I am Jolima.' The monster attacked, but Jolima stood his ground — he could not be pushed. The monster hit him with its claws but they fell out, then it tried to bite his neck, but its teeth fell out. Jolima's courage was the best magic. He took the monster by the neck, tied it up with rope and dragged it to the town where he showed it as 'my sheep'.

This story is exceptional in that it ends well. Often the hunter's magic is too weak for the fight against the hyena man so he will be devoured, or, if he escapes, he will be impotent. If a beautiful woman can be found prepared to offer herself and lie down naked in front of the hyena man, this will hypnotize the latter so that he can be ambushed and shot. Otherwise he is too wary ever to be surprised, for his talismans warn him. The hyena's tail is used by men who want to cast a spell on a girl who has jilted them. It is said that a hyena man has an irresistible influence on a certain type of proud woman so that she must submit to him, to be ravaged and torn to pieces.

The hyena men in southern Africa have two mouths; one for talking, which is set in a handsome face that can be shown in good company; the other with large, powerful jaws with enormous canine teeth for cracking human bones. The hyena face must not be shown in the presence of intended victims. When not hungry these hyena men look quite handsome and attractive. They are quite different from the hyena men in West Africa who always look and smell a bit odd, and change into complete hyenas at any time, to hunt. In Zimbabwe the hyenas are witches in disguise; some say they only *ride* hyenas, others that they are women who turn into hyenas.

I

Incubus demon from Nigeria

Ibo (Igbo). People and language in eastern Nigeria. See also *Earth; Gods; Spirits*.

Idols, statues and graven images (Swahili: *Sanamu*; Yoruba: *Ere*). Though the Ancient Egyptians created some of the finest art forms of stone carving in the world, little of this survives. Famous are the Benin bronzes, cast with a highly sophisticated method of moulding and smelting. Many bronzes are statues of gods. Wooden statues, some of considerable size, have been made and are still being made in almost all the countries of the tropical belt in Africa, from Sierra Leone all the way across to Madagascar.

In the museums of Europe and North America, many of these used to be labelled as 'idol' or 'ancestor image', until anthropologists discovered that behind each carved image there was hidden a wealth of mythology which was in many cases no longer known. Much African mythology has been so discouraged by the missionaries that the meaning of the statues is forgotten. Often it is secret and known only to the initiated in the rituals of the society to which the image belongs.

Traditional Islamic literature in Swahili and other languages, abounds in tales of idols that were adored by foolish kings. The best-known of these is Rasilighuli 'Demon's Head'. In the royal palace there was a statue that could speak because the devil lived in it so that he could tempt the king and his men to perpetrate evil.

Ifa (Yoruba). The Yoruba name Ifa has two meanings: it refers to the god and to his oracle; both are central aspects of the religion of Yorubaland. In the first meaning, Ifa is the name of the Yoruba god of wisdom, knowledge and divining; his other name is Orunmila (q.v.). The word Ifa may mean 'All-embracing', the word Orunmila may mean 'God knows who will be saved'. Both etymologies have been disputed. Several myths state that Ifa came to earth from heaven together with other deities, at the time when the earth was being created. The gods were establishing order in the world and needed Ifa's wisdom for their work. Ifa settled in Ile Ife in what is now western Nigeria. The localization of the original Ife as Ifa's residence is also disputed. While he lived on earth, Ifa married and had eight children; all of them became paramount chiefs, ruling the provinces of Yorubaland. In those days, heaven and earth were not yet separated by the barrier of great distance, so Ifa could travel to heaven frequently where he was consulted by Olodumare, the Supreme God (q.v.). One day, when he had been insulted by one of his sons, Ifa decided to leave earth and live in heaven again. His absence threw the earth into total confusion. Famine and disease took a heavy toll, no more children were born for a long time and many women remained barren. In despair, the elders sent the eight chidren to heaven to beg their father Ifa to come back to earth. They travelled upwards and after a long journey they found their father Ifa seated under a great palm-tree in heaven. He refused to come down to earth, but instead he gave each of them a set of 16 palm-nuts, *ikin*, which would be their divination tools.

Through the tools of divination, Ifa speaks to the people on earth. He announces the will of the gods to the people, and he conveys the prayers of the people to the gods.

Ifrit (Efreet, Afriit; Swahili: Afiriti or Ifiriti). Malicious spirit of Arabic origin, perhaps associated with *nifrit* 'wicked' and *ifr* 'cause to fall'; it also means 'antagonistic'. It occurs in the Koran only once (27: 39-40), when Solomon expressed the desire to own the throne of the Queen of Sheba, an ifrit, there described as one of the Jinn, offers to go and fetch it for the king. The ifrit has no difficulty in lifting the royal throne of South Arabia and carrying it through the air to King Solomon. This story, about which there can be no doubt for a Muslim, establishes that ifrits are very big and very strong. The Swahili word may derive from the Arabic plural *afarit*. The Swahili people believe that an *afiriti* lives in the rivers and creeks where the boys go swimming. It may suddenly grasp a boy by his legs and drag him down. It is therefore identified with leg-cramp. An ifrit can be made to work for a powerful man provided he has secured possession of King Solomon's seal, a precious stone from heaven with God's secret name engraved on it. This name will subdue all the demons except Iblis (the Devil) himself. Powerful ifrits may command armies of lesser ifrits who can do a great deal of harm together. They are divided into clans and are ruled by kings who go to war in order to take revenge for the slightest insult. They have males and females who can marry and have children, but they can also marry human beings, after having taken human form. Some male ifrits are known to have abducted attractive girls who were foolish enough to spend the night on the rooftop to get cool, but not all ifrits are wicked; some are capable of compassion for human children. Ifrits appear by rising out of the ground like an enormous pall of black smoke; they have huge batlike wings and live in ruins or in the earth, and they cannot be wounded except by sorcery.

Igbo see *Gods; Spirits.*

Ill luck and illness In medieval Europe, an 'ill' wind was thought to bring diseases like the plague but also other forms of misfortune, of ill luck. In Africa too, a 'bad wind' (literally so in Swahili: *pepo mbaya* 'evil winds, evil spirits') will carry misfortune in the form of sickness, infant mortality, barrenness in the women of the family, disease in cattle and goats, blight in the corn, failure of the crops. Evil is that which harms the lives of all those we need. Of course it is known in Africa that most diseases have natural causes, but the question remains: why are not all people affected by the same disease or other calamity? Why are some women barren while others have many children? Why do some people die young? These questions have led many people to conclude: misfortune is an evil spirit. It singles me out. Bacilli, viruses and other natural causes have no purpose, no will. A spirit is an invisible being with a will, it can think and choose its victim, it can select a method of destroying or torturing him. Such a spirit can be a living person, usually someone very close like a relative, or it can be a dead person, such as an ancestor who is angry over some oversight, or it can be an outsider spirit, such as a river-god, lightning, a thornbush, a pair of lions. We still speak of 'thunderstruck', 'moonstruck', 'lunatic', indicating the influence of heavenly bodies or natural phenomena on our fate. It is for this reason that many Africans call a diviner to diagnose illness instead of a doctor.

Ilomba (Barotseland, Zambia). Zambia and Zaïre seem to be filled with spirits of all kinds, but few good ones. An *ilomba*. (in Lozi also *ilomba-meme*, in Kaonde *mulombe* or *mulolo*) is a type of familiar (q.v.) in the shape of a water-snake; it is made, i.e. shaped and given life, by the *muloyi* (q.v.) for himself or for whoever pays him an agreed sum. The serpent's body is that of a normal snake but it has a human head, resembling that of its owner. Even the head ornaments are the same as those of its owner. In every respect the *ilomba* is so closely linked to its owner that if it is destroyed, the owner too, will die. To ordinary people it looks like a normal snake, but to its designated victim it looks like its owner so that he is warned, but paralysed with fright. The *ilomba* will then bite him swiftly and suck his blood. For the 'creation' of an *ilomba*, the *muloyi* takes blood from his client's back, chest and forehead, together with his nail parings, and mixes them with roots from the forest and perhaps puts these ingredients in a snakeskin. This operation will go on for weeks until the snake has grown to a yard or more. It will begin to live and eat eggs and milk in infancy, but after five years it will demand blood and begin to kill people if its owner does not 'give' it any victims, first a foetus from the womb of a young mother, then a baby, finally an adult. After each killing it will feast on the spirit of its victim and increase its size by doing so. Some say it will also grow an extra head after a good meal. The victims can be exhumed by the owner for 'reviving' so as to have obedient slaves (see *Zombies*). The snake lives in the river from where it arrives in the house of its victim through a tunnel. Once its owner has an *ilomba*, he can never get rid of it, for if he does not 'give' it human blood regularly it will starve and he will die with it. Inevitably one day it will be killed and he too will suddenly die.

Imana see *Burundi.*

Immortality Almost all the peoples of Africa believe in the immortality of the human soul after death. The Muslims believe that God makes the body of a child in the womb from pieces of earth which the angels bring him from where He tells them. When the child is born, or a little before, according to some, He places the soul in the body so that it lives. A person whose death is approaching will feel an irresistible desire to return to his native country because that is where his clay was taken, where God took his earth. His flesh wants to be reunited with its own kind. The soul survives and lives near the body in the grave until Doomsday.

For the reincarnation of Itonde as his son, see *Itonde*. A great man may come back as a lion or snake (see those words).

The Wafipa in western Tanzania relate that one day God came down to earth and was greeted only by the snake, since all the other creatures were asleep. God rewarded the snake by giving it a new skin every year so that it rejuvenates itself always. (See also *Chameleon; Death; Lion; Snake; Rebirth; Reincarnation*.)

Incubus In the Transkei, the most frequent appearance of an incubus is in the form of a Tikoloshe (q.v.), described as a black dwarf with a big penis, who can make himself invisible. If the woman refuses him he will choke her; if she gives birth to deformed children she will be accused of having yielded to a Tikoloshe while her husband was asleep or away. She will then be driven from the village.

The Impundulu is a large bird, sometimes described as a vulture, but with a penis, shaped like an ox tongue. Others say that it is a young ostrich with downy feathers, or like a secretary bird. If a woman who 'has' an Impundulu at night, takes a human lover as well, the Impundulu will attack him, suck his blood and so cause him to cough up blood and die. Vultures are generally considered bringers of war and disease. The woman who has an Impundulu will be accused of witchcraft if found out, but with her magic hands she can put her husband to sleep simply by stroking his face. One night a certain man who had been warned of his wife's 'habits', managed to stay awake and, to his horror, saw an Impundulu having intercourse with his wife. He waited for its climax, then thrust his assegai into its chest so that it died. He sold the feathers for much money to the sorcerers who make magical objects with them.

Women who yield to an Impundulu will give birth to vampires. Women may also have an incubus in the form of a snake, *inyoka*. There are two types of sexual snakes. The Ugatya may be given by a mother to her daughter. It lives inside a woman's vagina and makes her happy all the time so that she smiles and dances. Whenever her husband wants her she has to go out of the hut at night and quickly take it out, otherwise it would bite his penis so that he would get syphilis. An Ingumbane is a much more cruel sex-snake, always ready to destroy its human rivals.

Insects There are thousands of different species of insects in Africa, few of which are represented in any African language by a specific word. Most languages do distinguish bees, honey-flies, mosquitoes, hornets and tsetse flies. Different species of wasps are often distinguished, but flies and mosquitoes are not normally further specified. There is usually one word for all the numerous species of butterflies, but for ants and termites there are more specific terms, such as a word for red ants, one for large black ants, one for tiny house-ants, one for soldier ants, for white ants and one for migrating ants. Termites and locusts are commonly eaten, but grubs only by some peoples. The causal link between insects and diseases was not appreciated before the colonial period. Disease was caused by sorcery, they said.

The Alur of Lake Albert narrate that insects were originally stored in heaven in large closed jars. Some hungry visitors, believing the jars contained pickled food, took the lids off and were surprised by the contents. One jar contained flies, the next one mosquitoes, the third one wasps, etc. Though they ran back to earth as fast as they could, the insects kept buzzing around their heads and travelled with them to earth where they flourished.

The Nkundo of the central Zaïre Basin relate that the first insects were seen when the first man, Itonde Ilele-a-Ngonda (q.v.), had died. When his wife at home gave birth to his son and daughter, Lianja and Nsongo, the flies came out first, then the cattle, the goats and all the other animals, so that she, Mbombe, became the mother of all animals and human beings in one day.

The fly has a natural reputation for dirtiness in African folklore since it likes to sit on dung; but also for spying, since a fly can penetrate every room in every house and so, eavesdrop. The termites are admired for their tall (over 6 foot) chimney-type buildings of indestructible material, well defended by soldiers. Some peoples believe that a human soul may become a butterfly after death.

Islam see *Creation; Doomsday; Judgement; Swahili; Tijani.*

Itonde (Nkundo, Zaïre). Itonde was the name of a boy who had not even been born yet, but had already slipped out of his mother's lap to go and eat meat. Only gods can do that! Having satisfied his craving, he went and walked in the forest. No child would dare to enter the forest where all the spirits live, but Itonde was not afraid, he was already a grown-up man with a name and grown-up wishes. There he saw a little bird, it was Itoli the hummingbird. It perched on a branch and hummed a little mocking song, like this: 'You who eat/ your father's meat/ will a songbird black and white/ satisfy your appetite?'

'I am Itonde, son of Lonkundo (q.v.), king of the forest and all living beings. I was born in this night. What will you give me as a birthday present?'

'I am Itoli the Colibri. I will give you the world.' From under its tail, Itoli produced a small brass bell, such as dancers tie on strings round their arms and ankles. 'This bell has a name, it is called Bokili, the World. It will give you anything you wish for it contains everything. Look! It is all in here!'

Itonde looked closely at the small brass globe and to his surprise he could see the whole forest with all the animals and birds and all the streams with fishes in them. He could see all the birds' feathers and all scales on the fishes quite clearly. It made him very happy to see all that, knowing that he could get it at any time, even the big dark elephants hiding in the forest.

Itonde took the bell and started dancing, singing as he swung it: 'Oh Bokili, little bell, smaller than a baby mouse/ Oh Bokili, can you tell the way to my father's house?' At once he saw a path opening through the thick undergrowth in the forest. It led him safely to his father's village. Next to his father Lonkundo's house there was a shed in which the chief's drums are kept. Every king in Africa has his royal drum which only the king, the crown prince or a specially appointed drummer may touch. Itonde, knowing he was a crown prince, went up to the shed, took out the biggest drum, placed it in the village square, and struck it. The villagers hid in their houses, trembling, for it was said, 'If a stranger strikes the drum, trouble will come.' The big drum can be heard many miles around. All the village chiefs of the district heard it and prepared to go to the assembly which they assumed it announced. When the king calls, you go.

Finally, King Lonkundo arrived himself, having heard his own drum playing. There he saw a stranger, a handsome young man, sitting near the drum in his village square, playing his drum.

'Who are you, stranger, how dare you touch my royal drum? You must die for you have broken the taboo. Only royal hands may touch this royal drum, the voice of my kingdom. I rule here!'

Itonde rose before the chief, held up his hands and spoke: 'Look, Chief Lonkundo, these are your hands, your arms, your shoulders, your body is this. I am your flesh and blood. I am your son Itonde, I walk like you, I stand like you, I speak like you, I laugh like you. Ask my mother Ilánkaka. You went into her, you came out. All I am I have from you and from her!'

Chief Lonkundo looked in amazement and so did all the elders and all the chiefs from the distant villages: there was Lonkundo the king, and there was this young man, Lonkundo born again, the same features, the same manners, the same eyes, the same smiling mouth! Chief Lonkundo spoke: 'Elders, now that you have all seen that this young man is my son, I will fill his hands with royal presents. Itonde, you have come from the forest, your praise-name will henceforth be: Ilelangonda, Ilela of the Forest, Whose Charm Defeats All.'

Soon it was time for Itonde Ilelangonda to go and find a wife. One day he set out and after travelling many paths he saw a girl more beautiful than any he had ever seen. She was Mbombe the Elephant Girl, daughter of Kungoele, King of Thunder. She was so strong that she could throw any man. She said to Itonde: 'If you want to marry me you have to vanquish me.' So they fought, and Itonde from the Forest, Whose Charm Defeats All, won the Elephant Girl. Her father gave her 40 men and 40 women to serve her, and a catskin. They started out on their way to Chief Lonkundo's village but soon lost their way in the forest. Mbombe took the catskin, laid it on the ground and spoke to it: 'My father's catskin, open, so we can all travel safely to my husband's father!' The catskin grew until it was as large as a dance-floor and all the men and women stepped on it. Quickly the catskin folded itself around them like a tent, then it stood up. It had become a gigantic cat, the black panther of the Forest. With leaps and bounds it travelled over the forest till it arrived at the town of Chief Lonkundo.

Father Lonkundo was just watching the sky as he heard thunder approaching. A giant black she-leopard came down on the square. It gave birth to 40 men and 40 women, to Mbombe and Itonde. Lonkundo embraced his son and his new daughter-in-law and ordered 80 presents for her parents, which the 80 men and women carried home for them. It was a royal bride-price for Mbombe. Not long afterwards, Chief Lonkundo died and Ilánkaka, Itonde's mother, went back to her father's house in sunrise country.

There came a famine in the country as the game seemed to have disappeared from the forest. Mbombe was very hungry, so she spoke to her husband: 'Ilelangonda, if you cannot find meat for me, this child here inside me is going to die. It is your child, feed him.' So, Ilelangonda had to go on a long hunting expedition.

He penetrated deeper into the forest than he had ever been before. At last he found a few pygmy antelopes which he caught and brought back for his wife and unborn son. Soon she had eaten all that meat and was hungry again. Elephant Girl had a huge appetite! So, Itonde went back to the forest where he walked about for many days. At last he found a few bushpigs and brought them home for his wife to eat. They did not last many days.

Finally, when she, Mbombe the Elephant Girl, was hungry again, Chief Itonde spoke: 'I will go out and hunt for you again, but this time I have a feeling I may not come back. If you hear the monkeys wailing in the trees, if you see the leopards, one male and one female, close to the house, if you hear the elephants trumpeting close by, if you see that the gate of the enclosure will no longer shut so that the snakes can come into our garden, know that I am dying. If my bugle bleeds, then I shall have died.'

He went and disappeared into the forest, never to be seen again. He walked and walked until he found himself in the very heart of the forest, and he knew that that is the place where the spirits of the dead live. At last he found a bongo, a large antelope, and shot it. As it died, it cried, and soon Ilelangonda was surrounded by the invisible spirits whose game he was hunting. He fell in a ravine and died as his head hit a rock. The ghosts had made him one of their own by clouding his mind, so that he stumbled. The servants told Mbombe: 'Wife of the Chief! We can hear elephants trumpeting behind the house! We can hear the monkeys wailing in the trees! Two leopards have been seen near the gate, a royal pair! We cannot shut the gate, and there are snakes in the garden!' Mbombe looked at the wall where her husband's hunting bugle was hanging: large drops of fresh blood dripped from it.

Ivory Coast See *Peace*.

J

Jinn

Jackals The jackal is one of the most popular characters in the story-teller's repertoire: cunning, quick, eloquent, the ideal of the common man, the lonely boy who made good. Jackal shares this popularity with Hare (i.e. Bre'r Rabbit), Hedgehog, Tortoise, Spider and Squirrel.

In the mythology of the Dogon people of Mali, the jackal is the first-born from the union of the sky-god Amma (q.v.) with the Earth. From his mother, the jackal acquired 'words like water', i.e. the gift of speech, his mother-tongue. As the first possessor of the Word, the jackal is the god of diviners who will reveal the Creator's will. The jackal speaks to people by dancing, leaving tracks for the diviners to interpret. (See *Geomancy*.)

Janjero (Religion, Ethiopia). The little kingdom of Janjero was independent until 1894, when it was conquered by Menelik II, and added to his empire. It lies in the mountains between the Omo and Gibe Jimma rivers in the heartland of Ethiopia. Christianity came to the kingdom quite recently. Before that time, from the inception of the kingdom, human sacrifices were no exception, so the Ethiopian historians say. The kingdom was completely isolated since the rivers had to be crossed by travellers on inflated cowhides to reach it. Circumcision was the excision of the nipples and of one testicle of non-noble men, so they were disqualified from royal succession. The King, *tato* was the country's chief magical expert so that he was always busy practising. He was identified with the sun, so that he could go out only at night, 'since only one sun should shine at the same time'. When the king had a new house built for himself, a slave had to be sacrificed for every door. When the king died, his body was wrapped in the skin of a freshly killed cow and buried in the royal burial grove on top of the body of a freshly killed slave. A cow was killed every day there.

The Janjero used to worship a statue which fell from the sky during a storm, by offering it human and animal sacrifices. No one came into its temple because the lions there would devour every trespasser except the King, whose hands they licked. Once a year the King presided over a sacrifice of a cow to the crocodiles in the Gibe River. When he fell ill, the crocodiles would be fed human meat until he recovered, by their favour. The Janjero people also believed in the Supreme Being, Hao, whose visible manifestation was in the crocodiles in the Gibe. Young men were sacrificed to him; they were killed with spears and hung at the entrance gates of the kingdom. Foreigners and lepers were sacrificed as well.

Jinns, jinnies or djinns From Arabic *Jinn* or *Jann*, plural *Junun*; Swahili *jinni*, plural *majinni, jununi* or *ajinani*; Fulani *ginne*; Hausa *aljan*, plural *aljannu*; Nupe *aljenu*; Mande *aljine*. The word *jinn* or its derivatives is almost universal in Africa north of the Equator. The idea of what a jinn is also is fairly similar. The jinns are spirits created out of the air (the *shaitans* out of the Fire and the angels out of light), so they can travel in the air at the speed of the blinking of an eye, they can appear to human eyes at any time in any shape. Jinns may be good or bad though the bad ones tend to be identified with the *shaitans* (q.v.). Even the good jinns can be naughty or impish from time to time. The reason for this and for their monstrous shapes is their own sinfulness: they miscegenated with creatures of different kinds, which is sinful in the eyes of God. Hence the jinns with horns, snouts, hooves, fur or scales, which are probably remainders of heathen gods in the shapes of totem animals, now relegated to the world of *jinns* by the doctrine of monotheism. These jinns have great power over us by means of the magic arts which they possess. Jinns can put us to sleep, pick us up, and transport us through the air to a distant country, there show us miracles and mirages, then lay us in our beds again in a few seconds. That is what we call dreams. Jinns are of both sexes and can appear in human form, make a human being fall in love with them and marry them. The numerous reputed children from such marriages all have some magical powers such as the ability to walk through walls, to fly and to age slowly.

Jinns: their origin (North Africa). In the beginning God created the Light. Out of the Light He created the souls of the prophets, saints and angels; after that the souls of ordinary people, so we all have a little spark of light in us, but some angelic persons have a big spark. The satans (*shaitans*) were created from the Fire of God's Wrath, but the jinns were created from the hot Samoom or Simoon, the searing desert wind of the Sahara. The very first jinn God created was called Asoom Jan Tanushi or Taranushi. The Almighty taught him the laws which he and his descendants would have to obey, just as He gave Adam the laws for the human race to observe. However, after the centuries passed, the jinns no longer obeyed the laws of God, not any more than people did, since both races were deluded by their own pride. So, God sent the Deluge to Man, but He sent an army of angels to destroy the jinns, all blasphemous sinners. One of them, called Iblis, was captured and brought to Heaven, where the angels educated him. He was a good student so that he was finally appointed to teach the younger angels who flocked to his courses with great diligence. In the meantime, the dispersed jinns had reassembled on an island in the 'Southern', i.e. the Indian Ocean, where they settled. Iblis, more interested in power than in teaching, joined them there and was recognized as their king. He was called Azazil or Azazael, from then on. Scholars disagree as to which island or islands they settled on.

From their base in the Indian Ocean, the jinns fly out in all directions to delude people by whispering illusions (*ghuroor*, *ghururi*) into the already confused human minds.

Jok (Nilotic: Kenya, Uganda, Sudan). Jok is one of the most truly African concepts of the divine. It is a word, found with variations in all the Nilotic languages, as Jwok, Juok, Joagh, Joghi or Joogi. It is not always translated with the same English word, because the dictionary writers had different philosophical ideas themselves, which demonstrates the power of the spirit that we call Jok. Jok is God and the spirits, the gods, the holy ghost, the beings from the other world. It can be vague and precise, good or frightening, beneficent or dangerous, One or a multitude, legion.

If a missionary had chosen the word Jok to denote God in his Bible translation, he would defend the notion that the Nilotes knew the One God. If he had taken another word to mean God, then he might use Jok to mean 'the spirits', or 'gods', or 'devils', thereby embarrassing those missionaries of another denomination who had used Jok to mean 'God'. This, I think, is the origin of the confusion over Jok. This word incorporates all the contradictory ideas of the spiritual beings which in the minds of Europeans must be kept carefully separated. Jok is the unified spirit of God and the gods, personal and impersonal, local and omnipresent. (See also *Acholi*.)

Jollibe African name for River Niger. See *Ghana*.

Ju See *Bushmen*.

Judgement Day (North Africa). The first trumpet: That fateful day, the Day of Doom and Destruction, the sun will go out like a candle. There will be no trace left of human endeavour, no palaces or cities will stand up. A stormwind will blow dust in the eyes of the dying. The second trumpet: The wind will blow away the sand from all the graves and God will restore the skeletons to complete bodies again, recognizable for the souls that will be hovering overhead looking in all directions. For there will be no tombstones, no mausoleums, no rock inscriptions left. All the dead will be equal, but some will be distinguished by the light on their foreheads which is caused by incessant prostrations before God. For 40 years they will stand waiting on the dark plain in the cold wind, and the pouring rain which will gradually wash away much of the filth from bodies and souls. There will be millions and millions of people, like worshippers waiting for the imam to lead the prayers. Finally at the sounding of the third trumpet he will arrive, the Holy Prophet, on his white horse with a woman's head, led by the angel Jibril, light radiating from his face and a golden crown on his head. Suddenly, for all to see there will be the Pair of Scales, called Mizān, and behind it the Throne of God, of gigantic size will become visible, for this is Apocalypse, the Revelation of the Last Day: there will be no more hidden things.

Every soul will be worried over his or her own past secret sins. They will all be revealed and will be seen on the left one of the Pair of Scales. All the good words and acts will be there too, even the smallest coin you ever gave to a beggar boy will be there in the right one of the Pair of Scales. There will be no more darkness. In the dazzling light of the divine presence those who have lied to their neighbours, cheated their customers, oppressed the weak and forgotten the needy will be clearly visible by the dirt on their faces. Those who worked for their loved ones in secret modesty and shared what they had will be clearly visible by their shining faces, by the beauty of their kindness. What if the scales balance? What if your evil is as heavy as your good works? Pray to God. He may remember and send a sheet of paper fluttering down with the words: 'This soul is one of My servants. Once his mouth pronounced with honest conviction: "There is no god but God!" As soon as this note in God's own handwriting settles in the right-hand scale it will tip the balance and that soul will be saved for Paradise.

Juju The word *juju* is usually explained as coming from creole French *joujou* 'plaything, toy', referring probably to worry-beads or ornaments worn by people as amulets (q.v.) for protection. It may also refer to the captive spirit inside the juju, which was sometimes a small doll, i.e. a fetish (q.v.). One Muslim scholar said that juju came from the Koran (21:96), where it says that when Yajuju and Majuju come, Doomsday is nigh. The two different explanations of the origin of the word converge in the meaning of 'evil spirit'. The *Oxford English*

Dictionary gives as the first meaning 'a venerated object', and also the supernatural power residing in it. Juju can also mean 'divining to determine an auspicious day for an enterprise or journey'. As an object or fetish (q.v.) it is used, carried or worn on the person to protect its wearer against all sorts of evil. In West Africa where the word was first heard, it was also used for a horn stuffed with 'medicines' which will protect its owner against drowning and against losing his way in the bush. Perhaps juju comes from the Hausa Bori spirit *jigo* or *jigu*, the father of the hunters, who causes fits of shivering. Amanda Smith (1894) and Mary Kingsley were the first writers on the West African scene to use the word juju. A juju could be a large elephant's head used to bring good fortune to its owner's house. The juju priests needed a man's head to make their juju work, and their temple, called juju house, smelled strongly of the human blood that had been spilled in it.

K

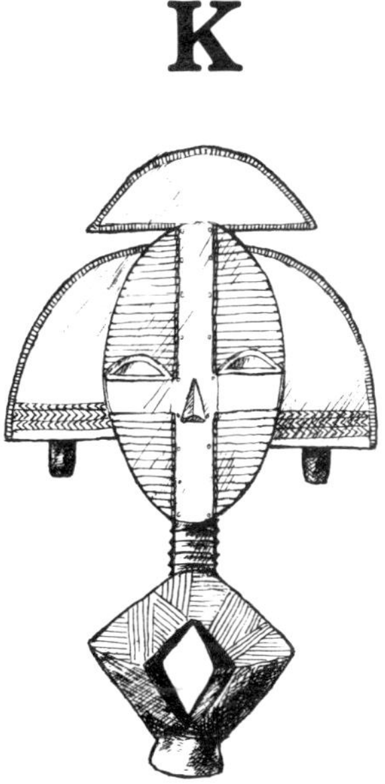

Kishi made of wood and copper of the Bangala

Kafa (Religion, Ethiopia). The kingdom of Kafa was founded in the Middle Ages, *c*. 1300, and lasted until the Ethiopian Emperor Menelik II conquered it in 1897 and introduced Christianity as the state religion. Kafa is also the name of the language of Kafa, which is quite unlike other Ethiopian languages and very old: witness its oral traditions.

The supreme deity of the Kafa was called Yaro or Yero. He was a sky-god and was later identified with the god of the Christians. Perhaps even today the clan-heads may still sacrifice to Yaro on the crests of hills and riverbanks of Kafa. The King of Kafa used to sacrifice to Yaro on the hill Bonge Dabbo near Bonga, the ancient capital. There was once a special cult for the fertility goddess (Atete?), later identified with St Mary. Her festival is now called Astar yo Mariam, 'the Epiphany of Mary' and consists of a number of fertility rites performed only by and for women, who, after collecting certain plants, go in procession to a riverbank where they throw the plants into the water, singing ritual songs. The people of Kafa remained faithful to the spirit rituals. The spirits are called *eqqo*; they live in the wilderness, in streams and trees. Some people can induce the spirits to descend into the body of a person and speak through his mouth, in answer to prayers, to predict the future. The hosts of such spirits function as shamans (q.v.) in Kafa culture. Devotees may go into a trance by means of drumming and dancing, uttering loud cries. This is the sign that the spirit has come, and those present can put questions to it. A priest will interpret the often garbled language of the possessed person for the people. The ritual takes place in the *Bare qeto*, 'House of Ritual', which is now also the word for the Christian churches. One of the spirits has been identified with St George; that is now the name of the church. In the old days the King himself was God.

Kalenjin see *Pokot*.

Kalunga (Ndonga, Namibia). Supreme god of the Ndonga who speak Oshindonga, in northern Namibia. Kalunga is the Creator and Benefactor of the Ndonga people who often invoke him, e.g. when they are ill, when they are planning a journey or a hunting expedition, or when they have to wage war against an invading enemy. They pray to him for victory in warfare and in despair after a defeat. They pray to him before planting and after harvesting. Kalunga may assume the appearance of a human being but he is many times larger so that he towers over the hills when he is visible for human eyes. Those who claim to have seen him, saw only part of him, the rest being hidden by the clouds and mists. They saw the face of an old man, sometimes his chest as well. Kalunga appears only to one person at a time, usually a woman, who is especially chosen by the god as his intermediary. Such a woman is called a *nelago*. She may be aroused from her sleep in the night by Kalunga's voice and will immediately go to the place, usually a hill, where she knows the god will become visible. There she will hear Kalunga's voice asking: 'Do you see me?' He will caress her face, and suddenly she will see his huge face in the sky. Kalunga will say: 'You are now my *nelago*, my child. Look!' There she will see all the god's treasures: baskets full of grain, beans, melon seeds and millet. Once Kalunga spoke thus to his *nelago*: 'Go to the King of Ndongaland and say to him: "The traditional sacrifices have been neglected. I will visit this nation with famine unless the King will slaughter an ox tomorrow and bring me offerings of grain, cowrie shells, glass beads, millet meal and pearls." Then I will give you as much corn as you can see in these baskets.' The woman hurried to the King and told him what the god had said. The King rapidly gave all the necessary orders and the next morning the *nelago* prayed on the same hill to Kalunga. The ox was killed and the famine averted.

Karina (Arabic *Ummu-Sibyani*, Swahili *Dege la Watoto*, Hausa *Uwal Yara*, *Nana Magajiya*). This demoness who appears often as a bird (see *Owl*), is feared in all Islamic countries and is known even in Indonesia, as Kuntianak. She may be the Berber Sheerree. It is related in Egypt that King Solomon when hunting in the wilderness, met a tall woman of great beauty who was naked except for her long hair. She spoke proudly: 'Who are you, hunting on my land? No man can vanquish me!' 'Who can?' 'Only the angel Mikail,' said she, not knowing that it was King Solomon. Solomon called out loud: 'Mikail, come and help me!' Mikail appeared at once and his shining armour so frightened the woman that she became old and grey, shrivelling up like an ageing witch. Now King Solomon asked her: 'Who are you?' She replied: 'I am Ummu Sibyani, the Mother of (dead) Children, the sender of the Evil Eye, the Bird of Illness. I have power over the children of Adam before they are born, and over their mothers before they give birth. I can assume the shape of a snake or a dog and enter their houses. I tie the wombs of the women so that they cannot conceive, and if they do they cannot give birth for the fruit will be lying athwart above the exit, and if it does come out it will be a stillbirth. And if it does live I only need to look at it and it will die for such is the power of my eye. I am Salmas, the Evil Eye. I can prevent the cows from calving and the ewes from lambing. If I look at a husband his seed will dry up and he will be sick. If I look at his crops they will wither, the grass for his cows will be chaff on the wind and his calves and his children will die or starve. His crops will not grow and his goats will have dead kids. I was once a human woman but I ate my children for the sake of magic, to own the power of sorcery. God condemned me to have only dead children and any woman to whom I show my blooded pudenda will have dead babies after that. Seeing me makes people sick. That is fate.'

Kenya see *Kikuyu; Liongo; Pokot; Sorcery; Suk; Swahili; Tobacco*.

Khadir *(El Khadir, Khidir, Kidhir;* Swahili *Hidhiri*, Fulfulde *Halilu*. The Arabic name is usually spelled Al-Khidr, or Khidhir.) This means 'the Green One', and since the name refers to a deity of the pre-Islamic period, it has been identified with Adonis, a Syrian deity adopted by the Greeks as the beloved of the goddess Aphrodite whose season was spring (early March). Adonis was killed but every spring time he rose from his grave with the vegetation. Khadir is immortal since he drank the water of the Well of Life (q.v.). Ever since, he has wandered about on earth, visiting the same place every five hundred years. He can see the changes which the local people do not know. In the desert they will tell him: 'Sir, this has always been a desert,' whereas Khadir remembers having seen forests there, and green pastures, and fine orchards. Thus the story of 'The Green Man' is the first lesson in environmentalism. With Alexander the Great, whose mentor he was, Khadir visits Africa. He is thus confused with Aristotle, while the Islamic tradition identifies with Elijah who never died. As a prophet of God, Khadir can speak all the languages of the earth, so he addresses the King of the Ethiopians, Azimu, in his own language. Deeply impressed by such scholarship, the King embraces Islam. The idols in his palace remain mute after that. The

King's wicked brother, Hakim, threw a spear at the holy man, but God turned it round so it hit Hakim's own ear: he converted. In the forests of Africa where there were many snakes and scorpions, they met a black nation living in reed huts. They took Khadir prisoner, but his iron chains turned into clay and crumbled away. After long marches, they arrived at a city gate which was guarded by a horseman made of solid brass, holding a long sword in his hand. An inscription, deciphered by Khadir, stated: 'This sword is for none but him who rules the world.' Alexander stepped forward, took hold of the sword and held it up. Khadir, riding a giraffe, entered the city of King Abud, who ordered his men to kill Khadir, but the men could not see him, and their swords bent round into their own hearts. (See also *Well of Life*.)

Khoi (Hottentots) (Gods, Namibia). The Khoi called the supreme God Tsunigoam, which is now pronounced Tsunigoab and translated as 'Wounded Knee'. The origin of this name is explained as follows: Tsuigoab was once waging war against his arch enemy the black god Gaunab. At first Gaunab was stronger and threw Tsuigoab several times, but each time Tsuigoab rose up stronger than before. Finally, Gaunab was driven away from this earth to his own home in the Black Heaven but only after he had wounded Tsuigoab in his 'walker', i.e. his knee. Since then, Tsuigoab has had a limp, like Hephaistos the Creative god. It did not, fortunately, prevent him from having a numerous family, and owning many sheep too. Another etymology for the name Tsuigoab suggests that it may be from *tsu* 'red' (originally 'bleeding') and *goa* 'walking', 'appearing', 'dawn', so the name would mean 'Red Dawn'. Long ago, the Khoi people would emerge from their huts at the first streak of red light on the horizon, go down on their knees and pray to the god of dawn who had just chased away Gaunab, the god of darkness after a fierce and bloody battle at dawn.

The god of light is also the god of lightning and thunder to whom prayers are addressed by the thirsty people at the end of the dry season when they are praying for rain to the sky.

Kianda (Kimbundu, Angola). Kianda is the Neptune or Poseidon of Angola who rules the Atlantic Ocean and the fishes in it. The Kimbundu fishermen around Luanda bring him offerings which they place on the rocks along the shore in the sea, and pray to him when they go out fishing that he may give them an abundant catch. Kianda once appeared to the elder of two sisters in the shape of a human skull and asked her to become his wife. She refused and hit the skull with a stick, but it did not fall. It flew to her younger sister with the same proposal. She received him with courtesy, offered food to the skull and promised to become his wife. The skull said: 'Follow me!' It flew in the direction of the sea. Its young wife followed him hurriedly. The skull flew towards a rock wall where suddenly a door opened. The young woman followed him inside, whereupon the door fell shut. Inside, they found themselves in a huge palace, where many servants rushed up to her, addressing her as their queen. They dressed her in fine clothes and served her delicious food. Her husband threw off his skull-appearance and revealed himself in all his splendour as Kianda the Sea-god. They lived happily ever after. They had many children, who had handsome human figures but could live underwater like fishes.

The elder sister met a handsome young man who proposed marriage to her. She accepted and he took her to his house far away from the village. After a time she became pregnant, and to her horror she gave birth to a child with two faces, one human and one a hyena face. She had married a *kishi*, a man-eating demon! She tried to escape, running to her old home but her husband overtook her and devoured her. The child grew up on human meat.

The appearance as a skull signifies that Kianda was an ancestral spirit who favoured the fishermen, his worshipful descendants.

Kibuka see under *Buganda*.

Kikuyu (Religion, Kenya). The Kikuyus are a nation inside a nation. They number two million, which is numerous for an African people. The speak a beautiful Bantu language and have lived on the slopes of Mount Kenya and surrounding districts for a very long time. The first Kikuyu was called Kikuyu and lived in a village called Kikuyu, which is still there. The word *kuyu* means 'a fig', and *mukuyu* is a fig-tree, a fertility symbol in Africa as well as in Asia. Kikuyu had nine daughters, who became the ancestral mothers of the nine major clans of the Kikuyu nation. The Kikuyu word for God is *Ngai*, which means the Apportioner. Thus during creation, God apportioned his gifts to all the nations of the earth. To the Kikuyus he gave the knowledge of, and the tools for, agriculture, at which the Kikuyus have always excelled. God controls the rain and the thunder, with which he punishes evildoers when necessary. Every person has a spirit, *ngoma*, which after death becomes a ghost. The *ngoma* of a murdered man will pursue his murderer until the latter has to come out of hiding and give himself up to the police, which is better than being haunted by a vengeful, persistent spirit. Burial rituals for the elders are executed meticulously, because their spirits are feared; the spirits of lesser members of society are less dangerous. Certain trees are inhabited by spirits which may have to be propitiated with food offerings.

Like Jupiter, Ngai punishes those who do not keep their oath sworn in his name, by striking them with lightning. It seems that the people also believed that a man's character was decided by God, so that his life, too, was predestined. The Kikuyus have a strong feeling of propriety; they will abstain from whatever they feel is untoward (see under *Taboo*). During the 1920s there was a prophet, Thiga wa

Wairumbi, who received direct messages from God for his people.

Kimpasi Kimpasi is a series of mystery rituals carried out on young people of the Kongo nation. The word Kimpasi seems to mean 'Place of Suffering, Ordeal', from *mpasi* 'pain'. It is, or was, particularly common in western Zaïre, in the region mainly south of the River Zaïre, and across the border into Angola. It used to be instituted when there were many deaths in the villages of a district. The elders, worried that the spirits were angry and made the people and children die, would fix a date for a Kimpasi 'bush school'. Each family in a village would designate one or two of its members, aged between 12 and 20, of both sexes but unmarried, to participate in this ceremony of ritual death and resurrection. At the place chosen for the purpose, near a river for the numerous ablutions, and in the forest because that is the habitat of the spirits called *nkita*, an enclosure would be erected from treetrunks, built in a square large enough to contain three dormitories and a Nzo-Lufumba or Initiation-House. At the gate a dozen or so *nkisi* (q.v.) would be placed, six-foot high statues of terrifying aspects representing different spirits, all known by name. The master of ceremonies is called *Mfwa-wasi* 'Dead of leprosy', a disease sent by God. The enclosure is called the village of Ngwa Ndundu. 'Mother' Ndundu is the mistress of ceremonies. Like the master, she must be old and wizened; she must once have had a child who died young, and she must have been possessed by a *nkita*. The *nkita* are spirits of the dead represented in the statues by a white and red stone, *tadi di Kalunga*, 'stone of Kalunga'. In the middle of the night, the young initiands would be led out of the enclosure to a ruined village now used as a cemetery, a haunted place full of spirits. The youngsters would be told to lie down in the pitch dark graveyard and would be beaten ritually with twigs that cause 'death'. Too frightened to get up, and believing themselves dead, the youngsters would then be carried back to their beds. During the following days or weeks they would be gradually brought back to life with numerous songs and ablutions, and then led back to their homes.

Kindness (Gongola, Nigeria). A certain chief had three wives. One day three visitors arrived, asking if they could spend the night there. Unfortunately it was a time of drought, so when the chief asked his senior wife she said: 'Impossible. We have no food. Tell them to go elsewhere.' The second wife, when consulted answered: 'I have no food even to feed my own children. Tell those travellers to come back next season.' However, courtesy forbade the chief to tell his guests 'Go away'. So, he consulted his third wife, who said: 'Guests must not be left outside, bring them in, yes, all three of them.' She went to grind the last grain in her granary. Miraculously, the grain seemed to multiply and by the time she had finished grinding she had enough flour for her guests and for all the children, and by the time she had filled her porridge pan, her flour basket was still full. She had only one little chicken but by the time she had cooked it, it was big enough for the family and the guests. The guests were very grateful, and after the meal the chief asked them to tell him their names. 'My name is Millet,' spoke the first guest; the second: 'My name is Prosperity.' The third guest spoke softly: 'My name is Kindness.' The first wife wished the guests goodnight but suggested that Millet might stay. The second wife invited Prosperity to her guest-hut, and the third wife asked shyly if Kindness wanted to sleep in the compound; she would give him breakfast — it would be nice if they could all stay together. At once Kindness agreed to stay with the third wife. Then the other two guests said that they would stay there too. 'We have to live close to our old friend Kindness. We cannot be happy anywhere without him,' they said. So, all three guests stayed with the third wife for ever after. From then on, there was always enough corn in her basket, no matter how much she gave away.

Kindoki (Kongo, Angola, Zaïre, Congo). *Kindoki* is the secret by means of which a man or a woman, but usually a man, becomes a *ndoki*, a sorcerer. If someone wants to become a *ndoki*, he has to find a master in the art of sorcery, who can cut bats' heads into two neat pieces. The pupil brings a pitcher of palm wine for the old wizard and says: 'This, I hope, will tie our friendship.' He will repeat this after a few days, entertaining the old man with small talk. Only after a few months, when they are already on intimate terms, will the young visitor say: 'I want to become mature.' 'But you are mature.' 'Oh, no, I have much to learn!' 'Are you quite sure?' 'I am sure.' 'How many are there in your clan?' The apprentice gives the number of members of his extended family and their names. 'Let us take your rich Uncle So-and-so.' When the young nephew hesitates, knowing full well that his uncle will die if he wants to become adept at sorcery, the old man says: 'Ah, you are not really determined to become an expert?' 'Very well, I'll let you have him.' 'In that case we will kill him and eat him together.' The old man takes a very strong fetish, *nkisi*, from his secret store and by means of it changes his pupil into an ant or a spider, or some other insect, and himself as well. Together they go to the rich uncle's house at dead of night, enter his sleeping body through the nose or the mouth, and creep down to the heart, where they suck the rich blood until the body dies. Afterwards they become normal people again, but now they are friends for life and when they meet they hold each other by the little finger. This is how one becomes a *ndoki*, a sorcerer.

Someone may be born a *ndoki* if his *mfumu-kutu*, 'ear-king', his migrating soul, is that of a *ndoki* entering his body at birth. This *mfumu-kutu* soul can leave the body at night and take any other form, insect or animal, good or bad, and travel about.

King killing (Hausa, Nigeria). In very old times, it was necessary for a tribe to be always on the alert, for enemies might be lurking anywhere and hostile tribes could attack at any moment. Every king must be strong, brave and quick. Without a strong-willed, iron-hearted commander the tribe would soon be defeated and scattered. The king was the strongest and most fear-inspiring man in the tribe. As soon as he began to age, he would be killed. This was merciful in times when only the strongest survived, while the weak knew they were doomed and slowly dying. Old age is suffering, says the Swahili proverb: *Kuzeeka kuteseka*.

In the days before Islam, the Hausa clans had totems. Every clan had an animal, fish, bird or plant to which it was attached in a mystic way, by identifying with its character, not fearing it. The royal clan's totem was the lion, and the King actually had a lion in his palace, which did him no harm, but discouraged burglars.

As soon as it became known that the king had failed to defeat an enemy tribe, or even omitted to march against an invading army, and in those days there were attacks almost every day, it would be time for him to go. No tribe could afford to leave the invaders unpunished, or else they would take the country and kill the tribe. A weak king was as bad as a traitor: someone who does not fight the enemy when it is necessary (see *War*). A weak king would not attract strong followers. Young men would go and serve other kings who could win battles, and come home with loot and fame. Five priests of the totem god would arrive one night accompanied by the lion, who was the incarnation of the clan-god himself. The King, who was himself the lion-god in human shape, would be tried by the priests, he would be accused of neglecting his duties of leader of the warriors and defender of the people. If found guilty the King would submit to the death sentence, and the lion would not defend him as it understood that it was all in the interest of the people. Then the King's throat would be cut.

Kishi (Kimbundu, Angola). A *kishi* is an evil spirit, a demon with a head that is constructed in such a way that there are two faces on it. One face faces forward in the normal human way, so that if one meets such a demon one is not aware that he is not an ordinary man. The other face is hidden by long thick hair which has been done up in an elaborate fashion which gives these black demons a modish outlook. The wise elders differ about the question: which way is the face looking? It may be facing upward, or backward, but they do agree concerning its shape: it is the face of a hyena (q.v.) with very strong, big and sharp teeth and very powerful jaw-muscles. The human face has a normal mouth and a glib tongue which talks nicely, but the hyena face has a different purpose: it is meant to crunch human bones. It is rarely seen by a human being who escaped to tell the story: all are eaten. One day three girls who used to go and fetch water at the river, decided to wade across it and explore the country behind the other bank, although they had been warned never to go there. It was Kishi country. The girls' little sister insisted on joining them, against their wish. They wandered until they saw a big house in the distance, well built with an upper storey and a palisade around it. Three *kishis* lived in that house and they were watching the girls approaching, like game slowly walking into a trap. The *kishis*' mouths began to water as they discussed methods to catch and devour the girls. They emerged from their house, dressed like gentlemen and with their long hair done up in the latest fashion. They talked charmingly to the girls, welcoming them to their house and inviting them to dinner. They even sang songs for them. After that, they went out of the room, and the little sister whispered: 'I am getting out, I have seen their other faces!' The other sisters would not believe her, until suddenly they saw them too!

Kongo See *Bakongo*.

Kuba (Bakuba) (Creation Myth, Zaïre). Darkness was over the earth which was nothing but water. Mbombo, the White Giant, ruled over this chaos. One day he felt a terrible pain in his stomach, and out came the Sun, the Moon and the Stars. The Sun shone fiercely and the water steamed up in clouds. Gradually, the dry hills appeared. Mbombo again brought up things from his stomach: this time it was the forest, trees, animals and people. The first woman appeared, the leopard, the eagle, the first falling star, the monkey Fumu, the first man. Then the first tools appeared too: the anvil, the razor, medicines.

The Woman of the Waters, whose name was Nchienge, lived in the east. She gave birth to a son, Woto, and a daughter, Labama. Woto became the first king of the Bushongo (Bakuba) and moved westward with his children, who were still white. He died their skins black because they had to live in the forest as hunters and white men are too visible for the game. He put a medicine on their tongues so that they could suddenly speak the Kuba language. He married his sister but he decreed that only kings should have the privilege of living with their own sisters. Ordinary people had to mix with other clans to make the nation more extensive. King Woto had a niece who gave birth to a lamb; this was the first appearance of sheep. Only the royal family may own them; so precious are they that they are almost human. Woto found the monkey Fumu licking palm-wine and so this delicacy was discovered. He also found a pair of goats who agreed to stay with people if they would protect them against the leopard. Since then, men have made war against the leopard. Woto could make the banana trees grow by blowing his horn; he could make the bamboo speak at night. He could even call the crocodiles from the depth of the river.

Kuzimu (Swahili *Alahira* (Arabic). The Hereafter, the Underworld, the world of the spirits, the ghosts of the dead who live under the earth in their own country where they lead a life similar to the one they had in this world. A cave or pit, river or pool may be the entrance to this spirit world, but only for brave characters. Some describe it as a dark and cool (*zimu*) place where the ghosts shiver as people do at night in the mountains (see *Hades*). Other myths describe the Afterworld as light and pleasant for the souls who can look down on earth. Other myths again describe the land of the dead as being below the surface of the rivers or lakes, where the spirits live on the bottom amidst weeds and waterplants like fishes. Many peoples, especially in West Africa, describe the Afterworld as a city, 'Dead-Town', right in the middle of an immense forest populated with all sorts of demons, ogres as well as a few friendly spirits. In Dead-Town, most of the ghosts are cunning and capable of seducing the rare living person who strays into their despair-filled habitation, into swapping his body or part of it with one of them in exchange for some worthless glittering object, so that they can escape but the living man cannot, since we all need a complete body.

Numerous ghosts remain for generations near their graves wherever that may be, haunting the place as spooks. That is why Africans will normally avoid ruins and deserted villages. The concept of Paradise (q.v.) comes with Islam and Christianity. In West Africa there is a belief in life *before* birth.

L

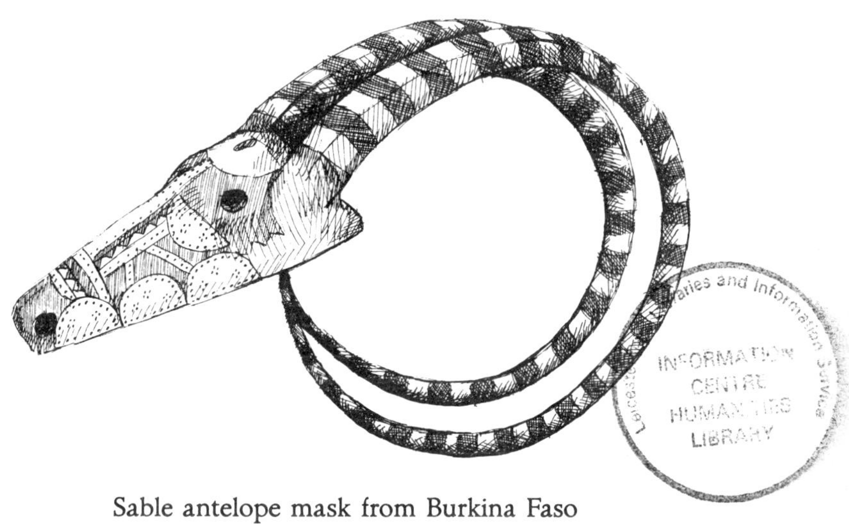

Sable antelope mask from Burkina Faso

Leopard Feared and universally admired for its fast and sure leap down from its tree onto its victim, never missing its grip, the leopard has a place in the mythology of most African peoples. In Zaïre, the leopard is a royal symbol and in southern Africa too, the kings alone were allowed to sit on a throne of leopard skins. A cap made of leopard skin was the equivalent of a crown. The leopard society in Zaïre and West Africa was usually the secret society of the chiefs and prominent witch-doctors who ruled the land.

In Zaïre there is the tale of the man whose flocks died, while his neighbour's goats increased in numbers. He grew so jealous that his hatred and aggression changed him into a leopard which started eating those goats. Only after many vain attempts could he be killed by magic.

The Yoruba of Nigeria tell the tale of a leopard-woman. A hunter had no children, so he promised the god Ogun that he would sacrifice a leopard if his wives would give birth. Within a year all the hunter's wives had babies, so the hunter went out to the forest in search of a leopard. After a long search he found a male leopard and shot it with a well-aimed arrow. (The tortoise helped him but that is another tale.) On his next visit to the forest the hunter met a very beautiful woman on the path. She invited him to follow her and they arrived at a fine house where the woman lived alone. The woman invited the man to sleep with her, and he could not refuse. It had been her intention to kill him and devour him in the night but she did not. She was lonely in the forest, her husband had been killed by the hunter. Perhaps she loved him, if leopards know love. She bore him three children, for he often came back to her. They were human beings in daytime, but at night they became leopards and hunted. They married human girls.

Lesotho See *Milk; Milkbird; Milktree; Water*.

Lianja (Epic of Lianja, Zaïre). Lianja is the eponymous hero of this epic who was indubitably a god in pre-Christian times, for the moment he is born he flies up to the roof of his mother's house together with his beloved twin sister Nsongo. The title of the epic is 'Nsongo and Lianja', and it seems that they were not only brother and sister but also husband and wife, like Jupiter and Juno, Isis and Osiris, or Shiva and Parvati in India. Gods live other lives than human beings. Osiris is reborn in his son the sun-god Horus, and Shiva and Parvati both die and are reborn in the different stages of their long and complex mythology. In the mythology of the Scandinavians we read how Odin (Wotan) is, after the gods have died in the Twilight of the Gods and the new day has dawned, reborn as Alfathur, the great Father God.

Lianja I and his grandson Lianja II are only two members of the epic dynasty which led the Bonkundo nation from the east, a point probably near the present Kisangani, towards their present habitat in the central Congo Basin where all the rivers flow to the west. Lonkundo, Lianja's grandfather (or great-grandfather in another version), was the progenitor, the Abraham of the Bonkundo nation. The miracle of rebirth or reincarnation recurs in this narrative several times. Both Lianjas are born on the day their fathers died. The father's spirit entered the mother's lap so that the child in the womb began to speak: 'The king is dead, long live the king!' A male voice was heard, calling: 'Mother, give birth to me, I want to come out into the world. Prepare for me a suitable exit.' Crying desperately, Mbombe replied to the voice inside her: 'My son, there is only one way for people to come into this world. You just come out that way.' But the strong male voice answered: 'Mother, I am the son of a chief, I cannot walk the path of commoners.' Suddenly, Mbombe's thigh began to swell up above the knee; it opened and out came a very handsome young man, armed with a spear and a ceremonial battle-axe. He jumped forward like a bird, leaping up to the roof of his father's house from where he surveyed the town, then he alighted on the ground in the square where his father had once beaten the royal drum. There he met the elders of the land and spoke to them in good language, not like a youngster: 'I am Lianja, son of Ilelangonda, son of Lonkundo. My father died an hour ago. Now I am your chief.' The elders all bowed and clapped as they admired his words and his strength, and paid him homage as the new king, Lianja I. 'And here is my twin sister with whom I was born together and with whom I will live together. She is Nsongo.'

After many adventures which are related in the great Nkundo Epic 'Nsongo and Lianja', in which Nsongo joins her brother on all his expeditions, Nsongo suddenly dies, perhaps because she had to wait too long for Lianja when he had gone out once on his own. At that time Likinda, Lianja's son, had just married a young wife called Boale. She was pregnant when Nsongo died and suddenly the women heard a girl singing a song. They looked everywhere, but no girl could be seen. The voice came from Boale's lap. It sang: 'I am Nsongo, Boale will be my mother. I am coming back to my brother Lianja.' She was born the same day; they called her Nsongo and when she grew up she was a great comfort to her uncle Lianja.

Liberia see *Hunger; Poro; Sheep; Totemism; Twins; Water; Women*.

Lion In many African religions the lion is revered as a god — or, better expressed, the god has taken the shape of a lion when appearing to human beings. The famous lions of Tsavo (*Simba wa Tsavo* in Swahili) who killed many people before they were shot were believed to be, by the local people, a king and queen of ancient times who reappeared to defend their territory, Tsavo. Several chiefs and kings in Africa traced their descent from lions, because it was believed that lions lay with mortal women and sired sons whom they taught the art of hunting, bushlore and, most important of all, the power to put a spell on the game so it could be killed, since no animal dies unless the gods will it so. Their magic art also enabled such boys to change themselves into lions and back again into men, so that they could go out hunting at night and rule their people in daytime. Men feared such princes since they were brave and fierce warriors possessing irresistible magic and charm. Women loved such lion men secretly and faithfully. Thus the scions of lions usually became rulers of men and women. Yet their powers also worked for the benefit of people since lions also possess the art of healing by magic. Their great physical and spiritual strength emanates from their beings and so restores the health of the sick by their very presence. Lions are also known to be very potent so that even one hair from the eyebrows of a lion is believed (in the Horn of Africa) to give a woman power over her husband so that she can have children from him by catching his mind. In the Sudan there are tales told of lionesses who meet the hunters in the bush and lie with them so that they give birth to half-human whelps. Many of these, if female, grow up to become irresistibly pretty women whose very appearance will make men fall in love with them. But beware! Half-lions live on meat alone, spurning all other food, and some lion women are known to have eaten their husbands. Others have helped their husbands and been faithful to them all their lives.

Sometimes a man may meet a beautiful woman in the wilderness who will invite him to make love to her after which she will resume her leonesque form and devour him, for she is the most voracious of all animals, the mother of lions, who loves hunting even more than love-making. Yet occasionally an experienced hunter may, with courage and cunning, outwit her and tame her, after which she will become quite amorous and also faithful to him. Her children, the lion men and lion women, are feared for their strength and ruthlessness.

The Egyptians called her Sekhmet, the lioness-goddess who loved to devour men in such great numbers that even her son, the young sun-god, had to ask her to let some men live. She is identified with Hat-Hor (Hathor), the mother of Hor, Horus the young sun-god; her name, which the Greeks rendered as Sakhmis, means 'powerful'. She takes revenge on the men who rebelled against the sun-god. Instead of human blood she was given pomegranate juice which is blood-red and is recommended as an aphrodisiac. Indeed the Greeks identified her with Aphrodite, the love goddess, who was in love with Ares-Mars the god of war. The warlike Arabs, too, worshipped her in pre-Islamic Mecca. They simply called her Allat, 'the Goddess'.

Lion-men (Bozo, Mali). The Fulani herdsmen of the Middle Niger Valley were concerned about their cows being attacked by a lion, so they went to a medicine man, paid him well for a remedy against lions and for a month suffered no losses. Then a fat cow was killed by the lion, so they went back to the medicine man for another magic remedy, promising him three fat cows if it worked. Unfortunately they later reneged on their debt. The man followed them but he could not wade through the river since he would lose his magic powers if he did. Water washes witchcraft off. So he had to find the ferryman, who was also the River Chief, i.e. the priest who performs all the rituals for the peoples along the river, for pilgrims on their way to the holy places praying for a safe return, as well as for the fishermen praying for a good catch. Naturally this priest, being himself an expert in the things of the unseen world, suspected his passenger and watched him while ferrying him across the Niger. He noticed that the medicine man spoke in a nasal voice, had sharp pointed teeth and a pungent smell of carrion about him which attracted a swarm of flies round his face. The ferryman had to force his passenger to pay for the crossing by stopping in mid-river, knowing that a lion-man could never jump in the water. So he paid. As the boat approached the bank, a herd of cows became visible and suddenly the eyes of the medicine man turned yellow like lion's eyes, as they saw all those fat cows. He jumped agilely onto the bank, growing short dun hair on his back as he did so; as his clothes slid off, his long tail with tuft appeared, steering his body in mid-air, like a true feline. Seconds after the tail, the long claws came out, the mane grew and, last of all, the sensitive whiskers and the cheek hair with which lions sense their prey.

Now the medicine man was a lion, ready to jump on a cow. The ferryman punted his boat to the Fulani camp and told them what he had seen. They knew it would be no use trying to attack the lion-man with their spears since his strong magic would protect him against their weapons. So they went and found a hunter who possessed a gun with copper bullets, the only sure instrument for killing a lion man. The latter, however, had got wind of their plans, changed himself back into a man and sat down in his village under a tree. A young Bobo hunter found him there and shot him with a magic arrow in his chest. The lion-man begged him to shoot again to kill him properly, but the clever hunter refused, knowing that a second arrow would revive the wounded lion-man. So, the latter died, for good hunters have strong magic for killing.

It is also reported that a young man who had just married a beautiful young wife received a visitor on the first night, who called that he was bringing a wedding present. When the bridegroom opened the door, he was attacked by a lion and devoured in a few minutes. The lion then forced the terrified bride to have intercourse. For three days he took his pleasure with her, then he devoured her as well, while the villagers could hear the bones being crunched by the powerful jaws. No one dared to break in and fight the lion, who quietly left the bridal chamber to have a rest in the bush. Later he came back as a man, to find another victim. The careful observer will always notice the nasal voice, the strong smell, the flies, the glaring eyes and the pointed teeth, still red with blood. Villagers are advised never to build near an abandoned site of an older settlement since it is there that the lion-men lurk. This indicates that these men with a double nature are 'really' the spirits of the dead chiefs who once lived there.

Liongo (Kenya). Mythical hero of the Swahili and Pokomo peoples of eastern Kenya. Historians have endeavoured to place Liongo in the chronology of the history of the Kenya Coast, as early as 1200 or as late as 1600. A large number of Swahili poems are attributed to Liongo, many of them popular wedding songs which are still performed at weddings, accompanied by special dancing, the so-called *gungu* dances, after the rhythm. Even the myth of Liongo is fragmentary and not a coherent story. Liongo was born in one of seven towns on the Kenya Coast which all claim the honour of being the great poet's cradle. He was exceptionally strong and as tall as a giant. He could not be wounded by any weapon, but when a needle was thrust into his navel, he would die; fortunately only he and his mother, whose name was Mbwasho, knew this. Liongo was King of Ozi and Ungwana in the Tana Delta, and of Shanga on Faza (Pate

Island). He was passed over for the succession to the throne of Pate, which went to his cousin Ahmad (Hemedi), probably its first Islamic ruler. It seems that the advent of Islam caused the changeover from matrilinear to patrilinear succession. King (Sultan) Ahmad tried to get rid of Liongo and had him chained and gaoled. By means of a long and self-laudatory song, the refrain of which was sung by the crowds outside the prison, Liongo caused enough noise to file through his shackles without being heard by the guards. As soon as they saw him unchained, they fled, for he was a formidable man. He escaped to the mainland, where he lived with the Watwa, the forest-dwellers. Each episode of this saga is marked with a song, which has been preserved. He learned to perfect his sureness of hand with bow and arrow, so that he later won an archery contest organized by the king to entrap him, and escaped again. Little is known about Liongo's successful battles against the Galla (Wagala), whose king decided to offer him his own daughter in marriage so as to tie the hero to his own family. With her Liongo had a son who later betrayed and killed his father.

Lokanda Bantu-speaking people of Zaïre. See *Tortoise*.

Lonkundo (Nkundo, central Zaïre). Lonkundo grew up and became a handsome young man. His parents died. One night his father Mokele (q.v.) appeared to him in a dream and taught him to make a contraption from the branches of a tree that he would find growing near the source of the river: the willow tree. The next morning early, Lonkundo went to the tree, cut off some branches and made that construction which his father had shown him in his dream. He set it up near the water's edge where the animals of the forest come to drink. The next morning the women told him: 'On our way to our fields we saw an animal caught in your construction. What is it?' Lonkundo told them. 'It is an *ilonga*, a trap!' One night Lonkundo dreamt that he had caught the sun in his trap. He rose and went to his trap in the forest. There he saw what looked like a fire. It was a woman shining like the sun, a sun-woman. He asked her what her name was. She said: 'I am Ilankaka, daughter of the Master of Copper. I lost my way in the night and was caught in this. I was led astray by a Bokali, a spirit in the night. Let us go to my father, he will give you copper to reward you for liberating me.' 'No,' said Lonkundo, 'I want you as my wife; that will be my reward.' He took her home and lived with her there, his sun-woman. She became pregnant, and had strange wishes, like all pregnant women. She wanted to eat nothing but *betomba*, forest rats. Lonkundo devised a special trap to catch rats, for a husband must find what his wife wants to eat, otherwise what will happen to his child? He caught dozens of forest rats and Ilankaka ate them all. One night, husband and wife were aroused from their sleep by a noise. It was darker than ever. Lonkundo touched his wife's belly: it was empty! 'Where is my child?' 'I don't know!' They were afraid. The child, their son Itonde (q.v.), had left his mother's womb because he felt a craving to eat meat like a real man. He slipped out and went to his father's meatstore where he helped himself and ate venison.

Lovedu Pedi-speaking people of Transvaal. See *Rain Queen*.

M

Mother goddess from the Congo

The Maasai The Maasai are famous for their refusal to adopt Western ways of life as so many other Africans have done. They still go clad in leather capes with plaited hair. They migrated into what is now northern Kenya from the area north of Lake Rudolf/Turkana from the first half of the nineteenth century onwards. With their 'flaming spears' they cut a swath of land for themselves through the Rift Valley, terrifying the Bantu peoples with their phalanx attacks, intended to occupy ever more land for their cattle, then to raid cattle in order to obtain wives.

The Maasai believe in the Sky-god, whom they call Ngai. One day God spoke to the first Maasai man after He had created him: 'Go into the bush and find a young calf. If you find it, come here to this hill where I am speaking to you, and build a *boma* (enclosure) of strong poles, 300 foot across. When you have built it, slaughter the calf, bring firewood and make a big fire. Burn all the meat in the fire, take none of it for yourself. Hang the skin in the gateway of the *boma*.' That night the Maasai man fell asleep in his hut and did not hear or see what happened. From the night sky there descended a herd of cows and some bulls, dozens of them, one after the other, until the enclosure was entirely filled with cattle, whose lowing woke the Maasai in the morning. His sons became cowherds and the

Maasai still hold nothing more precious than their cattle.

There are two more gods in the sky, the good black god who brings rain, and the evil red god who brings drought and dust storms. When the thunder growls, that is the red god trying to prevent the black god from sending rain.

Madagascar see *Diviners*.

Magic Magic is always defined in negative terms: its methods are non-physical, its results acquired by invisible means. The problem of magic is that it is incredible to the modern Westerner. The effects of magic are in the eye of the believer. One has to be brought up to be a believer, for those who have lived in their African environment all their lives cannot think that what they have always thought is wrong.

The first Europeans who described the performance of magical doctors in Africa were the missionaries, who regarded magic as mere deception of the people. The medical doctors who came to Africa with the first colonialists a century ago came to exactly the same conclusion for different reasons. They saw how the magical doctors had flourishing practices even though by any critical standards they could only be regarded as quacks. Yet, many people in Africa still flock to the magical doctors and come to the medical doctors when it is too late, and hopeless. The latter are then blamed for failing to cure the patient.

What induces people to remain faithful to a system of beliefs that has so often provably failed, and to treatments which are painful, dangerous and expensive? The answer must be that the magical doctor works within a local African system of thought and social structure. When someone has a known viral infection, the magical doctor will say to the patient: it is your kinsman so-and-so who is making you ill by his witchcraft because he is jealous of your wealth. That diagnosis seems to be more satisfactory than that of the provable viral infection. The therapy which the magical doctor prescribes is often extraordinarily far-fetched, yet the patient submits to it willingly and pays without complaint. The reader will notice that all references here are to the field of medicine. The reason is that most magic in Africa is performed — or pretended — in medical cases, and secondly, in medical science we have a chance of testing the case. The rain-maker (q.v.) and the drought-maker are not so easy to check. Even more difficult to verify is the 'work' of the killer at a distance. For the magic which (never in provable reality) turned bullets into water, see *Majimaji*. For the magic by which enemies become blind when attacking a town, see *Fingo*.

A saint in Somalia rescued shipwrecked sailors from certain death by drowning, while he was seen to be in his own town, by witnesses who later learned that the sailors had related how they were rescued by two hands coming from far away. Islam, if anything, has increased the tales of magic powers. Saints, we are told, can fly, see things that happen in other countries, walk on water, employ spirits and animals, etc.

Whether the numerous charms and amulets (q.v.) which are sold in all African countries, work, is impossible to tell. The exception again, is the medical evidence. A chapter of the Koran wrapped in a piece of skin hung on a man's neck does not arrest the progress of trachoma, as a man I spoke to in Dar es Salaam believed. His trachoma was making him blind. (See also *Diagnosis; Fetish; Illness and ill luck; Medicine; Medicine men; Nkisi; Sorcery; Witches*.)

Mahdi, The Muhammad Ahmad ibn Abdallah, known in the history of the Sudan as Al-Mahdi 'Guided by God', was born in Dongola on the Nile, *c*. 1840. From childhood he was deeply religious; he studied theology with several teachers and was initiated in one of the Sufi orders, one of the mystic brotherhoods. For a time he lived at Aba, an island in the White Nile, where he acquired a reputation for holiness and magic powers. He was attended by a small company of devout men and faithful believers flocked to his sermons. When he turned 40, Muhammad Ahmad, like the Prophet Muhammad at that age, decided that he must fulfil the mission which God had entrusted to him: he must cleanse the Sudan of all un-Islamic practices, re-establish the pure faith and the correct custom (*sunna*) of the Holy Prophet, then prepare the Path of the Lord, i.e. the Holy War, to make the world ready for Resurrection and Judgement.

In June 1881, Muhammad began writing letters to all the leaders of the Sudan, informing them that he was the expected Mahdi. It is believed that before Doomsday (q.v.) God will send the Prophet Muhammad back to earth as Al-Mahdi, the Islamic equivalent of the Messiah, who will, with Allah's guidance, establish the Kingdom of Righteousness, after destroying the Pagans, the atheists and all the other non-Islamic religions. Then he called his followers, the Ansar, to prepare for Holy War. In August 1881, the Sudan Government sent an army against Aba; when the army was miraculously defeated by the small band of Mahdists, thousands suddenly believed that Muhammad was indeed sent by God. The Government sent three more armies in succession, all of which were defeated, so that the faith in the Mahdi spread. He took El Obeid, the capital of Kordofan in January 1883, and in November annihilated an Egyptian army led by British officers. In January 1885, the Mahdi stormed Khartoum and took it. General Charles Gordon was killed. Suddenly, at the height of his glory, Muhammad died in June 1885, in Omdurman.

Majimaji (Tanzania). In July 1905, rebellion broke out in the area south of Dar es Salaam, against the newly instituted recruitment for compulsory work on the German cotton and sisal plantations. The senior German officer in command, Major Johannes, set out from

Dar es Salaam and on 5 August captured Mohoro, where he arrested the two men who were locally regarded as the instigators of the rebellion. They were *Zauberer*, sorcerers, of the Ikemba tribe and one of them who was known as Bokero, had been selling to his fellow Africans a *maji* (this word can mean 'water, sap, juice, any body liquid or vegetable extract') which, he claimed, had been given him by the Snake God to whom he referred as Koleo. (The word *koleo* literally means 'a pair of tongs', suggesting that this serpent was a python, well known for squeezing its victims to death; the worship of the python is widespread in Africa: see *Python; Snake; Water*.) Bokero, whose real name was Kinjikitire Ngwale, came from Ngarambi Ruhingo in the Rufiji Valley. He was well known for his magic powers, particularly for his ability to raise the spirits of the dead so that a man could see his own ancestors. Bokero and his colleague were hanged by the Germans. Bokero's last words were that it did not matter, for his *dawa* (see under *Medicine*) had already spread to other parts of the country and with it the spirit of independence. This *dawa*, the famous *maji*, was composed of water, *matama* (sorghum) and perhaps other millet as well as roots and various secret ingredients. It could be sprinkled over a man, or carried on his chest on a string round his neck, in a bottle made from bamboo, or it could be drunk as medicine. In whatever way it was taken, the man who had taken it was supposedly immune to German bullets: they would become muddy, *majimaji*, before hitting his body, and be harmless. Some women also took it, notably the Jumbess Mkomanira. The rebellion affected almost a quarter of the country and lasted for two years, until the summer of 1907, when the Jumbess Mkomanira was captured and hanged. Over a hundred thousand people died in the war, most of them from starvation. A Swahili poet, Abdul Karim Bin Jamaliddini, wrote an epic on the *Majimaji* rebellion in Lindi, in which we see the rebellion as a justified rising against the oppressors. It was published in Berlin in 1933, with a translation.

Malaika (East Africa). A good spirit sent from heaven to help people. Like the *shaitani* (q.v.) it can assume human form. The Malaika love people and will work for their benefit. God created them specially so that they might keep people on the straight path by sitting on their right shoulders and whispering in their ears what they should do or not do. The Malaika receive no food, because praying to God is their food. They have been created from the Light, God's first creation, so they are entirely transparent and cannot even think evil, let alone do it. They always obey God, who will send an angel whenever He wishes to help a human being in distress. Normally angels are invisible, but once God sent the Angel Mikail to defeat a very powerful evil spirit (see *Karina*). Mikail appeared in his full heavenly glory which was so dazzling that Karina was defeated by merely seeing him. She looked like an old woman after that encounter. Once Jiburili (Gabriel) showed himself in his real form: standing astride the earth, his feet suspended above opposite horizons, he towered above the clouds. The angels are constantly guarding heaven against the attacks of the *shaitani* by throwing rockets (*shihabu*) at them, which we see as falling stars. Death too, is a *malaika*, who serves God by taking the souls of those God has decided must die now. He may also send angels to do battle against his enemies the unbelievers. The *malaika wa vita*, the Fighting Angels, will drop burning stones on the enemies.

Malawi see *Chikanga*.

Mali See *Amma; Bambara; Dragons; Hippopotamus; Hydra; Hyena men; Lion men; Mande; Masks; Muso Koroni; Songhai; Sunjata; Vampire*.

Mamlambo (Zulu, Natal). Mamlambo means 'the River Mother'; she is the goddess of the rivers of Natal and will appear to those who sacrifice to her. In Zululand, at least in the old days, beer was mainly brewed by women, some of whom could make theirs quite strong and sweet. I was told the following story as a true report of the facts.

One day a beer-woman decided that she did not have enough customers in her beer-shop, so she went to the bank of the river Umgeni near Durban, after due preparations, and performed an elaborate ceremony, throwing much food as offerings in the water. She was calling the River Mother, and she succeeded. She watched carefully and after a long time she found what she had hoped for: a piece of wood no bigger than a matchstick came floating down the river. She picked it up and took it to her modest brewery in the firm faith that it was the River Mother. She placed the piece of wood on the bottom of the barrel in which she kept her beer. Then she made fresh beer and poured it into the barrel. From that day her beer-shop was always full of customers; her fame spread throughout the city. Nowhere was the beer so delicious. As they drank more of the famous beer, the patrons would feel ever happier, forgetting their worries at home and at work. They would just sit and sing nostalgic songs. This attracted the attention of the police. Brewing beer without a licence is illegal, so the police invaded the premises in search of illicit liquor. They found the barrel and opened it, knowing it was there to store beer. However, it was empty. On the bottom they saw a long snake, all coiled up, hissing at them. They quickly went away. That was Mamlambo, the River Goddess, protecting the beer-woman and her customers. The latter returned soon after the police had left. The beer barrel was full again, for Mamlambo had temporarily drunk the beer and now regurgitated it again. The beer was even better than before. Customers pawned their possessions to buy it. In this way the goddess ruled them.

Mande (Creation myth, Mali). God first created the seed of the *balanza* tree (*Acacia albida*). Then he created eleusine seed in twin varieties, as they say: He made the egg of the world into a pair so they could multiply. Next, God made three more pairs of seeds, and placed each pair in one of the four quarters of the earth. He enclosed them in a flower. In one of the egg-seeds there were two boys and two girls. The eldest boy wanted to rule the world, so he came out prematurely and descended to earth. Earth was his own placenta from which God quickly made the earth. Pemba, that was his name, sowed the seeds, but only the red eleusine germinated, because the earth was stained with placenta blood. Pemba's twin, Faro, became a twin fish, a pair of *mannogo*. One fish was cut into pieces and scattered on earth where they became the trees. From the other fish, God made a man, the new Faro, who had atoned for his brother's sins. God sent him down in a ship from heaven. It came to rest near the mountain Kouroula, where there was a cave, Ka, and near it the first pool was formed. Faro and the first eight people, four men and four women, disembarked. The eldest was called Kanisimbo, 'from the Womb of Ka'. There they saw the first sunrise. God had made the sun out of the other half of Pemba's placenta. Down from Heaven also came the first bard, Sourakata, playing the first drum. Then the first blacksmith came down and, seeing the drought, he raised his hammer and struck the rock, and rain poured down from Heaven filling the pool Kokoro with fresh, fertilizing water. Simboumba, brother of Kanisimbo, began to speak, saying *nko*, 'I speak', while he was sowing the seeds after the first rain. He took the clay from the pool and built the first sanctuary on the hill, the Egg of the World. Its roof was made of bamboo, Faro's hair. Kanisimbo sowed the first rice, *malo*. They built their first village called Kaba 'maize'. By causing floods from his body, Faro now created the Niger, so that river is his body, both male and female. In it, he left his seed for the future generation, which will be like fishes at first.

Mangu (Zande, south-west Sudan, north-east Zaïre). Witchcraft-substance. In the past, when a man killed his fellow with witchcraft (*mangu*), they consulted the oracles (*soroka*) about his death. The relatives of the dead man went to the chief with the verdict of the oracle. The chief consulted his poison oracle (*benge*) and if that also denounced the accused, the chief would order him to pay 20 spears and a woman to the victim's relatives. If, later, a kinsman of the accused happened to die, the accused would go to the chief and say: 'I have paid all this compensation, because I was accused of witchcraft. Now slit open the belly of this kinsman of mine to see that witchcraft-substance (*mangu*), with which, you say, we kill people.' He took a chicken, went to the poison oracle and spoke thus: 'We are about to cut open the belly of my kinsman; if we shall find witchcraft-substance in the belly, poison kill the fowl; if my kinsman is free of witchcraft, poison spare the fowl!' If the poison-oracle spared the fowl, they would announce that their kinsman's belly would be opened. An unrelated man would place a knife beneath the breastbone of the dead man and cut along the edge of the ribs and into the belly, first to one side and then to the other. After this they would loosen the lengthy intestines and examine them in vain for witchcraft-substance of which they found no trace. The accused would say: 'You see, I paid 20 spears and a woman on account of witchcraft, because they said we had killed a man and now there is no trace of witchcraft in us. We claim our compensation back: 20 spears and one woman we paid as blood money for the dead man.'

The witchcraft-substance may be an organ or a liquid; there are different words for it in the various languages of northern Zaïre and adjacent areas. It has been translated as 'stomach', or 'bile' or 'gallstone', but the real meaning eludes us, because there is no English word for a part of the body that makes its owner capable of killing people by magic, i.e. by non-physical means.

Marain Jagu (Soninke, Senegal). There reigned once a tyrant, Garakhe, who oppressed the people until they beseeched the great seer and preacher Bincigi to go and speak to the tyrant. Bincigi went and threatened God's wrath but Garakhe, unimpressed, gave him a day to settle his affairs before dying. Bincigi went home and entrusted his pregnant wife to the care of his most trusted servant whose (as yet unborn) daughter he promised in marriage to his (unborn) son. He, the seer Bincigi, knew the sex of unborn children. The next day, Garakhe had Bincigi executed. In due course his son was born; at the naming ceremony he named himself: 'I am Marain Jagu, son of Bincigi, Spotted Predator, Thunder of the Sky, Killer of Bulls.' He could walk in his first year, wrung a bull's neck and ate it. He challenged the seven sons of the tyrant Garakhe to a ball-game and killed them all with some quick bowling (balls were made of wood in those days). Killing the tyrant would not be so easy, for Garakhe was an accomplished sorcerer who possessed many fetishes (q.v.) that protected him, so Marain Jagu had to become apprenticed to famous magicians in order to learn the skills of killing by sorcery. As soon as he was big enough to wear his dead father's sandals, he spoke: 'The killer has forgotten, but the son has not forgotten.' He went to an old sage, who spoke: 'I can see you are avid for human blood.' Having learnt all the sage's tricks, Jagu went to meet the great sorcerer Dinga, who, after a magic competition, gave Jagu his most potent fetish, *korote*, a cow's stomach filled with mice, and the secret Book of Wild Boar Wisdom, and the left eye of a red dog. With these fetishes, Jagu overcame the dancing jinns (q.v.) of the forest and took their drum, Tonjo. After many strange adventures he came home to find his sister, Henten Kurube, who agreed to help him avenge their father. Then, Marain Jagu went to Garakhe's golden palace. He changed his fetishes into vipers who bit Garakhe's legs so that the tyrant died. Marain Jagu then became king.

Marriage Marriage is a most important institution in Africa. Most nations permit men to have more than one wife, except, of course, the Christian Ethiopians. Many kings and sultans have several wives, not for sexual reasons, but because it is useful to have as many in-laws as possible. Many African peoples regard marriage as a god-given institution. The Islamic peoples relate that Adam asked God how he should go about marrying Eve, since no one had married yet at that time. God sent his two archangels, Jibril to perform the wedding ceremony with the appropriate prayers, and Mikail to act as *wali*, the man who 'gives away' the bride to the groom.

In most African tribes, indeed in all patrilinear tribes which comprise the vast majority of tribal structures in Africa, the bride becomes part of her husband's clan (exactly as under Roman law); she owns nothing, except what she can carry. In the modern African states these laws have been replaced by Western-type laws, but in the Sudan Islamic law has been reintroduced, whereas in East Africa polygamy is still legal: a man may have many wives, while a woman may have only one husband. The basis of this difference is the need to produce sons so that the father of a patrilineal family will not die without heirs to sacrifice regularly for his spirit. The clan lives as long as its male ancestors live, and they, the spirits, can only live as long as their sons and grandsons offer sacrifices regularly: the body is fed by the hands.

Here is a tale from Lesotho to explain the origin of marriage. Long ago there were four young men who always hunted together. There was no one else on earth or so they thought, but one day God created woman and taught her to speak, to bake bread and clay pots, to grow grain and cook it. Thus, one fine day the four brothers met this young woman and wondered if she was a human being or an animal. One of them said he liked her and withheld his brothers from treating her as game. The three of them went away saying they were only interested in hunting game and if he wanted that animal all to himself he was welcome to it but that they would then also go and hunt for themselves. They were never seen again because, after years of hunting, they were caught by the lions and died in the wilderness when they were too old to look after themselves and defend themselves. Their woman-loving brother stayed with the woman who lived in a cave near a well in the rocks. She possessed fire, so she cooked his meat for him and gave him some porridge and boiled vegetables as well, which she had cultivated herself. The man was very happy and better fed than ever. They had many children, and in the end even grandchildren, who looked after the old people.

Masks (West Africa). A mask is the image of a god. A mask must have danced. Music and dancing bring the mask to life and make it divine. Yet at all times the mask is feared and respected for it always belongs to the god, even if he is not in it all the time. It hardly matters who is wearing the mask, together with the costume which usually belongs with it. Thus one says 'the mask behaves in this or that manner', as if the body in it was the body of the god himself. Indeed the person dancing the god has totally subjected himself to the will of the god, and identified with the mask he is dancing. Nor can he be seen, for the costume and mask conceal his body completely, so that he is anonymous. Yet the mask-wearer is often a high functionary in the hierarchy of the society which sponsors the dance, in its dedication to serve the god. Indeed, the mask-wearer becomes himself identified with the mighty god in the mask and derives often his power in the society and in the tribe at large from the authority and magic power of the god himself. For the duration of the dance he is the god.

Masks (Bambara, Mali). In many West African countries there are societies devoted to the worship of a god who is danced by means of a mask. Only initiated members of one sex may attend the annual or seasonal ceremonies. The drums will warn women not to approach the place where the god dances the male rites. Women have their own societies. The Komo society of the men in Mali celebrates the god of the waters, Faro, who created the fishes in the River Niger so that the fishermen can live. Every year a new mask is carved for the god, never the same. The mask has a face, either human or animal, representing a leopard, a stork, an eagle, an elephant or a vulture in the various towns of Mali, probably picturing different spirits. Sometimes the mask shows a combination of animal features, e.g. a buffalo's horns with a crocodile's jaws decorated with a duck's plumes. The ancient Greeks had centaurs and griffins which were once venerated, combinations of animals and men. Inside the mask there is a skull of a man or a hyena, the outside is painted white, red and black, intended to frighten the worshippers, reminding them that the god is claiming his due sacrifices. The black is obtained using clay from Faro's own river; the red was once the blood of young girls sacrificed to him annually. On the skull, which represents an ancestor, brass arrows are attached, intended to frighten away unauthorized spectators. The mask has big eyes, nostrils and ears in order to see, smell and hear people's bad deeds. The mask's mouth is often twisted since it is meant only to hum or whistle the sacred songs of the ritual, 'when happiness penetrates the god'. The square chin represents purity and firmness of decision. The man dancing the mask becomes himself god, or at least a semi-divine being inspired by the god.

Medicine All the words in African languages which are translated by 'medicine', also have the meaning of 'magic antidote'. In Nupe, a Nigerian language, *cigbe* means not only medicine, but 'an object or substance which causes remote and miraculous effects upon the outcome of human efforts and upon human fate'. It is always compounded of natural materials which anyone can collect and prepare if he has the secret recipe. It is not always possible to distinguish sharply between the empirical and the miraculous nature of African medicines, nor do the medicine men (q.v.) distinguish between the two functions of their remedies. Another anti-scientific aspect of African 'medicines' is that most are intended for good purposes but some serve evil intentions.

In Lingala, there are three words for 'medicine': *ebikiseli*, literally 'that which rescues or gives life'; *mono* 'medicine, amulet, magic object' and *nkisi* 'medicine, fetish, talisman' (see under *Nkisi*). The Nuer in the Sudan have a word *wal*, 'medicine, magic substance, fetish', which, however, is not effective except when administered with a ceremony. The Kpele (Liberia) word for medicine, *sale*, also means 'spirit, god'. In Zande, *ngua* means 'medicine, i.e. an object with mystical power usually of vegetable nature, used with magical rites, and also the treatment through the administration of drugs (empirical), medicines (magical) or 'surgery' (ritual). In both Nilotic and Zulu, one word denotes both 'tree' and 'medicine', indicating the origin of medicines. The Malagasy word *ody* is translated as 'medicine', but *ody tandroka* is a charm which prevents attacks by bulls, literally 'horn medicine'. *Ody basy* 'gun medicine' is an amulet for soldiers to prevent being hit by bullets. *Ody andoha* 'medicine for in the head' is a herb, *Ranunculus pinnatus*, taken against headache. This demonstrates that 'normal' medicines and magic charms are denoted by the same word.

In Zimbabwe, the *nganga* prescribes the heart of a lion to give a man strength, a portion of the body of a tortoise for security and solidarity, the sinew of a hare for swiftness, the milky sap of a certain tree for a woman's milk-flow. By touching the patient's body in a certain way, the *nganga* may transfer the strength of one part to the sick part, for rapid recovery, but just mentioning its name may already help. The *nganga* can even cure his patient by magic from a distance if he performs the right ritual at home.

Medicine man The function of the medicine man in an African society is quite different from that of a doctor. The medicine man has been compared to a quack and there are perhaps some who knowingly deceive, but the vast majority are serious, hard-working men. In some societies, women practise medicine as well; they are often called herbalists, though their function also includes much that is secret. The medicine man has also been compared to a magician, because his medicine (q.v.) works magically, not physio-chemically. In many societies the medicine man is distinct from the diviner, who can diagnose the disease but not cure it. The term 'medicine man' has been discouraged by some anthropologists because it is supposed to imply contempt of the man's primitiveness. However, it is the established English term; we have no other for this unique function in a non-Western society, i.e. a society where science does not yet dominate, and where medicine merges with faith.

In East Africa the *mganga* has many functions. He sells charms (q.v.) which protect the wearers against enemies of all kinds, not only illness but also burglars, arsonists, wild animals and famine. He will (for a fee) discover people who possess the evil eye (q.v.) and those who can change themselves into beasts of prey at night, men or women. Some are said to have the power to return stolen goods.

The medicine man is often depicted as dancing with his drum. This is associated with casting out evil spirits (see *Exorcism; Spirits*). The medicine man has been called a shaman (q.v.) because he receives messages from the spirits.

In the Transkei, a youth begins training to become a medicine man when he is called by the Abantubomlambo, the river spirits. They have to be obeyed for although harmless when undisturbed, they can cause disease when dissatisfied. From time to time they will claim a person as their sacrifice by right, and such a person will just go to the river and drown there, under the spell of the gods. His parents will try to stop him by tying him up, but the call of the spirits is so strong that he will often escape and join them. There below the surface of the water begins his period of training. After an unspecified number of days he may come back (many never do) and nobody will ask him whether he really lived underwater or what he saw there, for it is well known that disclosure of his knowledge will cause his death. After this initial period of study with the gods, the young doctor will wander off into the hills to collect the herbs, roots and fruits that he will need for his practice, guided in his quest by the gods of the rivers and pools. Dr Laubscher has found a high incidence of schizophrenia (both the catatonic and the hebephrenic type) and even of epilepsy among these persons who apparently hallucinated habitually. Whether suicide by drowning is normal in such cases is another question. Manic-depressive psychoses were also found among these 'wanderers'. Even witches whom Dr Laubscher examined appeared to suffer from schizophrenia in a state of progressive fixation, often sexual. The *igqira* or witch-doctor is not necessarily the same person as the *inyangi*. The *igqira* can smell (morally, not physically) the corrupting presence of a witch or sorcerer; in Zulu the witch-finder is called *isanusi*. He may be invited to cleanse an entire village of witchcraft by administering emetics, sneezing powder, and making incisions into which medicine is rubbed.

Mediumship Any member of an African society can become possessed by a spirit, except chiefs and heads of households. The medicine men themselves present a special case (see *Nganga* and *Shaman*). If a pregnant woman is possessed by a spirit, her child will be named after the spirit and will owe it worship. Few people become mediums voluntarily, as it entails many duties. Some mediums are possessed only once or twice in their lives, but the majority are visited repeatedly by the same or kindred spirits. As compensation, mediumship gives a person a higher status in society; e.g. women in a male-dominated society gain respect from their hosting of some awesome spirit, even chiefly status. Since much of the consultation of mediums during trance concerns medical problems, these people will also be approached at other times and be expected to diagnose diseases and suggest medicines. The commonest ailment they are consulted about is possession (q.v.) itself, which is a frequent phenomenon in Africa.

Once a person is established as a known medium, with a familiar spirit (q.v.), possession may occur or be induced at specially arranged sessions, presided over by the local 'doctor' as master of the ceremony, attended by all those who wish to consult the spirit. Drums and pipes are believed to be useful instruments for inducing the spirit to arrive. As soon as the medium shows signs of approaching trance, the 'doctor' will ask its name, since no man can have power over any spirit without knowing its name. The spirit will often speak a language which the medium does not know, so that the 'doctor' has to interpret its messages for the people. If the person with the familiar spirit is more independent and can go into a visionary condition without ritual or master of ceremonies, such a person is himself or herself a doctor, or even a prophet or prophetess.

Mganga see *Nganga*.

Milk Milk is almost a sacred substance in many parts of Africa, and always has been. Boys 'steal' the milk from the cow when drinking it directly from her udder, lying under her. Some African languages have special words for that 'stealing' and we can see them do it on the pyramid paintings of Egypt, where the cow was identified with the sky-goddess Nut, the rain.

In Burundi, the cows lived in the lake (Kivu), until God, Imana, sent one to Inaruchaba, daughter of Kihanga, the first king, the father of all the kings of the earth. First, the cows lived in the lake like the hippopotamus, but the first princess received the first cow seen on earth as a gift from God. She wathced it give birth to a calf, then she saw the milk come out of its udders and tasted it. She had a wound which was caused by a jealous woman when she had her son Kafomo, 'Wound', but when she drank the milk the wound soon healed. In her father's palace she had quarrelled with her father, so he had exiled her. Now she took the milk, put it in a pot and carried it to her father who was gravely ill. When he had drunk the milk he felt much better and forgave her. He asked her how she had found this medicine, and she told him about the cow. He went with her to the lakeside and there he saw an immense herd of cows. Suddenly a huge bull appeared, called Rutenderi, an incarnation of Imana (God). He approached King Kihanga and spoke: 'I give you these animals for your family, O King. Remember that only princes and noble ladies may drink the milk and own the cows.' In Bunyoro some princesses were fed exclusively with milk, so that they would be pure and noble.

Milkbird (Lesotho). The milkbird is one of the commonest motifs in the myths of southern Africa. The story goes as follows, with variations: A man and his wife decide to hoe a field behind their house, which has been lying fallow for a long time. They clear it in a day, but at night a little bird comes and sings the weeds back in place: 'Weeds, grow back, shrubs grow up, creepers creep.' The next morning the field is bush again, so they clear it again. The bird is an ancestor and the ancestral burial field must be left to itself, no one may cultivate on it or build on it. Finally, the man manages to catch the bird and put it in a cage which he hides in the house. There the bird agrees to fill a jar with milk every day provided no one outside the house knows. The bird is put over a pot and it produces *amasi*, a sort of yoghurt, a delicacy in southern Africa. They have enough for a daily ration. Inevitably, there comes a famine in the village and the neighbours begin to wonder how the man's children can have shining bellies while all the other children are starving. Someone is sent to spy; they catch the bird but it escapes and sings: 'I am your mother, I fed you in times of famine, now I go back to my land.' It flies away and never comes back.

Milktree (Lesotho). The milktree is another myth about a natural phenomenon that produces the holy food: milk. A certain chief has a daughter, Takane, and a little son. He and his wife go out to the fields and Takane has to look after her little brother. She may not come near her parents' milktree in their enclosed garden. But little brother cries and cries and begs for milk. She takes a knife and cuts a little slash in the tree. It bleeds a little milk which she catches in a jug and feeds her brother.

Mirage (Sahara). A discussion of the cause of mirages will be left to the physicists. This author can testify that he has actually seen one in the desert, in the Sudan. We are told by scientists that the oasis one sees in a mirage is there, it is only much farther away than it seems to be. What I saw, however, was definitely not there: a city on the lakeshore, with palm trees and skyscrapers. After I had observed this city for five or ten minutes, it vanished; nothing remained but sand.

No wonder then, that this strange phenomenon has stirred the minds of the travellers in the desert to conclude: We see what God wants us to see, and we are blind if He wishes. There are numerous tales of sinful travellers who saw before them palm-studded shores surrounding glittering lakes where attractive ladies were bathing. Hastily they ran in that direction until they were exhausted. Only their bones remain in the sand to bear witness to the end of all human desire.

There are sagas of armies which vanished in the desert; not a man ever returned to tell what had happened to them. Other tales tell of travellers seeing large armies of camel riders opposing them which, when they prepared to meet them, vanished. Legends are told of saints travelling calmly through the desert on foot, unperturbed by the thought of the immense distance to the next source of water, trusting in God. God folded the hills and valleys together like paper scrolls and led His friends (the saints) to fresh streams which He had just created for them there in the desert. God can make the desert bloom at any time and does so whenever it pleases Him. There are tales of cities in the desert like Irama, existing only by night when the moon is full. The traveller picks up some glittering stones, puts them in his pocket and travels on. At home he sees that the stones are diamonds. Hurriedly, he goes back with a caravan, but the city of diamonds has vanished.

Mizimu These are the ancestral spirits of the Bantu peoples, who are almost universally worshipped by their descendants, with the exception of those who have become Christians or Muslims. These spirits live under the earth or in the water, often close to their original homes, where their corpses may have been buried. In the lakes and rivers they may actually be seen in daylight by clairvoyant persons, living on the bottom where they have their own crops and cattle, sometimes in the form of fishes. They can be visited there by their descendants, provided the latter possess the right herbs to enable them to return from the realm of the dead, who are anxious to keep whoever swims in the river and drag him down to make him join their company. The terrestrial ancestors live in holes, hollow trees, pits, gorges and especially in caves which in some parts of Bantu Africa are very deep so that one can easily get lost in them. There, too, they can only be visited by doctors or shamans who possess the right magic to extricate themselves from the world of the dead. The shamans of the Amaxhosa in the Transkei may spend several days with the spirits in the rivers, to learn the art of healing by magic. Even though they have cattle and grain under the ground and fish in the water, the spirits are extremely hungry and must be fed regularly by means of offerings, of which they eat only the spiritual essence. They can often be seen in the dead of night, filing out of their caves like whiffs of mist, going in search of food. Do not travel at night without offerings. They can also take the shape of bats, lions, leopards or other animals, or even people, to punish or reward the living.

Modimo (Tswana, Botswana). The Tswana people of Botswana believe that there is only one Modimo — that is, God. The universe embraces the harmony of the opposites, life and death, light and dark. The order which holds life together is represented in the laws and customs which bind the people together for life. Modimo is mysterious, the Tswana people fear even to pronounce his name because Modimo is totally different from us.

The Tswana have no story of creation, since for them God and the world were always there. Modimo is rather the energy centre of the universe, radiating life in all directions into all creatures, so that Life continues to exist. Modimo is Mothlodi, the Source of Eternal Life, the river of existence which flows on for ever through time and space. He resides both in heaven and in the earth; in the sky, he manifests himself as lightning and thunder, as wind and rain. As an immanent divine being, Modimo rules all living beings on earth, preserving them in their proper place and order, which must not be disturbed, so that a ritual is required, even if only a small one, even when a man wants to cut a tree. It is every person's duty to preserve the sacred cosmic order, for instance by observing the taboos which the Tswana customary law imposes, such as not having intercourse before a proper marriage ceremony has been performed; or not leaving a corpse unburied, let alone exhuming it for sorcery. Modimo is praised as 'steadfast as rock', which means that his justice is immutable, so transgressors will be punished. It is thus not correct to say that Modimo created life and the law; rather He is Himself Life and the Law, the spiritual energy that maintains the order which permits us to live and have children. He is neither male nor female, yet he is a person, not an abstract 'it'. He possesses reason and knowledge.

Mokele (Ntomba, Zaïre). Wai was the first man; he lived near Lake Tumba. One day, he had to go out on a hunting expedition in the forest. He said to his wife Moluka, who was pregnant: 'When I come back, I want to see our son already born.' After his departure, days then weeks went by, but Moluka's belly did not grow round. Every day she had to go down to the stream to fetch water, and being very sad – for what woman would be gay without a baby? – she composed a plaintive little song, thus: 'Mother, mother, do you know/ Why my baby does not grow?'

One evening, at the riverside, she heard a rustling sound and, looking up, she saw a being in the shape of an old woman emerging from the reeds, who spoke to her in human language: 'Fear not, wife of Wai! I have come to answer your song.' The old woman touched Moluka's belly and lo! Out came an egg. 'Look,' said the woman, 'this is what you were pregnant of. Give it to me, I will keep it for you and care for it. Do not forget to bring me food here tomorrow morning.' After these words, the old woman disappeared and Moluka went home with her water jar, deeply shaken. The next morning she brought a dish of the finest food to the riverbank. Lo and behold! There was the old grandmother, holding in her arms the most beautiful baby you have ever seen! The woman ate the food which Moluka gave her, while Moluka took her baby and gave him the breast. Then the old woman said: 'Now I must take him away again, but come back tomorrow morning with more food.' She snatched the baby from Moluka's arms and vanished with him. Crying, Moluka went home. The next morning she was back at the riverside very early with a rich meal. There the old woman appeared with the little boy walking beside her. 'Here is your son, Moluka; he has grown well. You may take him now; I know that your husband is coming home today. But remember, don't show your son to anybody. Keep him inside your hut.' That night, Wai came back and the following morning all the women of the compound came out with their children to greet him. None of the children knew their father's name, for he had been away a long time. They all laughed when Moluka arrived at the chief's reception-cabin without a child. 'You, Moluka,' said the other women mockingly, 'you pretended to be the chief's favourite wife. Have you not born him a baby yet?' Chief Wai felt deeply disappointed with Moluka, and he felt dishonoured too, for a chief expects all his wives to bear him many children. He was about to divorce her and dismiss her when a noise was heard from Moluka's cabin and a male voice rang out: 'Door, open thyself.' The cabin door opened, and a tall handsome youth appeared. He stood in the doorway for a while, then spoke: 'How can I go and greet my father properly? Grass, disappear!' Suddenly, a path was swept between him and the chief's cabin by invisible hands. Then the young man ordered: 'Mats, unroll yourselves.' From nowhere mats were brought and rolled out, and laid down neatly on the freshly swept path by invisible hands. Now the young man strode over the mats towards the place where Chief Wai was seated, surrounded by his wives. He spoke: 'Good morning, my father, Chief Wai! I am your son Mokele, son of Moluka. You left me in her lap, and here I am!' The chief felt great joy upon seeing this handsome son and decided to make Moluka his most honoured wife.

Mokele Steals the Sun. In those days there was no sunshine yet, there was only moonshine, and the people of Ntomba called the moon the sun! One morning Mokele spoke: 'Father, does the sun not rise here?' 'We here do not know that thing you are talking about,' answered Wai. 'I will go and buy the sun for you!' exclaimed Mokele, and he started at once to dig out a canoe from a very large tree. When it was ready, the wild animals emerged from the forest to admire it. First came the wasps buzzing round Mokele's head, whispering into his ear: 'We want to go with you to find the sun. If the owners refuse to let you have it, we will sting them!' 'Bokendela,' shouted Mokele to the wasps, which means 'Come on board.' There arrived also the tortoise Nkulu who asked to be allowed to accompany Mokele to the Land of the Sun. 'What can you do? You are so slow!' replied Mokele. 'Slow?' wondered the tortoise, 'I am here first of all the wingless animals. I am the Sorcerer of Battle. I will be your war magician. I can divine where the sun is even when it is hidden from your sight.' 'Good!' exclaimed Mokele, 'Bokendela!' Next, there arrived the kite Nkombe. 'I want to travel with you!' 'What can you do, kite Nkombe?' 'If they refuse to give you the sun, I will pick it up and fly away with it.' 'Good! Come on board! Welcome!' In this way one after another all the animals of the forest were invited into the canoe so that it was quite full. They set off and after a long voyage they arrived in the country of the patriarch Mokulaka where the sun was hidden. Mokele greeted the old grandfather respectfully, then asked: 'Mokulaka, can I buy the sun?' Mokulaka answered: 'All right, but wait for Yakalaki, my son.' Mokele withdrew; the patriarch called his daughter and instructed her: 'Molumbu, go and brew poison for these strangers, I want them killed.' The wasps heard this and told Mokele what they knew, for wasps penetrate every house. Mokele followed Molumbu to her own cabin and started talking to her. She could not help liking him for he was a very handsome lad. Indeed, she fell in love with him and he seduced her, so they became lovers. She tossed the poison pot on the floor and sent word to her father that she had to go to the forest to collect fresh poison herbs. Meanwhile, the tortoise had kept his promise. He divined that the sun was hidden in a cave and proceeded to discover it, accompanied by the kite. The tortoise lifted the sun out of its hiding place and the kite grasped the tortoise in its talons and soared with his burden up into the sky. That was how the sun rose. Mokele and his crew saw this success. They ran to their boat as fast as they could, pursued by chief Yakalaki. Only the wasps did not run, they were raring for a fight. They stung all Yakalaki's men, who were thus forced to give up the chase. Yakalaki himself produced smoke to keep the wasps away, and attacked Mokele. Soon, Yakalaki had to run for his life but he had not given up yet. He went to the *elokos*, the cobolds of the Zaïrean forest, the wicked dwarfs who terrorize unsuspecting travellers in the woods. They managed to steal Mokele's boat, but Mokele arrived safely home with his bride Molumbu. His father Wai was overjoyed and all the people hailed Mokele as the hero who had fixed the point of the rising of the sun 'up-river' which for the Ntomba people means 'east', since all the rivers in their region of central Zaïre flow from east to west. Molumbu gave birth to a son whom they called Iyebelo, 'Whom no one can command'. Mokele possessed *iboke i molo*, 'a baglet with a medicine'. It had a name: *kangili kangili*, which means approximately 'jump, jump'. It was the powder of life. If a little of it was blown into the nose of a dead person, he would sneeze and revive. This mysterious powder became the heirloom of the Wai dynasty, as Iyebelo was to have many wives and numerous children.

Commentary. Wai is perhaps comparable to an ancient hunter-god, like Thor of the Norsemen. His son Mokele is reminiscent of Prometheus who stole the fire from the gods. As a sun-god the animals are his friends, agreeing to help him and serve him. The sun is hidden in a cave, as it is in other mythologies: in Greek myth the god of the underworld, Hades, retains it. Yakalaki resembles him as he has aspects of the god of death and is in alliance with the *elokos*, the evil spirits of the dark forest. He himself is responsible for the darkness on earth. Mokele by contrast is the god of life who rescues the sun and creates the sneezing powder that brings the dead back to life. He is born from the cosmic egg and grows to full manhood in a day, like the sun.

For society there are many lessons in this myth. A man who has many wives (and no one who hasn't is a great chief) will lie with all of them before he sets off on a hunting expedition. He has a right to expect that all his wives will bear him children.

Mongo-Nkundo (Religion, central Zaïre). The name Mongo or Mongo-Nkundo has been assigned as the collective appellation for the peoples living in the 'armpit' of the Congo, the hot steamy basin of the River Zaïre, where it turns round from north-west to south-west in its middle course, in a mightly swing across the Equator and back.

The Mongo believe in God the Creator, whom they call Mbomba Ianda or Njakomba, Wai or Komba. God is the Master of Life and Death, whose irrevocable decree commands us to be resigned and patient before the inevitable. God works and communicates with us through the mediation of spiritual beings, *bilima* and the shades of the dead, *bakali* (sing. *bokali*). After death, the *elimo*, soul, leaves the body and becomes *bokali*. The near relatives lament, the villagers dance and sing to honour the deceased. The *bakali* live in the forest in invisible villages, where they have their families; the living bring them small quantities of food at the graveyard, while at night the shades visit them. After two years the mourning period ends with a great feast. Some of the *bakali* may become elephants, hippopotamuses or crocodiles. The living, if they are sorcerers, may employ an animal, a snake or leopard, to steal for them and make them rich. The missionaries have discouraged the once widespread belief that the souls of the dead returned to life in newborn babies. A dead grandparent would be recognized in the new child who would receive the grandparent's name and be treated as the same person.

Numerous spirits (*bilima*, sing. *elima*) inhabit the region, especially, rapids and eddies in the many rivers, marshy valleys and big trees; women pray to them for children.

Monkeys (Pangwe, Cameroun). There was once a man who lived in the forest with his wife and baby daughter. He had made a large banana garden so they had plenty of food. In the same forest there lived 13 hungry monkeys who arrived one day at the house to beg its owner if they could have some bananas. The man gave them willingly, so the monkeys came back every day. When they saw the lovely girl they stole her quickly, rushing up into the trees with her. The man saw it too late to stop them. He went to consult a diviner who said: 'Those monkeys are all females and childless, so they long for a baby. That is why they took yours. There is only one way to get your daughter back: that is by joining those monkeys in their trees and winning their confidence; it will take at least a year. You can do it only by becoming a monkey yourself. Here is a medicine which will turn you into a monkey man. When you want to come back to us, here is another medicine which will make you human again.'

The man took the first medicine, became a monkey, climbed up into a tree with simian agility and joined the 13 female monkeys, one of whom was nursing his daughter, who was alive and well. He won their confidence by bringing them bananas from his own garden since they no longer dared to go near it now that they had stolen the girl. The man learned the language of the monkeys and heard them say they all wanted to marry him. So he married them, and in due course all 13 gave birth. Now they were all busy nursing and trusted him to feed his own daughter. One hot afternoon when they were all dozing, he ran away with her, arrived home, resumed his normal shape and his daily life. A year later, his own wife gave him a son.

The she-monkeys reappeared and threatened to steal his new son, unless he came back to the trees with them as a monkey. He did, and all the monkeys had babies again. This happened several times and thus a new race was born, the chimpanzees (q.v.).

Monsters and ogres Every nation in Africa has its own monsters; a monster is in principle a living being of unnatural shape or size. Giants are the commonest form of monsters, but dwarfs too, are often described as having unnaturally big parts, e.g. outsized heads. Some monsters are said to be nothing but an enormous mouth on a pair of legs. All it does is run from one victim to another, shouting: 'Hungry! Hungry!' Such a big mouth is so horrifying to see that people are paralysed with fright when seeing it and are easily caught and devoured. The Zulu people tell of a Basket Monster. It looks like a basket on the floor, ready to receive things like pieces of meat during slaughter time. One mother put her baby in a basket that seemed to be there just handy, to prevent the infant from rolling into the fire. To her horror the basket developed legs, got up and ran away with her baby in it. She never saw either again.

Ogres, that is, man-eating monsters, are richly sprinkled throughout African mythology. Most of them eat few men since men in Africa are usually strong and armed, alert and not afraid. Ogres are cowards, so they go for girls, since they are easily frightened and, what is even more important, are sweeter and softer in the flesh. Cunning characters, such as the Tortoise in Zaïre, easily outwit the ogres, by making them fetch water in sieves.

In central Zaïre the *biloko* (singular *eloko*, q.v.) are a very variable class of horrifying beings. Some are giants with snouts like crocodiles suitable for savouring human flesh, especially female flesh. They tend to specialize in what they prefer to eat. Some suck the eyes out, some devour only livers and hearts. Other *biloko* are nasty dwarfs with powerful hands like gorillas. The Islamic peoples are outdone by no one in their descriptions of monsters and ogres, for whom they have many names. (See also *Cannibals; Ghoulas; Ghouls; Jinns; Nundu; Shaitans; Tebo*.)

Months (Alur, Uganda). Many years ago the Alur of Uganda had kings; indeed the very first king of Alur was also King of the Universe. Yet, even he had to die. He sent messages to all his children: the Sun, the Moon, and all the edible species of ants. The Moon and the Muzale ants set out at once to join their old father at his deathbed, the Sun and the Naka ants waited until the next morning before departing. Each species of ants has its own time of day or night for emerging from their nests. The Moon arrived before the King had died. The King was pleased with the Moon and gave her the kingdom of the earth with all his children in it. When the Sun arrived the King had just died, so the Moon had been enthroned as Queen of the Earth. The Sun was so furious that he burnt her face by blazing at her, so that the Moon still looks ashen. Nevertheless the Moon is recognized as our ruler by all the people. That is why we count our lives in terms of moons, that is, months. The women who have marriage in their bellies will count the moons until their babies are born. When the cows are filled with calves we likewise count the moons until the calves' heads appear. The arrival and the duration of the rainy season and all the fruits and crops that come with it are also counted in moons. A girl becomes a woman when the Moon rises red for her, and goes on doing so until she marries.

It is said that one day the King of the Bats invited the Moon for a feast. He offered her a large piece of meat on a beautifully carved large wooden tray. The Moon coveted it, but the bat said no: 'Ask anything else.' The Moon took the tray anyway, for bats are not strong. Since then bats hang upside down with their behinds to the Moon, to show their contempt. The tray can be seen in the sky at Full Moon. (See also *Alur*.)

Moon Diana 'the Radiant One' was the Roman moon-goddess, identified with the Greek Artemis, well known for her temple at Ephesos in Asia Minor. The Egyptians identified her with Bastis or Bastet, the cat-goddess who was worshipped especially at Bu-Bastis, her own town. The association of cats, particularly black cats, with the moon is also found in East Africa, where the cat is the symbol of the pleasure-loving girl. The moon has always been associated with time-reckoning, in ancient Egypt with Seshat, goddess of the night sky and history. There are traces of the veneration of the moon-goddess in many parts of Africa; she may well be older than any other divinity.

In Cameroun, on top of Mount Cameron, explorers were shown the relics of a moon cult which may have flourished there for centuries. An eclipse of the moon was considered as a source of bad luck in many regions, because the moon is offended and no longer wishes to give us her light. During the 'white nights', when the moon is full, young people in Zaïre make music and dance all night. The Chagga (Wachaga) of the Mount Kilimanjaro region worshipped the moon by praying to the new moon every month after it appeared. The Kundu in Cameroun also pray to the new moon for good health. The kings of Burundi derived their ancestry from the moon-deity, believing that the king after his death would return to the moon.

In Central Africa, the spider is associated with the moon-cult. In Cameroun a moon-priest can take the moon down and plant her in his garden as if she were a banana tree serving his family. In East Africa some people relate that once the moon was much closer to earth so that she looked like a lovely white bird. Of course a Ndorobo ('Bushman') could not help shooting a poisoned arrow at her, so that she began to wane and soon died.

The Nuer in the Sudan say that the moon belongs to God; she is Nyadeang 'the Daughter of the Sky-Spirit'. When the Nuer see the New Moon they rub ashes on their foreheads and throw grain at the moon-disk, saying a short prayer, approximately: 'Ah Moon, Daughter of the Sky-Spirit, let us be at peace, we pray that thou mayest appear with goodness. May the people see thee every day. Let us live.' This is a relic of moon-worship.

The Bushmen of Angola pray to the New Moon, begging her for rain, game for the hunters and plenty of wild fruits, none of which will happen if the New Moon does not appear in time. Women and girls dance on one side, men on the other, to sing a hymn to the Moon Goddess: 'New Moon, appear, give us water! New Moon, come and thunder the waters down for us! Rain for us!' The Bushmen of Namibia also pray to the Young Moon in a fine hymn which begins: 'Wonder! Rejoice! The Moon has come back to us!' The worshippers blow an antelope horn to greet the moon, by whose bright light they frequently hunt nocturnal animals in the desert.

Moon King (Kimbundu, Angola). Long ago the King of the Earth had an only son. When the boy came of age his father told him: 'You must marry. I will help you find a wife.' The prince replied: 'I want to marry only the Moon King's daughter.' The King invited all the wise men and women of his kingdom to advise him how to find the path to the Moon, but no one knew it until finally the Frog arrived and spoke: 'Sire, I will travel to the Moon for you.' The King had no choice but to trust the Frog, so he gave it a letter for the Moon King. The Frog knew that the Moon King's water-bearers descended to Earth every morning before sunrise to fetch water from a certain very clear spring in the forest on a hill. The Frog went and hid in the spring and when the bearers arrived he quickly swam into the first pail they lowered for filling. When they arrived on the Moon the Frog jumped out, speaking: 'Take me to your King!' The surprised Moon-men obeyed and when he stood before the Moon King the Frog produced the Earth King's letter. The Moon King read it and wrote an answer which he handed to the Frog, who sat in the empty pail until the bearers took it down to Earth that same night. He quickly swam out of it when it was held in the water of the Clear Spring. He arrived at the Earth King's court saying: 'I am Mainu the Frog, Ambassador to the Moon King's Court. I bring a message from His Lunar Majesty.' The Earth King read the letter in which the Moon King agreed to the wedding of his daughter to the Earth Prince, as soon as the bride-wealth had been paid. The Earth King gave the Frog a bag of gold coins to take up to the Moon. As soon as the Frog arrived on the Moon with all that earth-money, he was regaled on a meal of pork and chicken. He was sent back with the message that the Princess of the Moon would arrive in the night after next. Nobody on Earth really believed the Frog but they did put on their best clothes and sure enough, the Moon Princess descended along a silver cord woven by the Moon-spider, and she married the Prince of the Earth.

Mother Goddess Although it has been said that at one time all the peoples of Sub-Saharan Africa worshipped a mother-goddess, only traces of such a universal religion have been found. The Zulu people have an image of the Mother of all the Zulus, who was a huge woman with enormous breasts with which she suckled her many children, all strong sons and daughters. Her husband was the first king of Zululand (see also *Python*).

The Ewe in Togo relate that before a child is born, its soul has to visit the land of Amedzofe, the People-Become-Place, where, high in the mountains of central Togo, there resides the Spirit-Mother who teaches every unborn child manners and good behaviour before she sends them down to be born on earth.

The Baronga of Mozambique relate that the first people came out of the reedlands or swamps near thc Mkomati, 'Cow River'. Every clump of reeds brought forth a different race, each with its own tools, e.g. the Venda popped out with their hoes. The first Baronga were a couple Gwambe and Dzabana, man and wife.

The Dogon scholar Ogotemmeli related how the Sky-god had intercourse with the Earth-Goddess who gave birth to twins. (See also *Ashanti; Earth; Goddesses; Muso Koroni; Oduduwa; Tanit.*)

Mozambique see *Frog; Hippopotamus; Rivers; Snake worship*.

Muloyi (Nande, Zaïre). Only a man can be accused of being a *muloyi* in Nande society; for women see under *sorcery*. The word *muloyi* is widespread in Central Africa: it is *moloki* to the Bangala (q.v.), *murozi* in Burundi, *ndozi* in Shaba. (See also *Ndoki* and *Warlock*). The *muloyi* can work harm on his fellow men and women by means of 'metaphysical' practices, though the Nande do not consider these practices as contrary to the laws of nature, but as part of their daily lives. The *muloyi* is wicked and works consciously, in contrast to the sorceress (see *Sorcery*), who may be unconsciously 'eating' the spirits of her victims, yet she too is evil.

The *muloyi* hates his victim; the rich are his special target, as well as people with large, happy families. He cannot be 'bought off' with presents, nor can he be appeased with kindness. He is ruthless, tenacious, cruel and never lets his victim go. He will bewitch even his own wife, his child or his mother, nor will he ever mend his ways. He can make himself invisible or he can work his magic at a distance. If one meets him, however, he is courteous, because he loves deceiving people with his tricks.

The *muloyi* works by means of an instrument of sorcery, *erirogho*. He makes this from the ashes of human bodies which he exhumes from graves after performing a secret ritual dance. The resulting 'poison' is mixed with food or, preferably, with beer. Pieces of nails and hairs, or even some earth from his intended victim's footsteps will give him power over the latter. He uses these things to make his *erirogho*, wrapping them in leaves; he will then bury the resulting parcel under someone's threshold, or under a stone near the house where the victim is asleep. The *kirimu*, spirit, of the victim will now be forced to go and live in the *erirogho*, while his body slowly decays. In the dark, the *muloyi* can be heard sniggering, laughing or howling.

Muso Koroni (Bambara, Mali). Muso Koroni, also spelled Mousso Coronie, is the earth goddess of the ancient religion of the Bambara people (q.v.). Her name means: 'the pure woman with the primeval soul'. There is more than one description of her appearance: some say she has the colour of the earth, others that she has the breast of an animal, which may mean she has many breasts, like Artemis of Ephesos. She may also have had the shape of the royal panther or black leopard, for she is the goddess of darkness. Pemba the sun-god is said to pursue her when he rises and she withdraws to the west, the land of the dead. She gave birth to all the living beings, plants and animals, after Pemba had 'penetrated' her, taking the shape of a tree, *balanza*, *Acacia albida*, sinking its roots deep into the earth. Like the Indian goddess of the forest, Kali-Parvati, Muso Koroni had a terrifying aspect: like a leopard she may attack unsuspecting people, causing women to menstruate with her claws. She also circumcized both girls and boys in this way. Since those primeval times the institution has been continued. Muso Koroni also taught people agriculture, for she is the goddess of both the cultivated land and the wilderness. Of the three types of corn cultivated by the Bambara, only millet is dedicated to her, the other two, rice and maize, being foreign imports. At harvest time, an old woman may, in certain districts, impersonate Muso Koroni by performing a dance near the grainstores, accompanied by calabash rattles.

Every human being has a certain wildness, a spirit of the wilderness, which is called *wanzo* and is associated with Muso Koroni. It is removed by circumcision, which tames or humanizes a youngster. In the same way, hoeing before planting makes the earth ready for cultivation.

Mvet (Fang, Gabon). The Mvet (Song) of Zwe Nguema is an epic poem, sung from memory by Zwe Nguema during an entire night, for 10 hours, until sunrise. It was recorded, transcribed, translated and analysed phonetically by an international team of scholars, and published in 1972 in Paris; its value was realized at once. Mvet is also the name of a stringed instrument, 5 foot long, which traditionally accompanies the recital, along with bells and sticks. Here is a condensed summary of the 12 cantos of the epic. In the Land of the Immortals, Engong, two souls, before their birth, choose their destiny. Akoma Mba chooses pride, while Medza M'Otougue chooses wealth. Soon, Akoma Mba is informed that King Zong Midzi of the country of Oku, is challenging him to war. Akoma Mba orders the beating of the drum called People's Blood. The men assemble in armour but the women are wondering what all the excitement is for, in their peaceful land of Engong. It was Angone Endong who by magic means had offended Zong Midzi who has sworn to kill him. One morning, Nkoudang, daughter of Angone Endong, tells her father that she had a dream in which Zong Midzi appeared to her (by magic) and now she wants to marry no one else. Angone Endong gives his daughter eight days to marry his arch-enemy Zong Midzi. If she fails he will have to die. At last her mother is prepared to accompany her to her uncle's home near the frontier with Oku. There she meets a very handsome young man, Nsoure Afane, whom Nkoudang agrees to marry for one night. In that night Nsoure Afane has a nightmare in which he sees the redoubtable Zong Midzi approaching, in search of Nkoudang, whom he wishes to marry, and her father, whom he wishes to eradicate. The dream is true, but only when dawn rises are Nkoudang and her mother persuaded to join him in fleeing to Engong. Zong Midzi has told his beautiful wife Esone Abeng to go first; he will follow close behind her. Thus, at the crossroads, the beautiful Esone Abeng and the handsome Nsoure Afane meet and admire each other's good looks. Soon, Zong Midzi arrives and finds his wife face to face with young Nsoure. He demands an explanation and Nsoure Afane points at Nkoudang, saying: 'She is my wife, whom I was accompanying with her mother to her father, Angone Endong.' These words do not allay Zong Midzi's temper; on the contrary, he is so incensed to see the daughter of his enemy married to another man that he slaps her in the face. This in turn arouses the anger of Nsoure Afane, since only a husband has a right to slap his wife's face. Nsoure Afane challenges Zong Midzi to a duel, but the latter creates a dense fog by his magic, and cuts off the head of Nkoudang. Furious, Nsoure Afane swings his sword, but instead of hitting his enemy he cuts off the head of beautiful Esone Abeng. He picks up both heads and creates a magic ball, on which he sits down, whereupon it rises up in the air and flies with him to Engong, where King Akoma Mba has seen all the events in his magic mirror. Nsoure Afane is accused of responsibility for the death of Nkoudang, but her mother defends him, and he escapes on his magic ball. Back home, he raises an army and attacks Zong Midzi, who is still in the vicinity. The battle is joined by the warriors from Engong; all the fighters use magic tricks. Zong Midzi escapes to his native Oku, but is surrounded again by the allies. In despair he disappears into the earth where his ancestors live. They keep him hidden for three days, after which they send him back to the surface with new magic weapons, including a gun that never misses. However, the warriors of Engong have iron wings and magnetic shields to which the enemies stick, paralysed. Zong Midzi is blinded by a magic plume. Then Akoma Mba explodes his belly after taking all his charms.

Mwindo (Nyanga, Zaïre). Mwindo is the hero of a long epic song which is recited by the bards of the Nyanga people in eastern Zaïre; it was recorded and translated by Daniel Biebuyck; four versions have come to light. Here are some episodes from version 2, abridged:

1. King Shemwindo of Tubondo decrees he wants no son to be born.
2. His wife Iyangura bears him a son, Mwindo, and a daughter; Mwindo is born with his sceptre and medicine-bag, from the palm of his mother's hand. The King orders Mwindo to be buried alive, but at night Mwindo rises from the grave and sits by the fire.
3. They grow up; Mwindo's sister Nyamitondo marries Lightning, who takes her to Heaven where he teaches her to grow bananas. A Dragonbird devours all the people and their animals. Mwindo climbs up to Heaven through a hollow tree to ask Lightning for help. Mwindo and his sister, who has received iron tools from Lightning, descend to earth. Nyamitondo is at once devoured by the Dragonbird, but cuts her way out with a knife and so liberates all the people the Dragonbird has swallowed.
4. Mwindo buys two dogs for his Pygmy friend Shekaruru, to hunt.
5. Shekaruru meets Hawk who is being attacked by the Red Ants; he liberates Hawk, who promises to help him in the future.
6. Skekaruru is pursued by a herd of warthogs, but Hawk appears, picks him up and carries him safely to his village.
7. A neighbouring king, jealous of Mwindo's fame, attacks Mwindo's unarmed citizens and destroys them. At home he celebrates.
8. Mwindo returns to his town full of corpses. He prays to the beings

of the subterranean world, the earth, the sky and the air. Then he throws his sceptre down on the ground and all his dead citizens rise up, alive. Mwindo goes to the town of the jealous chief, throws his sceptre down and destroys it.

9. Mwindo visits the subterranean world by descending through a fern. He meets the beautiful Kahindo, daughter of the god of fire, Nyamurairi. Kahindo warns him of her father's tricks. Mwindo climbs up to Nyamurairi's house, where he is told he must go and harvest honey in a tall tree. Bat gives him nails for climbing and Spider gives him threads strong enough to hold him. Nyamurairi hits Mwindo with his belt so that he dies but his sceptre revives him. He spends the night with Kahindo. The next day he is told to grow bananas for the town. He creates a hundred axes to cut trees, the banana trees plant themselves, and bear ripe fruits at once, enough for the town. The next two days there are further trials and battles but Mwindo survives them all. He is even burnt to ashes but when the ashes fall into a pool, Mwindo rises up whole and healthy.
10. Mwindo comes home and his father gives him nine wives as part of the welcome-home celebrations for the hero and his men.
11. A young man goes hunting with Mwindo's dogs. He meets Ukano daughter of the cannibal Kirimu. She gives him food; he plays the *zanza* for her. Kirimu tells him to play the *zanza* all night, which he does without falling asleep so that Kirimu cannot catch him. In the morning the dogs are released and kill Kirimu, Ukano marries the young man.
12. Mwindo's war against the Mburu apes. They fall out of the trees when he points his sceptre at them. He points it at the sky and so causes hail to fall which destroys the apes' town.
13. This canto describes seven adventures of the Pygmy Shekaruru hunting with Mwindo's dogs. He meets Nyamwanda, wife of the god Muisa in her iron house. She gives him the whistle that brings people back to life. From there he arrives in the town where the king's son has died. Shekaruru revives him and is given a girl as a present. Next, he arrives at the ghost town of Mpacha. He falls asleep there and the ghost puts nails in him but he frees himself by means of magic glue which repairs people.
14. Finally Shekaruru returns to Mwindo's town. Mwindo is enthroned as king.

Myth See Introduction.

N

Nkisi fetish of the Kongo in Zaïre

Namibia See *Bushmen; Kahunga; Khoi; Moon; Ovambo; Ram.*

Ndoki *(Kongo, Lingala; Angola, Congo, Zaïre). The word ndoki* is widespread in Zaïre and surrounding countries, even though other words are also in use (Mongo *boloki*). *Ndoki* is the sorcerer, a man or woman who can harm others with invisible means, or by changing themselves into insects. There are two types of people: the good and the *ndoki*, the wicked destroyers of life, health and happiness. A *ndoki* is not like the normal friendly African who loves his peace of mind. *Ndokis* are nervous people, constantly shifting place because they want to avoid being bewitched themselves; their faces also twitch all the time. People with shifty eyes, a stare, or a squint are particularly suspect. A squint, *ntala zole* 'double glance' proves that a person cannot have normal relations with his neighbours. At night such a one will come and dance in front of their houses. That is the first spell. Or the *ndoki* will stare at his or her victim with *disu difwa* 'an eye that kills', until the victim can no longer move or think freely. *Ndokis* also have double tongues, one normal visible tongue and an invisible one which puts a spell on the listener. With sweet words will the *ndoki* invite his or her intended victim to come and have a meal. The *ndoki* has dirty hands which serve the delicious-looking food to the unsuspecting guest. Under the *ndoki's* nails there are hidden tiny grains of magic substance. Soon, the victim will get indigestion, a headache and fever and will go home and die. The *ndoki* 'eats' his victims, not the flesh but their blood. At night a *ndoki* will penetrate the victim's bedroom in the shape of an ant or mosquito and suck his victim's blood like a vampire. Then, the *ndoki* will take the body and make magic poison with it, leaving a dead goat in its place. A male *ndoki* will have a special love for young girls, not to rape but to devour. When the *ndoki* has died, the eyes continue to stare and cannot be closed. *Ndoki* spirits wander about and are seen as falling stars.

Necromancy Divination by studying corpses. See *Diviners*.

Ngai see *God; Kikuyu; Maasai*.

Nganga (Southern and Central Africa). The word *nganga* (Swahili *mganga*) is used in most Bantu languages to translate 'doctor'. Europeans refer to the *nganga* as 'medicine man, witch-doctor, magician, herbalist or shaman'. In Zimbabwe, a young man becomes a *nganga* if his father, grandfather or uncle is one and will train him in the art of recognizing diseases and their causes, their cures and the spirits whose influence, good and bad, is everywhere in human society. Aspiring women doctors are usually trained by their mothers or aunts. The *nganga* has to go the forest himself to collect the herbs, roots, bark, flowers and leaves he needs for his practice, often accompanied by his son, whom he will teach the names of all the plants. This knowledge of African botany is not secret: scientists have access to it. What is esoteric is the application of the herbs to expel the evil spirits which cause disease; this knowledge is inherited in every family of medicine men and women as the trade by which they live. The *physical* application of the herbs is open to study by pharmacologists who have published some of it. Some *nganga* families have a tradition of healing going back many generations. The living members receive messages from their ancestors, who speak to them in dreams about the illnesses they are called to cure in the villages. The spirit of a grandfather may tell his grandson where to find the herbs that will cure the illness, and which spirit has caused it. This knowledge is all the more important since many cases involve not just one patient but a whole family or even a village or a clan. The authority of the ancestors, to whom some of the people in the village concerned may be related as well as the *nganga*, is necessary in order to make the therapy acceptable. The spirits also tell the *nganga* how to prepare the herbs, usually by pounding, drying, boiling or rubbing. More important still, they reveal to him who the human agent, alive or dead, of the disease or misfortune has been, and why.

If the spirits point (e.g. through the oracle bones) at a living person as the cause of the illness, then such a person is a witch, i.e. someone who 'eats' the flesh of his or her victim in a magical manner-without actually touching the victim, but by putting a spell on him or her so that the victim will waste away. Western doctors would diagnose tuberculosis, which is quite common in Zimbabwe, but to the Zimbabweans the cause is evidently spiritual.

Ngbandi (Gods and spirits, Central Africa, Zaïre). Toro is the supreme god, or tribal spirit, of the Ngbandi, who live in northern Zaïre and partly in the Central African Republic. When twins are born amongst them, they believe they are snakes, because their god is a snake-god, a divine serpent. Toro was born to Kangalogba, the dragonfly, a female spirit and symbolic for the waters of the great River Oubangui (Ubangi). The snake is the first-born of all the animals, and as such he has seniority even over the royal leopard. It is believed that the spirit of a king will, after his death, become a leopard. The eldest son in every family has the duty to perfom the sacrifices to the ancestral spirits, so he is a priest for life. He can sell his rights to the royal title but never his priesthood.

The Li is an evil spirit who comes to live in the stomach of a man or woman and makes them restless and mischievous. Li-men can steal children and devour them in the forest. They also love eating dead bodies so they often open the graves of the recently dead and have a feast with drums and dancing, but they cannot be seen. If a Li-man knocks on a man's door one night, that man will call his wife and children and say goodbye to them for he knows he will soon die. Suspected Li-men are tried and executed. Autopsy will disclose some tumour in the small intestine: that is the Li!

Mbomba or Sangu is the name of a huge water-monster, the river-god of the Wele and king of all the fishes and frogs. All the fishermen will pray to Sangu and throw offerings of food in the water before starting their work. If Sangu seizes a man, if he calls the name of his grandfather his spirit will save him. Nzapa is the Creator, the Father of all human, animal and other beings. He set the law and rules all our lives and destinies. Seven gods are invoked every morning in a special prayer: Nzapa, Yayu the Sky, Sese the Earth, Banga, the white or clear waters, from which the white men were to spring, and Mbongo, the black waters from which the black people originated, Ketua the god of fortune and Lomo the goddess of peace. Ketua, the deity who rules good and bad luck, had seven children: Morning, Noon and Evening, Night, Moon, Sun and Water. During the season when the ants swarm, Ketua went and visited all his children with their wives and families, but none of them offered him a dish of fried ants, which is a delicacy in their country. Finally, Ketua arrived at the house of his son Water, the youngest, who immediately spread out his finest mat for his father to sit on, and told his wives to stew a portion of fat ants for his father. The latter was gratified by this and decided to give Water the rights of the first-born son. That is why today the Water-spirit is the most powerful deity. One of Ketua's other children, Nze, the Moon, is also widely worshipped by the Ngbandi, when the Moon is renewed at the beginning of his cycle, preferably in the company of Venus, his wife. When a girl has her first period, people say that she has 'seen' the Moon, who has 'cut' her. When they say: 'The moon stays dark for her', she is pregnant; she 'has a drum'.

Nzapa the Father-god, had four children, all palm-trees: Raffia-palm, Liana-palm, Wine-palm and Oil-palm. When Nzapa felt old and weak, none of his sons sent any food to him, except Oil-palm, so Nzapa spoke: 'Henceforth, Raffia-palm will be woven into a bed for man, Liana-palm will be twisted and plaited into a basket by the women, Wine-palm will be cut and carved by the tapsters, but Oil-palm's nuts will be gratefully admired by man.'

The Ngbandi people believe in the soul which can be seen in a peaceful pool when you look down. Old people do not want to be photographed, for that means having your soul taken and the photographer can make you ill. At night the soul travels, an experience which we call dreaming.

Niger see *Dausi; Songhai; Swords; Twareg.*

Nigeria see *Bachama; Bori; Earth; Edo; Ehi; Goddesses; Hausa; Hunting; Ibo; Kindness; King killing; Nupe; Oba; Predestination; Pre-existence; Tiv; Yoruba* (which also gives list of gods).

Night witches (Botswana). Night witches, *baloi ba bosigo*, are not really witches, because they act with malice aforethought; their motives are envy, greed and vengeance. They are mainly women, we are told, who in daytime do their normal work, but at night, when their husbands are fast asleep, their spirits leave their bodies as soon as they hear the call from the coven. They can hear this call only after they have been initiated with special medicine being injected into their bodies. They can only be initiated when they have sacrificed a close relative, preferably a first-born child. When seen at night, they look as white as ashes, or red like their victims' blood. These *baloi* converge in the graveyard where the new graves will magically open for them. The corpses will come floating to the surface. At once the witches start carving out the parts they need for their evil work. They have special medicines (powder or liquid), which they blow into their victims' faces so that a deep sleep debilitates the victim. They cut open the body and insert pieces of flesh from the corpses, or bones, or teeth, into the living bodies, which will invariably become sick and emaciated. The *baloi* can go in and out through closed doors.

The owl is the ally of the *baloi* for it warns them when someone is approaching. It is said that witches can construct a flying machine which looks like an animal but is made from porridge, vitalized by means of special medicines. Most witches, however, ride on hyenas, the corpse-eating scavengers capable of running and jumping at great speed. These night witches must return to their sleeping bodies before dawn, or else they will surely die. Very similar tales are told in Zimbabwe, Zambia and Zaïre. (See also *Sorcery; Witches.*)

Nile, River The Nile is the longest river of the world and the most famous river of Africa. The Ancient Egyptians related that the Nile rose in an ocean called Nun (pron. *noon*) in the far south. They may have heard of Lake Victoria. Several gods were associated with the Nile, most prominent among them was Khnoum or Khenemu, the god of the Cataracts, whom the Nubians called Doudoun or Dodonu, represented as a buck with wavy horns. He had two wives, Sati and Anuket. Hapi or Hapy was an androgynous Nile-god, protector of the boatmen, represented with fat belly and hanging breasts. For the Nile goddess Thoueret or Taweret, see under *Hippopotamus*.

The people of Burundi relate that once upon a time there was a terrible drought in the country. The people implored their king, Intare I, to make rain or provide water in any way. The King went with his court to the highest mountain, Mfunda, in the forest district of Kibira in north-western Burundi (q.v.). There was a yellow stone on the summit, which the King struck with his copper hammer. The stone, which is called Iyogera, at once opened and out poured a river, which is still there, the River Ruvubu, which flows into Lake Victoria, so that it is geographically the beginning of the Nile, and Iyogera its source. The yellow stone still bears the King's footprint, and he was buried near the stone, by his grateful people.

The Nubians, who live between the First and the Fourth cataracts, relate that there are spirits living in the Nile (see *Dogir*).

The Nilotic peoples all live along the Nile: the Luo, Padhola, Acholi (q.v.), Alur (q.v.), Nuer (q.v.), Dinka, Shilluk (q.v.), and Anuak. They are among the tallest Africans, keen boatmen and fishermen, who have numerous traditions about the mysterious creatures who populate the Nile, its lakes and its swamps, the Frog Drink-All who can empty a lake, and Jokinam, the Lake-God who owns lake-cows which graze on the bottom of Lake Albert, herded by fishermen who drowned.

Nilotic see *Alur; Jok; Nuer; Shilluk.*

Njuzu (Karanga, Zimbabwe). The Shona Dictionary of Fr. M. Hannan gives for *njuzu*: 'water-sprite'. That simple translation hides many mysteries. All marshy places where water rises, wells, pools and lakes, are sacred in Zimbabwe because they are inhabited by the *njuzu*, the guardians of the pure water. Girls must fetch water in a well-cleaned jar, or else the *njuzu* will get them. Aspiring shamans (see *nganga*) have to spend some time with the *njuzu*, who will teach them the magic of healing better than anyone. If a boy dreams that he is swimming in a pool it is a sign that he has reached adolescence.

If man has a dream that he must perform a sacrifice for the *njuzu*, he should do so at once. If he does not, then when he comes near the water's edge he will suddenly see a beautiful naked woman rising out of the water. She will seduce him. He will willingly go with her and will later be found drowned. The *njuzu* rule the creatures of the water, the crocodiles, the snakes and the fishes. A *njuzu* may appear as a fish with a human head. They are born in the mountain caves where the rivers rise. The *njuzu* do not like noise, so that, when the Europeans arrived with their noisy machines, the *njuzu* left many pools and swamps which subsequently dried up for ever. These spirits, when travelling, wrap themselves in dark clouds and, rising up in the air, cause terrible winds which destroy everything in their path (see *Tornado*), causing rain. In the old days, in a time of severe drought, a child had to be sacrificed to these water-gods who would take it and make it their own child, so the child would become a *njuzu* himself. Other people maintain that the *njuzu* are themselves the spirits of the dead who now live in the mountain caves where they were buried in the old days. Some say that the snakes are the female *njuzu*, while the crocodiles are the males. Both snakes and crocodiles are death symbols. Ghosts often appear as snakes (q.v.).

Nkisi The word *nkisi*, also pronounced *mkisi, kisi* or *kishi*, plural *mikisi, minkisi* or *nkisi*, depending on the dialect, is widespread in northern Angola, western Zaïre and the Congo. The usual translation for *nkisi* is 'fetish' (q.v.), 'talisman' (q.v.), or 'idol' (q.v.). It can also mean: witchcraft, magic force, or 'disease caused by magic'. Properly defined, a *nkisi* is an object in which a spirit lives, or which has spiritual power in it, and which is controlled by a person, usually a sorcerer. The spirit may be someone who has died and now lives in a statue, or it may be an independent spirit. A *nkisi* is not a natural object like a tree, plant or a well. For the tree-dwelling spirits of the Bakongo, see *Tebo*. A *nkisi* may be a spirit locked up in a calabash, a shell or an antelope horn. Spirits roam free in the forest, where they may be caught by the spirit-experts, the *nganga-ndoki*, the 'spirit-doctors', who possess the magic power and the right formulas to capture the spirits which fly around at night like bats. Some are dangerous, like vampires. Sometimes the *nganga*, called to a sick-bed, may put a handful of the ingredients of a *nkisi* in a pouch, for the patient to wear on his neck, arm or hips. This then becomes an amulet, *mbambi* in Kongo. These ingredients, *mfula*, are: clay from the river containing spirit substance, herbs, leaves, roots, bark, nails, claws, bills, hair or tails of animals or birds, menstrual blood, feathers, excrement, gall bladders preferably of leopards, poisonous juices and seeds of plants. From all these the *nganga* may make a *nkisi* which cures or prevents illness, one which helps a woman to become pregnant or to give birth without trouble, one which makes the crops grow, the fish bite or the animals walk into the traps. A very powerful (and very expensive) *nkisi* may make an enemy ill or kill an evil spirit. There are more than 150 different types of specialized *nkisi*, each for a purpose, which is determined by a specialist, the *nganga ngombo* or diviner, a very powerful person in the community, since he not only indicates the diagnosis but also the causative agent of the disease or disaster.

Nkundo see *Mongo-Nkundo*.

Nosenga (Korekore, Shona). Nosenga is known as a *mhondoro*, a god or tribal spirit, who selects a medium whose name is Hore, through whose mouth he will speak to the people. Hore lives in the town of Chief Chakoma and whoever wishes to consult the oracle of the god Nosenga has to request permission from Chief Chakoma. The chief will call the *nechombo* (acolyte or priest), and the latter will speak to Hore, the *svikiro* (medium), to tell him who has arrived for consultation. The medium goes to sleep and, usually early in the morning, wakes up the priest with strange noises that betray the presence of the god. The visitors may ask their questions which the god will answer through the medium. The questions usually concern drought, the proliferation of aggressive lions in the area, an epidemic or the necessity of electing a new chief.

Nosenga has a number of wives, human women who are dedicated to the god and have to lead a life of complete chastity. In 1922 a man raped one of these women and as a result, so the people said, no rain fell after that. The god was consulted and demanded the burning alive of the culprit. The man was duly killed but of course the British authorities considered this as murder. However, the matter was explained and the chief who was responsible for the 'execution' of the rapist, and who was already under sentence of death, was subsequently released. The following season (1924-5) more rain fell than ever before in recorded history.

Nuer (Gods and spirits, Sudan). The Nuer, who may have been influenced by the Christianity of the Nubians to their north, and who have certainly been very strongly affected by Islam, believe in the Great God, whom they call Kwoth, 'Spirit'. He is regarded as the Judge, the Creator and the Father of humankind, and the one who gives us all we need, and takes from us, by His right, what He wishes, yet He is compassionate. God lives in the sky, from where He sends rain, wind and thunder. The spirits of the air are called His children and these include some birds. Twins are regarded as birds and so are also God's children. God is praised as Tutgar, literally 'Strong and Limitless'. Long ago there was a rope hanging down from Heaven and all old people who felt weak climbed up along it to meet God in Heaven. God would rejuvenate them after which they would return to earth. Alas! One day the hyena, who is known as a troublemaker, cut the rope, so God, indignant, pulled it up. Death reigned on earth from that day onward since people could not rejuvenate.

The other spirits of the sky are Deng and his daughter the Moon goddess. Deng is regarded as a foreign god and therefore the bringer of disease, which is caused by possession by a spirit. Col (Chol) is a spirit who brings rain and thunderclouds (the word *col* originally meant black). It loves the *colwic* (cholwich), i.e. the souls of people who were killed by lightning.

Rang, the Wielder of the Spear, is the god of hunting, also associated with the rays of the sun, which are flaming spears. West of the Nile, Rang is also called Garang, also a giraffe name. Wiu is the war-god; the word *wiu* means 'spear'. The word for war in many African languages is derived from the word for spear. Buk is a female spirit ruling the rivers and streams. She is sung as 'Leopard of the Night' and 'Daughter of Fire-flies'. She protects from crocodiles those devotees who sacrifice a goat to her.

Nundu (Swahili, East Africa). Swahili *Nundu Mla Watu* means 'People-eating Nundu'. Among the Bantu peoples of eastern, southern and south-western Africa, the Nundu (also called by other names) is a sometimes invisible man-eating monster. It is sometimes represented as a gigantic lion or leopard, but its description and size make it similar to the European dragon, or the Anglo-Saxon Grendel, an equally mysterious monster that devoured people and can only be slain by a true hero. Like Grendel, the Nundu has been compared to an epidemic, a disease that strikes unseen and 'eats' the country.

The saga is fairly similar in most parts of Bantu Africa: village after village is laid waste by the Nundu, a monster that no one can describe because few escape from its onslaught. It devours not only people, but cattle as well as goats and even the trees and the crops, so that one might think it symbolizes a drought. Nundu strikes periodically, and all the people know about it is that it is as big as a hill, it has a mouth like a cave, and it walks so noisily that its approach can be heard many miles away; yet people pay no attention to what they hear, thinking it will not hit them.

The hero of the saga is the orphan boy, or the child who grew up in the wilderness, or the lonely hunter, or the young man who is the son of a god and a mortal mother, who was expelled by the community. He acquires some good weapons from his divine father, a spear, sword or axe. With this he slays the dragon, or he tilts a boulder from a high rock so the dragon's head is crushed. In another version, the hero is himself swallowed up, but he comforts the many people who are alive inside, by telling them to start a dance. The endless dancing and drumming in his stomach makes the monster sick so that it has to lie down. With his good weapon the hero pierces the stomach and the outer skin of the Nundu, so that finally 'they see light'. They all come out, people, cattle, goats, hundreds of them. The hero and liberator becomes the owner of all the animals by right, and is made king. He marries many wives.

Nupe (Religion, Nigeria). Soko is the Nupe name for God, which word may originally have meant 'dark sky', for it seems to have referred to the beginning of the rainy season, when God gives his long awaited rains without which the crops cannot grow. However, many etymologies of gods' names are speculative. Though the Nupe may refer to God as Tsochi 'Our Lord', they regard him as a remote and aloof lord, who has only a marginal interest in human affairs. He is invoked and appealed to in everyday life, but Nupe notions about God's omnipresence are vague. God is certainly regarded as omnipotent, i.e. He is the ultimate cause of all things, the Creator of the earth.

Next, there is Sheitan, the Devil, clearly a word of Arabic origin (see *Shaitani*), who is regarded as the origin of evil and bad luck, such as a quarrel between good friends or people lying to each other. Another name for Sheitan is Abilii (cf. Swahili *Ibilisi*, both from Arabic *Iblis*). Sheitan has the power to seduce, but God may forgive people, which implies that there is an expectation of retribution.

Kuti is a mysterious magic force in the world, generated by ritual and sacrifice, a spiritual emanation from God. *Chigbe* is translated as 'medicine' but, as in other African languages, that word implies a magic power, a spirit-force. *Rayi* 'life' is what God sends or withholds to a newly born child. A person's *rayi* increases with growth and diminishes with old age and disease. In sleep, *rayi* and body are separated. *Fifingi* means 'shadow' of living, moving beings, and then also 'shadow-soul'. It survives a person's dying body and may appear to his survivors in dreams, sometimes causing nightmares. It may haunt houses and scare travellers if its body was not properly buried. A symbolic burial ceremony will lay such a ghost. *Kuchi* is the spirit of an ancestor which is waiting to reincarnate.

Nyame God. See *Akan; Nzambi*.

Nymphs (Congo). A mother had 10 children. The eldest was very pretty and had many suitors, so that the mother was jealous of her. One day she sent the girl to fetch clean, clear water from the river. The obedient daughter went to the river and waded into it, since all the water near the bank was muddy. Suddenly the Water Girls grabbed her feet and dragged her down into the cold mainstream. These river nymphs cannot be seen for they are made of water; only at nightfall and early before dawn can they be seen rising from the water as faint mists.

When her daughter did not come back, the mother told her eldest son Mengi to go and fetch water. He went and found his sister's jar floating empty on the water. Upstream he heard bells and his sister's voice singing: 'Come, Mengi my brother!' Suddenly Mengi saw his sister's hand rising up from the water, holding a pearl necklace, and her voice said: 'Give this to Mother!' Mengi took the necklace home and was, of course, accused of having stolen it. He had to go back, accompanied by the elders of the village, who wanted to hear the girl's voice and see the hand with the pearl necklace. They did: a second necklace was left in Mengi's hand. The men quickly built a dam in the river to divert its water. When the bottom became dry, they saw a coffin; when they opened it they found the girl, still very pretty but looking blood-red, a frightening sight. They heard voices singing: 'If you are strong enough, take her back, if not, we the Bisimbi will keep her.' Strong men lifted the unconscious girl out of her coffin and onto the bank, but a violent storm arose suddenly which broke the dam so that one man was drowned. However, the girl was safely on dry land. A voice was heard: 'Take her but never feed her pork.' Pork is the meat which the dead eat. The girl opened her eyes.

The men helped her up and took her home. There she lived on and soon she was as beautiful as she was before, yet she had changed, as if she was dreaming much of the time. Her mother was still jealous of her beauty and one day she gave a feast for which she secretly slaughtered a pig. As soon as the lovely girl, without knowing it, ate a piece of the pork, water began swirling round her feet, it soon rose to her knees, her thighs, her breast, her neck, as if there was a stream in the house. Finally she was carried away, out of the house and down the path to the river, where she disappeared, this time for ever. The house remained damp ever after, for water is a powerful element. Mengi was so attracted by the voices from upstream which he could still hear, joined by his sister's voice, that he one day jumped into the river and never came back. For 'mother' we may have to read 'stepmother' in this tale.

These Bisimbi (singular *Kisimbi*) are the *Bisimbi bi Masa*, the Water Nymphs, as there are also other types. As in Ancient Greece, the Nymphs were the spirits of the dead, hence the reference to the food of the dead, which incidentally explains why the Semitic peoples may not eat pork. The Bisimbi prefer to live in wells and ponds which form the sources of the rivers. They are so dangerous that only the *nganga* (q.v.) will go there in search of roots and pebbles for his practice; for the purpose he brings protective medicine. Only after special rituals can he pick some of the waterplants which are considered excellent medicines against skin diseases, which, they say, are caused by the Bisimbi. When someone is ill in the village, an elder will come and pray to the Bisimbi every night until the patient is better.

Nzambi (Other forms: Zambi, Nyambi, Nzambe, Yambe, in different dialects and adjacent languages, even Njambi, Jambe). This word for God is widespread in West Central Africa, between northern

Namibia and Gabon to Central Zaïre, Angola and Zambia. It was noted by the first Portuguese scholars in the sixteenth century as the word for God in Kikongo, the language of the Bakongo. The Bakongo express their devotion to their Creator in didactic riddles such as: 'Nzambi has made a field with two light patches in it. What is it? The sky with sun and moon.' 'Nzambi has made a knot in a string that will never be undone. What is it? The navel.' 'Nzambi has made a path and keeps it clean. What is it? The throat.'

Nzambi has given intelligence to both people and spirits. He is often referred to as Nzambi Mpungu, the Supreme God. Perhaps the name comes from a verb *yamba, zamba* 'to cause, to shape, form'. Numerous proverbs refer to God. 'Nzambi has made us with fingers and nails; he has made us with hunger and thirst.' 'Death cannot be bought off: when Nzambi wills it, it will take you.' Or, 'Nzambi takes what belongs to him already: our lives, when no healer can help us.' A man who, while working in the forest, was missed by a falling tree, exclaimed: 'Nzambi has spoken to me, or I would be a dead man!' The mother says to her daughter: 'Nzambi has made you in my womb, one day he will make a little child in yours, we hope.' (See also *Akan*.)

O

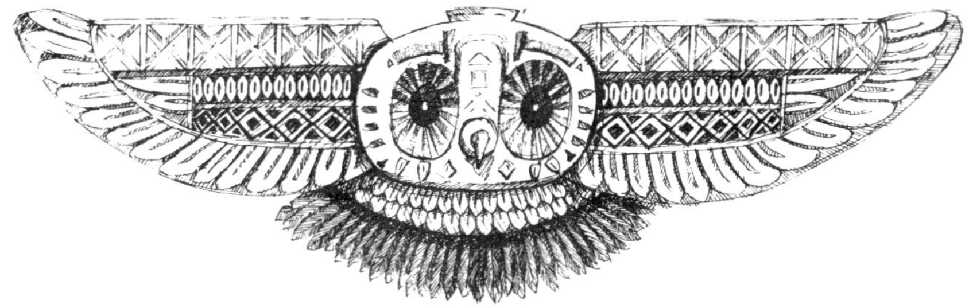

Owl mask from Burkina Faso

Oba (Benin (Bendel), Nigeria). The *oba* is the traditional king of the Edo people in southern Nigeria, whose capital is Benin City (to be distinguished from Benin further west, formerly Dahomey). The *oba* was once a divine king who lived in a vast palace which was destroyed in 1897. He had shrines for the gods in his palace, where he worshipped Olokun, Uwen and Ora in private. His worship of his own ancestors was public and national, not in the sense that the public could watch the rituals but in the sense that the rituals were benefiting the people. The living king ruled by virtue of the tradition that he is the eldest son of the eldest son (and so on) from Oranmiyan, the first known King of Benin. That king who lived more than 700 years ago, entered the waters where he found the god Olokun (q.v.) and stole from him (as Hermes stole the graces from Pluto) the costume of royal coral beads. This costume or, rather, this waistcoat made of coral beads is still worn by the *oba* on ceremonial occasions. When the King is wearing that costume he does not shake or blink but stays still and unmoving. When he sits down in it on the royal throne, he is not a human being but a god. He alone had the right to take human life. In the court of law he was the final arbiter of the death penalty while in the course of the ritual he alone made the human sacrifices to the gods. Thus the King was feared and revered by the nation. As king of the dry land the *oba* was the equal of the god Olokun, who ruled the waters of the rivers and the ocean. The *oba*'s palace was considered the centre of the world and so it was there that all the major rituals of the nation were performed. Some of these rituals lasted for several days, during which whole oxen would be slaughtered. All the dignitaries had to wear special costumes which were tailored for the purpose.

Obatala (Yoruba, Nigeria). Obatala was the first god to be created by the supreme God Olodumare (q.v.); his name was at first Orisha-nla, a sort of collective name for 'divinity'. Obatala is worshipped in many towns of Yorubaland under different names: Orisha-Popo, Orisha-Ogiyan or Orisha-Ijaye. Yet, the form of worship is fairly homogeneous. A well-known hymn to Obatala has the lines: 'Obatala will make his worshippers strong and healthy; he will support his children and make them prosperous and numerous, and give them cause for laughing.' He makes barren women pregnant and shapes the babies in their wombs like a work of art. He is called a sculptor god. Obatala loves cleanliness; he is always pictured wearing clean white robes, living in a whitewashed palace, pure and clean, with his consort Yemowo. In his sanctuaries, too, there is always a jar of clean water, which is freshly collected every morning by a virgin or an old woman, carrying a bell as she walks through the streets, speaking to no one while on her sacred errand. The water is given to worshippers and will make barren women fertile. Kola nuts, coconuts and maize are offered.

Oduduwa (Yoruba, Nigeria). The myths depicting Oduduwa as a female *orisha* (divinity) are original in character and are widely accepted. She is the wife of the great god Obatala (q.v.) and together they created the earth, or perhaps it is better to state that Oduduwa *is* the earth as primeval matter, and that Obatala moulded her, or, better still, created her offspring together with her. The name Oduduwa means: 'the Self-existent ruler who created all beings'. Yet, the existence of Oduduwa has not always been peaceful and motherly, since there are also traditions of Oduduwa leading tribes and armies into war. The great war took place between the people of Ugbo, who were defeated by the people of Ife, a battle which is still celebrated, and Oduduwa is still worshipped in Yorubaland, in particular in Ife-Ife, where the chief priest will point out the very spot where she alighted when descending from heaven.

One of the sons of Oduduwa is Ogun (q.v.) who is therefore of earthly origin. Ogun became a great warrior who fought many victories, so Oduduwa gave him the kingdom of the town of Ire in the land of Ekiti. Many people believe that Oduduwa was the mother of the entire Yoruba nation, signifying no doubt that the Yoruba people came out of the earth where they live today and did not invade the country from abroad. Others maintain that Oduduwa was not a female deity but a god, but in mythology such seeming contradiction is not a problem. In many mythologies of the world the earth deity is androgynous, and is capable of giving birth by itself to all creatures without fertilization.

Ogres see *Monsters*.

Ogun (Yoruba, Nigeria). One Yoruba tradition holds that Ogun was the son of Oduduwa (q.v.) who helped his father fighting their enemies and for his valour was rewarded with the Kingdom of Ire, or Ilesha and Ondo, as other scholars maintain. The present King of Ire descends from Ogun, who was last seen there sinking into the ground with his sword, telling the citizens they could call him in time of need. His sanctuary stands today on that very spot, where he is still worshipped. The King of Ire sends offerings for Ogun regularly. Another, perhaps older tradition relates that when the gods decided to settle on earth they found thick impenetrable forest barring their way. Ogun, the god of iron, made an axe and also a hatchet and with these tools he cut a path through the bush, so he is still honoured with the epithet Oshinmale 'Pioneer of the Gods'. Those who neglect to worship Ogun are told: 'You cannot eat yam without a knife,' referring to Ogun as the god of iron and forging. He is, for that reason, the god of metal, wealth, prosperity and the protector of work in the beginning of the day. He is called: 'the Owner of the House of Treasures'. Ogun is the god of all the skilled men who use metal tools, the blacksmiths, the goldsmiths, the butchers, the hunters and the soldiers too, since he is the god of warfare. Even in our modern times Ogun is worshipped, especially by the drivers of lorries and taxis, by mechanics, barbers and haircutters. Soldiers on their way to the battlefield will perform sacrifices to Ogun to invoke his protection against injuries. Lorry-drivers believe that if they do not pray for offerings to Ogun before they set out on a long haul across the country, Ogun might cause an accident on the road. Is he not the God of the Path? Yoruba scholars have compared Ogun to the Roman god Mars and this seems to be an apt comparison. Mars was not only the god of war, but, more important, the god of pioneers who open up new land.

Oko (Yoruba, Nigeria). Oko (the name means 'hoe') is the Yoruba god of agriculture who is worshipped by every farmer as well as by his many children's children. Oko, as the people of Ibadan used to relate, was first seen near Irao, where he lived as a venerable farmer. He was not born on earth: he had come from Heaven. This explains why he was sometimes visible but at other times invisible, even for his own descendants. He could often be seen slowly walking through the fields as a very old man with a stick, often squatting down to rest. Later he went to live with his relatives in the city of Irao, but even there many farmers came to him with baskets full of yams and other produce of the land to honour him and thank him for giving them good crops. One day the old man Oko had disappeared; only his staff was still there in the house, so the people went on honouring the staff. Once a year a feast is held for Oko during which the faithful have a big meal; only after this day may the new crop of fresh yams be eaten. His followers may not touch the snake; the guinea fowl is considered the worthiest offering for the earth-god. Oko is often represented by a staff hung with cowrie shells.

A few days before the beginning of the rainy season, Oko's followers celebrate a feast in the forest; it is called Odu-Osha-Aruru. By nightfall a large number of women and girls, who have cooked the best food, proceed to the selected clearing, led by the priestess called Yemo. The men are led thither by the priest called Olo. After the meal, when there is no moon, some women will select a man by whom they would like to have a baby. Without this unofficial behaviour no rain could fall, or so they say. This fertility rite commemorates the conception of the god Shango in his mother the forest goddess Yemaya or Yemoya, sister of Orungan or Oranya.

Olodumare (Yoruba, Nigeria). Olodumare is the supreme god of the Yoruba pantheon. His name means the Great Everlasting Majesty. He is also called Olorun, 'the Owner of Heaven', Eledaa 'the Creator', Alaaye 'the Living One', Elemii 'the Owner of Life', Olojo Oni 'the Owner of the Day', i.e. the One who controls our daily lives. When Olodumare had decided to create the solid earth out of the primeval marshes, he created a snailshell full of earth, a hen and a pigeon, and gave these to Orishanla (q.v.) (who may originally have been identical with him) who threw the earth down, whereupon the pigeon and the hen began diligently to scatter it; this became land. Olodumare then sent the chameleon (q.v.) to inspect the earth. The chameleon reported that the earth was wide enough but not yet solid enough, so more sand was added. Chameleons tread carefully. Olodumare then created the first oil-palm to be planted by Orishanla on earth, for food. There followed the coconut tree from which palm-wine is tapped, and the Kola nut tree as well. Then Olodumare created 16 human beings whose leader was called Oreluere. Orishanla moulded the forms out of the earth, after which Olodumare put life in them which he alone can do. Orishanla then led the people to earth; they came down at a place which they called Ile-Ife, which is the oldest Yoruba town. The Yoruba say: *Ishe Olorun tobi* 'God's work is great.' Olodumare is immortal since he is himself the owner of life, so he is described in a hymn as 'the Great Immovable Rock which never dies'. He directs all things, so there is a proverb saying: 'Whatever Olodumare approves of is easy, but if he does not like someone's plan it is impossible to carry it out. He is the Compeller, the One whose compulsion never fails. Our illnesses can be cured but when Olodumare has determined our death it cannot be averted. Olodumare hears everything, he is always listening to our complaints.'

Olokun (Benin, Nigeria). Olokun was the eldest son of Osanobua the Creator. Olokun is the Lord of the great Waters, the most popular and the most worshipped god of old Benin, now called Bendel. Olokun is associated with the Olokun or Ethiope River in south-east Benin. This river is considered the source of all the water on earth including the ocean, on the other side of which there is the land where the dead souls go. The souls of as yet unborn children come from there. Thus Olokun is the provider of children. Before arriving in their birth-house, the children are blessed by Olokun, for good luck. He also gives good luck to ships and sailors on the ocean, so he is the god of wealth and commerce. He loves beauty in all forms: he likes fine statues, graceful movements in dancing, rich fabrics, sweet songs and elaborate decorations on his temples on earth. It is said that women owe their beauty to him, for he loves beautiful women and gives them children. More women pray to him than men. When a girl is born, her parents will install a shrine for Olokun in their house; when the girl marries, she will take the shrine with her to her husband's house, where it is venerated even more. It contains an earthenware pot with river water that has to be renewed regularly. If she fails to conceive she will become even more involved in his worship. Some women are possessed by Olokun, so they become members of local cult groups which are led by priestesses. The interior of a temple dedicated to Olokun is beautifully decorated and filled with numerous statues. It is intended to represent the gods' palace under the sea, a paradise of beauty and purity. There, too, is the treasure-house of all the riches on earth, which the god will give to the people when and where he may decide they deserve them. He is a good god, so he is called 'cool', like his father Osanobua.

Omens An omen is a sign shown by the deity to a person who wishes to undertake something and is unsure what the outcome will be. In Egypt there are diviners who can be consulted, for a fee, to predict whether a certain day is auspicious for some important enterprise, such as a wedding. The diviner has diagrams full of numbers and letters, on which he will put his finger without looking, meanwhile reciting verses from the Koran, hoping that his finger will be directed by God.

Swahili scholars in East Africa have similar methods for determining whether a certain girl is a suitable bride for the young man who says he wants to marry her, and vice versa. The girl's parents will consult a scholar (*mwalimu*) regarding the prospective bridegroom. Their names have to match.

Hunters are particularly concerned about seeing the right omen when setting out on a hunting expedition, and so are fishermen. Birds often signify good or bad catches, storm, calm or good wind.

Prayers are needed to bring the fish to the surface; demons may keep the fish away from the nets.

Among the Tumbuka of northern Malawi, if a fox (*Vulpes chama*, also, but incorrectly, called silver jackal) is seen or heard it has to be questioned by the elders of the village: 'If there is to be an enemy attack, keep silent!' If the fox barks, the next question will be: 'If there is witchcraft in the village, keep silent!' If the fox barks, that is believed to mean 'no', and the next question is asked; if it stays silent, that means 'yes', and the people will take measures as necessary. If the warning is repeated, say, by the Great Hornbill Mngombwa, the village may be deserted for fear of attack or witchcraft.

If a traveller sees a puff adder or a chameleon on his path, he will return home and consult a diviner to avert the evil.

Oracles The English word oracle originates from Latin *oraculum* 'announcement', from *orare* 'to speak, announce, pray'. The best known oracle of Antiquity was the one at Delphi in Greece, where Apollo, the god of sunlight, clarity and knowledge, announced the future through the mouth of a medium, the Pythia. African gods, too, give their oracles in this way, by means of possession (q.v.) of a medium (q.v.), often a woman, who will speak with a strange voice words which she does not even understand but which have to be interpreted by a priest who is appointed for the purpose (see *Buganda; Bunyoro*). Hundreds of people come daily, but especially on festive days, with a goat or other sacrifice to consult the oracle regarding illness in the family or in the animals, barrenness, drought and other problems. The medium usually resides in the god's temple; she has a special seat when she gives oracles to the worshippers.

Usually the god himself chooses his medium who becomes as it were his spouse, possessed by the deity whenever it so wishes. In East Africa, the gods are usually known; in West Africa even unknown gods may select a medium and possess him or her, whereupon this person will establish the worship of the new deity by building a temple and instituting rituals. Most gods give their oracles through a medium who may also function as the priest (see *Akonadi; Ashanti; Ifa*). Oracles in written form (as used to be given by the Greek priests) are extremely rare in Africa. The *hakata* or oracle tablets of the Shona in Zimbabwe are not consulted by the geometric signs carved on them but by the type or identity of the tablet as it lies in relation to the others.

As we have seen, an oracle is given essentially in a language. When the deity does not speak but gives signs which can be read only by trained diviners, we should speak of divination. Yet the term oracle is widely used in Africa for the answers to many forms of divination (see *Diviners*).

Orishanla (The Birth of Sun and Moon, Yoruba, Nigeria). The King of the Forest had a lovely iroko-tree. One day it fell down because he forgot to sacrifice to the gods, but it did not crush his house. Instead, the god Obatala (q.v.) appeared and with his magic power he turned the tree into the secret precious metal (gold?). Then he called the blacksmith of heaven and told him to make a jar and a boat from that precious metal. Then he called his slave, whose name was You-don't-hear-what-I-say, and told him to travel in the boat with the golden jar in it, up to the top of the sky and then down again on the other side.

Thus the sun began its first journey. Olodumare the god (q.v.) created also the moon like a flintstone, with one thin side and a round side. He sent it up in the sky where it slowly spins round, showing us its full round side only during three nights of the month. Half a month, 15 days, was the time needed by God to create people and trees. In that time the New Moon becomes full.

In the beginning there was only Orisha the Divine Spirit. He lived in a house at the foot of a sheer rock wall. He had a slave called Eshu who cooked for him and served him all his days. Eshu hated his master for having to serve him, yet he was himself a god, the god of fate. One day Eshu climbed up the rock and moved a big boulder that was perched on the edge of the precipice. He pushed it so that it fell down on Orisha's house. Orisha was crushed and, with the splinters of his house, was scattered and flew in all directions. Thus fragments of the divine spirit can be found in many places, in all living beings, even in the winds and rivers. That is why there are now 401 *Orishas* or gods, the sacred number called collectively *Orishanla* 'the great Orisha', i.e. all the deities together.

Oromo (Religion, Ethiopia). The people known to the Ethiopians and Europeans as Galla call themselves Oromo, plural Oromota, and their language Afan Oromo, or Afan Orma, 'language of men'. Galla means 'wanderers'. The Oromo belong to the speakers of the family of Cushitic languages and they worship Waka or Waqa, the common god of the Cushites. Next to him there is Borenticha, who may be the arch-ancestor. They also know Saytan, the evil spirit (see *Shaitani*), and a long list of other spirits, *ayana*. Waka is the Creator of the earth and the people to whom he used to speak; in western Ethiopia Waka is identified with the God of the Christians. The Arusi in the south pray to Waka in the morning, saying: 'O Waka, you have given me a good night, please give me a good day.' They have more fear, however, for Saytan or Shaytan, the Evil One, who is always hungry and thirsty, so that frequent offerings of meat are made to him. Other evil spirits are Ibissa Shayto, the spirit of fire, to whom a black goat is sacrificed: and Karandala, to whom an ox is offered. Evil spirits may appear as dangerous snakes called *jini* (see *Jinns*); some say there are 44 of them, others say there must be 88, all busy inflicting misfortune on people. They may be appeased by smoking, dancing, singing or the sacrifice of a red hen. Spirits of the mountains and springs are called *kollo* or *qollo*, and also receive sacrifices. The *ayana* or *awulia* are said to be guardian spirits who live in a kind of terrestrial paradise. Some of these move from the animal bodies in which they live, into the bodies of newly born babies, which explains why so many people have the obvious characteristics of certain animals. The *kollo* have the form of cocks with four horns on their heads. When a man sets eyes on them, he will soon die. Another type of spirits are the Dache, who live in trees and may cause rachitis to children. Before a feast, ritual offerings are placed at the roots of certain trees with invocations: 'O Dache, O Kollo, take away all sickness and bad luck!'

Orunmila (Yoruba, Nigeria). Orunmila was one of the original celestial gods of the Yoruba pantheon, one of the Yoruba Olympians, who accompanied Obatala (q.v.) on his first descent to the swamps of Earth. He has the epithet Gbaye-gborun, 'He who lives both on Earth and in Heaven', because he travels around as the Counsellor of Olodumare (q.v.) to plead with him for the alleviation of human suffering. He also counsels human beings, by means of many oracles in which he presages the future and so, eases life. The oracle and the method for obtaining it is called Ifa (q.v.).

Orunmila was present in Heaven when Olodumare fixed the destiny of every man, woman and child on earth, so that he knows all our histories before they have happened in real life. For this reason he is called 'He who bears Witness to Fate'. By means of the Ifa oracles, Orunmila can speak to the people and inform them concerning the decrees of God, i.e. Olodumare. He decides which ceremonies are necessary and which animals must be sacrificed. His advice is always studiously followed. Orunmila is also consulted on behalf of sick people, for which reason he is also the god of healers; when he still lived on earth he was surrounded by students anxious to learn his art, and from these he selected 16 to become his disciples.

Orunmila has his shrine in almost every Yoruba household where he is worshipped, and where his emblems are kept: the 16 sacred palm-nuts called *ikin*, pieces of ivory, cowrie shells, the divining tray *opon ifa*; all these objects are hidden behind a screen which is opened when the divining begins, sometimes daily. There are also sacred groves devoted to Orunmila, called *igbodu*, where he is worshipped and where initiation rites take place. The priest of Orunmila is called Babalawo, 'Father of Mysteries', who is highly respected. Orunmila's functions are comparable to those of Hermes, who also travelled between the human and divine worlds and was the god of diviners and healers.

Osun (Yoruba, Nigeria). Osun is the Yoruba goddess of the river of the same name. In the towns along the river Osun she enjoys special worship. Her father was Oba Jumu and her mother was called Oba Do. Once a year a feast is celebrated in her honour, called Ibo-

Osun. Yams are cooked and eaten in abundance after which a dance party is given. During the dance Osun will select one or more of the women dancers to serve as her medium, 'she will come and live in them'. These women will receive new names, such as Osun Leye, 'Osun's gift', Osun Tola 'Osun's Treasure'. Henceforth all the people will come to consult one of those women concerning illness or other problems in the family. Most of these worshippers who come to consult Osun are women; many come from far away for help and advice to the goddess, not only during her festival but throughout the year. The Tola or chief priestess will officiate during the year by sacrificing the pigeons, chickens and sheep which people bring.

The goddess Osun was the spouse of the god Shango, though no one knows for how long. She had human children whose descendants still live along the riverbanks and in the towns. They have special dietary laws; they must not eat snails and beans, nor drink *otioka* (sorghum-beer).

The goddess Osun is widely loved for her willingness to help people to alleviate the burdens of their lives and cure their illnesses. She gives to the poor what they need, we are told.

In Osun's temples weapons are kept: bows and arrows and daggers which are placed on the riverbank during festivities in town. The central object is an earthenware plate or dish in which white pebbles from the riverbottom are kept. Her symbol is the women's stool, and her metal is brass; her followers wear brass bracelets.

Ovambo (Angola-Namibia). Ovambo is the collective name for fourteen tribes, of whom seven live in Angola, and seven have migrated to Namibia during the last two centuries. The largest group are the Kwanyama, who live mainly in Angola but who have recently 'spilled over' into Namibia, where they almost have a majority. Each of the fourteen Ovambo groups has its own language and myths. The myth of origin of the Ova-Ndonga in Namibia is as follows.

God created the earth, the planets and the animals, the trees and the termites. The termites got busy at once and built a huge termite hill. When it was finished, God made a hole in it and called: 'Come out!' Out came the first man and his wife; his name was Amangundu. They lived on earth until the wife had a son, whom they called Kanzi. After a time she had another son, whose name was Nangombe. Kanzi married and had a son called Mshindi, who travelled north and settled in a country with numerous animals, so he called it Kwa-nyama 'Game-land'. He became the ancestor of the Ova-Kwanyama in Angola. The descendants of the second son of Amangundu stayed in the plains where they acquired cattle which are called *ngombe* in many Bantu languages. Nangombe's descendants became known as the clan of Ekwa-Nangombe, but today they call themselves Ovandonga and their language Oshindonga.

In the old days, when the (semi-nomadic) Ovandonga had to move to a new village, they would first await the harvest festival. Then the oldest member of the tribe would draw the outline of the new village in the earth, after which the *ofindilo*, the sacred doorposts would be hammered into the ground. During this work, the clan chief would recite a prayer: 'Our Lord of our forefather Nangombe! Come with us, come and chase away all evil! Come, let us enter our village through this gate in safety! Help us to bring in good harvests through this gate in peace! Bring food inside, keep hunger far away, we beseech thee!'

Ovimbundu (Spirits, Central Angola). The Ovimbundu believe in a Supreme Being, Suku, who created the mountains, the rivers, the sky and the people on earth. Every person has an *ocililemba* (spirit or soul) which in daytime becomes visible as one's shadow, but which during sleep has adventures of its own, which the sleeper experiences as dreams. It leaves a dying body and becomes a ghost, *ocilulu*, wandering freely. Sometimes it flies through the village like a whirlwind, screaming. Finally, it will choose a home, usually the home of its descendants where sickness will signify its presence. The inhabitants will then call the diviner, *ocimbanda*, who will, of course, identify the spirit, which will cause the patient to go into a trance in order to 'receive' the spirit. This latter has now become an *ondele*, an ancestral spirit: it will stay in the home. The paternal ancestors are satisfied by a beer feast and a hunt; the maternal ancestors, however, are malignant and may 'eat' children. A long-established spirit becomes peaceful and is called *ehamba*.

The oldest spirit is Osande, the founder of the family who is always kind and generous, warning his or her descendants of dangers. Kandundu is the most senior of the ancestral spirits who is worshipped at a shrine in Bailundu. No one is allowed to see the contents of that shrine for fear of becoming blind. Kandundu gives dreams which have great significance. Another shrine is dedicated to Huvi, the god of the hunters; there all the hunters' meat is kept. Dances are held in front of it, amidst poles topped with skulls. A priest and priestess are in charge of supplications for success in the hunt, and of receiving offerings.

Owls In many African countries the melancholy call of the owl is associated with bad luck. Already in the Bible, the screech owl or barn owl is associated with death and desolation (Isaiah 34:14); its name, Lilith, means the Goddess of Night. The Carthaginians and Ancient Egyptians also associated the owl with a goddess, Neith, identified with Athena. In Botswana, people believe that the owl is associated with the night witches (q.v.) and warns them when humans approach.

In East Africa the hooting of an owl in the night is particularly disastrous for a baby. If later the child has an illness or defect, people say in Swahili: *ameliliwa* 'He or she has been hooted over.' Preventive magic is used to protect the child. In northern Malawi, when the owl is heard, the headman will ask it if there is witchcraft in the area, or if the enemies will attack soon. The owl will answer. (See also under *Omens*.)

In Ghana it is believed by some, that witches have owls as familiars or can change themselves into screeching owls and fly out to pick off the limbs of their victims, not physically, but in essence, e.g. a man's penis, which will then surely become weak and useless. The proverb says: The daughter of the screech-owl will have no nice voice.

The Yoruba of Nigeria relate that there is a type of people, whom they call *aje* 'witches, sorcerers', who can leave their bodies at night and fly away as birds of prey, that is, owls, *owiwi*. In daytime they sit dozing harmlessly in the shade, but at night they fly into their victims' houses through a hole in the roof, and suck the blood of the unlucky doomed persons. The latter will wake up the next morning feeling weak and depressed, unable to get up and even to speak. Quickly the kinsmen have to send lavish gifts of cloth to the *aje*, at the advice of a diviner, as a sacrifice to redeem their relative.

P

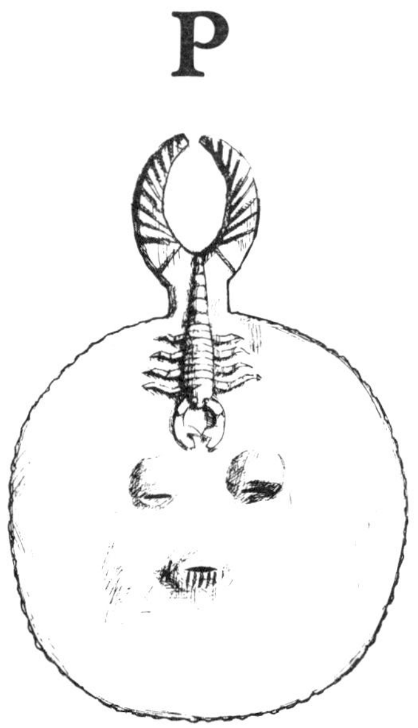

Poison scorpion mask from the Ivory Coast

Peace (Gai, Ivory Coast). *The Wise Spirit Fe.* It was many years ago in the district of Tobbe-pleu in what is now the Ivory Coast, that the Mask-spirit called Fe was first heard of. It was called a 'masked devil', but that was only because the Muslims thought it was Satan being worshipped. Fe was the god of the clan of the Gai who appeared in the shape of a mask. When the clans of Chuilo and Nyaio were fighting a long-standing feud, Fe was called to arbitrate and reconcile the contending parties. Fe came, a very large mask, attended by two men from Mano, Satumba and Suape. The Nyaio, however, refused to accept the arbitration of Fe and continued the war, but they were soon defeated.

Thus Fe became the god of the Chuilo people and the Nyaio became their vassals. Whenever an enemy approached Chuilo, the mask of Fe would begin to dance and look in the direction where the enemy came from, long before human eyes could see any people on the path. Before the enemies could attack, their eyes would be blinded by Fe's terrifying face and they could no longer see the village. Or their minds would suddenly go mad and they would wander off in all directions, forgetting their intention. Whenever it did come to a battle, the enemies would throw their javelins first, but they would all miss. Then the people of Fe would throw theirs and all the enemies would flee in panic. The god Fe would never allow his people to make war, that is, to go out on a raid. The great mask used to say: 'Peace is better for you than war, just as rain is better than drought.'

Pokot (Religion, Uganda). The Pokot believe in a supreme God in Heaven whom they call Tororut and to whom they sacrifice animals. The son of God, Ilat, has to fetch water for his father in heaven; whenever he spills some we earthlings call it rain. Tororut's blessing must be asked at least once a year for the crops and for the cattle. During this ceremony, the priest performs the sacrifice *amoros*, of a specially selected ox, after which the participants, all men, partake in the ceremonial meal. In times of drought and epidemic, a similar ritual is performed in the hope of propitiating God and restoring the good relations. Tororut has a younger brother, Asis the Sun-god, and a wife, Seta, the Pleiades. Apart from Ilat, they have two more children: Arawa the Moon, and Topoh the Evening Star. The appearance of the Pleiades in the sky marks the beginning of the planting season.

After the birth of a child, both mother and child are washed ceremonially, the ritual being repeated after five days, when the spirits who threatened the mother and her baby, will have gone. Personal illness is blamed on the *oi*, the Spirits of Disease, who can be expelled by emptying the sick man's house: all his pots, boxes and baskets must be carried out so that the evil spirits have nowhere to lurk, after which the priest or the clanhead circumambulates the house, making much noise to frighten the spirits away.

After a man's death, his spirit may be seen in the shape of a snake. In the bush, snakes may be killed, but in the house a snake, if it enters, must be given milk and meat, for it is the spirit of an ancestor who can intercede with God on behalf of the living, in order to avert disease and famine. Death is believed to 'infect' a place, therefore, when an aged person has died, the body is buried under a heap of stones in the house or in the yard, after which the place is abandoned. Before the colonial period the Pokot never built permanent settlements.

Poro (Kpele, Liberia). Poro is a generic term for the secret societies which have acquired great power in some West African countries. Poro in particular is the men's secret society; the women's secret society is called Sane or Sande. There are, of course, special words and names for each autonomous society. These societies hold regular meetings in the forest, where they must not be disturbed. A specific rhythm of drumming indicates the place and time of the meeting and all those not invited will stay well away for fear of being harmed by the strong magic for which the Poro societies are notorious. The Grand Master of the local Poro society is invariably a powerful dignitary in ordinary life in his district. His function during the official procession is to carry the Great Mask, Ngamu, which personifies the deity whom the Poro members worship and serve. It may not be mentioned in public, so it is referred to in whispers as Loo Seng 'Forest Thing', since its bearer is wrapped up in reeds, leaves and branches, concealing his true identity. Many Poro societies never display the Great Mask to ordinary citizens, only to members. Only a small inner circle of peers know the identity of each other and of the Grand Master. Some Poro societies possess magic regalia, including skulls which ensure power and frighten the people. Dancers and stilt-walkers may accompany the procession. The mask itself is called *sale*, which is translated as 'medicine', but originally must have meant 'spirit'. An aspiring member will have to be initiated first, after which he may climb the many ranks and grades of the Poro hierarchy. Some of the high offices may be hereditary. The top panel of the Poro may sit in judgement over certain offences against morality and punish the culprit, after hearing the Great Mask, which will speak in a high falsetto voice so that no one can recognize the speaker.

Possession Possession is a way of dying temporarily, for the owner of a body who is prepared to be possessed must vacate his body; his soul has to go into oblivion so he can remember nothing later. There cannot be two souls or spirits in one body, so that receiving a spirit from outside is, in a way, dying. In addition, the guest spirit usually remains in command and can return at any time to make his presence felt and speak through the mouth of the borrowed body, so that the original person remains, forever after, a servant of that dominant spirit. One of the Swahili words for being possessed is *kubeba* 'to carry', as a woman carries a baby. The spirit is also said to 'mount' the host, as if he were a male animal mounting a female; in Swahili the possessed, even if he is a man, is referred to as a woman, and the spirit as a man 'having' her. In Swahili, possessed persons are called *watege* which literally means 'trapped persons', like animals in a snare. In Haiti, the *loa*, spirit, mounts (*monte*) his host but here the image is that of riding a horse; or they say, the *loa* is *installé* in its host, as if the latter were no more than a house for the god to live in. This happens after a brief period of *débatment* 'squirming', during which the angelic soul of the host tries to resist the intrusion of the stronger *loa*. This attitude agrees with the Swahili view that the good soul must and can fight the threatening spirit, with God's help. Where the spirits are themselves *the* gods, the host is the truly religious soul, carrying the bodiless but heavy god, caring for him.

For the scientists, the psychiatrist and the psychoanalyst, the custom of spirit possession poses a vexing problem. Although it is almost universal in all the countries of Africa and the Caribbean, it is by no means confined to peoples of African type or extraction. The easiest type of possession for modern science is the Swahili type. Here the possessed person is called *muwele* 'a patient', indicating that the Swahili scholars, like Western doctors, consider their condition abnormal. 'Patients', a majority of whom are women, often display symptoms of hysteria or other affectations caused by the need to receive attention in the family. The 'spirits' descend upon them suddenly, and make them behave oddly: leaping, dancing, whirling, talking nonsense. The ceremonies for the exorcism of the 'spirit', paid for by the husband, place the woman in the centre of attention when the *m-ganga* 'doctor' speaks to the 'spirit', which answers through the mouth of the 'patient'. It is even rumoured that the 'patient' is invited by the 'doctor' into a special cabin for his private use, to be 'interviewed' without witnesses, to expel the 'spirit'. All these phenomena can be fitted in a pattern of neurotic, mainly female behaviour, which makes possession by malicious, one might even say naughty, 'spirits', explicable in medical terms. In other Islamic countries, too, women are known to be frequented by *shaitans* (q.v.), but these are dealt with by beating, as in Europe before 1800.

Much more problematic for science is the special type of possession which is called mediumship (q.v.).

Tanzanian Coast. When a woman is ill and lies in bed, groaning and complaining of pains, her husband will go to the local *mwalimu* 'teacher' or 'scholar', who often functions as *mganga*, doctor. He will consult his sandboard (see *Geomancy*) or his book of *Falaki* – astrology (q.v.). Finally he will give the diagnosis: 'Your wife's illness is caused by two spirits, one is a Kinyamkera, the other is a Kilima. Go to the exorcist who specializes in the Kinyamkera spirits; he will prescribe a medicine for drinking, incense for burning, herbs for rubbing into the skin, and an aperient. We hope she will sleep well. After two days you must go to the exorcist of the Kilima spirit. He too will give your wife some medicines so that she may recover, if God wills.' The treatment may last for two weeks and will be far from cheap. A *ngoma* 'dance' will be organized which will last a week for each spirit. A goat will be slaughtered for the last and biggest dance which will take all of the last night of the exorcism ceremony. At the end of this dance, towards dawn, the patient will have to drink raw goat's blood, she will be draped in cloths of three colours, red, white and black, and she will dance in the centre of the circle of women dancers. Suddenly she will have an attack of the shudders. Trembling all over her body she will shout and scream; this is the sign that the spirit wants to speak. The exorcists will ask the spirit: 'What is your name?' The spirit will shout out its name, what it wants, etc., through the woman's mouth. Finally, the exorcist will command the spirit: 'Go away, leave this woman in peace.' The spirit will rise to the woman's head and go out through her mouth and disappear. Some people say they have seen a spirit that looks like a little devil. The spirit also has to be given food before he can be persuaded to leave the woman. The husband has to pay the two doctors or exorcists, plus the teacher who is only a diagnostician; he has to pay the dancers, the drummers and the pipers. He also pays for the food, the goat and the cloth.

Predestination (Edo, Bendel, Nigeria). In a certain town two brothers lived with their mother. The elder was so poor that his cloth would not meet round his waist. He had neither servants nor slaves, so he had to carry his own water and firewood. The younger was so rich that he did not know all his slaves; he had 40 wives, so that when he wanted to dine, each wife had to bring only one dish. Whenever he spoke he was obeyed; his brother was ignored, whatever he said. So, the elder went one day to the diviner to ask for a medicine that would kill the younger. The diviner gave him a calabash, telling him to smear some of its contents, an ointment, on the belly of a pregnant women, then look carefully at it. The elder left and was stopped in the street by a man who asked him to help his pregnant wife. He entered her hut, took out his calabash, smeared the ointment on her belly and saw to his astonishment a boy fully armed with a matchet, snares, an axe and arrows, signifying that the boy was destined to become a hunter. A moment later the child was born as a normal naked baby. The people, believing that the elder was a doctor, called him to another pregnant woman, where he also applied his ointment. To his surprise he saw a girl wearing beautiful clothes. He told the people what he saw and a moment later the girl was born normally. Now, the elder brother perceived that wealth and poverty are predestined in the world before birth. He went back to the diviner apologizing for his wicked intentions. The diviner told him to make friends with his younger brother rather than to envy him. The elder brother took a hoe, went to his brother's land, hoed the soil and began to plant yams for him. He had never done this. When the younger saw him, he embraced him gratefully, took him home, gave him food and drink, invited musicians and made a feast for their friendship. He gave his elder brother whatever he needed from then on.

Pre-existence (Yoruba, Nigeria). Sanku, Temere and Afuwape were three unborn children. Before Afuwape was born, his father consulted the oracle, paying a goat to the priest, in order to learn what his future child must do. The priest said: 'It is good. Your child will be a son and when he grows up he will be rich. But you must make a sacrifice of a thousand cowries on his behalf.' The father did as the priest had told him and went home to his wife, whose baby was due any moment. In the meantime, far away in the land of the unborn, Sanku and Temere had given up waiting for Afuwape and proceeded to the house of Ajalamo, 'the God Who Moulds New Children'. In that house they saw rows of shelves with innumerable *oris*. An *ori* is the spirit of life of a person, his character as it is expressed on his face, his personality which shapes his life and his deeds. Literally, *ori* means 'head', so the unborn children saw the faces from which they could choose one for themselves, to wear for life.

The two children chose two nice faces for themselves and left heaven for earth. They were duly born, grew up and lived in poverty all their lives. Afuwape arrived later in the House of Faces. He saw a poor old woman sitting on the floor and asked if he could help her. She said that she had worked hard hoeing for the proprietor, who owed her a thousand cowries but would not pay her. Afuwape suddenly found a thousand cowries on his person; they were, of course, the cowries which his father had donated to the priest. Afuwape gave them all to the woman. She thanked him and shuffled away. Suddenly the god Ajalamo appeared from above and spoke: 'Afuwape, thank you for what you did. Now choose this head here, it is the one that will make you happy and prosperous.' Afuwape thanked the god, took the face which the god had indicated, and suddenly he was born. He grew up in a good family, learned many things and became a very rich chief.

Priests There is, in many African communities, a very highly developed priesthood, which in many cases is hereditary. It is the duty of the priest to serve as an intermediary between the divinity and the devotees, to which end he has to perform the regular rituals, ceremonies and sacrifices. Whereas the diviner, the shaman and the prophet, each in his own way, are also intermediaries between the divine world and the people of their faith, it is the priest who is responsible for carrying out the ritual necessary to ensure the continued goodwill of God or the gods towards the worshippers.

In the smaller ethnic groups the priest may combine his functions with those of the diviner, the shaman or even the healer-herbalist, and in many areas, as also in medieval Europe, the priest is often consulted as a scholar and medical expert. That is not, however, his main function. In other small communities the priest is, as with the Ngbandi of Zaïre, always the oldest son of the oldest branch of the chiefly dynasty, more senior than the King and therefore more acceptable to the ancestral spirits whom he serves. As in most religions, the priest must undergo a long period of training in order to become familiar with all the details of all the ceremonies, their timing, their sequence, their purpose and their quantity. Whereas the diviner, the shaman, the healer and the magician may work in private, even alone, the function of the priest is almost invariably to officiate in public. This is why he is also concerned with morality and good behaviour. Usually the young man or woman receives a call, a vocation to the priesthood in a dream or as a voice in the wilderness. This call must be obeyed to avoid dire consequences for the individual and the community. A priest is always highly honoured and respected by the believers, because his main function is the sacralization of the community, their reconciliation with the divinity.

Prophets There is some confusion, in writings on African myth and religion, on the nature of prophecy. Some people are referred to as prophets who are, for example, merely diviners (q.v.) or inspired preachers. Prophets can prophesy the future, like diviners; they know things which are hidden for normal people, like fortune-tellers and soothsayers; they receive messages from the other world, like shamans (q.v.); they may even cure patients by laying-on of hands, like faith healers. Yet, the prophets are more than any of these: they create religion and sometimes they even create a nation. There is always a very special relationship between the deity and the prophet who conveys the divine message to his people in the name of that divinity. Consequently, the latter is usually not an impersonal spirit but a personal god, creator, law-giver and good father of his people. The Islamic tradition recognizes only 24 prophets before Muhammad, beginning with Adam. Every prophet is inspired by God to preach God's will to his people, to teach them God's law, to warn them of the dire consequences of disobeying God, and to uphold the moral principles when the people have fallen into sin and indifference.

Prophets have a special relationship to their nation as a whole, not just to one clan. Sometimes kings function as prophets, like Solomon (q.v.) and sometimes a prophet becomes a ruler, like Muhammad. Muhammad received God's revelation through an angel, but most prophets receive it directly by hearing God's voice, while they are conscious and in full possession of their mental powers, in contrast to a medium (q.v.), who hears and repeats voices from the spirit world without knowing it. The shaman (q.v.) travels himself to the other world to hear God's word. A prophet receives a vision while on earth, in which God shows him heaven and hell. Unlike the shaman, the prophet does not have to go into a trance to see and hear his divine master. Finally, a prophet often defies accepted views of his people, so he may risk his life by speaking up. The others, shaman or diviner, operate within the social system which supports them. (See also *Mahdi*.)

Purification Ritual purity is of the greatest importance to all the peoples of Africa, many of whom perform elaborate ceremonies to achieve it or to restore it. The Muslims have to wash with water, if it is available, before beginning their prayers; without these ablutions, *tawadhu*, no prayers are valid. In addition, repentance, *tauba*, is necessary, for God accepts no prayers from a man who hides his sins from God.

Among the eastern Bantu elaborate ceremonies follow the death of a man, especially a chief. His wives, his brothers, his children and other relatives have to be purified from the 'contagion' of death. The Tsonga of southern Mozambique used to invite a stranger to sleep with the widow, so that he would take the 'ill luck' (q.v.) away with him. Evil spirits which are often considered to be the cause of ill luck, disease and sin, may be 'loaded' onto a goat or chicken and left outside at the crossroads. There, the unsuspecting traveller will find the goat, and happily take it home — and with it the evil spirit, thus ridding the village of it, while being 'contaminated' with it himself. Shaving the head, both of men and women, is often practised to purify people both from sin and from ill luck. Spraying people with water serves the same end. Water, without which no life is possible, is a powerful magic weapon; in West Africa it is used to 'cool' the power-laden bodies of great hunters, warriors and women who have had twins. Menstruating women require ritual 'purification' in many communities, including Islam.

Pygmies The Pygmies are the remainders of an ancient race of human beings which was once far more widespread than today. Some old people in Kenya could remember, a generation ago, that they had seen Pygmies (in Swahili *mbilikimo* 'half a man'), which takes us back to a century ago when Kenya had less than 4 per cent of its present population and was still largely covered in forest. The Pygmies live in the forests, now mainly in the Ituri Forest in Zaïre, and also in Congo.

The Pygmies are divided into several tribes speaking distinct languages. They are generally shy and peaceful people, but they do not like intruders in their forest habitat. In pre-colonial days, unsuspecting travellers would be ambushed and eaten, or would be hit by poisoned arrows from unknown directions. But this information comes from the surrounding Bantu peoples who destroyed much of the forest. They gave the Pygmies a reputation as magical experts whose medicines were much sought after, especially those which put a spell on game, for the Pygmies had great fame as hunters. Even elephants could not escape their magic but were literally spellbound by it. The details of such hunts are rather sanguinary.

The Pygmies believe in a Supreme Being known as Kalisia, and in an ancestral hero called Tore, which may mean the Spider. Kalisia is the Lord of the Forest who protects the hunters, if they have performed the correct rituals, and leads the game into their snares. He also appears in dreams, telling them where the game is hiding. Thus Kalisia selects the hunt-leader, the pioneer pathfinder who has premonitions about things to come. The Pygmies are intimately acquainted with the animals of the forest, who, they say, are intelligent, powerful beings with the ability to work magic upon the hunter, such as making him temporarily blind. The Bantu chiefs often employ Pygmy ritual experts who will perform the correct ceremonies without which the hunt cannot be successful.

Pyramids (Egypt). Many tales are told concerning the ancient pyramids which, it is said, contain uncounted treasures and therefore constitute an irresistible target for thieves and robbers. However, the ancient kings and queens knew this, and defended their tombs so effectively that only a few intrepid adventurers who managed to penetrate the pyramids, ever emerged to tell the tale. One such young man, knowing that the pharaohs had built a slide behind the main entrance, told his accomplice to hold the rope, the other end of which he tied round his person. He walked into the corridor and sure enough, soon the floor curved downwards and he slid down a hundred yards. He would have fallen to his death if his comrade had not held him, so he landed safely on a floor deep in the earth. He walked into a corridor, and suddenly a door shut behind him. He had to untie himself and walked on.

After a long time he saw light and found himself in a green garden full of exotic trees and flowers. Suddenly he saw a princess of great beauty coming towards him. She greeted him with a smile and invited him to share her meal. She led him to her palace where an abundance of food was waiting. When he felt tired she showed him a bedroom where he soon fell asleep. When he woke up she was there, offering him beverages. He stayed with her and they had children.

One day he said he wished to see his own town again, but she warned him that once he left he could never come back. So he stayed and did not mention it again for a long time. Their children were already grown up when he finally decided to go home, but no one wanted to come with him. His wife showed him a door he had never seen, and through it he found the outside world, but he never found that door again. When he drank from a pond he saw that he had white hair, and in his home town no one he had once known was alive: they had all long since died.

Python There are three species of the genus *Python* (family of the Boidae) found in Africa: the Ball python, which, when disturbed, rolls itself into a ball; the Angolan python, *Python anchietae* and the African python, *Python sebae*. A python may grow to a length of well over 7 metres (20 feet) and swallow over 50 kg (120 pounds) of food in one meal. One python is known to have swallowed a leopard whole, but this was exceptional. In Zaïre it is believed that the oil of the python (*mafuta ya nguma*) will make its owner rich, and that the sperm of the python (*mani ya nguma*) will make a man irresistible to women and very fertile.

Many generations ago the King of Zululand had a queen who did not give birth, although her body kept on swelling up, until she was enormous. When she finally began to give birth, out came the head of a python, so that all the women present fled from the room. For hours and hours the python went on coming out of the queen, until at last, when the women asked her from outside: have you given birth? She answered: 'I have now finished.' The King decided to emigrate with his entire household, leaving the Queen alone with her offspring. She had to grow her own corn to feed herself and the python, which went to live in the river. After many months the python's skin began to peel off, and there appeared the head of a baby boy. As the snakeskin flaked off further, there appeared a baby girl, then a boy again, and so on, until there were five boys and five girls. The queen called the first boy Uhlathu Yesiziba, 'Python of the Pool'. As they grew up, he became the chief of the village; together they repaired all the houses. Many people came to live there as retainers. Finally the King heard of it. He went to visit his old capital and found no python but 10 handsome children. He was delighted and made Uhlathu Yesiziba his successor. His clan still lives there.

In the old days, whenever the Nyamwezi of Tanzania encountered a python in the fields or in the bush, they would address it with veneration and render it homage by clapping their hands as if greeting a king. Libations of water and oil are offered when the python enters a house, and in such cases the local chief is informed, and he will order a goat to be sacrificed to the reptile. If one sees a dead snake, one has to bury it like a human being, and one keeps the rings from its skin, to be worn as talismans (q.v.). When a python blows in a man's direction that person can expect to receive great wealth and other blessings.

If someone killed a python, its spirit might take revenge by destroying the killer's whole family. To prevent such a disaster, the chief would impose a stiff fine on the perpetrator. The python was addressed as 'our king' and people knelt in front of it. The king was informed of such encounters with the words: 'Sire, your brother has come.'

R

Ram mask made of ebony from Cameroun

Rain cloud Everywhere in Africa, except in the rain forest zone, rain clouds are viewed with great joy. They are eagerly expected at the end of each dry season, and greeted with jubilation when they arrive. Prayers are sent up to the sky, not only by the traditionalists but also by Christians and Muslims, when rain clouds remain invisible or linger on the horizon. Black or very dark blue are favourite colours for many peoples simply because they are the colour of rain clouds: the blacker the better. There are proverbs like: 'Clouds are better than lightning.' (Lightning is often observed long before the rains begin.) Rain clouds are often regarded as gods or as the expression of divine power and recompense. There are traces of an old Bantu goddess of rain, comparable to the ancient Egyptian Nut.

Rain-making Rain is considered by many African peoples the most precious gift of heaven. The worshippers of the One God will pray for rain whenever He withholds it. There are some very beautiful Islamic hymns of supplication for rainfall, in Swahili. Many other African peoples believe that rain can be made, i.e. that if the correct rites are performed, the sky is forced to drop rain, by the sheer magical power of the rain-maker. The Alur (q.v.) of north-west Uganda recognize the King of Ukuru as their chief rain-maker because he is in possession of the rainstones and the rainspears. These spears are made of metal, not wood, and will make rain if planted in a stream. If they are pointed up at the sky and swung to and fro, they will prevent rain. The Abira clan have a rain-dance by which they dance naked, after the sacrifice of a goat. They sing the songs of Jokrut, the god of twins, and when the goat's blood and the contents of the stomach are poured into the god's own vessel, rain will fall. The rainstones which were long ago found in the heart of a deceased king, Uchak, must be boiled in oil during the recitation of certain prayers in order to make rain in abundance.

In southern Mozambique a hundred years ago, the magicians used the bodies of exhumed deformed babies to make rain-medicines. In Transvaal, as in Uganda, the rain-maker uses an antelope horn stuffed with 'medicines' including seashells and seaweed. The Nandi of Kenya, in times of serious drought, appeal to the god Asis, while a white sheep is pushed into the river. The sheep is then left to scramble on the bank again and shake itself so that the drops fly in all directions, causing rain. For the rain-making in Barotseland, Zambia, see under *Sitondo*. In Burundi, the Bavurati 'Pluviators' are a clan of rain-magicians who undergo a long, hard apprenticeship. They make rain with the lightning-flesh and tar which floats on Lake Tanganyika, mixed with honey. (See also *Chiefs; Gishu*.)

Rain Queen (South Africa). We must distinguish between the queens of the Lovedu people in what is now eastern Transvaal, who were a succession of female rulers named Modjadji or Mujaji, and the great goddess whose incarnations on earth these queens were. Only then does the incredible reputation of *the* Rain Queen make sense as a religious phenomenon. The Lovedu people were protected by their Goddess of Rain against the invasions of the Zulu hordes of the early nineteenth century, since just the mention of her name struck terror in the hearts of her people's enemies, who, when they approached her kingdom, would be struck by magic and die of unknown causes. She could send drought and even swarms of locusts to her enemies.

The mist-covered slopes of the northern Drakensberg ('Dragon') Mountains were the home of Mujaji the Rain Goddess who appeared only very seldom to human beings, but demanded sacrifices of cattle and even human daughters from those who came to supplicate for rain. She was the Transformer of the Clouds who could send torrential rainstorms to destroy the homesteads of her enemies and let gentle rain descend beneficently on her devotees' crops. Her fame as an immortal goddess in the body of a fair queen was used by Rider Haggard for his novel *She* (1886), which made him famous. The Lovedu pride themselves on their female ancestry and give a high status to women, which is quite exceptional in Africa. There are numerous legends about the wisdom and cunning of the Rain queens in playing off the Boers and the British against one another in the late nineteenth century, so that the Lovedu were not deported, like their neighbours after they rebelled. She never showed herself to white men, but had a woman who impersonated her. The first queen was Dzugudini who came from the north in *c*. 1600, from Zimbabwe, with her son Makaphimo, grandson of Monomotapa. They taught the local people the use of fire and became their rulers.

Rain spirit see *Alur; Chiga; Rain-making*.

Rainbow (Kongo, Zaïre). For the Bakongo, the rainbow is a protecting deity, to whom they address a beautiful hymn when they see it in the sky: 'I am Lubangala the Protector/ I guard the earth, I guard the sea/ I guard the village in daytime/ I guard the ancestors' graves.' The Rainbow has more power than the protecting deity of the clan himself has against the power of the Thunder-god. Thunderstorms, when they came raging in from the Atlantic, were feared by the Bakongo of ancient times. When they saw the Rainbow, they saw it as a strong giant arching his body over their village to protect it, like a mother protecting her child against the hyenas. Hence this hymn, in which the Rainbow is introduced singing his own praises, like a hero in battle.

Rainstones see *Alur; Rain-making*.

Ram The ancient Egyptian sun-god Ammon-Ra, whom the Romans later identified with Jupiter, their supreme god, was venerated in the shape of a ram at Siwa in south-western Egypt, where people still speak Siwi, a Berber language. The association of the sun with the ram is well known in the astrology of Antiquity, especially. The Swahili still begin the New Year on 21 March, when the sun enters the sign of the Ram, i.e. Aries, whom the ancient Persians once venerated as Mithra the sun-god. New Year's Day is still called Nairuzi in Swahili, from the Persian *Nau Ruz*, 'New Light'. Sheep are rare in tropical Africa except on the highlands in Kenya where the Kikuyus keep them.

The Berber sheep-shearers still sing a hymn to the rising sun in their Moroccan mountains, calling it 'Our great Ram'. Underneath their Arabic veneer there is still much ancient myth.

The Hottentots or Khoi (q.v.) of Namibia have a myth about the Sun-ram, whom they call Sore-Gus. A man called Giri (Jackal) was once hunting in the wilderness when he saw a wild sheep. It was a huge ram with long fluffy wool which shone golden in the sun, as if it emitted light. After a long pursuit he hit it with his last arrow, so it died. He cut some of its meat and went home but he felt so thirsty that he asked people for water. However all the water he touched dried up. A wise old man said: 'You must have killed the mighty Sun-ram. Do not eat its meat for it will kill you. Go back at once to where you have hidden the body and put the meat you cut out back in its place. Then pray: 'Ram of the Sun, Ram of the Sun,

Please stand up! Please become as you once were. Please live again as before!' Giri did everything as he had been told. He put the flesh back in the body, sang the prayer and to his relief the shining ram rose up and walked away. The water then came back in the pools.

Rebirth We may distinguish between reincarnation (q.v.), which is the continuation of the same soul in a new body, usually by means of being born from a woman as a baby and so without knowledge of any previous existence, and rebirth, which is the resumption of our physical existence, perhaps in a different shape, but by preserving the identity of the substance we were created from. African peoples believe that some ancestors are reborn in their descendants. Thus the mother sings to her newly born baby son: 'How shall we name you, little one? Are you your father's father or another? Whose spirit is in you, my warrior? Whose little spear-hand tightens round my breast? Your eyes glow like a leopard's in a thicket!' (Pygmy, Zaïre).

The dead are impatient to be reborn and sing while waiting: 'Moon, moon, shine on our way, shine on the homeward path, Shine brightly on the path of our return, the stream we have to cross, so we can travel in the night, home to our loved ones, where a woman will give birth.' (Ewe, Ghana).

A Wolof man in Senegal prayed to his revered totem-ancestor: 'Root of our life! Root-sap which will enrich the life of our tribe and all its branches! Give me a little of your lion-breath! I hear you roaring, lion of my blood, I need your strength to help the tribe to grow.'

Reincarnation The belief in reincarnation is widespread in Africa. In North Africa it is related that many saints, including the Prophet Muhammad himself, have been seen walking upon earth centuries after their death, because according to the Koran, God may restore a person's body whenever He wishes.

In South Africa and in Zimbabwe, I have been told by several persons that Jesus has been seen, and not just in a dream. They said that on Easter Sunday morning he appeared to churchgoers and spoke to them, telling them: '*Ngipfukile* I have risen,' then walking away.

Reincarnation does not, however, normally refer to brief periods of a person's presence on earth, but to being born from a woman in human form. The spirit so reborn may be either human or divine. A god who has lived on earth in one body may reincarnate in another body to begin a new life, like the Buddha. In the epic of Lianja (q.v.) among the Nkundo of central Zaïre, Itonde (q.v.) is the god of death and the first being to die. His spirit reincarnates at the moment of his death in his son Lianja, who is being born at that moment from Mbombe, the Mother Goddess. The son comes out holding his father's spear as a sign of authority. He in turn is reborn as his son Lianja II. Thus the ideal is established of a dynasty of divine kings each of whom is born at the moment his father dies and is reborn as his son. Whether the dying father's spirit flies home and enters his wife's womb to be born at once, or whether his sperm already contained the essence of his spirit is unclear.

The belief that a child is a reborn ancestor, uncle or aunt, is widespread in Africa. The parents will look for some resemblance in the child's face or body to a recently deceased relative, or one who appeared in a dream announcing his or her return to earth in human form, and name the child accordingly. Some ancestors and kings are believed to be reborn as animals, especially lions, birds and snakes.

Revelation Every religion necessarily begins with some communication from the Other World, a voice or vision of that spiritual reality telling the people what they must do or believe, through an intermediary, a medium (q.v.), a shaman (q.v.), or a prophet (q.v.). A medium speaks the spirit's words without knowing; a shaman visits the spirits in their abode and is taught by them there. Revelations are usually reserved for prophets, though some scholars maintain that God reveals in some way also to saints and other holy persons of His choice. The Somali have many tales about holy sheikhs who received knowledge from God so that they could rescue drowning sailors from the rocky shore of the ocean while continuing their lectures, or send a messenger to a man in the desert who was about to be robbed. God had revealed to them what normal people could not see because it was far away and hidden behind rocks, such as the robbers lying in ambush. God may 'fold the distance together' like a cloth, and 'make rocks like glass', if He wishes, to show the truth to His friend (*wali* = saint). God may also show the truth to His servant by shedding light inside the brain so that things which are already there, can suddenly be seen. Or, God may transform the desert temporarily into Paradise, so that His servant can tell his followers what he has seen. In the Bible, God spoke in the whirlwind (to Job) and in a soft breeze (to Elijah), or came himself (to Abraham).

In Africa, there are many tales about voices in the desert (Swahili *hatifu*), though most of these are capricious *shaitans*. By far the largest part of all revelations comes in dreams, in the world of Islam as well as in the world of the African gods and spirits. Dreams are taken very seriously in Africa, so much so that some dreams have changed history. Some medicine men, shamans and *ngangas* do their work while in the company of the spirits, *mizimu*, who talk to them all the time.

Rivers In most parts of Africa the rivers dry up during the dry season and this observation has caused the people of southern Mozambique to believe in Chipfalamfula, the big fish who can 'shut the river', i.e. stop the flow of the water.

Chichinguane was a little girl who was left behind on the dry river bed when the water began to rise. When the water had risen to her breast, she knew she was dying but suddenly she saw a large mouth and heard a voice: 'Come in, my daughter, and live in my belly where you will lack nothing.' Chichinguane entered the mouth of the big fish and settled in its belly. There she met many people who had cattle and fruits and lived in plenty. When she had become a big girl and was ready for marriage, the fish gave her a magic wand and told it to take Chichinguane to the palace of the King, for she would marry the Prince. She stepped out of the fish's mouth onto dry land but at once she was attacked by ogres. She called out: 'Chipfalamfula, shut the water.' The river became dry and she walked across. When she was safely on the other bank, she called out: 'Chipfalamfula, open the water,' and, while the ogres were right in the middle, the water burst forth again, so they were all drowned. Chichinguane continued her journey guided by the magic wand which shone like a torch in the night. It guided her to a cave where she found fine clothes and precious stones, so she was rich. When she arrived at the palace the Prince fell in love with her and married her.

The Baluba of Kasai tell the tale of Tangalimlibo, she who walks by Moonlight, who was born after her mother begged a favour from a riverbird. When her father-in-law ordered her to fetch him fresh water in daytime, he knew he was commanding her to break her taboo. The river held her until her own personal cow was slaughtered and given to the river-god.

Rwanda (The Lion Goddess). Nyavirezi was the daughter of a chief. She loved walking about in the wilderness. One day she felt thirsty, but the only water she found was a puddle in a hollow tree. She drank a little from it but it did not slake her thirst. It was lion's urine. On her way home she saw her father's cattle with some fat calves that gave her a funny feeling. She shook herself and suddenly she grew tawny hair all over her body, a tail with a brush, and long eye-teeth in powerful jaws: she had become a lioness, big and strong. She leaped on the calves and devoured them. After that meal she felt better and resumed her human form. This happened again: when her craving for meat and hunting became strong again she found she could become a lioness as soon as she felt the urge to hunt. After several calves went missing, her brother, who was responsible for their father's cattle, became suspicious and began to watch her. He told the chief, who forbade Nyavirezi ever to go out again. Fortunately, not long afterwards a young chief arrived wanting to marry Nyavirezi, as she was big and strong. Her father told her: 'Love your husband but never tell him your secret!'

Nyavirezi was married and in due course gave birth to a daughter whom she called Nyavirungu. Vigara, her husband, heard the servants whisper: 'At least it is a human child, without claws or teeth.' Vigara took his spear, went to his wife's room and demanded to know her secret. She refused to tell him, and when he, furious, thrust his spear at her, she avoided him in a skilful sideways jump. The spear grazed her side and the sight of her own blood made her a lioness again. With one stroke of her front paw she broke her husband's neck and devoured him. Then she resumed her human form, cleaned the floor, and went home to her father.

In spite of the rumours that circulated about her, young men were attracted to her for her great beauty and strong looks. The winner among the many suitors was a tall and handsome man, Babinga, King of the Mandwa people who, it was whispered, were spirits or at least experts in magic. But who is never slandered? Nyavirezi married Babinga and in due course gave birth to a son, Ryangombe, 'Buffalo Horn' (q.v.), who grew up prosperously. When he came of age his father died so he had to go and claim the far kingdom of Mandwa. On his journey he was attacked by a leopard, but he killed it skilfully. An old herdsman appeared to him and told him what he must do. Soon after, Ryangombe met a pretty girl and offered her the leopard skin if she agreed to marry him. She did, and in due course she gave birth to a son, Binego, who grew up prosperously and one day set out in search of his father. He met the same old herdsman who told him: 'Your father is still contending for his kingdom of Mandwa; he is not winning, but you can help him. The key to that kingdom is a magic formula which I will teach you. When you enter it, under this mountain, Bihama, you will see your father engaged in a game of *bao* (East African backgammon) which he is losing. I will teach you all the rules and tricks of the game, so you can help him to win. The usurper of the kingdom is a traitor called Mpumuti Muchuni.'

Binego stayed with the old herdsman who taught him the game of *bao* which is so difficult that few Europeans have learned it. Finally, Binego set out to find the entrance to the Mountain of Bihama and opened it, by speaking the right words. He found himself in a vast hall, the palace of Mandwa, where his father was playing *bao* against a monstrous opponent. Binego walked up to his father and quickly told him the winning moves. Ryangombe won and when Muchuni protested, Binego took his father's spear and stabbed him to death. Father and son went home to Nyavirezi.

Ryangombe, King of Rwanda Ryangombe, 'Buffalo Horn', was the son of Babinga who was King of Mandwa, the kingdom of the spirits, and Nyavirezi (q.v.), Queen of Rwanda, the woman who could become a lioness whenever she wanted, and hunt. He had a son, Binego who, like his parents, lived through many adventures. One day father and son decided to go hunting, but Queen Nyavirezi told them: 'Do not go out today, my King Ryangombe! I had a dream in which I saw what will happen today. You will see a hare without ears or tail. Then you will see a river without water. Then you will see a girl with hair all over her body. If you go out today you will be killed by a buffalo horn.' King Ryangombe was unmoved: 'The men are waiting, the dogs are yelping on the leash. If I call the hunt off because my mother had a dream, all the people will say I am a coward, a sloth.' The King set off with his son and all his men. Soon they saw a hare with neither ears nor tail (a hyrax). The men said: 'Let us turn back, O King, this is the omen your mother mentioned.' The King went on. Later, they saw a river overflowing, but without water: it had only blood in it. The men pleaded: 'Your Majesty, please come home with us.' Ryangombe said: 'Shall I fear my fate?' Finally, they met a girl who was all covered in lion-coloured hair. 'Sire, let us turn round, this is a bad day for hunting. The signs spell doom.' Ryangombe spoke: 'This girl will marry my son Binego. She is a lion-woman, like my mother. Well met, daughter-in-law!' They began to hunt. The King speared a leopard, then a lion. Finally the men said: 'There is a solitary buffalo in the bushes. It is an angry bull. If you come near it, it will charge, O King.' Ryangombe spoke: 'I killed a lion and a leopard. Shall I fear a bull?' He went forward and thrust his spear between the bull's ribs, but it did not die, it charged. Ryangombe jumped aside, but a root caught his foot and he stumbled. The King fell on the buffalo's horns. One horn stabbed the King in his side. The hunters soon finished the bull off, but King Ryangombe did not rise again. He spoke his last words to his faithful followers: 'Who can battle against fate? Go to my mother with my son and the lion-girl. Tell her that everything happened as she foretold. We shall see each other on the summit of the great Fire Mountain (the Volcano Ruwenzori). There we will rule the spirits as we have till now ruled human mortals. The child that does not listen to his mother will listen to the Crickets.' After these enigmatic words the king expired. He died as a human being, but he rose up as a spirit king and flew to his father's kingdom of Mandwa. His mother at home saw a leaf come whirling down from a tree. It was not green but red. That is how she knew her son had died.

When the hunters arrived, she recognized the lion-girl from her dream. With her magic powers she gave the girl a smooth human skin. Prince Binego married her and in due course they had a son, Ruganzu, who ruled after his father had died. Many epic tales are told about the campaigns Ruganzu had to fight for his throne against the king of the evil spirits, Inzira. When, finally victorious, Ruganzu came home, he found his way blocked by a huge rock. On top of it there stood a throne, and on the throne sat his grandfather Ryangombe, King of Mandwa, the realm of the spirits. 'What shall I give you that you may let me go home in peace with my tired warriors?' asked Ruganzu of his grandfather. Spoke Ryangombe: 'I desire no burnt offerings, but in every town of your kingdom there shall be a priestess through whose voice I will speak to the people, and there will be a priest in attendance to interpret the oracles and to pray to me for the people.' Ruganzu promised to do his grandfather's behest, and the vision vanished. Thus Ryangombe, King of the Spirits, still speaks to the people.

S

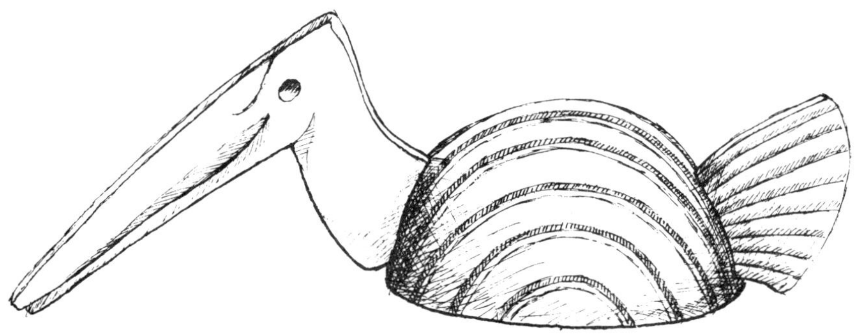

Soul-bird head-dress

Sacrifice In many African clans, the eldest son has the duty to sacrifice to the clan-spirits, those of his father and grandfather. Without those sacrifices the clan will wither and die like a tree whose branches have been cut off. This is the essence of the patrilinear system: the continuity of the lineage for ever. That is why the sacrifice of the first-born son is the highest sacrifice for a man, and even for God. Essentially a sacrifice had to be made for redemption: one had to die so that the others might live. Life is based on a balance in nature, so there must be as much giving as getting.

The rule is that a sacrifice must be offered gladly, readily and happily, otherwise it is not acceptable to God, who does not need our sacrifices, since He owns all things already. Thus the position of the sacrifice in Islam and Christianity is fundamentally different. In Islam, man is always the slave and supplicant of God, in Christianity he shares with God. In Antiquity the votive offering was the commonest preliminary to a sacrifice. Modern worshippers would dismiss such 'bargaining with God' as irreligious, yet it is still very common in many religions. Soccer clubs in Dar es Salaam are said to offer sacrifices to their gods or spirits if they let them win the next match and to place fetishes (*hirizi, kago, fingo*) under the opposing club's goal, hoping their spirits will let all their balls pass. This may well be propaganda from Islamic clubs!

The common true sacrifice is made in Africa to create, to celebrate or to restore good relations with the deity or the ancestral spirits. Usually the gods are not satisfied with less than the slaughter of an animal (Genesis 4, 4-5), in Swahili *muhanga*, which is part of the great feast of the *tambiko*.

The Dogon people of Mali have a very special sacrificial rite called *bulu*, from *bulo* 'to revive, resuscitate'. Thus the sacrifice in principle revives the relations of the community with the universe of life and living beings. These living (*omo*) beings have souls (*kikinu*) and a vital strength or force of life (*nyama*). The essential moment in the sacrifice is the victim's death. First, the agent of the sacrifice, the sacrificiant, alerts the deity, the aim of the sacrifice, by means of his prayers; secondly, the blood of the victim (an animal) flows onto the altar, carrying its *nyama*. The Dogon elders say that the altar drinks the blood like a baby drinking his mother's milk. In other words, the altar itself is a living being, functioning as an intermediary between the sacrificiant and the deity.

The deity is thus also fed, nourished by the sacrifice, especially by the blood, and so, in turn, has the will to feed, i.e. to give energy, *nyama*, to the sacrificiant, by pouring his (the deity's own) energy into the liver of the sacrificed animal. The sacrificiant subsequently eats the liver during the sacrificial meal, thus consuming the divine energy which he needs to live. There is thus a complete circle of the flow of energy, one might say, a circuit of energy that has to be closed in order to work. The victim's death sets in motion a series of events by liberating its energy for the benefit of both the deity and the sacrificiant.

The Songhai (Songoi) people in eastern Mali offer a sacrifice for rain to the sky-gods, in particular the Rainbow-god, Sajara, who is a serpent with all the colours. It is represented by a forked tree where a white ram is sacrificed, after which the priest sprinkles the blood carefully over the tree which represents the Rainbow-god on earth, and so, functions as the altar. A dance takes place during which the sky-gods possess some of the dancers and speak through their mouths, thus announcing their wish. This verbal contact makes a covenant possible which is in fact a vow pronounced by the gods: 'If you sacrifice, we will give rain.'

The Mofu in northern Cameroun have so many gods that there are sacrifices in their country every day. Each head of a household (*Bi-ay*) has seven spirits to whom he has obligations: his deceased father, grandfather, great- and great-great-grandfather, his mother and father's mother, and finally the spirit of the field, without whose consent he cannot cultivate successfully. Sacrifices are necessary after a funeral to remove the contagion of death; to the ancestors to remove *madama* 'impurity', the result of sins against the clan laws; to God, *Bi-erlam*, and the mountain spirits *mbolom*, for rain. In the case of sickness a diviner, *mbidla*, inspired by a spirit, has to be consulted regarding a sacrifice.

Sahara The name *sahara* means 'deserts' in Arabic, which implies correctly that the Sahara is composed of several deserts. The word *desert* originates from Terra Deserta, the name the Romans gave to the territory south of Carthage, implying that it was deserted land. Indeed we now know that the Sahara was once inhabited by numerous tribes, before sand was blown over their crops and grazing land. From time to time the sand is blown away again, revealing orchards, walled cities, palaces and castles. Such events have given rise to uncounted legends of doomed cities whose citizens were punished by God for their sins. Rock paintings in the central Sahara show men and women herding cattle on lush pastureland where no grass grows today. Lake Chad was several times larger than it is now 2,000 years later. The gods and demons of ancient times still wander at large for the travellers in the Sahara are often deluded by visions, mirages, also called Fata Morgana, the Italian name for the Arthurian Lady of the Lake; the Arabic name is Marjana from Greek Margara (whence the flower Marguerite), perhaps from Indian Mangala, the name for Demeter, the Roman Ceres, Egyptian Isis, the goddess of vegetation, who caused the weary travellers to see green oases full of flowers, to give them hope. Travellers also hear voices in the desert, Arabic *hatifa*, plural *hawatif*, male and female voices, some telling them where to go and so saving them, others seducing them from the Straight Path into sin, some reciting poetry, others disclosing the future or the place of hidden treasures from the past. Thus the travellers were often led to the remains of caravans where they found gold and pearls, only to be themselves trapped in the endless spaces without water or guide. Some ancient cities are visible only by night when the pearl-studded walls gleam in the moonlight. Travellers arrive, fill their bags with treasures and leave in a hurry. They open their bags at home; nothing but sand; they travel back, but the accursed city is invisible by day. Whirlwinds looking like huge monsters, travel across the desert, destroying all in their path. African languages have special words for these obvious evil demons.

San see *Bushmen*.

Senegal see *Marain Jagu*.

Serpent (Nigeria). A girl called Jaliya lived near the river Gongola in a small village. One day the village girls teased Jaliya while they were fetching water on the bank. They pushed her into the water as a joke, but she disappeared. The girls fled and told Jaliya's father that she had jumped into the river and drowned. Meanwhile, Jaliya felt herself being pulled gently down by a mysterious force. When her feet stood on the bottom she saw a splendid palace; its gate was open, there was no guard. She walked inside, admiring the fine furnishings, when she came upon a huge serpent sitting on a throne with a crown on its head, in a huge throne room. The serpent bade her to sit down and to sing for him. She began to sing and since she knew very many songs she could go on a long time. Now it so happened that the King of Gongola arrived on the riverbank with his men, and heard a soft young voice singing the old songs of his youth. At first the King would not believe that the singing rose up from below the surface, but when he realized that, he ordered his men to build a dam and lead the river water round through another channel. A king in love can order anything. When at last the water level began to fall, the serpent raised its huge head out of the water and breathed steam in billowing clouds so that soon rain began to fall. Then it opened two enormous wings and flew away, followed by its 40-foot tail, to another part of the river where it was now deep. Meanwhile the singing went on and finally a very beautiful girl became visible, playing a big golden harp, sitting on a golden stool, wearing a golden crown. She told the King that the serpent had made her Queen of the River and had given her all the golden treasures which surrounded her. The serpent knew that the King wanted to marry Jaliya; the serpent had given her permission to live on earth again and to marry the King of Gongola on condition that he performed an annual sacrifice to the serpent.

Shaitani, Shetani (Swahili). *Shaitsani* (Hausa), *Eshu* (Yoruba), *Essitaani* (Ganda), *Zavolo* (Lingala), Shetani (Malawi), Sathane (Zulu), Sheitani (Sidamo), Sintanaa (Malinke, Mali). Evil spirit, devil, satan, demon. Evil spirits are of many kinds in Africa. They may be deceased persons who have not been properly interred or who have an unfulfilled need on earth, such as the duty to take revenge on a murderer or tormentor; many are spirits of women who died in childbirth. Some are nature spirits who live in caves or rivers where they molest innocent travellers. Many demons appear in the shape of snakes or leopards, scorpions or owls threatening people or simply being evil omens. Many evil spirits devour all the people they meet: they are ogres of enormous size and ugliness. Islam teaches that *shaitans* were created by God out of the eternal and infernal fire as the instruments of His punishment for our sins. These satans have simply been added to those already known in Africa. Many of them were released from bottles found by fishermen in Morocco who imprudently removed King Solomon's seal. Some evil spirits are whirlwinds in the desert which may make the traveller insane; others are seductive voices in the desert. Some satans live in oases and take the shape of pretty girls to seduce travellers, whose bones will be found many years later. Some look like ordinary human beings and speak normally, but they tempt people to do evil. Some *shaitans* possess people so that they behave like madmen, dancing and whirling round. A doctor, a saint or a shaman can cast out such a spirit and make the patient normal again. This requires an expensive ceremony, to exorcise the spirit in the patient and persuade him to leave his 'mount' in peace. In Sidamo, the *Kalicha* does this, in Central Africa the *nganga*, in East Africa the *mganga*, but many evil spirits are too powerful to be subdued except by the Almighty Himself (see *Exorcism*).

Shaman The shaman is the intermediary between the two worlds of the spirits and of the people. A shaman has direct contact with the spirits; usually this contact takes place only after a special series of rituals have been performed, or while the shaman is in an 'elated' state of ecstasis, also called trance or dissociation. 'Ecstasis' describes the state of a person whose spirit or soul is 'away', 'above himself', experiencing things unheard of on earth. Possession (q.v.) describes the state in which, conversely, the spirit or spirits have come down from heaven, or have risen up from the earth, to enter the head and/or the body of the person. Not every possessed person is a shaman, however; some are 'only' mediums (q.v.), whose will is replaced by the spirit. The purpose of the shaman's life, especially of his visits to the other world, is to help his own people, who will consult him or her whenever they are hard-pressed by mortality as a result of disease or disaster (war, famine, flood or fire). In Africa, many healers are shamans because they are in contact with the spirits, often the spirits of their ancestors (see *Nganga*) or others, either constantly or only when entering a state of trance. These spirits may accompany the shaman in the wilderness where he must find the medicinal herbs for his patients, and in the houses where they may tell him the diagnosis of the patient's ailment. Other shamans have to go and consult the spirit(s) in a particular dream; in Islamicized communities the spirit will be a Muslim saint. The best-known type of shaman is the one who, after drumming and singing has brought on the right conditions, will leave his body behind to travel to the other world where he will meet God or the spirits who will tell him what must be done to relieve the suffering of his people. Some shamans have to be ritually buried to visit the spirits of the nether world. Only by his miraculous power can he come back from that world of the dead spirits.

Shango (Yoruba, Nigeria). Shango, or Sango, is one of the earth-gods of the Yoruba, as opposed to the sky-gods Olodumare, Obatala, Oduduwa, Ogun and Orunmila. The earth-gods were born on earth and lived originally among the human population. They did not die but transformed themselves to be ready for a post-human existence; some went to live inside the earth, others travelled to heaven along a chain.

Shango was King of Oyo, where people whispered that he owned a talisman (q.v.) that could call Lightning to destroy his enemies. Shango's subjects were dissatisfied with what they called his tyrannical rule, so he relinquished his kingdom, mounted his horse and rode into the forest. From there he later rose up to the sky along a golden chain. He is now the god of thunder and lightning. Even while he lived on earth, fire would burst from his mouth while he was speaking to his frightened subjects. Today he is remembered as the god of justice and fair play. He punishes those who steal, lie, bewitch others or work sorcery. When he was born on earth, thunder and lightning were observed. Even today, thunder and lightning are hailed in Yoruba society with the respectful words: *Kabiyesi*! 'Your Majesty, hail!'

Some worshippers of Shango can, it is believed, even now, make the lightning strike their enemies by magic means. Yet, it is also strongly believed that only the wicked are struck by lightning. Therefore there is little sympathy for whoever dies in that way, and his body is carried to the forest and abandoned there by the Magba, priests of Shango, because he was a sinner. Shrines dedicated to Shango are found in many towns and villages, where the god is often depicted with a ram's head and horns, in the company of his three wives, Oya, Oshun and Oba. Shango is clearly comparable to Jupiter-Zeus, the classical god of thunder and lightning; in Egypt he was called Ammon-Ra. He was often depicted with a ram's head. (See *Ram*.)

Shankpana (Yoruba, Nigeria). Shankpana, or Sankpana, is one of the names of the god of the smallpox and perhaps of other epidemics as well. For those who are surprised that a mythology contains a deity of disease it will be good to remember that Apollo, son of Zeus, was also the god of the plague in Homer's *Iliad*. Shankpana was the son of Shango (q.v.) the god of thunder; his taboo is the sesame plant, *nyamati* (Hausa *sure*), which must not be found in the house of any of his followers: if it is, then Shankpana will send disease. All those struck by smallpox may go to Shankpana's temple where the priests will wash them and rub their skin with a secret medicine. The god's special feast-day takes place in September, when goats, chickens, palm-oil and bananas will be offered to him. His followers never touch horse-meat and marry exogamously. It is related that Shankpana was once a war-god who conquered Yorubaland centuries ago, invading from the north or north-west. This legend may be a graphic description of the first smallpox epidemic in the country, sweeping across southward.

Once a woman in the town of Oru, who was an Orun worshipper, gave birth to a child with a neck tumour, who soon died. She had a second and third child with the same ailment. All died. The father consulted a diviner (q.v.) who sent him on to the priests of Shankpana in the temple with the Osoko statue of cowries, holding a tin sword. The oracle of Osoko is made up of 50 cowrie shells, all cut in half. These shells are thrown in a particular manner and from the way in which they fall, the priest can conclude the nature of the disease and its remedy. The priest spoke: 'In the future you must per form the sacrifices you have hitherto made for Orun, for Shankpana. They are the same god.'

Sheep (Glau, Liberia). The ancestor of the Glau people was Muy. His wife gave him many sons, all strong boys, except the last one, who was a lamb, a young ram. When that lamb was born, Muy called his sons together and spoke: 'You have seen that your little brother is a sheep. From now on we will eat no mutton. Can anyone eat his brother?' So, sheep became the friends of the family. One day a stranger arrived with a young ewe which he offered for sale to the family. Chief Muy agreed to buy it, but instead of eating it, he gave the ewe to his youngest son, as a wife. They lived happily ever after and had many lambs, who were well looked after.

In that country there lived a wicked king who demanded every year an animal from every hunter and farmer. Whenever a man brought him an animal, the king would ask: 'Where is my girl?' In addition to the animal tax, every family also had to offer a girl to the king, not to marry but to devour, for he was an abominable cannibal. When Muy arrived to offer the king a prized leopard he had shot, the king demanded his daughter. When Muy protested that he had no daughter, the king shouted: 'I want to eat all the sheep on your farm!' Muy was so enraged by this sacrilege that he raised his spear and stabbed the king to death. Of course he had to flee to escape the king's son, who was now king. With his family, including his flock of grandchildren, they ran for their lives until they came to the bank of a river, where there was no boat in sight, and no bridge. Chief Muy bowed down in prayer to a very tall tree that grew on the bank. Slowly it bent down until it reached all the way across the river so that they could all scramble across to safety, even the lambs could run along the large trunk. As soon as they were all safe, the tree righted itself just before the king's men arrived who had to swim across. Just at that moment a flood-wave swept down the river, so they all drowned. (See also *Ram*.)

Shilluk (Myths, Sudan). The Shilluk are the northernmost Nilotic people; they live along the west-side of the Nile. They believe, like the related Nuer (q.v.) in the One God, Jwok, who created the world, its plants, animals and people. A tradition says that God created people in three types, black, white and brown, because he used different types of earth. The white man (*Turuk* 'Turk') was made from white loam, the brown man, i.e. the Sudan Arab, was made from the desert sand, and the black man (the Shilluk call themselves Chol which means originally 'black') was formed from the fertile riverside clay. One day, when God came back from heaven, he called his three men, but two of them hid. Only the white man obeyed and arrived to greet God, so God gave him many favours. Thus the whites are rich. God owns two loaves (what we would call pancakes, flat disk-shaped objects), i.e. heaven and earth (says the riddle). The third element in the cosmology of the Shilluk is the Nile, their only source of water, where they catch fish. Their myth of origin describes the land in which they first lived as the 'head-land', i.e. the source of the Nile, 'where there was a great lake', which may have been Lake Albert, the focal division point between the Alur (q.v.), the Acholi (q.v.) and the Nyoro. Each of these peoples took a different migration route from Wi-kwach 'Leopard's head', where the Nile emerges from Lake Albert. God sent Omara to earth from heaven as the first man. He married the cow-goddess Diang, who gave birth to a son, Okwa, who married the crocodile-goddess, Nyakaya. She gave birth to a son, Nyikang, who was the first Shilluk king. The Shilluk still sacrifice to the goddess Nyakaya in the Nile. Thus, the royal house of the Shilluk nation descends from the three elements of their world: sky (man), earth (cow) and water (crocodile).

Sin In African religions, sin is a transgression against one or more of three things:

1. An agreement, a covenant with a deity or with a person. The Yoruba god Orisha-nla expects his devotees to abstain from drinking palm-wine and becoming drunk. Anyone breaking this prohibition is a sinner.
2. A custom, a traditional habit or taboo, or a ritual. A person neglecting the ceremonies which are incumbent upon him as a result of his social or sacral status is also a sinner and will be visited by the deities.
3. The expected code of behaviour which a person in a given category (adolescent male, married woman, etc.) must show. Society prescribes behaviour, usually formulated in the form of proverbs which are repeated to make morals sink in. The Ewe say: 'God does not help a sorcerer.' The Yoruba say: 'You who steal in the night, if the king of the earth does not see you, the king of heaven sees you, so beware!' The Mongo say: 'It is better to be hungry than to steal.' The Nuer say: 'A wife must obey her husband.' The Zulu say: 'The sorcerer will one day poison himself.'

In Africa, many concepts of sin coincide with those in other continents; these sins include some of the sins in the Ten Commandments: adultery, theft, murder, disobeying one's parents, dishonesty, especially when witnessing on oath, coveting one's neighbour's property or his women, and taking any of the divine names in vain, i.e. in an untrue oath. It is also implicitly believed by Africans (as well as by most religious people on earth) that they must not worship other gods than those which their parents taught them to worship. Thus it appears that eight of the ten commandments in the Bible refer to sins that are universally regarded as such by traditional African religions.

Sitondo (Barotseland, Zambia). A *sitondo*, plural *basitondo* is a rain-maker who works on behalf of the village headmen or other authorities. Kings do not need him, for the kings of Barotseland were believed to be demigods who could protect their subjects and their herds from rainstorms, lightning and thunder. The *sitondo* is also called *ngaka wa pula* 'rain-doctor', because he is often asked not to make rain, but to stop it, for rain often causes severe damage and flooding in Barotseland. It follows from this that he is able to withhold rain where it is needed or to cause floods where he wishes, so that he is held in deep awe by the people. Likewise, the word *sitondo* is applied to the *ngaka wa litau* 'doctor of lions', to the *ngaka wa likwena* 'doctor of crocodiles', to the doctor of hyenas and to other specialists who produce and sell amulets (q.v.) to protect their clients against attacks by those wild animals. They are believed to be in some way identified with those animals, for how would a man be able to keep a lion at bay if he could not speak to the lion in his own language? So, he can call a lion to devour his enemies for him! Thus the *sitondo* is also able to strike his opponents with thunder and lightning whenever he wishes, but he may also be asked to treat injuries caused by lightning, such as burns. So he is a real doctor, as well as a potential sorcerer who possesses the power to kill his enemies with a *siposo*, a fiery missile, or an invisible bullet from a *kaliloze*, a magic rifle or spell-gun. The *sitondo* digs up the eggs of the lightning-bird and uses them to make remedies against diseases caused by thunder and lightning. The Bird of Heaven lays its eggs in the ground where lightning strikes. A *sitondo*, also known as the 'Shepherd of the Clouds', will sing to the clouds to bring them together and persuade them to drop rain, then disperse them, when the fields are soaked. (See also *Rain-making*.)

Snake worship (Ronga, Mozambique). The following account of events was given to Henri Junod by Chief Nkolele, son of Mawatle, in 1895, as the simple truth: 'As chief priest of this religion it was my duty to go to the forest and perform a sacrifice for our ancestral god Mombo wa Ndhlopfu (Elephant Face), who lives in that forest. I went ahead with my offering, a cock which I had prepared for the purpose, until I reached the place in the heart of the forest where we customarily perform our sacrifices. Suddenly, he appeared: Mombo wa Ndhlopfu, father of Makunju, master of the forest, in the shape of a long viper, raising up its head. When the women came nearer and saw him, they panicked and fled, and so did most of the men, but we, the elders, stayed. The snake crept slowly around the place where we were standing to bless us and to thank us for the offering. It was only a cock but he showed his gratitude as if it had been a cow. We had also brought some fruits and other food for him to eat. In silence he was saying to us: 'Thank you, my children, it is good to see that you are remembering me and that you have brought me presents. Well done!' The viper, which was as thick as my leg, crept up to me and stayed quite close, looking at me but doing no harm. I looked at him. He was saying: 'Thank you, good to see you, my grandson!' This is the truth! Then, I prayed to him, saying: 'You, Mombo wa Ndhlopfu, Master of this country, which you have given to your son Makunju, who has given it to his son Hati, who gave it to his son Makhumbi, who gave it to his son Kinini, who gave it to his son Mikabyana, who gave it to his son Mawatle, my father, who gave it to me. Here is my sacrifice, a fine cock. Here I am, I am the last of the lineage. If I had not come, who would have offered you anything? You are the master, we ask trees to make our houses and our boats, we need trees for our fires and it is you who own the forest.' (See also *Gishu*.)

Snakes Snakes enjoy a special status in Africa because many are believed to have a relationship with the spirits, or to be inhabited by spirits, to carry them, or to be spirits themselves. In the Bible snakes are always evil (e.g. Isaiah 30:6), but in Africa, snakes may be messengers of the ancestors and therefore good. The Zulu king may reappear after death as a powerful mamba. In Luanda, a man may be possessed by a snake-spirit called *gola*, which will make him creep and writhe like a snake on the floor. Near the Lualaba River there is a pool where there lives a big snake called Kabwe which sometimes speaks through a medium. The Zimba of Mozambique have a ritual for praying to the ancestors for rain, during which they carry the women, who are at that moment possessed by the snake-spirits, into the forest to pray. These snakes, *malombo*, love the dance and give oracles when asked about diseases which they themselves have caused.

The Cokwe (Chiokwe) of Kasai believe that a pregnant woman has a snake in her belly, an ancestral spirit, helping the growth of the baby. Many people regard the sperm itself as a spirit. On the banks of Lake Tanganyika there is a cult of big snakes (*insato*); each snake has its own priest and possesses him from time to time. The Yao on Lake Malawi had the cult of the rain-snake, a statue of which was shown at boys' initiation ceremonies. It was called *tsato* 'python' (q.v.). The Lenge of Mozambique also had a water-spirit, which attracted young people and possessed them so that they plunged into its sacred pond where the spirit would teach them its secret lore. They came back from this ordeal with a snake, *ndzundzu*, wound round their necks. For the spirits in the pools of Zululand, see Tornado. Snakes are often teachers of medicine, like the serpent of Asklepios, which was probably his grandmother Python. (See also *Wute*.)

Sodza Sky-god. See *Ewe; Hua*.

Solomon, King In Swahili and other Islamic languages: Nabii Sulemani. God had given Solomon the entire earth as his kingdom, so that he ruled Africa as well as Asia. He was also king over the animals, the birds and the reptiles, whose kings were the lion, the ostrich and the crocodile respectively, three African animals. In addition, he was king over the jinns (q.v.) and other spirits, many of whom live in Africa. Numerous tales circulate in east, north and west Africa, about the miracles seen in King Solomon's days. He used to travel on a carpet carried by flying jinns; it was so large that there was a kitchen on it complete with cooks, fires and cauldrons. Upon arrival in a given country, Solomon could invite its king to share his meal which had been prepared during the flight, without spilling a drop during take-off or landing. If the local king or his subjects refused to accept Islam, Solomon would order some of his jinns who are normally invisible, to show themselves in their true shapes; as tall as the tower of Babel, very ugly, with long horns and tails, with large piercing eyes and enormously long teeth, and many hands. The population would be so frightened that they all confessed Islam.

One day, King Solomon was invited by the Queen of the Ants, but when he alighted with his party in the Valley of the Ants, they saw with horror that the ants were as big as wolves. However, the ants were equally terrified by the monstrous servants of the king. Their queen, as soon as she realized who her guest was, ordered her subjects to pay him their respects, so all the ants sang in unison: 'Long live the king of all the animals and insects. Praise the Lord.' Solomon asked his hostess if there was anything she wished. Proudly she answered: 'We fear God alone. He will provide whatever we need.'

Songhai (*Creation myth I*, Niger). The Songhai or Sonrai live in the Niger valley just north-west of the Nigerian border, where they once formed the great empire of Gao, at its peak in the thirteenth-fourteenth centuries. The Zerma speak a dialect of Songhai. Though influenced by Islam, they still have their own living oral tradition of myths about the ancient gods.

They relate that: 'In the beginning there was the earth, with in it Isa, the Niger-mother which flowed towards the Lebo-tiki, (which means literally 'Land's end'), into the ocean which surrounds all the land. Above us there is a winnow (a shallow, open-topped basket used in winnowing) upside-down, made of stone, forming the slate-blue sky, from which sometimes pebbles fall down. These are stone axes, thrown down by Dongo, the god of thunder, who brandishes an axe with a bell, the sound of which is perceived by us as thunder. Dongo has his smithy in the sky where he forges lightning, and whenever a person has been struck by it, people will search for the axe that hit him.' Invariably they will find one of the numerous polished stone hand-axes which were left there by the neolithic peoples. Rain is received from the goddess of water, Hara-Ke, i.e. Mistress of Water, who is assisted by Goru and Godi, two dragons, who live in two Niger tributaries. The kingdom of the goddess Hara-Ke lies under water and is inhabited by numerous genii as well as the spirits of the dead, including the drowned, who live in beautiful cities and palaces on the bottom of the Niger. Other spirits live in the bushes of the vast savannah; these are the Ganji-bi 'black spirits', as opposed to the more exalted spirits of the air called Hole-Koara or 'white spirits'.

The Songhai knew God before the arrival of Islam; they called Him Irke 'our Master' and Kutiumo, the One who knows all. He is also called the Deceiver, Zambanta, like Hermes and the Sumerian god Ea. The reason for this curious epithet is that the gods kept immortality for themselves, while making us mortal.

Creation myth II (Niger). Clearly influenced by Islamic or biblical elements is the following account of the Songhai story of Creation. After God had created the universe, he created Adama and Hawa, i.e. Adam and Eve. God told them He would give them children but they must bring them up for Him. In the following years they had 40 children (this is in accordance with the tradition of Islam) but they were disobedient and tried to hide 20 of their children. Incensed, God appeared to Adama and Hawa, saying: 'I know everything. For your punishment I will place between you and your children a wall so you will never see them again. The 20 children you have hidden will become My children.' These 20 invisible children became the Holê, the higher spirits as opposed to the Ganji. It is these Holê spirits who cause possession and epilepsy. They are also seen in the whirlwinds, a common phenomenon in the desert; some sudden winds are also caused by the spirits of women who are dying in childbed. The fishermen along the river sometimes see a Holê, sitting on the riverbank and looking like a lovely light-skinned girl. One of the Holê spirits is Faran Maka, a giant who fishes the river using his beard as a net; he is also quoted as the great story-teller of old. The persons who are possessed by the Holê spirits are called *Holê-tam* 'slaves of Holê' or *Holê-bari* 'Holê's steeds'.

Faran Maka became the ancestor of one of the Songhai clans, of the Faran fishermen. He lives on the island Toru, 'Magic', where he has to eat a hippopotamus every day, lest he starve. He will uproot a baobab tree when he wants to brush his teeth. One day, Faran Maka wanted to make a floor in his house, so he went to dig clay from a termite hill. Inside it he found a lovely girl and fell in love with her. They had two children, Weikare and Wango. Later, she went back to live in the river.

The Myth of Musa Jinni (Mali). This myth from the region of Timbuctoo is still sung in epic form by the Songhai bards. Musa Nyame or Musa Jinni, which means Musa the son of a Jinn, a spirit, is the great hero of the epic, comparable to Hercules or Beowulf in European myths.

One day when she is tired during a long journey, a young girl goes to sleep under a tree, a very foolish thing to do. In the tree there lives a jinn, which comes down to have his pleasure with the girl so that she conceives and gives birth to a boy whom she calls Musa, i.e. Moses, whose father was also unknown. So he becomes known as Musa Jinni, Moses Spiritson. Later, however, Musa meets his father, who teaches him all the magic jinns know, which is terrifying, and also enviable!

One unlucky day there arrives the Hira which is an enormous monster. It is so hungry that it devours the countryside, eating whole villages. Musa has to slay it; he is accompanied by his fiancée who is as well-versed in magic as he is, and as courageous. Together, they manage to kill the monster. But for Musa, conquering his fiancée is much more difficult. He tries to tie her with magic chains, but she breaks them. When he finally constructs a chain that she cannot break, she agrees to marry him. Then a second Hira appears, which, it seems, is a sort of giant elephant. It appears that Musa's fiancée is herself an elephant in secret. She goes and changes herself into an elephant and lies down near a pond, feigning sleep. When the big male Hira appears to drink, it begins licking her and quickly she pulls four hairs from his tail. The next day Musa, who has received these hairs from his faithful elephant-bride, only has to show them to the big Hira, and it lies down, ready to be killed, so strong is the magic of a monster's own hairs. (For she-elephants marrying men, see under *Elephant*.)

Sorcery A sorcerer is more powerful than a witch (q.v.). A witch is born with witchness, like a congenital ailment or aberration. A sorcerer does not have to perform black magic; he does it out of love for working evil, and hatred for people, often his own people whom he may sacrifice in order to learn his nefarious profession. The sorcerer's purpose is power over his fellow men, and wealth, the more the better. His methods are ruthless killing of whoever is in his way, and spreading disease and sterility.

The sorcerer's tools are the spirits he can control. He can enslave people by making them die, then reviving them and making them work for him (see *Zombies*). He is often seen at night on the graveyards, digging up freshly buried corpses of people who died a mysterious death because he made them ill previously. He can make the dead bodies walk with his black magic incantations and with herbs from the forest. He will slit their tongues lest they talk about him to the people who meet them, though such people are usually terror-struck and nailed to the ground, unable to speak. It is not only for whole corpses that the sorcerer visits the graveyards but also for parts: skulls, hands, hearts, livers and other organs are useful for his practice. He makes fetishes (q.v.; see also *Fingo; Kindoki; Ndoki; Nkisi*) i.e. statues which actually live as soon as the sorcerer has forced one of his serving spirits to enter them and stay in them. Such statues can fly through the air and attack the sorcerer's selected victim, while the sorcerer's identity remains a secret. No need to add that the victim, seeing such a wooden monster approaching, dies of fright even before being hit. Yet sorcerers are very popular since their services are in great demand.

The Nande (q.v.) of Zaïre believe that among them live the *avali*, singular *omuli*, literally 'one who eats'. An *omuli* is a woman or a girl who 'eats' the soul, *kirimu*, of another person who will subsequently die, of 'consumption'.

One young woman, whose sister had been 'eaten' by an *omuli*, went to consult a very powerful *omuli* in order that she could 'eat' the brother of her sister's eater, and so take revenge. In the middle of the night, she, that is her *kirimu*, 'spirit', went to the forest, where she met six *avali* who, sensing the purpose of her visit, invited her to join them: 'Would you like to become like us? Remember the condition: you must bring one *kirimu* for us to eat.' The young woman knew the condition and went to the young man who was asleep. With her secret power of *omuli* she 'took' his *kirimu* and brought it to the coven to be devoured communally. The *avali* recognize each other, yet their powers are not conscious; what is conscious is their hatred and desire for revenge against others. The young man whose *kirimu* had been 'taken' died the same night. Many women accused of this witchcraft confess that they have 'taken' the spirits of others and 'eaten' them. Curiously, it is the pretty girls with a gentle character who tend to be accused of this witchcraft. Under pressure from her fellow villagers, such a girl may even give a convincing description of the feast she and her coven had in the middle of the night. One girl is reported to have commited suicide because she believed in the truth of the accusations. An *omuli* is not born as such, although presumably she has the inclination to this nefarious practice from birth. She can become an *omuli* at some stage in her adult life, and she may also subsequently forswear her habits of eating spirits and even denounce the other members of the coven when she is converted.

Tanzanian Coast. 'If a man is rich, has a good wife, many children, a roomy house and fine clothes, his neighbours will get together and say: 'That man brags about his money, let us make him ill, so he will have to spend his money to get better.' So they go to a sorcerer and pay him to make the rich man sick. The sorcerer will go with his apprentices in the middle of the night to the graveyard, open the grave of someone who has just been buried, drag the body out and carry it to the forest. There each member of the coven carves out a piece of the dead flesh for his own use. This flesh is burnt, together with secret herbs and the ashes are scraped together and kept in a safe place. Now the sorcerer has to wait for the rich man to spit on the ground. As soon as it is dark, the sorcerer will come and scrape up the sand with his victim's saliva in it, mix it with those ashes and scatter the resulting powder on the path which the rich man uses daily on his way to work, if possible near a baobab tree (q.v.). This will make the victim ill as soon as he passes over it. Then his wife will go to the wicked neighbours and plead: 'Please remove the spell,' and they will refer her to the sorcerer, without saying, of course, that any of them was involved. Nobody knows who the sorcerer is. In public life he is a well-known and respected doctor, a *mganga*. The doctor will tell the patient: 'Go and walk past that baobab tree along the path.' The patient goes and falls down under the tree, because of the powerful powder. This is the 'evidence' the doctor needs. He has the patient carried to his home, where he tells the sick man to step over his back into his house, while the doctor lies down on the doorstep, to remove evil. The doctor will then make 30 incisions in the patient's skin with a razor, after which he will rub 'medicine' into the wounds. He will then organize a dance, *ngoma*, which will go on for several days, until on the last day, after many rituals, the evil spirit will rise up from the belly of the patient, or whichever part of him was sick, and depart.

Soul The nations of Africa have extremely diverse concepts of the human soul. Each culture has developed its own cosmology. In Swahili, *roho* means 'soul' in the sense of what leaves the body at death, *nafusi* in the sense of what is rewarded or punished in the afterlife for good conduct in this life. The word *ruhu* means 'spirit', e.g. *ruhu ilahi* 'divine spirit'. In Tsonga, *moya* 'spirit' is that which leaves the body at death, and in Luba the related word *moyo* means 'life, good health', but in Swahili *moyo* is the heart, the seat of moral decisions.

In English, 'soul' implies humanity, whereas 'spirit' may be found in animals too. The soul is a personal, individual being, the spirit is more a life-source and centre of mass energy. In Hausa, *kurwa* 'life-soul' is what can be eaten by sorcerers. In Zulu there are three words normally translated as 'soul': *idlozi* 'guardian-spirit', departed spirit'; *umoya* 'wind, air, breath, life'; and *isithunzi* 'shadow, influence, personality'.

In East Africa it is said that the departed soul hovers in the house of the deceased like a bat fluttering aimlessly. The Basuto of Transvaal relate that the soul leaves the body in the form of a scarab beetle (*Copri*), the Ronga think of a falcon as the incorporation of the soul. Both beliefs were also present in Ancient Egypt. (See also *Hyena; Lion; Mizimu; Snake*.) In Natal it is said that the souls of the dead become butterflies.

For some peoples the soul is tied to a part of thc body, liver, heart or stomach, or body liquids, especially blood or sperm. Others believe that the soul is free (see *External souls*) to go where it wishes, while the body seems to be asleep on its bed. The soul's journeys are later remembered as dreams. In Namibia, the Bushmen (Ju) believe that the soul after death lives on in a monitor lizard or a pygmy antelope, but the very good souls live on in the Moon. All the peoples of Africa believe the soul is immortal.

South Africa see *Hlakanya; Mamlambo; Medicine man; Nganga; Python; Rain Queen; Tikoloshe; Tornado; Zombies; Zulu*.

Spell Putting a spell on someone is paralysing that person's will, the power to think and act independently. A spell is a ray of energy directed at a person or an animal which makes the victim incapable of moving other than in the direction which the more powerful spirit wishes it to move. The more powerful spirit is usually the doctor. In science-conscious societies the doctor can induce hypnosis in his patients, which is the scientific form of laying spells on people.

In Africa, the expert hunter possesses magic by means of which he can put a spell on the animal he wants to catch, so that it will run into his nets or his traps, or show itself in the open field so that he can shoot it. But the most popular form of spell is love-magic, the means by which a person can make someone of the other sex fall in love with him or her and no one else.

A Somali woman went to a doctor telling him she wanted her husband to love no other woman. The doctor said he needed three hairs from a lion's eyebrows for that. The woman came back with the hairs, so the doctor said: 'If you can put a spell on a lion so that he does not wake up when you snip off his eyebrows, you can put a spell on your husband as easily.'

In Nigeria, a business woman put a spell on a young man, so that he served her devotedly until he finally drowned himself. Among the Hausa, numerous methods are known to put a love-spell on someone of the other sex; the most effective are those containing parts of the target person's body such as hairs and nails. Stealing a garment from the beloved and then treating it with magic is a method used in southern Africa.

Even a dead person can be put under a spell (see *Zombies*). Spirits who may appear as birds or lizards can put a spell on people by singing to them, or by staring at them, as snakes do. (See also *Magic*.)

Spider see *Anansi the Spider; Tule, the Spider God*.

Spirit hut see *Chiga; Temple*.

Spirits Spirits are living beings with or without bodies; those without bodies may 'enter' a body individually or collectively, or even several bodies; some spirits can revive dead bodies by 'entering' them and by the energy which is the essence of a spirit, make it move and speak, in that way communicating their message to the living. People visiting a cemetery in the middle of the night have reported seeing the dead bodies and skeletons walking or even dancing, moved by their own or other spirits. The 'life' of a spirit, which is in principle immortal, is evident from the 'fact' that it moves and so has 'life-force', that typically African concept of our experience. Secondly, a spirit has will; it goes somewhere purposely, whether walking or flying, and it may move things. *Telekinesis* is, for the African spirit-expert, the removal of an object by a spirit-master without touching it. He simply commands his servile spirit to move it for him, invisible for other spectators. Even for Islamicized Africans, trees, animals, plants, etc, have spirits which obey God and can speak to us if He so wishes. He ordered the palm-trees to uproot themselves and worship the Prophet Muhammad. A man who can fly is being carried by the spirit he commands. Sorcerers may control several spirits to steal and murder for them, or to stay inside a statue (see *Fetish*) or to 'enter' dead or half-living bodies and work for them (see *Zombies*). Some spirits are individuals with their own names which they will pronounce through the mouths of the mediums they possess (see *Possession*). At the other extreme there are collective spirits leading a cloud-like existence together, undivided into individual identities. (See also *Ancestors; Mizimu; Nkisi*.) Spirits, we are told, exist in many types and variations, apart from the spirits of the ancestors (q.v.). Spirit tales are told by all the tribes of Africa and there are numerous words for spirits in every language of Africa. Many spirits belong to the country, the savannah and the swamps, such as the Nyamwezi spirit King Katavi, the Nubian Dogir (q.v.) and the lake spirit Mugasha of the Ziba people on the shores of Lake Victoria. (For the spirits of the earth and the forest, see under those words.) Sun and moon are regarded as spirits or gods, and some of the planets, e.g. Venus (see *Tanit*). Natural phenomena like thunder and lightning are, or have, spirits, according to many people in Africa. Many trees are believed to be inhabited by spirits, or to *be* spirits. In the former case, there are several spirits lurking in the branches of one tree; in the latter case, the whole tree is the abode of one spirit which lives in its wood and has a purely arboreal character (see under *Trees*). Important events, especially great disasters in the lives of the peoples, can be regarded as spirits or gods, such as war, disease and famine. Thus the Ewe have a war-god, Koliko, and the Nuer god or spirit Wiu causes not only war, but also rainstorms, thunder and lighting. Next to physical illness, especially psychic diseases are caused by spirits, often by a plurality of spirits, *junun* in Arabic, *wazimu* in Swahili.

Many animals are associated with spirits (see under the individual animals). Spirits can hear and see, speak and appear in dreams to people, in human form or disguised as animals, angels or devils, or as a mist, a cloud of smoke or a will o' the wisp. Spirits are clever: they usually outwit people.

Spirits (Kongo). The Bakongo believe that every person has a body, *nitu*, and a spirit, *moyo*. When life ends, the spirit leaves the body and lives on in or near the water, preferably the rivers in the forest.

A person also has a soul, *mfumu-kutu*, literally, the king of the ear, because one can hear it whispering in one's ear. When someone faints or swoons, they say: his soul has gone away. A sleeping person's soul wanders about. What he sees is what we call his dreams. Meanwhile his body may have marital relations while asleep. The soul is the cause of a person's shadow.

A sorcerer (see *Sorcery*) is a man who has the capacity to change his soul into a *kiolu*, a tiny animal which can penetrate someone's body and kill that person from inside. The sorcerer's body stays at home all the time, peacefully asleep, so that no one suspects him. The sorcerer, *ndoki*, sucks the blood from the heart of a person while he is inside that body, until the soul flies away. It is said that the *ndoki* sucks like one sucking an egg, so that only the empty shell remains, a comatose body that will soon die completely. The spirits of the ancestors are called *bakulu* (singular *mukulu*); only the spirits of those who have led a virtuous life are *bakulu*. They are not black but white and live underwater in their own towns. A *nkita* (plural *bankita*) is the spirit of a person who has died a violent death, in battle, by suicide or murder. Na Ngutu is the king of the heroes fallen in battle. Ma Kiela is the queen of the female spirits who died of knife wounds. Dinganga rules the other *bankita*. These spirits are white, immensely strong and very dangerous; they live in rivers and in the jungle. They often appear in the shape of *ngembo*, bats, or as swallows. When someone sees a flight of swallows, he will stay quiet, spit on the ground and whisper: the spirits! The *bankita* play a vital part in the rites of revival of the sect Kimpasi and are entrapped in calabashes by the *nganga-nlaba* (doctor). A *kisimbi* (plural *bisimbi*) is a spirit who attacks people and makes them ill. (See also *Tebo*.)

Sudan see *Dogir; Jok; Mangu; Nuer; Shilluk; Tule; Zande*.

Suk (Religion, western Kenya). The Suk (pronounce Sook) once had a great reputation as fierce warriors, beating even the dreaded Maasai-Samburu in *c*. 1850. The Suk are the first branch of the Kalenjin family of tribes to leave their original homeland of Mount Elgon's slopes. Originally only hunters, the Suk now herd cattle in Kerio Valley, living in peace with their neighbours if they can.

They believe in God, whom they call Tororut, offering him animal sacrifices. God's son is called Ilat; he has to fetch water for his father in Heaven. When he spills it, it rains on earth (*ilat* means 'rain'). Tororut's blessing must be invoked at least once a year for the crops and the cattle. An ox is selected by the priest, *tusin*, to be slaughtered; he rubs its blood on the chests of the participants, all men. In times of drought, famine or epidemic, similar rituals are necessary, to propitiate God. Personal illness is blamed on Oi, the spirit of disease, who may be expelled by emptying the sick man's house, after which the priest casts the evil spirit out, since it has nothing left to lurk behind inside. Tororut has a wife, the Pleiades, and a brother, Asis, the Sun-god. Tororut's wife Seta has three children, Ilat, 'Rain', Arawa, 'Moon', and Topoh, the 'Evening Star'. The appearance of the Pleiades marks the beginning of the planting season.

After death, a man's spirit may travel in the shape of a snake (q.v.). In the bush, snakes may be killed, but if a snake enters a house, it must be given milk and meat since it is the spirit of an ancestor who can intercede with God on behalf of the living, in order to avert disease and other disasters. After death an old man or woman would be buried in his or her own hut, after which the descendants would move house; this was no hardship, since they were nomads anyway. Death 'infects' a house. The bereaved shave their heads, but when the New Moon appears, mourning ceases.

Sun The Kamba of Kenya tell the tale of a man who wanted to see the place where the sun rises every morning. He travelled east until he came to a wide river. He swam for a long time, frightened by the thought of crocodiles. At last he arrived on the other side and went on until he came to a second river, even larger than the first. He plunged into it and after a long time the strong current deposited him on the opposite bank. There in front of him he saw a hill, the crest of which seemed to be on fire. It was a mountain, much higher than he had thought but at last he reached the top. There he saw a vast palace made entirely of gold shining so strongly that the eyes blinked. Since the journey had taken him much longer than he had thought, the sun had risen and was already high in the sky, but the Sun's wife was there and she received him very kindly with refreshments.

Finally he saw something red coming towards them, which grew larger and larger. It was the Sun himself, home from a day's work in the sky. He greeted his guest courteously and invited him to supper. After the meal, the Sun showed his guest round his palace. The domes were made of copper, the arches of cloud-pearls. The next morning the guest was up before sunrise so that he could see the actual bed from which the Sun rose. This was permitted so he saw the Sun lifting off and soaring up into the clear morning sky. Mrs Sun gave her guest a loaf of freshly baked sun-bread. Then she said: 'Close your eyes,' and when he opened them again he saw his own house and his family just coming out. Together they ate the sun-bread and they have never been ill since that day. The more they shared, the more there was.

Sun-worship is not widespread in Africa, though the word Iruva, Izuva, Lyuba (= Swahili *jua*) for God in several languages of Congo, Cameroun and Tanzania, means 'sun'. The Jagga (Wachaga) of north-east Tanzania greet the rising sun with a prayer. The Duala of Cameroun pray to the sun-god Loba after sunset. On the island of Sao Tomé, the name Lube, 'God', also meant originally 'sun'. The islanders speak Bubi which is also a Bantu language. The Nyamwezi in Tanzania may refer to God as Kazyoba, an old word for 'sun'. Only vestiges of sun-worship remain among the Bantu.

Among the Yoruba Orun is worshipped as the sun-god, but it seems that this veneration has long been in decline. They relate in the north of Yorubaland that one night the young hunters pursued some game until they came upon a clearing where they saw a great light, brighter than any fire. They ran away and consulted the diviner in their town. He spoke: 'Long ago your ancestors used to bring sacrifices to the sun regularly but you have neglected these, yet you are Omo Orun, "Children of the Sun", that is, descendants of the sun-god.' Then he explained to them what to do, how to worship the sun-god, which taboos to observe, and how to live.

For the sun-myth of the Mongo-Nkundo peoples, see *Falcon; Mokele*. The Yoruba myth likewise seems to echo an older myth in which the sun was discovered while previously there had been darkness. For the myth of the sun-ram in Namibia, see under *Ram*. The Khoi (q.v.) and the Bushmen both have a myth which likewise begins with the primeval darkness.

Sunbirds (Zimbabwe). The sunbirds are two golden birds, which were found among the ruins of Zimbabwe about a century ago by one of the first explorers. They were probably discovered in the remains of a building which may have been the sun-temple of the ancient Bantu religion of the Shona people of Zimbabwe. These birds which form a pair, represent, it appears, two swallows, whose high and swift flight is praised by many poets of the old Bantu tradition, and about which the story-tellers relate that they can fly better even than the eagle.

The swallows, as is well known, are migrating birds. They arrive in southern Africa from Europe around the beginning of October, when spring is at its most beautiful and thousands of flowers are blooming. The sun is on its way up. The myth of the Shona people relates that the sunbirds belonged originally to the goddess Dzivaguru, the goddess of the earth, of the darkness of night, and of the rain clouds, of the pools and streams. The rainy season begins usually also in October, or later, when the gods are displeased.

We cannot live without sunshine, nor can we live without rain, yet we cannot have them at the same time, for rain and sunshine do not normally descend together. The great goddess Dzivaguru, whose name seems to mean 'Great Sun', ruled both heaven and earth in what may have been the oldest form of the Bantu religion, i.e. the religion of the peoples who speak Bantu languages. They have many myths in which the first man and woman on earth lived in darkness because the sun had not yet been discovered. The sun, the primal source of light, has to be captured so that people may have light to live by. The secret of the sun is that its light penetrates even in the darkest room, just as a swallow can fly through a house before any-one can catch it. Nosenga (q.v.) caught the sunbirds in his trap, and so day broke. (See also *Falcon; Lonkundo.*)

Sunjata (Mandinka, Gambia, Mali). Sunjata (Sonjara, Soundiata) was a prince of the Keita (Kaita, Keta) dynasty in ancient Mali and probably its founder. His long campaigns to establish the Mali Empire and defeat his lifelong enemy, the old king Sumanguru may have taken place in *c.* 1235. As a result of Sunjata's conquests, his capital Niani became the richest city of the Western Sudan. The heartland of the Mali kingdom lay between the rivers Senegal and Niger. The exploits of Sunjata and his numerous magic battles with the tyrant Sumanguru have become the subject of an extensive epic tradition well known in all the countries where Mande and its dialects are spoken, especially Mali, Senegal and Gambia.

Sunjata was the son of Fata Kung Makhang, whose diviner advised him to marry Sankarang Madiba Konte's daughter Sukulung, which he did. She soon became pregnant but it lasted for seven years. When Sunjata was born he did not walk before he was 7 years old. When he was fully grown he put on trousers that were intended for the King of Mande. No one else could wear them. When his father died, Sunjata became a hunter (his name means: Stealing Lion). He was so generous that he once cut off part of his leg to feed his hungry companion. Sunjata was told that Sumanguru had killed his (Sun-jata's) brothers and usurped the kingdom. Sumanguru was said to be a jinn who could not be killed like a man, but only by magic. Sunjata's sister Nyakhaleng Juma Suukho offered to give herself to Sumanguru for one night in order to find out the secret of his life-spirit. Sumanguru fell in love with her and revealed to her that his father, a seven-headed jinn, could only be killed with the spur of a white cock, which had to be put on an arrow, together with cer-tain leaves and magic powder. If the jinn, the father of Sumanguru, was hit by that arrow, he would die and his son Sumanguru would lose all his magic power. Then he would become a palm-tree, an anthill, a whirlwind, and finally a songbird.

Juma found her brother Sunjata and told him the secret of his enemy. He found the cock, the leaves and the powder. He shot the arrow, hit the jinn who died. Sunjata's men entered the fortress but found no man. Juma said: 'He is in that palm-tree!' They cut it down, but Juma cried: 'There, he is in that anthill!' They broke it up, but a whirlwind raged suddenly and flew away. They went into it with swords, but a songbird was all that was left of it. It flew to the forest, mocking them. But Sunjata was king of all Manding.

Swahili (Creation myth, Kenya). In the beginning there was only one God, century after century. When He decided to create the light, that was the first morning: light spread to the horizons of the night-sky in all the colours of the rainbow and the Lord was pleased with its beauty. Out of this light He created the souls of all the human beings who would live in the future, for God already knew all the things that had not yet come. The souls of the prophets were created first, then the souls of the saints and holy men, the pious and devout worshippers of the One God who would live only for Him. Their souls shine in darkness forever. After these, the Lord created the myriads of souls of ordinary people, like the stardust in the sky, the silver river of the night. The angels, too, were created out of light, so that they can never lie, for their luminous bodies are transparent so they contain only purity and no other desire than to worship God and help people.

After the light, God created seven great things: the Canopy, the Throne, the Pen, the Book, the Trumpet, Paradise and Hellfire. First, the Canopy, Arishi, is like a tent or pavilion above the immense and immutable Throne, Kurusi, upon which the Lord resides. Then, God created the Pen which reaches from the sky to earth and writes, day and night, the fate and destiny of all men and women. Next, the Book, the Well-preserved Record in which all events that will ever take place, are written down for all the centuries to come so that whatever misfortune happens, the pious man will not rebel against God but exclaim: It is written, it is His will! After this, the Trumpet of the Last Day which will announce the End of the World and God's final Judgement over all the souls He created. Then God created Paradise, the Garden of Delight where the good and obedient souls will live in eternal bliss, loving God and each other. Then, God created the great fire of Hell, Jahannamu or Gehennom, where the wicked will live in eternal torture, suffering consciously.

Beneath His Throne, God created a gigantic tree, the Cedar of the End. Even about the nature of this tree there is disagreement among the scholars. On this tree there are millions of leaves, some fresh and green, others old and withering: our lives. On each leaf, God has written a name, for He knows every one of us by name. When He wills, a leaf comes whirling down, but before it reaches the earth, an angel arrives, reads the name on the leaf and tells the angel of Death. The Angel of Death, called in Swahili *Nduli Mtwaa-roho*, the Taker of Souls, will descend immediately to earth, find the owner of that name wherever he is hiding, trembling for the approach of inevitable death, and announce: 'Your hour has come, your time is past.' Death will then part body and soul forthwith, for death gives no delay.

Finally, God created the earth, and the sun to rise above it. The earth was one vast ocean and the warm sun-rays made the mists rise up and form themselves into colourful clouds which travel from one end of the sky to the other. Then God called the continents to rise out of the ocean. They rose up: Arabia, Ajamia (= Iran), India and the Swahili Coast which the whitemen call Africa and the Arabs, Biladu-z-Zanji, the Zanji lands. There are sandy beaches, vast plains and towering mountains piercing the clouds. For God it is easy. Then He called the islands and they rose up quietly in the midst of the foaming waves, surrounded by coral rocks. Surveying the barren lands God caused green vegetation to sprout. Tall trees rose to form forests, covering the steep sides of the mountains; waves of plumed grasses decorated the hills, rows of whispering palm-trees nodded along the seashore.

Then God made the sun decline in the west, painted the skies red and gold and took the light out of the world. He suspended numerous bright lamps in the sky, which He called stars and caused each of them to move along a path that He had assigned to it. Only He knows how many stars there are and where they go. For God everything is easy, since the unfathomed sky is far beneath His presence.

Next, God created an enormous cock with many-coloured feathers. It stands in Heaven and crows every morning before dawn so that the cocks on earth can hear it. They too, will begin to crow so that the people will know that it is time to rise and worship the Lord. After the cock crowed, the sun rose and the day began on the earth which looked like a flat pancake floating in the world-ocean. Now, God created the animals in four classes: those that swim, whose king is the whale; those that creep, whose king is the python; those that fly, whose king is the eagle, and those that walk on four legs, whose king is the lion. Likewise there are four classes of creatures gifted with intelligence: the angels made out of the light; the jinns or wind-spirits made from the element air; the satans or evil spirits made from the fire; and finally human beings made from earth. God knows what all his creatures eat and makes sure that every one of them receives its food. All His creatures are born and so they all must die, for nothing will live for ever except God himself. He feeds one creature with another. It is therefore right that we eat what God has destined as our food: the animals which He taught Adam to tame or to hunt.

The flat earth with the surrounding world-ocean is like a filled saucer which God placed on the four horns of a bull (some say it is a cow but only God knows). This bull stands on the back of a huge fish which swims in another ocean, the depth of which no man ever saw.

Swallows see under *Sunbirds*.

Swazi (Swaziland). The Swazi or Swati believe in a god in heaven, Mkulumncandi, The Great First One, and his messenger, Mlentengamunye, One Leg, but they do not worship these beings. The sun is also a god, and his wife, the moon, follows him every month after a period of invisibility; this happens 13 times in every solar year. The Swazi king, it is believed, descends from the sun, so his family are called the Mlangeni, the People of the Sun. Once a year, when the maize, gourds and pumpkins are ripe and the moon is full, the Big

Incwala is celebrated, a great feast which lasts for six days during which the king is given new strength and vigour to face the new year. On the last day of the feast rain should fall to extinguish the fire in which the king has to burn objects representing the past year. The ancestors, *emadloti*, are believed to wield great power: they may send dreams and they are concerned with the good health and the prosperity of their descendants. If a person starts a quarrel in the family or neglects his obligations to his kinsmen, the ancestors may send bad dreams, scarcity or sickness. For such crimes as incest within the immediate family, or murder of a close kinsman, they may inflict the 'bite of the dead' as punishment. The ancestors on a person's father's side watch his fulfilment of his moral obligations; the ancestors on one's mother's side try to prevent harm from befalling their descendants on earth. Ancestors may appear to their descendants in waking time, in the form of snakes; the great African mamba is the manifestation of a dead king's spirit. For the interpretation of such portents the Swazi have to consult diviners, *tangoma*. There are no ordained priests; every head of a family has to maintain the good relations with the ancestors on behalf of his sons, and after his death his eldest son will fulfil that function. Mother-ancestors are also frequently appealed to, since mothers have a high status in society. The king appeals to his ancestors on behalf of the nation.

Swords: Dama Ngile (Djerma, Niger, Burkina Faso). Dama Ngile is the title of canto 5 of the great Epic of Dausi (q.v.). Its meaning is 'Great Bull', which was once the name of a mighty king of Jerra and Old Wagadoo. He had had his name inscribed on the sword, which bore his name and fame ever since.

Daibu was a humble hunter who lived well away from the towns. One night he had a dream in which he heard a voice saying: 'Your wife will give birth to a son and you will call him Dama Ngile.' Indeed, a son was born as big as a bull calf who soon grew up to become as strong as a bull, so he could fight a lion. One day he walked all the way to the city of Mande in the kingdom of Mali. There he boldly asked King Sunjata (q.v.) for the sword Dama Ngile. The King did not want to part with his sword even though he possessed a hundred swords. He told his armourer to put it at the bottom of a great heap of swords and told Dama Ngile he should find it in the blinking of an eye. But the sword Dama Ngile rose up by itself and entrusted itself to Dama Ngile's hand. Sunjata perceived that Dama Ngile would one day be King of Jerra and Old Wagadoo, for that is how God shows signs to perceptive men. How Dama Ngile became King of Jerra is a long tale; it was through his hospitality and generosity rather than through his sword.

Many generations later there reigned in Jerra Wagadoo a scion of Dama Ngile's dynasty, Sila Mabo, who coveted his brother's wife. This prince, Bey Tergisi, was ugly, since his face was full of scars and pockmarks. His wife was persuaded to unveil her husband's face which he always kept veiled in daytime, out of shame. Of course Tergisi discovered his brother's vile schemes, so he hatched revenge. Two parties formed and the fraticidal war became a civil war in which the king and all the princes perished. The citizens found no honest man to become their king. At last they became humble hunters and foreigners became their kings. A Fulani herdsman found Dama Ngile lying in the grass and gave it to his king. Then Al-Hajji Omar conquered the land and the sword.

T

Tebo mask from Angola

Taboo The word taboo comes from *tapu* in the Polynesian languages, which means 'untouchable'. For instance, if someone had used the wrong word to a king, he would become *tapu*, someone to be avoided, and had to go into exile for ever. It was not because the King was offended, nor because he was too rude and ignorant to be tolerated, but because bad luck attached to him; he was infected with danger, which could not be 'forgiven'.

The Swahili word for this is *kisirani*, a person who spreads bad luck in the house by his mere presence, as if he had germs. It is nobody's fault except the invisible black demon's whose presence can only be guessed at, sitting on the jinxed person's neck. Some kings had the bringers of bad tidings executed, because bad luck adhered to them, as the messengers knew themselves, so they agreed to be killed, for who can fight his fate?

The Kikuyu word for taboo is *thahu*, for which Benson's Dictionary gives: 'Ceremonial uncleanness incurred by violation of tribal code; state of psychosomatic ailment due to the breaking of a taboo or through some mischance bringing a person under the displeasure of ancestral spirits; freedom from incurred uncleanness is obtained by ceremonial purification, in the case of animals by slaughter, or by demolition and rebuilding of a house.'

According to the Chuka and Mwimbe peoples of Mount Kenya, *thahu*, ritual impurity, is caused by one of the seven following events:

1. Touching a corpse, e.g. by functioning as an undertaker for the family. When a person dies, someone has to 'throw out' the body, i.e. carry it out of the house and into the bush, where it is left. So, a good deed makes a person taboo for his family. Likewise, murder and manslaughter makes a man taboo, or *thahu*, for others, which proves that uncleanness is neither moral nor hygienic, it is caused simply by touching death without regard to illness or intention.
2. Killing a hyena or other 'name animal', i.e. a clan totem.
3. Having intercourse with a woman during her period.
4. If a child jumps on the marital bed, or if it breaks by itself, then its owner is in a state of *thahu*, uncleanness.
5. If a hyena leaves its dung outside the house.
6. If a wife has stepped across her husband's legs.
7. If a tree has fallen on a man, or if his hut has collapsed.

In all these cases, the medicine man, *mundu mugo*, is called, and the affected person has to go through elaborate rites to remove the 'contamination'. As long as this is not done, the society refuses to tolerate that person in their midst. He has to take time off from his work to see the 'doctor' in order to have the 'infection' removed. Most of these events causing a state of being taboo are associated with death: the hyena for instance, eats the bodies of the dead. The collapse of one's house or bed would be regarded as ill luck by anyone. The jumping of a child on the bed, or the wife stepping across her husband's legs are no doubt symbolic for the fear of sterility.

Taboo can also refer to things one must not touch. In Islamic societies it is *haramu* (taboo, forbidden) to touch pork or wine. This is not a health rule since the use of alcohol for disinfecting a wound is equally inadmissible. Meat must be *halali* (= kosher). Every person belonging to a clan with a totem ('clan-name') may not eat the animal, so, someone called *Nyati* ('Buffalo') may not hunt or eat buffalo.

Talismans A talisman is an object which protects its owner and gives him strength, good health and magic power. The origin of the word talisman is the Greek *telesmena*, lit. 'completion', i.e. of the ritual that was necessary in order to make the talisman work. From this word the Arabs made *tilism*, from which comes Swahili *tilisimu*, but the common word is *dawa* 'medicine' (q.v.; see also *Amulets; Charms; Fingo*). Amulets are passive objects, i.e. they just protect their owners against evil, whereas talismans may cause harm to whoever attacks the wearer, by 'throwing back' the evil upon him, especially when it is a magic attack by a sorcerer or a witch. In Africa, a dried cricket has magic power, as has the tail of a lizard, much in use by fetishists and amulet-makers. An elephant's hair is considered an extremely powerful talisman because elephants have powerful spirits. It is taken from the elephant's tail and worn like a finger-ring by women who want sons, in Central Africa. In Uganda, some women wear tails of giraffes suspended from their belts like tails on their behinds, swishing them to and fro as they walk to market. This will make them irresistible and is guaranteed to attract a lover. In North Africa the Hand of Fatima is believed to be the most effective protective talisman against the Evil Eye (q.v.). There are metal plates with the sign of a heavenly body engraved on them, e.g. the sun (gold), the moon (silver), Mars (copper) and Jupiter (iron), which protect the wearers against bad luck. In East Africa the mallams write passages from the Koran on scraps of paper, preferably on Friday, which they sell for much money wrapped in cloth to be hung round children's necks. There are also very elaborate silver boxes containing entire chapters, *hirizi*.

Tanit (Goddess, Tunisia). The ancient goddess Tanit may well have been of Berber origin and her cult already widespread in North Africa when the Phoenicians arrived to build their North African Empire. They soon identified Tanit with Astarte, the biblical Ashtaroth (Judges 2:13-17), the consort of Baalim (Samuel 7:3-4). Baalim was the Phoenician Baal, widely worshipped in North Africa until well into Christian times. The Ram-god Baal-Hammon was identified with the Egyptian Ammon-Ra, the Hellenistic Ammon-Zeus or Ammon Jupiter, worshipped by the Ammonites in what is now Amman in Jordan. Probably for this reason the Greeks and Romans identified Tanit with Hera-Juno, Jupiter's consort, the goddess of marriage, home and family.

However, Ashtareth (I Kings 11:4-8) or Astarte is usually identified with Venus-Aphrodite, the goddess of love and sex. Astar-te means star, in particular Venus, and one of the symbols of Tanit seems to be crescent, the usual representation of the planet Venus, called in Hausa Matar-Wata 'the Moon's Wife'. The crescent shape of Venus can be seen by some clear-eyed people. The symbols of the goddess Tanit that have been found on the archaeological sites of North Africa all point to her being identified with Aphrodite-Venus: the dove (q.v.) as a symbol of love is still used in Egypt. The Swahili proverb says: Two doves feed one another when they love one another. The palm-tree as the symbol of youth, beauty and fruitfulness is the second Venus emblem; the pomegranate is a well-known symbol of sensual love and fertilization: there is a Swahili song about its symbolism. The fourth symbol is the fish; as ruler of the zodiacal sign of Pisces, Venus is the goddess of the fishermen, the Stella Maris or Guiding Star of the Phoenician navigators.

Tanzania see *Bena; Majimaji; Possession; Sorcery; Zaramo*.

Tebo (Kongo, Angola-Zaïre). *Tebo*, plural *matebo*, is a type of evil spirit among the Bakongo of western Zaïre and adjacent regions. They tell the following story: a certain man had many goats and pigs. One bad year a disease broke out which killed his pigs. In the same year leopards carried away his goats. His yard was silent! After that he heard bleating and grunting only in his neighbour's yard and his heart turned black with jealousy. A *kindoki*, an evil spirit, had become king of his ear so he heard nothing else. He brooded over his neighbour's prosperity and refused all food. Finally he took his gun and went into the forest where he tracked down a leopard. After many hours he ambushed it and shot it. He cut its belly open and took out the bile. This he smeared along the rim of a pot, after which he invited his neighbour for a pot of beer. Soon after, the neighbour fell ill and died of a stomach ache. His wife called the diviner (q.v.) who revealed that the jealous neighbour was the culprit. He was subjected to the poison ordeal: he was locked up in a cage and forced to drink *nkasa*, the poisonous bark of a tree. He died but the clan's ancestors refused to admit his soul to their Dead-town. So, the sorcerer's soul became a *tebo*. Ugly dwarfs, their skins ash-coloured and wrinkled like warthogs, *tebos* wander around their old homes, terrifying the villagers whenever they are visible. If one meets a *tebo* on a lonely path in the forest, it is too late already. The *tebo* will leap on his victim, beat him to death and drag him to his cave to devour him. *Tebos* will also steal pigs and goats from the village, which they can do unseen; only some *ngangas* (witch-doctors) possess a *nkisi* (q.v.) by means of which they can distinguish a *tebo* in the dark, even if he has taken the shape of a leopard or a vulture perched on top of a tree. Some sorcerers have enslaved *tebos* with strong *nkisis* and can force them to carry out their murderous work for them, unseen and unsuspected.

Temple In modern times a temple is regarded as a place for meditation ('temple of wisdom'), insight, prayer and worship. The original function of a temple, however, both in Europe and Asia, was to house the deity. Usually the worshippers were not even admitted to the temple, and only the supreme priest was authorized to enter the inner sanctuary, alone.

The primary function of the temple is to be the House of God. The faithful remain outside waiting patiently their turn for their sacrifices to be accepted and, as in Buganda and Ghana, for the deity to give an oracle in answer to their urgent questions (see *Oracles; Sacrifice*). The medium (q.v.), the person who is possessed (see *Possession*) by the deity and so speaks the divine words, lives in the temple or is in attendance on special days.

Many African peoples have no temples but shrines, i.e. small edifices where food, beer or other offerings are placed by the believers, usually the descendants of the spirit who lives in the shrine or is buried under it. The believers hope to propitiate and pacify the powerful spirits. These shrines are called *maisonnettes d'esprits* in French-speaking Africa (see also *Ghosts*). The Bakongo inter their chief in his own house, then move and build another village for themselves. The chief's house, *Mbansa*, becomes the place where his spirit is worshipped, his temple. Other important personalities will be buried around him as time goes on.

Like the ancient Egyptians, some African peoples place statues of their ancestors or other deities in their temples; these statues or statuettes, usually made of wood, sometimes of bronze, rarely of stone, represent the deity. Usually the divine spirit is believed to be inside the effigy, at least in part.

Teso (Religion, Uganda). The most important ceremony in Teso-land is the ritual of rain-making (q.v.), for which the elders and the people gathered near a certain rock where they slaughtered a cow. The meat was eaten on the spot, while the medicine man (q.v.) sprinkled holy water on the participants, after which the people danced and sang during the remainder of the day. Rain would soon fall.

When a prominent member of the community died, a sheep and a cow would be slaughtered; the sheepskin would be wrapped around the dead man's head, the cowskin around his body. He would be interred inside his own cabin where he had lived. His wives could go home or stay on as the wives of his heir, normally his eldest son. Offerings of food and beer are often placed on the graves of the elders, otherwise they might be offended and cause harm, such as sickness or crop failure.

The sky-god is called Apap or Akuj; he is the Good Creator. There is also an evil god, the dreaded Edeke, god of disaster to whom the people prayed in times of sickness, blight or prolonged drought. Sacrifices are still offered to propitiate him, even though the majority of the Teso are now Christians.

The 'medicine man' referred to above, is called *emuron*; he possesses magical powers which he uses for good purposes. He can predict the future and diagnose illness, cure the sick and cause rain to fall. He sells charms and love potions. The *emuron* is often called upon to undo the work of the evil *echudan*, the sorcerers. Sickly children are considered to be endowed with superior powers, which makes them suitable for the profession of *emuron*. *Emurons* are normally women, dressed in bark cloth and cowrie shells. Only they can talk to the *ajokit*, the spirit of a patient who alone can tell her what causes the disease: an evil spirit in the form of a snake, or insect sitting in the patient's stomach, which has to be exorcized.

Tikoloshe (Xhosa, Transkei). A *tikoloshe* is a hairy monster, no taller than a baboon, and walking in the same odd manner, with long arms and an ugly face. Although it once lived only in the rivers of the Transkei, it has since been seen in Natal and even in the city of Johannesburg. It can make itself invisible for a time and it can look like a human child for it possesses magic powers and is very vicious. I was told the following story as a true one.

One day a woman saw a *tikoloshe* while she was filling her water-jars at the riverside. It emerged from the deep water, stared at her while floating downstream, then swam to the bank and leaped out of the water. It shook itself like a dog and walked towards the woman, who fled, leaving her bundle of firewood behind. The *tikoloshe* picked it up and capered after her, easily keeping up, until she was home. It was so quick that she could not fasten the door in its face, so it slipped in, jumped on her back and started mating with her, because *tikoloshes* are as sexy as satyrs. That was the moment the husband came home from a hunting trip with his spear and bow. He thrust his spear at once into the *tikoloshe*'s back, or so he thought, but it was quick and agile, so it jumped up into the rafters and sat on a roofbeam. The spear went deep into the woman's back and made her husband a murderer: she died. While the husband stood there gazing at her bleeding body, the *tikoloshe* jumped down from its perch onto his back and fastened its long black fingers round his neck, forcing him to leave the house and walk to the town.

Subsequently a series of murders were committed which baffled the police. Most of the victims were women who had been raped prior to being strangled, but some were rich men whose money was stolen. No one had seen the murderer even though one man was killed in broad daylight. He was the woman's husband.

Tiv (Religion, Nigeria). The Tiv live in central Nigeria; their language is very complex and yet logical. They number about one million. For the Tiv, the sky is an abstract, or rather, distant power. They say: *'Aondo ta iyange'* every morning, which means: Aondo, the sky, sends the sun, i.e. the sun rises. Similarly they say Aondo roars when there is thunder, or Aondo is coming with a storm, when bad weather is brewing. To many, Aondo now means the Creator. They say: 'Aondo made the Earth', Tar, which includes everything on it and in it. Tar is pictured as a man lying with his head towards the east, similar to the ancient Egyptian god Geb, lying down as the earth. In the extreme east of Tiv-land there is a large, bald round rock called Swem, which is the place of origin of the Tiv, they say, and so the focus of radiation of Tsav, vital energy.

The seasonal migration of birds to this rocky area is seen by the Tiv as the Mbatsav, the spirits of the ancestors, who use the birds as their vehicles, flying to the fountain of life-energy for recharging their spiritual powers there.

They may visit the houses of their descendants at night in the form of owls, in daytime as a cow, a wild animal or snake. Chameleons, lizards and frogs may bring messages from them. The spirits of the dead are feared; they hover near their former houses. In the marshes the spirits can be seen as fireflies. Anyam the Leopard, being the most powerful night animal, is especially feared, and seldom mentioned. When a man's millet has been eaten by monkeys, he calls them spirits too.

The Por (*poro*) was a bin or tray in which the skulls of the ancestors were loaded. No ordinary person could look at it. This Por was surrounded with ceremonies; when a clan head died, his skull would be added to the Por in an elaborate ceremony.

Tobacco (Kamba, Kenya). A man found porcupine quills in his field one morning, so he concluded that a porcupine had come to eat his maize. The next night he hid and sure enough, he saw a porcupine. He hit it with his spear but it escaped, with his spear. He followed it till it disappeared into a hole in the ground. He climbed down the hole and found himself in a large tunnel. It seemed to be endless but he persevered, walking for two days, until the tunnel opened onto lush countryside. Suddenly the farmer saw his father, who had been dead for years. They greeted each other and the son asked the spirit of his father if he had seen his spear (which had once been the father's property). The father said: 'That porcupine you hit was your mother.' 'Where is she?' 'In yonder village. You may go and greet her.' The farmer walked on and entered the first hut in the village. There he saw his spear in a corner, and there was his mother's spirit, sitting on her stool. She recognized him and asked him how he was. He asked her how she was, and she said: 'Last night I was hit by that spear.' The son asked her what she wanted as a present to make good. He also apologized, saying: 'I did not know that that porcupine was my mother. Please forgive me.' She said: 'Put a stone in the fire.' He did and when it was hot he suddenly saw his best and fattest ram appear, there in the Underworld two days walking from home. No one can explain how things happen in the Spirit World. The ram served as an offering to his mother's spirit and the son could now take his spear back. As a farewell present his mother gave him a box and a bag of seeds. 'This box contains snuff,' she explained, 'which people will love to sniff. It is made from the dried leaves of a plant for which these are the seeds. Grow them and pound the dried leaves into powder which you can sell for much money. It will make you rich. It is called tabacco. Shut your eyes.' When he opened his eyes again he was on earth.

Togo see *Ewe*.

Tornado (South Africa). The tornado, a terrible revolving storm, was regarded as a god in many parts of Africa where it occurred. In southern Africa it is represented in the shape of a long snake because that is what it looks like, a snake reaching from heaven to earth. The Zulu name for this deity is Inkanyamba and many Zulus have seen it themselves. Whoever has built his house in the path the tornado is taking will have to flee, for it destroys everything in its way. It tends to disappear as suddenly as it arises, so they say: it hides in a pool when not active. From there it will often take the same route, from Witbank northwards to Hartebeespoort and beyond. It grows when it rises out of its pool to a serpent of enormous size, then shrinks again when descending.

Once upon a time a man was caught by the Inkanyamba who, according to some Zulu wise men, is female, a goddess of the waters, of hail and storm. She picked him up and carried him through the air many miles away to her own pool where she hid, together with her quarry. Police searches were fruitless: the man remained missing, until a man from the Nyanga tribe offered to find him. He dived in a certain pool and persuaded the man who was now living in it to come back with him to the world of earthlings. Finally both men emerged from the water. The missing man had become as white as a fish under water, with long hair looking like seaweed and a long white beard. He seemed to be strong and healthy, but he refused normal human food. He only ate seafood, crabs and toads.

Not long afterwards the Inkanyamba came back to her pool, missed the old man and went in search of him. This caused such a terrible storm that the authorities requested the old man to give himself up to Inkanyamba. This he did willingly, since he no longer liked living on earth, but preferred life with the water-goddess.

Tortoise In the tales of all the African peoples the tortoise is never defeated. Its slow movements and wrinkled skin give it an appearance of being very old and very wise, cautious and prudent. There is a Swahili song in which the tortoise sings of himself, 'I move house and yet I never move house, I am at home wherever I travel.' The 'shield' which the tortoise carries on his back is another sign of wisdom, for no one can kill the tortoise. Well known, even in America, is the African tale of the tortoise being caught by the lion. It said to the lion: 'Uncle, if you are wondering how to soften my shield and make it good for eating, just put me to soak in the river.' The lion thought that a good idea, and put the tortoise in the river. There, in its own element, the tortoise escaped and hid in the mud. Its ability to live underwater gives the tortoise familiarity with the spirits of the other world who live in the water, and with the rain-god.

The Lokanda of central Zaïre relate that one day all the animals went out hunting, leaving the tortoise in charge of the foodstore, after the bushpig had been eaten by the mysterious Totonge, a monstrous, voracious, unknown animal. No sooner had the animals gone than the Totonge arrived — enormous! The tortoise offered it some honey, and when the Totonge wanted more, the tortoise said: 'You will have to get it from my *esote*.' The *esote* is the anus of the tortoise which he can open and shut at will by pressing his back-shield and his belly-shield together. The Totonge put its hand in, and was caught. It beat the tortoise but tortoises do not feel that. When the animals came back they found the Totonge as the tortoise's prisoner. They carved it up and divided the meat but gave the tortoise nothing. Tortoise then took a piece of glowing coal from the fire and started making rain. Rain fell abundantly and extinguished all the fires, so the animals had to give tortoise a big piece of meat each to buy new fire from him.

Totemism This word is sometimes used as if it was a religion, like Hinduism or Buddhism. However, totemism can only be part of a religion, one segment of the total system of beliefs. Totemism is the belief (i.e. it is regarded as a matter of course) that there is a special, supernatural relationship between a human being and another being, usually an animal, sometimes a plant or another natural phenomenon, such as a river or lightning, which are also living or spirit-beings. The strength and power of the totem-being flows into the human being protected by it, so that the latter's life is closely tied to this totem, without which he cannot prosper.

Everyone is accompanied by his totem all the time, like a shadow, and when he transgresses against the laws of his totem's taboo, it will punish him; if it is a leopard, it will give him spots; if it is a snake, it will make him mad; if it is a tortoise it will give him sores; a banana, fever, etc. No one may eat his totem animal or plant. A totem is inherited from one's father, who will protect his children even after his death, through the animal.

Many learned authors have analysed the 'primitive' and 'tribal' thinking which explains the existence of totemism in Africa. A totem belongs to a clan, i.e. a group of people who are related to each other through a common ancestor, and this ancestor often has the name of an animal and sometimes a tree or a plant. Modern African nations have their emblems, such as the Tanzanian giraffe, the elephant of Natal, the Zaïrean leopard, or the lion of Ethiopia. Yet, a totem is something much more intimate for the members of a clan than a national symbol. Camara Laye reports that he could swim in the river with his brothers and cousins, because their totem was the crocodile, so the crocodiles would do them no harm. Were they not themselves the crocodiles' cousins? Special myths explain how a particular clan descended from an animal, a concept that seems alien to Western thinking, because Westerners have lost the closeness to nature, the intimacy with the source of life itself. A human woman living on her own was visited regularly by a lion, who did her no harm; on the contrary, he brought her meat. When she had a son, the lion took the boy and trained him in bushlore so he became a hunter, the ancestor of the Lions' clan. Very similar stories are told about many other animals who became clan ancestors (see e.g. *Buffalo; Elephant*). Carnal contact with animals of either sex is abhorrent to modern people, but quite common in African mythology.

In the African tales of the jungle the big animals are clearly superior in brains and especially in the magic arts. It is therefore not demeaning for a man to give his daughter in marriage to an animal, as happens frequently in the tales. Usually animal husbands are as good as human ones, if not better. Animal wives too, are faithful to their human husbands until the desire to go back home to the forest becomes too strong, but that happens to human wives as well. It is often assumed by the mythologists that these tales explain the presence of the clan-totem, but this is not always stated in the story. In any case, often the clan 'totem' is a plant (like the roses of the Lancastrians and the Yorkists) or even an object, like a spear or a knife, so there is no 'descent'.

Trees Africans know they depend on trees for firewood, without which their wives cannot cook their food. In some areas the goats can climb trees to eat the green leaves. The leopard lurks in a leafy tree to fall upon the lonely traveller at night, and vipers do the same in Uganda. In some trees the bees make their nest where they store honey. Every big tree has a spirit. Some trees house many spirits (see *Baobab*). Whether a tree *is* a spirit or is inhabited by a spirit is not an easy question. The people will say: The tree *has* a spirit, or: *in* the tree there is a spirit. The spirit has a voice which the careful listener can hear and even understand if he knows the language of the spirits. This voice has to be preserved carefully by the drum-maker (see *Drums*). The boat-maker too, wants to keep the spirit of the tree in the wood, so that it will protect the boatman against drowning in the treacherous rivers, when the tree has become a boat. The appearance changes, the spirit remains (see *Boats*). Together in a forest, the trees have a collective spirit, powerful enough to be revered as a god (see *Forest*).

Trees can be tricky. With their roots they can trip up the unsuspecting traveller, who will often believe that his enemy bewitched the root to do that. Thorny branches have the same function. In Namibia there is a tree that is believed to eat people: it catches them with its branches, opens its bark and swallows them up. Inside the tree, the victim can be heard singing a goodbye song to their relatives and friends. Only the Woodpecker can save them, for it possesses magic powers. For a fee, it will open the tree with its sharp bill. A man in Zaïre was married to a tree. It gave birth to his children, a healthy boy and a girl who were human but knew the spirits of the forest and so became famous herbalists, for it is the doctors who need the trees for their medicines.

Tuareg see *Twareg*.

Tule, the Spider-God (Zande, Sudan-Zaïre). Just as the spider descends from the top of a tall tree, so Tule descended from the sunny sky. From his abdomen, the clever spider makes the rope that enables him to travel between heaven and earth. When Tule (also called

Ture) arrived for the first time from heaven, he carried in his bag the seeds of all the plants and trees, for the earth was still empty wasteland. Tule scattered the seeds in all the countries, then he rose up to the middle-sky and began to play his drum, as the magicians do it. Soon, all the seeds germinated and sent green stalks, sprouts, shoots and stems up into the air, leafing and flowering. Alas, the earth was dry as there was no water anywhere, so Tule went in search of water. Finally he came upon a hut in the bush. There lived an old woman who had discovered yams and planted them; then she scraped them and cooked them and was just ready when Tule arrived. He asked her for water but she denied that she had any. Tule knew that she must have used water for the cooking, so he changed himself into a spider and crept up the doorpost. There he saw that the contents of the woman's jars was water. He took a reed from the wall and sucked water up from the jars. The woman approached with a knife wanting to punish him for stealing her water, so he rocked the jar. It fell over and broke so that the water flowed across the earth. Tule then resumed his human form and talked sweetly to the old woman, promising he would dig her fields if she cooked him a meal. She cooked him a dish of yams while he made a hoe and an axe to cut the trees and hoe the fields for cultivation. Then he made a bow and arrow, went into the bush and shot a guineafowl which he gave the old woman as relish for the meal. The woman was pleased with this, so she gave him the ripe fruit of the Zamba-lindi tree, telling him to throw it on the ground at the crossroads and then look behind. He did and saw a lovely woman, whom he married.

Tunisia see *Tanit*.

Twareg (The Origin of the Twareg, Niger). Once upon a time there was a people called Gaawo in what is now desert country, who were attacked by a strange race, and defeated. As tribute, they had to pay seven virgins every year in perpetuity, to their victors. One year the Gaawo elders decided to send a sage with the virgins, since they had heard there were many jinns in the desert. The sage was a marabou, a holy man of great age and wisdom. Before sunset of their first day of travelling he told the girls to stay on top of a hill where he could keep an eye on them, while he explored the valley, before it was safe to pitch the tents. In the valley, the sage found what he had feared: traces of jinns, which are unnoticed by normal people. So he went back to the hill, but when he arrived at the top, the girls had gone. They had decided to explore the valley with its alluring oasis of green palm-trees. They pitched their tent right on the edge of the water, the very thing the sage had wanted to prevent. They refused to move, saying they were tired and wanted to sleep. Sleep they did, so much so that they did not feel the jinn, which rose from the water like a faint mist, entered their innocent bodies, all seven of them, and rose to their heads as well. The next morning the girls told each other their happy dreams, giggling. The sage perceived that his precautions had been in vain. He could see they were already pregnant, since he was a learned doctor. All he could do was stay with them in the oasis until they had had their babies. So, he looked after them, growing vegetables and breeding camels for a living. In due course of time seven healthy boys were born, and grew up prosperously. The old scholar taught them all the arts and skills he knew: reading and writing, archery, riding camels, woodwork, leatherwork and cultivation.

They became so adept at riding camels and shooting arrows that they conquered all the lands of the Central Sahara between Tunisia and Timbuctoo. They called themselves Iwillimedan 'Students' or Imagheghan, 'the Sons of Maghegh', the name of their father, the jinn, who met them from time to time in the desert and taught them his art, magic. When they had come of age they entered the service of the big tribal chiefs of the Sahara, fighting and winning numerous local wars and battles. For their bravery and loyal services they were rewarded with wives by the tribal chiefs, who wished to tie such strong warriors to their own clans by marriage. Thus each of the seven warrior sons of Maghegh became the ancestor of a clan, and the day came when the Imagheghan became such a strong and numerous tribe that they defeated even the Songhay and Zerma, driving them away towards the south-west. It was no doubt the powerful assistance of their father Maghegh who could make men mad, which helped them to succeed in their conquests, their never-ending battles for living space and for the ever-receding green pastures for their camels. He it was who looked after them from conception to old age; that is why they were all so healthy and strong. They used to travel at night when the desert air was cool and pleasant and the stars showed them the way, as their learned teacher had pointed out.

This is why the Arabs called the Twareg, that is Tawāriq, plural of Tāriq 'Traveller by Night'. By this means they could face their adversary at dawn, as it were appearing out of the desert sand. It is said they once founded a kingdom in the Amahaggar Mountains where they were at one time ruled by a queen who possessed immortality as well as irresistible beauty, but no trace of her palace has ever been found.

Twins As in ancient Europe, so in Africa, the birth of twins was greeted with mixed feelings of joy and fear. In Nigeria some people used to leave twins in the bush, according to Chinua Achebe. Some said, twins brought ill luck; it may be that twins were regarded as too great a burden on the poor mother. It was often believed that one of the twins is the child of a god, or of a devil, and that only one is his own father's child. In Uganda, however, the greeting: 'Welcome, O Mother of Twins', is a great honorific, when said to a guest. In Bantu Africa, some peoples say, if twins are of different sexes:

'They may marry together, they slept in the womb together.'

The Gola of Liberia relate that one day when a terrible war was 'eating' the land, a pair of twins caught it, because twins possess magic. Unfortunately they dropped the war on a rock so that it broke into a hundred pieces, and each piece became a new war, as terrible and devastating as the first war.

Once a pair of twins went out to build a town, each in a different country. One town prospered because the twin-man who was its chief, was kind and friendly. The other twin was hard and cruel to his people, so they killed him.

Twins are feared by the Kpelle in Liberia, because they possess magic powers, more than any medicine man, because they are born with a magic horn which shows them the way through life, and protects them against forest devils. Twins may be compared to sun and moon, the twin children of heaven. It is perhaps for that reason that twins are permitted more than other children. They have a tendency to perpetrate naughty tricks, like breaking their mother's pots and dishes, but then they catch some big game with their magic, and all is forgiven. (See also under *Ngbandi*.)

U/V

Vervet monkey mask from the Congo

Uchakijana see *Hlakanyana*.

Uchawi (East Africa). Not far from Mombasa there lived a retired missionary who one morning found a doll hanging in her garden, made from hair, human hair, it seemed. She called the servants but none came: they had all fled. Finally she did the right thing: she asked the local scholar, Mwallim Musa who came and spoke: 'This is *uchawi*. Someone wishes you to fall ill, suffer and die. But you have nothing to fear: *uchawi haramu*, sorcery is forbidden by God. You are well known for your good works, your charity and compassion (*huruma*) with the people. God sees us.'

The sorcerer, *mchawi*, is a wicked character who commits secret crimes by means of special tools and *dawa* (medicine, q.v.) including *sumu*, poison, which he may put in someone's beer or food. Phsyiologically these substances are ineffective. Their effect is in the fear they inspire which is so intense that people who feel threatened by it will desert their jobs, their families or even their hospital beds to escape from *uchawi*. Sorcerers may be either men or women but some people say that they are more often men because women have more pity than men. Sorcerers develop a special relationship with their *dawa* in which there lives a secret spiritual power, so that the *mchawi* can no longer escape his own evil tools but has to go on perpetrating evil for ever, until a wise *mganga* (medicine man) prepares a *tego*, a trap, i.e. a counter-charm which will harm the sorcerer himself by his own evil forces. The Colonial authorities used to try not those accused of sorcery, but the accusers, yet many sorcerers, when brought to the headman's court, have confessed the wicked deeds of which they were accused.

Uganda see *Alur; Ankole; Buganda; Bunyoro; Busoga; Months; Teso*.

Vampires Vampires are evil spirits who, as spirits, are immortal, but who make use of the bodies of people or animals. Human beings have to be 'recruited', for the vampires to obtain a human body to live in, or to appear in when visiting normal people, who are all prospective victims. The animal bodies in which the vampires live, or rather, appear, are those of bats (q.v.), but in Africa they appear in a great variety of shapes, (see *Crocodile; Hyena men; Leopard; Lion men*). True vampire bats (family: *Osmodontidae*) live only in South America; the Old World bats of the family Megadermatidae are incorrectly believed to suck the blood of the victims. The origin of the word vampire as well as the myth is, in Europe, Turkish *ubyr* 'ghost'. In Africa the belief that some persons (who may be of mysterious origin) 'eat' the lives of human victims, is widespread, from Zimbabwe to West Africa. The myth of Dracula, a man who has died, lives in a coffin, but rises to suck human blood, is also Turkish. In Africa there are sporadic traces of this myth, both in Western, Southern, Central and Eastern Africa. Such a man can be recognized by his corpse-odour, or by his fang-teeth.

The Bammana of Mali relate that the Subaga are persons who can leave their bodies to fly into their victim's house, where they descend noiselessly on his body and take his *ni* 'life'. The first Subaga was a man called Kenimbleni, who stole from the sorcerer Korongo three secret powders. One enabled him to change his skin like a snake and so, to become immortal; one to fly during the night like a bat; and one to speak the birds' languages. He had to learn to change into a lion and into a bird with red talons, after which he had to take off with the wind. The Subaga call each other by drumming on skulls covered with human drumskins.

Vodu (Fon, Benin). Vodu or *vodou*, from which the Caribbean peoples have made *voodoo*, is the word for the gods in the Fon language of Dahomey, which is now called Benin; Fon is related to Yoruba. The Fon people relate that there are three regions for different *vodu* or gods, the sky, the earth, and the clouds in-between. The first god, the Creator, lives far away in the sky and is not worshipped. When he started creating he began with twin gods. The god Lisa is the sun-god who causes the day and its heat, when people have to work hard; he is the god of strength and endurance. His sister

Mawu is the moon-goddess who causes the coolness of the night, peace, joy, fertility and gentle motherhood, and rain. Age is the god of the animals in the savannah and so, is worshipped by the hunters. Loko is the god of the trees, the forest and he is therefore invoked by the herbalists who need the bark and the roots of trees for their medicines. His sister Ayaba is the goddess of the hearth, where wood is burnt daily to cook food. Legba is the youngest son of Lisa and Mawu. He is the god of fate. The two eldest children of Lisa and Mawu were Sagbata and his twin sister. Lisa and Mawu sent these two to earth to live there and populate it with their children. Their younger brother whose name was Sogbo, was sent to the clouds to become the ruler of thunder and lightning and so, the god of fire and of rainwater. In spite of his tremendous power and his vast domain in cloudland, Sogbo was jealous of his elder brother the ruler of all earth. Therefore he withheld rain so that nothing could grow on earth and the people were starving. The people's prayers moved Mawu to send Legba to earth for Legba knows all the languages of gods and of people too, so he is often sent out as a messenger and ambassador. He brought the Otutu, a songbird to earth and told it that it must begin to sing as soon as a fire broke out. Soon, the angry Sogbo caused a fire on earth with his lightning. Otutu began to sing and Mawu, informed by Legba, quickly sent showers of rain, so the earth was saved.

Vulture In Swahili the vulture is called *tumbuzi*, 'the one who disembowels'. The black monk vulture is feared because seeing it brought disaster to the travellers in the wilderness. Some East African people say that the vultures carry the souls of the bodies they have eaten, so vultures are called 'soul-birds'. The Yoruba believe that vultures live to a ripe old age, so they must possess great wisdom. If a vulture eats the meat which is put on the altars for the gods, it is supposed that the vulture does so with the permission of the gods, so they regard the vulture as a sort of mediator between the gods and the worshippers. Indeed, without vultures the sacrifice cannot be performed successfully. So, the Ifa priest has a special prayer to the vulture, Igun Salagereje: 'Come and eat our sacrifice! So that the sacrifice may be taken away by the gods! Without the vulture no one can perform a sacrifice or propitiation, nor can we perform divination. Vulture, come and eat!'

In Ancient Egypt, the vulture was a goddess, Nekhebet, who was identified by the Greeks with Illithyia, the protectress of childbirth, and the protecting goddess of Upper Egypt, the oldest kingdom in the south. As a mother goddess, Nekhebet suckled the royal children; she is often depicted dispensing wisdom to the Pharaoh himself, hovering over his head holding in one claw the flywhisk, still today in Africa the symbol of royalty, and in the other the seal containing the king's name.

In later times she was identified with Mut (pronounce *moot*) the spouse of Ammon-Ra the sky-god whom the Greeks identified with Zeus, so Mut was the same as Hera-Juno. Mut means vulture. For the Egyptians and many peoples in Africa, the vulture is a bird who makes life out of death by eating dead bodies, so that she must possess great wisdom; she also has a wide vision and sharp eyes for she can detect food far away.

W

Water jar made in the mother image from Nigeria

War 'War,' says the Swahili poet, 'is like a savannah fire: once it starts it is almost impossible to put out.' This is as true today as it was a century ago, when he was writing this in Mombasa. War is already shown on the walls of the tombs and temples of Egypt, e.g. Rameses II (XIXth Dynasty) conquering Libya. Yet the Egyptians did not engage in war for amusement but to prove to the world that the favour of their gods cast a magic spell on their helpless enemies. Rock drawings in the Sahara show men guarding their cattle while other men attack them, perhaps the oldest record of war in Africa. Some African peoples described the war-god as a voracious lion, who 'eats' people. Onuris in Ancient Egypt was associated with the lioness Mekhit, his consort; he wore plumes like an African warrior. In southern Africa the god of war is sometimes described as an enormous monster, trampling on people's homes with its many heavy feet, devouring people and their animals, consuming entire villages as it wandered on from valley to valley to satisfy its unending hunger. Only a divine hero could slay it and bring prosperity back. The King of the Shangane in Mozambique used to be awakened every morning by his praise-singer with the words: 'What have you won? Your forefathers fought great battles and conquered nations!' This exhortation to war was functional. Cattle-owning tribes have to conquer fresh pastures in every generation, or perish. No king would wage war without consulting the oracles and the diviners regarding the most auspicious time and the probable outcome: will it end in victory or defeat? All the warriors would wear war-talismans or charms to protect themselves against spears and arrows; or they would by sprayed with a liquid which would turn iron into water as soon as it touched their skins (see *Majimaji*).

The spirits of the ancestors usually encouraged wars against neighbouring tribes who were encroaching on the ancestral land. Villages and towns were protected by amulets and fetishes that were buried under the gate, so that the attacking enemies would be blinded. (See *Fingo*.)

Warlocks Warlocks are called *walozi* in Swahili, *varoyi* in Zimbabwe, *baloi* in Zambia, Botswana and Lesotho, *baloji* in Kasai and Shaba. In Ganda the word for warlock is *mulogo* and in Hausa a *maiya*. All these persons have one thing in common: they 'eat' human beings. In Kasai, the spirits of warlocks congregate in a tree while their bodies pretend to be asleep in their beds. Or a warlock can leave an object, such as a broom, or part of his body, such as a buttock, behind, to answer for him in the night if someone calls. No one must be known to be out in the night: that is a sure sign of witchcraft. In their meetings, the covens partake in a communal meal which is also spiritual, not physical. They eat the soul substance, the energy principle of their victims; the latter will not even be present, yet after a short time, they will show signs of illness, and soon they will wither away and die without hope. Every member of the coven has to contribute a victim in his turn, which will then be 'consumed' at the next convention. Usually the warlock will have to offer a member of his own family, if only because it is easy to get pieces of nails, hairs or other parts of the intended victim's body. It may even be lethal when a warlock puts a bewitched piece of meat in the soup. All those who eat from the soup will surely die, and warlocks will consume their lives. (Note that in Swahili the word for 'life' and 'soul' is the same, *roho*, whereas in Luba, *moyo* means both 'life' and 'good health'.) Warlocks do their destructive work because they have to; it is congenital to them. When caught they may confess their crimes with resignation since witchcraft is their inborn nature. In Zambia, two warlocks confessed to have eaten the flesh of babies but that does not normally happen. The soul-energy suffices as their food. Many peoples believe that witchcraft is hereditary, it runs in the family, it is not a craft, i.e. a skill, but an inherited evil, like aggressive madness. The Zaïreans believe that a warlock is born with a witch-substance in his body. (See *Mangu*.)

Water In Africa, water is more precious than any other element. In almost every pool and stream, we are told, there lives a spirit (see also *Ifrit*) and in the rivers and lakes there are many spirits including the spirits of the dead and drowned.

The Kpelle of Liberia have reported that there are Water People in their rivers, people with human heads and long hair, but with the abdomens of fishes. Early in the morning they sit on the rocks sunning themselves. If you see one, they say, ask him for money. The Water Spirit will say: 'If you want money, we will make you King, but you must bring us a white ram every month, a length of white cloth, and your wife, your mother or your daughter. Only if you bring us the women you love most can we make you rich for the rest of your life.' If a man comes back from the water and soon after his old mother falls ill and dies, and he spends money like water, people will say: 'He has given his mother just to be rich.'

A woman whose totem was a big fish, once lured such a fish with rice; while it ate the rice, the man killed it with a knife. They cooked the fish and ate it. They both died.

It is not true that fishes cannot talk: they not only speak human language, they can even sing and put a spell on people.

The water-god may be a crocodile (q.v.); she may also be a goddess, the hippopotamus (q.v.) who protects pregnant women. The Basotho tell the story of the terrible drought, when the river which had always 'suckled' the kingdom, was totally dry. The King sent messengers to the mountains where the river rises. They met the river-god who told them: 'I will give you water, if your king gives me his daughter.' Reluctantly, the King sent his only daughter as a bride to the pool in the mountains where the river-god lives, where they left her to face the god. She had many children by him and the country never lacked water. (See also *Njuzu*.)

Well of Life The Well of Life has exercised the minds of many scholars in the past. One draught of its water suffices to give any creature immortality, i.e. he or she will live till the Last Day or Doomsday (q.v.), the day when God will destroy all living beings on this earth. Possession of even a small bottle of this water would ensure a doctor fame for life as it would enable him to cure the sick: one drop put on the lips of a dying man would revive him and ensure long life. However, so far as is known, God has granted only one man to drink from the Well of Life. His name is Khadir, 'the Green Man'. Where is the Well of Life? Some scholars point at Asia, others at Africa. But where in Africa? Some writers believed that the source of the Nile was the Well of Life, under the Mountain of the Moon. Others have pointed to the Atlas Mountains, under which God's angels lead the Atlantic waters to feed all the wells and springs of Africa. Others have argued that if we can find the well that feeds Lake Chad, we must come upon the world's richest and best-hidden well, in the middle of the Sahara. We do know that under the Sahara there are vast hidden lakes full of fresh water, the remainder of the immense swamp that once covered Africa from the Nile to the Niger and the Senegal.

The myth of Alexander the Great relates that God had given him the power over all the countries of the world but not the power of life. So, Alexander went in search of the Water of Immortality under the earth. After he landed in Africa he was told that the entrance to the Well of Life was a cave in the mountains, and that he should ride a mare, for only mares can find their way in the dark. Accompanied only by Khadir, Alexander entered the cave leading to the Land of Darkness. There, the two men lost sight of one another, so Alexander never found the well. Khadir saw El-Dabba, the Beast of the Apocalypse, then he saw the Angel of Death. Finally he saw the Devil who tried to prevent him from reaching the Well. Suddenly, in the dark, Khadir stumbled and fell headlong in a pool. That was the Well of Life. Somehow he found a way out of the water and out of the caves. Khadir is still alive, they say; some people have met him.

Witchcraft In Africa, there are two types of witchcraft, the conscious and the unconscious. A witch (Swahili *muroji*) can be an old woman who by her mere presence makes a child ill. She does not do anything, though she may later be accused of casting the evil eye (q.v.) on the child, supposedly because she is jealous, not having any surviving children of her own. There is also, in East Africa, the *kisirani*, a person — he might be a boy — who by his mere presence causes misfortune, like precious earthenware falling to pieces when he enters the room. Here, witchcraft cannot really be called a craft; it is simply a disastrous influence, the result of being born with ill luck, which is contagious like the radiation of death.

As a conscious craft, witchcraft is indistinguishable from sorcery (q.v.) (see also *Muloyi; Warlocks*), the sinful art of causing harm by means of magic tools and/or evil spirits (see *Nkisi*) or slaves (see *Zombies*). A sorcerer in Zaïre used to place a *nkisi* on the path of a woman every day until she died of fright and despair.

An important type of witchcraft is the ability to change into an animal. A witch does this unconsciously at night. He or she may even be unable to prevent this from happening, like Dr Jekyll. (See *Crocodile; Hyena men; Lion men; Wolf.*) The night-witches (q.v.) are invisible in daytime, but can be seen flying at night with fire coming out of their behinds. They devour human bodies, dead or alive, during the night. The sorcerer can change not only himself, but others too, into animals, if they disobey him and in order to own them and use them. The sad tale of the tired donkey who was once a beautiful woman, and who can still speak human language, is well known. The most common form of witchcraft is brewing poison and secretly putting it in the intended victim's food. The victim will die and his spirit becomes a slave. (See also *Mangu; Muloyi; Uchawi; Warlocks; Witches.*)

Witch-doctor There is much confusion concerning the English word witch-doctor since it is often used in a situation where it does not fit. A woman called Mwaringiseni who lived in the south of Mashonaland, was accused of sending a snake to bite her brother, by a *nganga* named Muchurhuru in April 1961. On the strength of the witchcraft suppression act of Southern Rhodesia (1899) she took the *nganga* to court for false accusation of witchcraft. She won her case. This type of *nganga* has been called a witch-doctor, but he is no more than a diviner: he threw his bones or his *hakata* sticks, and pretended to read in them that the woman had sent her familiar snake to kill her brother.

The word witch-doctor is also used in the sense of a healer who uses magic medicines or even harms people by sorcery (q.v.). The only correct use of the word is to denote a person who cures witches. The exorcist (see *Exorcism*) cures patients who are possessed by an evil spirit, and such patients may indeed by driven to crime. The man who was cured by Jesus had been put in chains to prevent him from attacking people (Luke 8:29). However, not all persons possessed by evil spirits are witches, so most persons called witch-doctors are no more than witch-finders, or, as they say in South Africa, 'witch-smellers', for a witch smells of death and magic poison. Very few 'real' witches are curable, since it is an inherited or innate inclination to be a witch and to cause misfortune by black magic. The Zande *binza* or *ira avure* is a 'true' witch-doctor since he knows which trees and plants produce the medicines which, if eaten, will give him power to see witchcraft with his own eyes and to drive it away from its intended victims. He does this by means of singing and dancing and then extracting the witchcraft object from the body of the alleged witch.

Witches Witches seem to be more vicious in Africa than in other continents. In modern England the word is loosely used in the sense of a woman with spiritual abilities, but in Africa witches are always evil, though not always female. A European missionary once said to a very naughty boy in his class: 'You must have a stomach!' The result was a stunned silence. The word 'stomach' in that language (Ngombe) was not only used to denote a wicked nature (as the young priest thought); it is the organ of witchcraft. A witch, when found out, must take the poison ordeal, which is usually lethal. That is, they believe, proof of being a witch and can only be punished by death. Afterwards an autopsy may reveal the 'stomach' or however we translate the word; in Zande the word is *mangu* (q.v.), which has been translated as 'appendix' or 'gall-bladder', though the correct translation is 'witches' extra organ'. Thus witchcraft runs in the family, and this belief is found in Zaïre, the Central African Republic and right through to Zimbabwe and Southern Africa. One is born a witch and cannot be operated on, so that there are families of witches in Africa. Such persons are believed to have a natural inclination to work evil by their mere presence, without necessarily doing anything. 'Evil' means that they make people ill and cause their death by casting what in Islamic cultures is called 'the evil eye' (q.v.).

In daily life witches can be normal, friendly, even charming people, and their very social success makes them most suspect. Witches 'eat' people, not physically, but they devour the spiritual strength, the life-force of their victims so that they die. In Zimbabwe the witch, *muroyi*, is called to the profession by a dead ancestor, an aunt or other relative in the night, who appears as a shadow or in a dream, or as a cobra. The call must be obeyed. Witches are believed to ride on hyenas to their dances.

Wizards Wizards are men who know more than others and who have unusual skills to do the incredible. Among them are the sooth-sayers (from Old English *sooth*, from Swedish *sant* 'truth'), the speakers of truth, usually referring to the future; such men are now called diviners. Fortune-tellers are more often women in both Europe and the Orient, e.g. Egypt; in eastern Africa they used to be Indians who enjoyed a large clientele. In South Africa too, the fortune-tellers and diviners (q.v.) are popular among all races. Wizards (the word is derived from 'wise') are not normally represented as wicked, just as extraordinarily skilled in the magic arts. Only a wizard is able to construct a contraption by means of which an evil spirit is caught. The trap looks like a cage; inside some human blood is sprinkled under the lever that closes the door. A piece of human flesh is even better. The wizard knows the incantations which will attract the imp or *tebo* (q.v.) to risk itself in the trap. The next morning it will be there, looking hungry and angry, its appearance is that of a wizened child or an old monkey, or it may look like a big bat, with huge black wings and sharp teeth. The only way to dispose of it is the fire; make sure no piece of its body remains unburnt for it would grow into a new devil, and plague people by sitting on their necks and sucking their blood. The wizard can also save his friends from the ogres (q.v.) (Swahili *walawatu*) by constructing a flying machine (Swahili *kiruka*) which looks like a basket made of catskin; it easily accommodates a dozen people. It flies just a little faster than the ogres (also called *mazimwi*) can run, and a little higher than they can jump, but if you speak a word when you are in it you will fall out and certainly be eaten by the ogres. One of the marvels which a competent wizard can construct is a door through which one can go and visit one's dead parents in the Other World.

Women (Gangwi, Kran, Liberia). In the beginning of time, we are told, there was only one woman, whose name was Gonzuole. She lived by herself, cultivating her land with no one to help her. No man ever visited her and yet she gave birth to a succession of children, all girls, and all very pretty. They grew up prosperously and built a village for themselves, in the middle of the forest, well defended. Some men who lived on the edge of the forest penetrated the forest and saw glimpses of the attractive girls, but none succeeded in entering the well-guarded village. So, the men consulted a diviner, Debome. He advised them to pick the most delicious mushrooms they could find and place them near the women's village. The men thought this an excellent stratagem. They collected loads of tasty mushrooms and put them on the path leading to the female village. Soon the girls came out and, seeing the mushrooms which they did not know, they tasted them and liked them. While they were picking them up, the men suddenly came out of hiding and surrounded the lovely girls. The oldest of the men, Chief Utompe, captured Gonzuole herself. She, however, said: 'You may each have one of my daughters, if you promise never to do her any harm. As for me, I am unfit for a husband, so let me go and live by myself in the forest.' The men agreed and each man married one of the girls. The girls, however, were not happy with their husbands for they could not forget that they had taken their mother prisoner. One woman put a spell on Chief Utompe so that he died, for women are experts at witchcraft. Another woman wanted to punish her husband, so she went and robbed another man, hiding the stolen goods under her husband's bed. The effect surpassed her wildest dreams: two parties formed, those who believed that her husband was guilty and those who believed in his innocence. Soon the two factions went to war with spears so that many died.

Worship A person who believes in God does not have to do anything in our modern world, where religion is a matter for the individual. In old traditional societies this was and still is, different. A child was born into a community and he or she worshipped with that community the god whom they adored. Gradually the child would be told who it was for whom all their ceremonies were celebrated. So, whereas a modern person may begin to worship after he has been converted to a religion, a member of a traditional society has to participate in worship long before he understands the reason why. What is worship? The Swahili say: *Ibada ni kazi* 'Worship is hard work'. That is, or should be, true, but there is another interpretation possible as well: 'Work is also worship.' Like most Swahili proverbs, this one has two meanings. For a Muslim, worship is not only praying, fasting, remembering God all the time, paying *sadaka* and going on the pilgrimage. It is also building mosques, digging wells for the people to perform their ablutions, teaching the Koran, also just reading it to the people, and just listening to it. Giving food to the poor, bringing up one's children in the fear of God, reconciling quarrelling parties, all those actions are acts of worship, as much as reciting God's holy names, or more.

For Christians, worship is going to church, listening to the sermon, praying together or individually, reading the Bible, singing hymns, receiving the sacraments, and even just being present at all these good acts. But the best of these is prayer.

In African religions, there are prayers and hymns, both individual and communal; there are processions with singing; there is also dancing and making music with drums and stringed instruments (Psalms 81:2), bowing and kneeling down (Psalms 95:6); moreover spirit possession is a form of worship, and talking to the god one worships. Even being circumcised or sacrificed is a form of worship.

Wute (Origin of death, Cameroun). One day, the Lord God called his special messenger the chameleon (q.v.) and told him: 'Go to the peoples on the Earth and tell them these good tidings: they will have to die like all the animals but later they will rise from their graves again. Now go quickly!' The chameleon travelled down to Earth, but chameleons always tread very carefully along the branches downwards, and they have a habit of stopping frequently to rest, reflect and look around. So it took the chameleon 14 days to travel from God's city to the Town of People. In the meantime, the snake (q.v.) had heard of God's favours to People, and he decided to trick them. He went to the People's town and announced: 'God has sent me to you with the following message. All people who have died will remain in their graves for ever after. They will never come back. Death will keep them for good.' Death heard the snake say this and rejoiced for Death is a greedy character, coveting ever more people as his prey.

When the chameleon finally arrived he called the townspeople together and announced solemnly what God had told him to say: 'People will rise after death.' The people, however, called him a liar: 'We believe in what the snake has told us, for he was here first.' The chameleon replied: 'Impossible, I am God's truthful messenger.' The people then called the snake from his hole in the earth and asked him who had told him that people die for ever. 'God told me that,' lied the snake without any scruples. So, the chameleon defied him: 'Let us go to God's city together and let Him decide who is right.' So they went and appeared before God together. God heard both parties and spoke: 'The snake has lied. I never gave him a message. Yet the message delivered first to mankind will have to stand. It cannot be undone. Death has already begun to kill many people, since he overheard the message. For your punishment, snake, you will be hated by people for ever after, and they will kill you as soon as they see you'. Thus it happens that people die and never rise again. (See also *Death*.)

X/Y

Yoruba mother goddess from Nigeria

Xhosa People and language of the Transkei. See *Mizimu; Shaman; Tikoloshe*.

Yemoja see *Goddesses*.

Yoruba (How Yorubaland was Created, Nigeria). In the beginning there was only Olorun (q.v.) the god of the sky in his heavenly abode. Down below there was nothing but water, there ruled Olorun's brother Olokun (q.v.), ruler of the sea and the lagoons, like the Greek Okeanos. Olorun ruled the sun, Orun (q.v.) but there was no earth yet. Then Olorun sent his son Obatala (q.v.) down with an immense globe, the earth, which he placed in the sea, where it broke up in big fragments, forming mountains and islands. The first living creature to grow there was Agbon the palm tree, from which Obatala made palm-wine. He drank it and fell asleep. Indignant, Olorun sent his daughter Oduduwa (q.v.) goddess of the earth, down to put matters right. She was accompanied by Aje, the goddess of wealth and money, who, like the Roman Juno Moneta, the goddess of money, had the form of a fowl. At once the fowl started scratching the earth in all directions like a good chicken, for which purpose she had five toes on each foot. This is how the earth became wide and habitable. The water ran away through a hole where people still fetch water today. Olorun gave Oduduwa a bag of *oka*, corn or millet, which she sowed on the new earth, together with other seeds. Soon, the earth sprouted plants and trees in verdant abundance. Finally Olodumare the Creator, who is often identified with Olorun, descended to earth and set foot near the old palm-tree, where there is now the ancient city of Ife, the centre of the earth. He assembled all the 16 gods around him in the first great Council of the Gods on earth: Obatala or Oshala, Ogun, Eshu, Shango. Each of the gods became a clan ancestor, whose descendants built one of its 16 suburbs around the centre, which is ruled by the Supreme God himself. Thus the city of Ife-Ife (also called Ila-Ife or Ilife) is the city of the 17 divinities. As a result of numerous quarrels among the citizens, and even civil wars, the composition of the clans in the city is now very different from what it was at the beginning of its long history. This tale of turbulence explains also why the names of the gods and goddesses of the Yoruba clans are not the same in all the traditions; while some seem to have been identified with each other, others seem to have been split off. The same phenomenon can be observed in the great mythologies of ancient Rome, Greece and India. Thus Obatala is also referred to as Orishanla, which is a collective name for the gods who descended to Ilife together; he is further known as Olufa, a name which is also used for God by the Muslims. Obatala and his sister-spouse (only the gods may marry their sisters, just as in ancient Greece) Oduduwa, still live in the earth under Ilife, where they are venerated as two stone images. In another tradition the gods may even have different genders, for instance in one version of the creation myth it is said that Oduduwa is Obatala's (here called Oshala) brother, who marries Aje and has with her a son, Oranyan. The following Yoruba divinities have been described in this work in separate articles: Eshu, Obatala, Oduduwa, Ogun the God of Iron, Oko (Agriculture), Olodumare, Olokun, Orunmila, Orishanla, Osun, Shango and Shankpana. Various traditions have been followed, because the myths of the same deity are sometimes quite different in different parts of Yorubaland. (See also *Doves; Earth; Eshu; Goddesses; Ifa*.)

Z

Zambian rhinoceros head-rest

Zaïre see *Alur; Bakongo; Bangala; Chimpanzee; Death (Mongo); Eloko; Falcon; Itonde; Kindoki; Kuba; Lianja; Lonkundo; Mongo-Nkundo; Muloyi; Mwindo; Rainbow; Sorcery*.

Zambia see *Ilomba; Nzambi; Sitondo*.

Zande (Ghosts and omens, Sudan, Zaïre). The Zande (pl. Azande) live just on the watershed between the Nile and Oubangui (Ubangi) rivers, and so, just astride the border between the Sudan, Zaïre and the Central African Republic. The old hills of Zandeland are worm-holed with caves where the numerous streams rise, and in those dark caves, obscured by gnarled roots, there live the gods and ghosts of the dead. The medicine men have to go there to find the plants and roots for their medicines which the ghosts will show them, if they receive proper gifts. Otherwise, the ghosts will be heard wailing when plants are pulled out. They may also send a great serpent to attack the intruders. Only the medicine men dare to enter those caves, because they can protect themselves with their strong magic.

The most feared of all the wild creatures in Azande myth is the Adandara, a sort of wild cat, which hunts at night in the bush. They say that not only its eyes, but its whole fur gleams in the night because it is a witchcraft-animal. Male Adandaras have sexual relations with human women who then give birth to kittens whom they suckle like babies. It is considered a bad omen if one sees such a feline or even hears its shrill cries in the night. Only witches meet and make love to them. A remedy against ill effects is to blow the magic whistle.

If someone sees an iguana or a tortoise (q.v.), one of his relatives will die; likewise if one sees a chameleon (q.v.), or a chimpanzee (q.v.). Bats (q.v.) contain the souls of witches; if a man possesses strong magic he can make the bats fall down when they steal his corn. Ghosts can be benign (*atoro*) when they are dead ancestors, but the ghosts of witches (*agirisa*) are vicious: they may put a spell on travellers in the bush so that they lose their minds. If a man hears an owl cry he knows there is a witch around and blows his magic whistle; hearing a jackal howling is an omen of death. (See also *Tule*.)

Zaramo (God, creation, witches, Tanzania). God, in Zaramo (or Zaramu), is called Kyumbe. They are not sure whether God created the sky and the earth or whether they were there already. They do believe that God created all the animals in the beginning without tails. When God had prepared all the legs he called all the animals back to have their tails fitted and fixed. The snake, however, was too lazy, too proud and too greedy to come, as he was busy devouring a frog which could not jump away since it had no legs yet. When its brother arrived, God gave it strong legs so it could hop into the water and so save itself from the snake. The millipede was the last to arrive because without legs it just coils and uncoils, getting nowhere. God gave it all the remaining little pieces of legs, a thousand of them. When the snake finally arrived, all the legs were taken. So, the snake envies the other animals their limbs and hates them. The snake was disobedient, it sinned against God by being slow. All the other animals were still peaceful. Even the lion never attacked people, until one day it was stung by a hornet, which likes to make the animals angry. Furious with pain, the lion attacked a man and devoured him. His brother later killed the lion.

God is invisible and so powerful, say the Zaramo, that no *dawa* (talisman) helps against him. When he calls, we all have to go. God takes the dead spirits to Kolelo, a huge cave in the mountains. There is a pool inside this cave where women go to bathe in order to conceive, men go there to slaughter a sheep praying to the spirit of Kolelo for rain. Underground streams can be heard there. Persons accused of certain offences are taken there and the Voice of Kolelo will pronounce them guilty, if fright has not already made them confess. Witches were put to the test by one of nine ordeals: they had to swallow boiling water, or they had to put a foot seven times on a red hot iron. If burnt they were guilty.

Zigula (Religion, Tanzania). The Zigula have the same words for 'High God' as some of their neighbours, namely *chohile* or *mlungu*. Ritual centres around the propitiation (*mviko*), of the spirits of the dead, *wazimu*, who live in *uzimu*, the country of the dead, but they will cause disturbance among the living if they are offended or neglected. Both maternal and paternal ancestors are worshipped, at shrines in the bush where two paths cross. In addition, there are the spirits of the forest and the hills, such as Kinyamkera, a malevolent spirit with only one leg, one arm, one eye and one foot, who causes misfortune. Furthermore the Zigula believe in witches (q.v.), persons who can turn themselves into animals. If found out by a diviner, a witch must undergo an ordeal (*mvaha*), such as not being burnt by scalding water, or licking red-hot iron. If burnt by these tests, the witch was considered guilty and burned alive.

A magician *mgonzi* possesses the art of divination (*mviramoro*), and of preparing medicines and charms which ward off evil-intentioned trespassers from fields, gardens and houses, or protect their owners against the evil eye (q.v.), theft and sterility, or make their owners' sweethearts fall in love with them. There are elaborate ceremonies with dances and songs to cure a person who is possessed by a spirit.

Zimbabwe see *Goddess; Nganga; Nosenga; Sunbirds*.

Zion The origin of the new churches of Zion in South Africa was the Christian Catholic Church in Zion, founded in Chicago in 1896 by John Alexander Dowie, who was reputedly a faith healer, following in the footsteps of Jesus, baptizing his new converts, inspired by St Peter's words in *Acts* 10:37-8. As early as 1897, a Revd. J. Buchler left his Congregational church in Johannesburg and started ministering on the basis of the Christian Catholic Church, 'baptizing by triune immersion, preaching that God hears prayers and will heal the sick if we have faith, by laying-on of hands' (see *Baptism*). Buchler and his earliest collaborators, Roux and Mahon, were Afrikaanders who preached to the coloured people in Afrikaans and to the black people in Zulu and Sotho, urging them to be clean in body and spirit, to pray and work hard. They soon had a flock which in 1904 numbered 5,000, growing rapidly into a congregation of black people with hope and self-confidence. The name Zion was based on Psalms 68:31: 'Ethiopia shall soon stretch her hand out to God.' 'Ethiopia' was thought to refer to all of Africa. Zion was the hill where David brought the Ark of God to rest in the City of David (II Samuel 5:9; 6:12). On this Hill of Zion, St John in his vision saw the Lamb and the Saints (Revelation 14:1). Finally, St Paul promised the Christians: 'Ye are come to Mount Zion and to the city of the living God, the heavenly Jerusalem, and to an innumerable company of angels, to the general assembly and the church of the Firstborn. . .to God. . .and to the spirits of men made perfect (Hebrews 12:22). The Zionists also mention the 'Banner of Zion', probably referring to Isaiah 11:10-12. The Zionists call themseles in Zulu, Amazioni, and in Sotho, Bazioni. Today, there are well over a hundred thousand churches of Zion organized into 4,280 congregations with well over four million members. Many are baptized in the Ocean near Durban. All believe in healing by faith in Jesus and casting out devils in his name.

Zodiac see *Astrology*.

Zombies (Bantu). Zombies are heard of in many parts of Africa. The word *zombie* comes from Kongo *zumbi* or *zombi* 'fetish, enslaved spirit'. A sorcerer, i.e. a malicious character with a strong will, magic power and knowledge, may 'catch' the spirits of living or dead creatures, human or animal, and make them work for himself. His magic power keeps the spirits in his power so that he can even imprison them in a statue to frighten others into submission. (See for this, *Fetish; Idol; Nkisi*). Nowadays the word zombie refers only to human beings who keep their bodies and are still alive but have lost their souls and characters, so they no longer distinguish between good and evil: they obey. I was told the following as a true story in Natal: Sipo and Vamba were two brothers living together. One day Vamba became sickly — he 'walked *zombe*', as they say in Zulu: he wobbled like a very old man, and soon he died. Sipo buried him but he did notice that Vamba's body was still soft. He had died by the magic power of a distant sorcerer. The next morning the grave was open and the body was gone. That was the proof of sorcery. Determined to save his brother, Sipo visited all the villages in the district, asking people if they had heard of a powerful sorcerer. At last someone answered him in whispers and pointed a trembling hand in the direction of the hills. Sipo travelled on with grim perseverance until he found the large farm owned by the sorcerer. At dusk he saw a strange sight: an army of silent labourers came shuffling to the fields and started working, hoeing without the usual singing of African farmhands. Suddenly Sipo recognized his brother among them, though Vamba's face looked grey and his eyes were sad; nor could he talk since his tongue had been slit. Sipo took his brother in his arms (he was very light) and took him home, but Vamba died soon after; this time he did become stiff.

Zulu (Creation myth, Natal). The Zulu people who live in Natal, had an elaborate cosmology. Their creation myth was recorded by Dr Wilhelm Bleek, Librarian at Cape Town, during his research tour in Zululand in 1855-6. Today these myths have died out. An abridged version is given here.

I

The Great One came out of the Earth beneath.
He came out with the sun and he came out with the moon.
He placed them in the sky, saying: Let the sun travel by day...
Saying: Let the moon appear after sunset.

II

The Great One rose out of the Earth underneath.
He brought forth people (Bantu) and white people;
He brought forth cattle, goats, sheep, dogs.
He brought forth the animals of the wilderness
and many other things.
The Great One called Unwaba the Chameleon.
Saying: 'Go to Bopapa on Earth and tell him: People shall not die.'
The Chameleon went on its way downward, treading carefully.
The Great One called Intulo the Lizard.
Saying: 'Go and speak: The people (Bantu) shall die.
The white people shall die as well as the black people.
The cattle, the sheep, the dogs will all die. Nothing will remain.'
Intulo the Lizard set off running rapidly down to Earth.
There it spoke: All people must die, all who inhabit the Earth,
and all the animals who live upon the Earth.
Meanwhile Unwaba the Chameleon trod carefully.
Then it stopped and nibbled the leaves of the shrub Bukwebezane.

III

Meanwhile the Lizard Intulo ran in great haste, because
The Great One had spoken: 'Intulo, arrive on Earth
and say unto the people that they must all die.'
The Lizard Intulo arrived on Earth, obeying the Great Lord.
It spoke there: 'All the people shall die, white and black.
All the animals will die, tame and wild. Nothing will remain.'
The word of the Great One cannot be taken back. It stays.
People and animals die, leaving behind their little ones.

IV

The Great One created: a white man and woman
Saying: The white man shall marry the white woman
and they will beget more white people.
And He created the Bantu-people, man and woman,
Saying: The woman be married to the man, both black
and they begat the Bantu, the black people.
The Great One spoke: the White people shall live near the Ocean
And the Black people shall live in the middle of the land,
They shall build kraals to keep cattle, goats and sheep;
They shall breed dogs and go hunting.

V

The Great One spoke: The White people shall own clothes and guns.
The black people shall wear skins and the men will carry spears.

The married women shall wear a red headdress,
The married men shall wear a headring.

VI

The Great One broke out of the Earth, out from beneath.
He rose up from the reeds, from the water's edge,
He created many nations: the Sun people, the Elephant people,
the Bushmen, the Whitemen and the Black people, the Bantu,
In many tribes did he create them: the Zulu, the Swazi,
the Ba-suto, the Xosa, the Sembu, Tembu and Pondo
and twenty-four other tribes.

VII

The Great One spoke: Let water come forth that the people
may drink from it and the animals as well.
Let fire come forth so that people can cook their food.
There is the Earth, let the women dig it.
Let the men cut trees and build houses.
The men shall make hoes and give them to the women
so that they can plant seeds, so that the millet may grow.
The women must fetch firewood, grind the corn and cook food.

VIII

A woman shall be obtained from her father in exchange for
cattle.
If a man dies, his younger brother shall marry his wives
Lest they be married by men from other tribes.
If a man knows how to keep his people
he will know how to keep his cattle
So that his sons may inherit the shining beasts after he dies old.

(See also *Hlakanyana; Mamlambo*.)

Bibliography

U. Beier, *A Year of Sacred Festivals in One Yoruba Town*, Lagos, 1959.

W. H. Bleek, *Zulu Legends*, ed. J. A. Engelbrecht, pub. J. L. van Schaik, Pretoria, 1952.

M. Bloch, *Placing the Dead, Tombs, Ancestral Villages and Kinship Organization in Madagascar*, Seminar Press, London, 1971.

H. Callaway, *The Religious System of the Amazulu*, 1888, reprinted London, 1971.

E. Casalis, *Les Bassoutos*, Paris, 1859.

H. Cory, *African Figurines*, London, Faber & Faber.

J. B. Danquah, *The African Doctrine of God*, K. Dickson, London, 1908.

M. Deren, *The Voodoo Gods*, Thames & Hudson, 1953.

R. M. Downs, *Tiv Religion*, Ibadan University Press, 1971.

E. E. Evans Pritchard, *Nuer Religion*, Clarendon, Oxford, 1962.

——, *Witchcraft, Oracles and Magic among the Azande*, Clarendon, Oxford, 1963.

D. Forde (ed.) *African Worlds, Studies in the Cosmological Ideas and Social Values of African Peoples*, OUP, 1966.

M. Fortes and G. Dieterlen (eds.) *African Systems of Thought*, OUP, London, 1965.

M. Gelfand, *Shona Religion*, Juta & Co., Cape Town, 1962.

——, *Witch Doctor*, Harvill Press, London, 1964.
——, *The African Witch*, E. and S. Livingstone, Edinburgh, 1967.
M. Griaule, *Conversations with Ogotemmêli, An Introduction to Dogon Religious Ideas*, OUP, 1972.
P. Hadfield, *Traits of Divine Kingship in Africa*, Watts & Co., London, 1938.
C. W. Hobley, *Bantu Beliefs and Magic*, Witherby, London, 1938.
J. H. Jahn, *Muntu*, Faber & Faber, London, 1961.
Journal of Religion in Africa, (ed.) A. F. Walls, University of Aberdeen (pub.) E. J. Brill, Leiden, Holland.
C. G. Jung, *Man and His Symbols*, Aldus Books, London, 1964.
H. A. Junod, *The Life of a South African Tribe*, 1959.
M. Kilson, *Kpele Lala, Ga Religious Songs and Symbols*, Harvard University Press, Cambridge, Mass., 1971.
N. Q. King, *Religions of Africa*, Harper & Row, New York, 1970.
J. Knappert, *Myths and Legends of the Swahili*, Heinemann, London, 1970.
——, *Myths and Legends of the Congo*, Heinemann, London, 1971.
——, *Bantu Myths and Other Tales*, E. J. Brill, London, 1977.
——, 'Central and Southern Africa' in *Mythology* ed. R. Cavendish, Orbis, London, 1980.
E. J. and J. D. Krige, *The Realm of the Rain Queen*, London, 1943.
I. M. Lewis, *Ecstatic Religion*, Penguin, 1971.
G. Lindblom, *The Akamba in British East Africa*, Uppsala, 1920.
L. Mair, *Witchcraft*, World University Library, London, 1969.
E. L. R. Meyerowitz, *The Sacred State of Akan*, Faber & Faber, London, n.d.
J. Middleton, *Lugbara Religion*, OUP, 1960.
E. G. Parrinder, *Religion in an African City*, Oxford, 1953.
——, *West African Religion*, London, 1961.
——, *African Mythology*, Paul Hamlyn, London, 1967.
——, *African Traditional Religion*, Hutchinson, London, 1954.
——, *Witchcraft, European and African*, London, Faber & Faber, 1963.
R. S. Rattray, *Religion and Art in Ashanti*, Oxford, 1927.
J. Roscoe, *The Baganda*, London, 1965.
A. W. Southall, *Alur Society*, Heffer, Cambridge, 1953.
L. W. Swantz, *The Zaramo of Tanzania*, Distributed by Nordic Tanganyika Profect, P.O. Box 2530, Dar es Salaam.
P. Tempels, *Bantu Philosophy*, Paris, *Presence Africaine*, 1959.
H. W. Turner, *Living Tribal Religions*, London, Ward Lock Educational, 1977.
V. W. Turner, *The Forest of Symbols*, Cornell University Press, Ithaca, NY, 1967.
A. Werner, *Myths and Legends of the Bantu*, Harrap, London, 1933.
J. Williams, *Africa's God*, I-III, Boston College Press, Mass., 1936-8.
W. C. Willoughby, *The Soul of the Bantu*, London Student Chris-

tian Movement, 1928.
——, *Nature Worship and Taboo*, Hartford Seminary Press, Hartford, Conn., 1932.